BACKFIRE

BACKFIRE

A HISTORY OF HOW AMERICAN CULTURE LED US INTO VIETNAM AND MADE US FIGHT THE WAY WE DID

LOREN BARITZ

THE JOHNS HOPKINS UNIVERSITY PRESS
Baltimore and London

TO THE YOUNG AMERICANS WHO FOUGHT THE WAR AND THOSE WHO FOUGHT AGAINST IT

Originally published in 1985 by William Morrow and Company, Inc.
Johns Hopkins Paperbacks edition, 1998
9 8 7 6 5 4 3 2

The Johns Hopkins University Press
2715 North Charles Street
Baltimore, Maryland 21218-4363
The Johns Hopkins Press Ltd., London

Library of Congress Cataloging-in-Publication Data

Baritz, Loren, 1928–
 Backfire : a history of how American culture led us into Vietnam and made us fight the
way we did / Loren Baritz.
  p.   cm.
 Originally published: New York : W. Morrow, 1985.
 Includes bibliographical references and index.
 ISBN 0-8018-5953-0 (pbk. : alk. paper)
 1. Vietnamese Conflict, 1961–1975—United States. 2. United States—Civilization—
1945– I. Title.
DS558.B37   1998
959.704'3373—dc21   97-51946
                                                                                        CIP

A catalog record for this book is available from the British Library.

CONTENTS

PREFACE, 1998

I wrote this book in 1983 and 1984. Since then, especially in the last few years, several key players in the Vietnam War have supported my criticisms of the conduct of that national calamity. Especially thoughtful and candid are the memoirs of Robert McNamara, secretary of defense in the Kennedy and Johnson administrations, and Colin Powell, who served two tours in Vietnam, first as a major in the American division and, long after Vietnam, as chairman of the Joint Chiefs of Staff in the Bush administration.

These and other memoirs center on our monumental ignorance of the enemy—the Vietcong and North Vietnamese—as well as of our presumed friends in South Vietnam. There is no longer any serious debate about the ignorance of the men who made the war. McNamara acknowledged that he and his colleagues in the Pentagon, and also in the State Department and the White House, had played a lethal game of blind-man's buff: "Our misjudgments of friend and foe alike reflected our profound ignorance of the history, culture, and politics of the people of the area, and the personalities and habits of their leaders."[1]

But there is still a disturbing silence about an even more debil

---

1. Robert S. McNamara with Brian VanDeMark, *In Retrospect* (New York: Times Books, 1995), p. 322.

itating handicap. Wars start with political decisions, not combat. We did not understand the Vietnamese and we did not, perhaps do not yet, sufficiently understand ourselves—what it meant and means to be Americans. We did not intercede in Vietnam because we failed to know the enemy; we went to war for the reasons every nation does, to satisfy a need perceived to be so great as to justify, to demand, bloodshed. There are many reasons why we lost the war—why we had to lose it—but even more complex reasons why we felt it necessary to fight in the first place.

In a sense, Vietnam developed gradually, as wars usually do. Decisions made by FDR and Harry Truman unlocked the gates. Eisenhower and his secretary of state pushed them open. JFK drove through. Johnson made it a gargantuan and deadly parade, and Nixon blew up the countryside. Yet they were all good and decent men, devoted patriots, and taken as a group representative of mainstream America. None, however, leveled with the American people or Congress, or dared to talk sense in public about the war.

The war presidents believed in what they were doing. I have no doubt they were sincere. Victims of Cold War jitters, they meant to curtail the spread of communism. With deep-seated American idealism, they intended to engineer a more sanitary and more democratic Vietnam. LBJ desperately wanted to "win their hearts and minds," and Nixon described the war as a "noble cause." They wanted to save the Vietnamese, sometimes from themselves, always from their ideologically crazed brothers. Our sense of moral superiority to the rest of the world, our missionary compulsion, is a story as old as the settlement of America.[2]

The way we fought illuminates everything else. The military, especially the army, never solved the strategic equation of Vietnam, although some of its tactics succeeded. Our commanders lusted for a massive conventional battle that we could easily win, but the enemy refused to oblige us. There was never a front line—never any line at all—and no territory to be won and held. The Vietcong looked exactly like our allies in South Vietnam, never appearing in uniform and easily blending into the village life of the countryside, where they were undetectable. Conventional armies and advanced technology were nullified by guerrilla warfare.

2. I have written about the background ideas and myths in *City on a Hill* (New York: John Wiley, 1964).

For the GI grunts in the field, it was a grisly nightmare. Think of the soldier lucky enough to have his laundry done by a sweet old woman who, after dark, changed into a Vietcong guerrilla laying mines on the path to the mess hall. And, if he was still alive the next morning, she brought him clean underwear. What is the right weapon to use against such an enemy?

Henry Kissinger, secretary of state under Nixon, finally got it right: "America's material superiority was largely irrelevant."[3] The clouds of B-52 bombers, the omnipresent choppers, the best equipped war machine in the world, and it was all beside the point. That is because "the point" was always the sweet old laundress. Why was she a VC fighter? Was it humanly possible to identify her as a mortal enemy before she killed? The answer was almost always no. The nature of guerrilla warfare is precisely that guerrillas can become invisible. Their weapon of choice could be a knife, a rock, or a sophisticated rifle made in China or the USSR, or perhaps lifted off a dead American soldier.

How do you destroy an enemy you cannot find? JFK thought the Green Berets were the answer. LBJ sent half a million men. Nixon spread the war to Laos and Cambodia and dropped 36,000 ton of bombs on Hanoi during Christmas of 1972. So we lost. It was impossible to win. How could rational and patriotic men not see?

The problem of determining who was winning plagued the military command in Saigon. Finally they defined progress by the gruesome numbers, the infamous body counts. The goal of the war became an inflated number of enemy corpses, real if possible, invented if necessary and convenient. Colin Powell wrote the truth: In Vietnam "our senior officers knew the war was going badly. Yet they bowed to groupthink pressure and kept up the pretenses, the phony measure of body counts, the comforting illusion of secure hamlets, the inflated progress reports. As a corporate entity, the military failed to talk straight to its political superiors or to itself."[4]

Many but not all of the people on the home front who protested against the war were also sincere and idealistic. The antiwar protesters were almost as diverse as the nation, including radical

3. Henry Kissinger, *Diplomacy* (New York: Simon & Schuster,1994), p. 700.
4. Colin Powell with Joseph Persico, *My American Journey* (NewYork: Random House, 1995), p. 149.

students, wispy hippies, wispier movie stars, draft evaders, clerics, professors (I was one), returned veterans, politicians, and ordinary Americans who were moved to take a stand for a wide variety of reasons. Many believed they were more authentically patriotic than their president. Some fled the country; others became deadly terrorists. But there was no doubt that the link between the people and their government had been broken. In 1968, the majority of Americans were opposed to the war.

Draft evasion is still the sorest issue of Vietnam. Politicians continue to vent their resentments against political foes, especially men who evaded the draft—as Bill Clinton knows. As with so much else about the Vietnam era, they aim at the wrong target. The indefensible political decision to exempt students from the draft was not the students' fault. The consequence of that political decision was the corruption of the army and the shame of the nation. The draft was aimed at black kids and poor white kids. Colin Powell's outrage is entirely justifiable:

> I can never forgive a leadership that said, in effect: These young men—poorer, less educated, less privileged—are expendable . . . but the rest are too good to risk. I am angry that so many sons of the powerful and well-placed and so many professional athletes . . . managed to wangle slots in Reserve and National Guard units. Of the many tragedies of Vietnam, this raw class discrimination strikes me as the most damaging to the ideal that all Americans are created equal and owe equal allegiance to their country.[5]

To understand our present role in the world, we must understand the Vietnam debacle. Enemies change, and we must, too. We did not lose the Vietnam War—called the American War by Vietnamese—merely because we were ignorant of the people we wanted to befriend and other people we wanted to kill. We lost because we made the mistake of entering and failed to seize the moments when we could have, and should have, withdrawn.[6] We lost because deep American fears took over and fighting and dying were seen to be better choices than "losing our credibility" or "watching the dominoes fall." The names of 58,000 dead Americans are carved into the Vietnam Veterans Memorial ir

5. Powell, *American Journey*, p. 148.
6. McNamara, *In Retrospect*, pp. 320–21.

Washington. To make that number comprehensible, think of the 168 people who were killed in the Oklahoma City bombing, and then imagine the same number of deaths in 345 additional American cities.

As usual, we demonized the enemy to strengthen popular support, but, as usual, the result made peace harder to achieve and normal relations impossible for years. We lost the war because of pride—we assumed "they wouldn't dare" try to hurt us and that they would come to their senses and see that what we wanted to do to them was really in their best interest. And no American president wanted to be the first to lose a war.

So this book is about America. It focuses on our national myths, political assumptions, the nature of our political and military bureaucracies, and the personalities of the managers of that war. It seeks to unpack American culture as the way to understand what happened, and why.

PREFACE

I write about the Vietnam War to clarify American culture. This war was a magnifying glass that enlarged aspects of some of the ways we, as Americans, think and act. Such a glass not only makes things easier to see, it also focuses light so it will burn. A child can learn from touching something hot. Can a nation?

I wrote this book to explore the answer to that question, to see whether our Vietnam experience could be made to reveal what there was, and is, about the condition of being an American that promotes or retards the discovery that fire is hot. Americans build international fires differently from the rest of the world. Again there is a question: Why? As a people, we are not unique. But we have so many matches, and some of us may not have had proper instruction about the dangers of playing with them.

In the summer of 1982, when I began writing this book, I realized that I had been agonizing about Vietnam for almost twenty years. I had read every major book and article about the war. I was always disappointed by them. The writers, whether they were scholars or journalists, were always describing the war. They did not explain the war, or why it happened, or why we waged it the way we did, or why we negotiated the way we did, or why it eventually became such a disaster for us. What I was reading concentrated on the shooting war. None of the books or articles concentrated on America, and I wanted an explanation of how and why America became involved in its worst political and military defeat. I came to believe that the book I was looking for had to be about us, about our American culture.

One GI in Vietnam believed that "the experience of war revealed what men are made of and those that came out badly usually had problems going in."* Just so, not only for the individual soldier, but for the entire nation.

Different cultures go to war for different reasons and fight in different ways, but the intricate connections between war and culture are present in all nations. I will argue that there is an American way of war that is congruent with the American way of life, with American culture, and that is the way it must be. We cannot understand war without understanding culture. That is what this book is about.

I have divided the book into three parts: cultural myths, political assumptions, and bureaucratic behavior. I first recognized this as the necessary architectural principle for thinking about our Vietnam experience when I was building a tool shed for my mountain house in Vermont. I had this house as a retreat from the bureaucratic pressures of my job as a provost, first with the central office of the State University of New York system and later at the University of Massachusetts at Amherst. Before I became a bureaucratic administrator, I taught American intellectual history. During those earlier years, I wrote several books and articles about cultural myths. I also taught political history and became a political participant in opposition to the Vietnam War. With thousands of others, I was involved with teach-ins, marches, more speeches than was consistent with sanity, and political organization. In 1968, I was elected as a delegate to the terrible Democratic National Convention in Chicago, and later managed Paul O'Dwyer's losing senatorial campaign in Rochester, New York.

I have a tendency, dangerous with power tools and often ruinous to the result, to daydream when I build things. When

---

*Peter Goldman and Tony Fuller, *Charlie Company* (New York: William Morrow, 1983), p. 186.

I was calculating the angles of the rafters on my tool shed, it occurred to me that the three phases of my own career matched the three organizing principles of a book I thought had to be written. As a scholar, I knew American mythology; as a professional historian and amateur politician, I understood American political history; as a bureaucrat for thirteen years, I had learned about life in the corridors.

Like other senior bureaucrats I had no time for sustained thought, but in fugitive moments I wrote some notes about how the triangulation of myth, politics, and bureaucracy might locate this war. Unwilling to stop, I resigned my bureaucratic position to write this book. At the time I had no idea where this would lead. Those first scribbled notes became an obsession that had two important results. First, the rafters don't fit properly. Cutting snugly fitting angles requires a certain serenity of soul. Deep meditations about Henry Kissinger's diplomacy, in my case at least, disturbed this serenity. The second result was less aggravating, but perhaps equally important: I spent the next two years abusing my word processor.

The first part of the book is called *Tinder*. In it I state that to understand the Vietnam War it is necessary to explicate the assumptions we make about our country. These assumptions are made up of the values and self-perceptions that are so deep, so traditional, that they are taken for granted and are rarely discussed. They live under the skin rather than in the mind; they support our pride in our country, our patriotism. They are inhaled in our youth, reinforced in school, by mass culture and by the apparent satisfaction they give us throughout our lives. The attitudes that flow from these deep assumptions help to organize the way we think about ourselves and about the world. They are the old American myths that form the basis of American nationalism. The central myths are those of "the city on a hill," American idealism, and our technological invincibility. In discussing these myths I show specifically *why* we became involved in Vietnam.

The second part of the body, *Fire*, concentrates on our assumptions about politics and power. It shows how the pressures of domestic politics shaped concrete war decisions. It is an examination of *what* Americans decided to do for and to Vietnam. This section is the most traditional, as it examines the Vietnam connection from Franklin Roosevelt through Richard Nixon.

Some of the events described will be familiar to readers who were attentive during the period. Although the political narrative of the war decisions is important so that the reader may follow the twisted path, I am always more interested in the assumptions that lay behind the actual decisions. These assumptions—about the nature of the cold war, the theory of containment, the threat of McCarthyism, the meaning of massive retaliation, the domino theory, the importance to Presidents of always seeming tough-minded, and the religion of secrecy, as examples—are the stuff of which our political culture is made.

Our national political culture is a product of thousands of small and not-so-small ideas. They exist in the collective wisdom of the agencies and departments of the government, of the players in the political parties, of the press, the Presidents, their wives, and their aides, and of congressmen and the public. This political culture is built slowly, bit by bit, so that future decisions always have a precedent, probably several. The architects of our involvement in Vietnam, for example, remembered Munich too well. They *assumed* that on this model it was vital for America to avoid similar appeasement. They remembered and acted. But they failed to understand that the assumed model in their minds was inappropriate, that whatever else he might have been, Ho Chi Minh was not Adolf Hitler.

My focus is on the usually unexamined assumptions of men in power that led them to make specific decisions, rather than on what they actually decided. Because the assumptions behind decisions cannot be analyzed unless the decisions are examined, both must be discussed. These political and military decisions, in short, are the results from which we can try to tease out the political culture of the men who were making war. Mistaken assumptions obviously create bad decisions. I show the bridge between the impact of our national mythology and the results that flowed from the bureaucracies in Washington.

Part III of the book is called *Backfire*. I argue that concrete political and military decisions must be considered in the real-life bureaucratic context in which they occur. There is sometimes a very great difference between the decisions that leaders make and the way those decisions are carried out, or not carried out, by the thousands of people working in the Defense and State Departments, the military, the CIA, and the White House. More important, there are internal rules in any large bureaucracy that tend to shape decisions, and pity the free spirit who tries either to rewrite or ignore them. I concentrate on the role of the bureaucracy in making war in Vietnam and in managing the armed forces (and the corruption of the army officer corps), the reactions of the fighting men, and on the spread of the bureaucratic personality throughout American life.

I wrote this book with the conviction that truth is more important than evenhandedness. There are, after all, some controversies, such as the Vietnam War, whose inner meanings cannot be disclosed by the sort of irresponsible impartiality that is allergic to a conclusion. I do not apologize for the fact that some of my conclusions are passionate. We are considering matters of life and death, not merely an intellectual exercise. Worse, we are considering whether there was some acceptable justification for the deaths, Vietnamese as well as American. The time may come when enough scar tissue will have formed to permit a cooler detachment, but not yet, not for me. I also believe that passion is an appropriate response to war, that something real is lost when the battlefield is sublimated into the thinner air on top of Mount Olympus. The emotional involvement of the author may enlighten as well as distort. Whether I have succeeded is not for me to judge.

After the war, our first reaction was to purse our lips and walk on tiptoe. It looked as if we were determined to erase the memories through silence. Our embarrassment seemed to lead to some sort of collective amnesia. Finally, this eerie hush has been disturbed from several directions, including television and newspaper coverage. Our attention was caught by the beautiful and touching monument the Vietnam veterans had built on the Washington mall. There are now dozens of recent scholarly studies of America's strangest test of arms, most of which focus on the military history of the shooting war, not on the question of American culture. Perhaps we are now ready to take another step, to think about what it meant to be an American during the thirty-year period of our war in Vietnam. The solution to the puzzle of the relationship of American culture to that war has relevance to how we think about ourselves in the present, how we think about other nations, and how we think about the next war.

I have been enormously fortunate in my critics. The people who read this book in manuscript made suggestions that improved my work. I thank Susan Sontag, Richard Minear, Joseph

Ellis, Walter Goldstein, Theodore Behr, Murray Schwartz, and Phyllis Baritz. Ellen Joseph's editorial art was indispensable. Vincent Demma, a historian with the Southeast Asia Branch of the Center of Military History of the Department of the Army, made several key documents available to me, as did David Boies of the law firm of Cravath, Swaine and Moore. Captain Paul "Buddy" Bucha, a Congressional Medal of Honor winner, and Sam Adams, a former CIA analyst, were generous with their time. In the mid-1970s, the late James F. Kelly was my friend, my boss, and during countless happy sessions over a drink(s) after work, was my mentor in the ways of complex bureaucracies. Lawrence Bassett helped with bibliographic matters. Gerard McCauley provided steady encouragement and amusement far beyond reasonable (but not my) expectations of the conduct of a literary agent. Bruce Lee, my editor, helped with substance as well as style. When periodically I wrote myself to the very edge of a cliff, he had an annoying tendency to suggest that my next step might be sideways. I quote from one of his sly little letters: "What you're going to do here is saunter along, keeping in the shade and out of the hot sun, moseying on down to the salt lick where at sunset, in chapter five, you're going to shoot the reader through his goddamned head."

L.B.

Sunderland, Massachusetts, and Poultney, Vermont
July 1984

PART I

TINDER

THE MYTHS WE TAKE TO WAR

ONE

GOD'S COUNTRY AND AMERICAN KNOW-HOW

In 1972, while worshiping in a temple near an American air base, Colonel Chuc sank into a trance and received a battle plan and a magical sword from the spirit of the Vietnamese general who defeated Kublai Khan's Mongols seven hundred years earlier. Followed by a sergeant who carried the ancient sword on a velvet cushion, Colonel Chuc went to fight the North Vietnamese according to the plan he had been given. An American officer who was there at the time said that the South Vietnamese soldiers knew that the spirit of the ancient general who had crushed the Mongols breathed in Colonel Chuc. They engaged the army of North Vietnam and did what fifteen years of American training failed to do. They won. They were victorious because they were following an authentic leader, a man greatly favored by the heroic ancestors.[1] It was not easy to understand such a people.

America was involved in Vietnam for thirty years, but never understood the Vietnamese. We were frustrated by the incomprehensible behavior of our Vietnamese enemies and bewildered by the inexplicable behavior of our Vietnamese friends. For us, this corner of Asia was inscrutable. These Asians successfully masked their intentions in smiles, formal courtesies, and exotic rituals. The organic nature of Vietnamese society, the significance of village life, the meaning of ancestors, the relationship of the family to the state, the subordinate role of the individual, and the eternal quest for universal agreement, not consensus or majorities, were easily lost on the Americans.

Most of the Vietnamese were so poor, American GIs said that they lived like animals. Some said they were animals. They did not bathe, had no toilets, and ate food whose smell made some young Americans vomit. There was something about the very great age of Vietnamese culture that seemed to resist our best efforts to understand. There was something about the exhausting heat, the depressing rainy seasons, and the red dust that made even the geography of the place seem out of reach. Most of all, the peasant in his rice paddy, his young son in a pointed hat sitting on a water buffalo, represented what peasants had done forever. They seemed eternal, immune to change. They were not part of our century and not part of our world.

When we did try to impose changes, for the better of course, the resistance of the people could seem like ingratitude or stupidity, as it did to a young GI, Steve Harper. The Vietnamese enraged him. "We were there to help but Vietnamese are so stupid they can't understand that a great people want to help a weak people." He said that "somebody had to show poor people better ways of livin', like sewer disposal and sanitation and things like that." He once watched an American team enter a village to teach the peasants sanitation while members of South Vietnam's army stood around laughing because they thought it was a pointless waste of energy. His worst experience was his R&R tour in Tokyo, "the greatest sin city":

> I would walk down the Ginza, their main street, and look at all the slant eyes and I swear I'd start to get sick. I was even tempted by some of the prostitutes but one look at their faces and I'd walk away in disgust. . . . I began to get angry at Asians and at my own country. Why couldn't they take care of their own problems?[2]

Americans who were most responsible for our Vietnam policies often complained about how little they knew about the Vietnamese. They mistakenly thought they were especially uninformed about the northerners. For example, General Maxwell Taylor, America's ambassador to Saigon, admitted that "we knew very little about the Hanoi leaders . . . and virtually nothing about their individual or collective intentions."[3]

General Taylor sent a cable to President Johnson that included the western cliché that the Vietnamese were "well aware we place higher value on human life than they do."[4] General Westmoreland also believed that "life is cheap in the Orient."[5] This bigotry was a result of the Americans' ability to use technology to protect our own troops while the North Vietnamese, too poor to match our equipment, were forced to rely on people, their only resource. This did not mean that a Vietnamese parent did not grieve the loss of a child. It meant two other things: Nations fight with whatever they have; and, what we had was not enough to compensate for our cultural ignorance.

Beyond the usual American preference for European culture, manners, and languages, the Far East was, as the cliché has it, "mysterious" to American policymakers. The fact is that Americans were monumentally ignorant of that part of the world where they were attempting to build a nation in our own image. A young man then in the Defense Department, Daniel Ellsberg, admitted this ignorance: "It is fair to say that Americans in office read very few books, and none in French; and that there has never been an official of Deputy Assistant Secretary rank or higher (including myself) who could have passed in office a midterm freshman exam in modern Vietnamese history, if such a course existed in this country."[6] Such a course did not exist.

In the summer of 1970, after twenty-five years of American involvement, Henry Kissinger, then Mr. Nixon's security adviser, met with Dr. Ellsberg in San Clemente. Dr. Kissinger asked for the name of someone who knew "anything" about North Vietnam because "as you know, no one in this government understands North Vietnam."[7] Nine years later, Dr. Kissinger wrote about the opaque strangeness of all of Vietnam. He believed that the land and people of that faraway place were mysterious, beyond the reach of strategic planners and geopolitical policymakers, even beyond the reach of reason:

> Psychologists or sociologists may explain some day what it is about that distant monochromatic land, of green mountains and fields merging with an azure sea, that for millennia has acted as a magnet for foreigners who sought glory there and found frustration, who believed that in its

rice fields and jungles some principle was to be established and entered them only to recede in disillusion. What has inspired its people to such flights of heroism and monomania that a succession of outsiders have looked there for a key to some riddle and then to be expelled by a ferocious persistence that not only thwarted the foreigners exertions but hazarded his own internal balance?[8]

Our difficulties were not with the strangeness of the land or the inscrutability of its people. Modern, secular, well-educated people, such as we are, such as General Taylor and Dr. Kissinger were, can learn about exotic people in distant places. Our difficulty was not with the peculiarities of the Vietnamese. The problem was us, not them. Our difficulty was that the foot soldier slogging through a rice paddy, the general in his Saigon office planning great troop movements, the official in the Pentagon, and the Presidents who made the war were all Americans. Peer de Silva, a CIA chief of station in Saigon, said, "The American official posted in Asia very often finds himself, whether he realizes it or not, standing solemnly before the Asians, his finger pointed skyward and the word 'repent' on his lips."[9] We wanted the Vietnamese to repent for being Vietnamese. There was something about the condition of being an American that prevented us from understanding the "little people in black pajamas" who beat the strongest military force in the world.

In common with most Asians, the Vietnamese had one custom that American soldiers could not tolerate. The people of Vietnam hold hands with their friends. Two Vietnamese soldiers would walk down the street holding hands. An American marine from south Boston noticed this custom: "They all hold hands, see. I fucking hated that."[10] The intensity of this marine's reaction was characteristic of America's fighting men. The custom proved to the GIs that South Vietnamese men were homosexuals, and this diagnosis explained why the Vietnamese were incompetent warriors, raising the question about why Americans had to die in defense of perverts.

A traditional technique for turning American teenagers into soldiers at boot camp was for the drill sergeants to accuse slackers of being queer. The formula was that only "real men" could become soldiers, and the military's first job was to teach youngsters manhood, not soldiering. Relying on deep cultural shame, the drill instructors shouted, "Ladies, attention." The novelist Tim O'Brien described what happened to him during basic training at Fort Lewis. He and a friend were sitting alone polishing their boots. Their sergeant screamed at them: "A couple of college pussies . . . Out behind them barracks hiding from everyone and making some love, huh?" The sergeant stared at them: "You afraid to be in the war, a goddamn pussy, a goddamn lezzie?" They were given guard duty for that night, and the sergeant thought he had the perfect punishment: "You two are gonna walk 'round and 'round the company area, holdin' hands, and you can talk about politics and nooky all the goddamn night." But "the bastard didn't have the guts to order us to hold hands."[11]

For American teenagers struggling "to measure up" to the military's definition of manhood, or not struggling because the standard had been earlier absorbed on the street corners, football fields, or in local bars, the handholding Vietnamese were repulsive and dangerous. If a Vietnamese took the hand or touched the leg of an American grunt, as the foot soldiers were called, the gesture, if unchallenged, would call into question the American's "manhood." In an attempt to deal with this, the marines gave lectures to the men about this custom, saying that all Vietnamese do it. The lecture made things worse because its implicit message was that all Vietnamese were homosexuals. General Westmoreland observed that the handholding struck the GIs as "odd and effeminate."[12]

This could all be dismissed as just another example of American cultural ignorance except that it occasionally had hideous consequences. A marine's truck was stopped by South Vietnamese soldiers who wanted the Americans to take a wounded South Vietnamese soldier to a hospital. His leg had been shot off. One of the marines said, "Fuck him. Let him hop." But the commander of the truck told the wounded man to climb in. "The fucking little slope grabbed my leg." The truck commander said that he had been in Vietnam long enough "to know that most of them are queer. They hold hands and stuff." One of the Americans "whacked" the wounded soldier and told the driver to get going. They threw the wounded man out of the moving truck: "The poor fucking bastard was screaming and crying and begging us. 'Fuck you, you slope. Out you go.' "[13]

The Americans did not see guerrillas or North Vietnamese strolling hand in hand down the street, or if they did they did not realize they were North Vietnamese. It was usual for grunts to respect the enemy more than the ally. As GIs watched our gunships pulverize an area, one said, "You couldn't believe that anyone would have the courage to deal with that night after night . . . and you cultivated a respect for the Viet Cong and NVA. . . ." He also told of a lone sniper firing at a marine base from his hole in the ground. The marines fired everything they had at him, but he always reappeared to fire another round. Finally, napalm was dropped on his position and the entire area was burned to the ground. "When all of it cleared, the sniper popped up and fired off a single round, and the Marines in the trenches cheered. They called him Luke the Gook, and after that no one wanted anything to happen to him."[14]

Thomas Bailey, an interrogation officer stationed in Saigon in the early seventies, believed that Americans did not understand themselves well enough to understand the Vietnamese. He became frustrated because "their civilization was so much older than ours, although we would characterize them as being uncivilized. I would have a difficult time defining the way in which they were more civilized than we were, but they were. It's my gut feeling."[15] It was difficult for the young Americans who were sent to save the South Vietnamese both from themselves and from North Vietnam to encounter people who did not want to be saved in the way we intended. "Government is not important," a villager said, "rice is important." America corrupted the urban elites of South Vietnam by dangling riches in front them. But it was the city dwellers, especially the Buddhists, who struggled hardest against the other corruption, the cultural pride and myopia of the Americans. They were as proud of their traditions and culture as we were of ours.

This question of whether we thought they were civilized had grisly side effects. This is illustrated by the case of Sven Erickssson, a fictitious name given to an American GI. One month after Sven arrived in Vietnam, he became part of a five-man reconnaissance patrol. The night before they were to start, the sergeant told the others that they would take a girl with them "to have some fun." He said it would "be good for the morale of the squad." The next morning the patrol kidnapped a young woman from her mother and sister. After a day's march, with the woman carrying much of their gear, they settled in for the night. Four of the men raped the woman, but Sven, a serious Lutheran from Minnesota, refused, despite the sergeant's questioning of his manhood, and despite accusations that he was betraying his buddies. The next day the patrol got caught in a fire fight with a few guerrillas, and the sergeant gave the corporal permission to kill the woman. He stabbed her three times, twice in the chest and once in the neck. She still did not die, so he blew away part of her head with his M-16.

Sven brought charges against his buddies, despite the commanding officer's extended attempt to cover up, by finally getting a chaplain to help. All the others were found guilty. Part of their defense was that the gang rape and murder "did not occur in the United States." "Indeed," their counsel argued, "there are some that would say it did not even occur in civilization. . . ." After several levels of review, all got substantially reduced sentences. The fear of what the released men, especially the sergeant, might do to Sven explains why his real name was not used.[16]

Even Sven experienced the difficulty of thinking of Vietnamese as human, let alone civilized. When he earlier walked through a village only to discover guerrillas shooting at him when he got to the other side, and the supposedly friendly villagers had not warned him, he was naturally bitter. As he put it, "All that many of us could think at such times was that we were fools to be ready to die for people who defecated in public, whose food was dirtier than anything in our garbage cans back home." This could change some of the GIs, he said. "It could keep them from believing that life was so valuable—anyone's life, I mean, even their own."[17]

Finally, the question descended to a different level: Were they human? Later, at a place called My Lai, this question was answered again. It was a question that had to be answered over and over. But the answer depended on the personal values and interdictions of the individual grunts. Neither the American government nor the military helped them. As we will later see, both encouraged the wrong response.

Americans were ignorant about the Vietnamese not because we were stupid, but because we believe certain things about ourselves. Those things necessarily distorted our vision and confused our minds in ways that made learning extraordinarily difficult. To understand our failure we must think about what it means to be an American.

The necessary text for understanding the condition of being an American is a single sentence written by Herman Melville in his novel *White Jacket:* "And we Americans are the peculiar, chosen people—the Israel of our time; we bear the ark of the liberties of the world."[18] This was not the last time this idea was expressed by Americans. It was at the center of thought of the men who brought us the Vietnam War. It was at the center of the most characteristic American myth.

This oldest and most important myth about America has an unusually specific origin. More than 350 years ago, while in mid-passage between England and the American wilderness, John Winthrop told the band of Puritans he was leading to a new and dangerous life that they were engaged in a voyage that God Himself not only approved, but in which He participated. The precise way that Brother Winthrop expressed himself echoes throughout the history of American life. He explained to his fellow travelers, "We shall find that the God of Israel is among us, when ten of us shall be able to resist a thousand of our enemies, when he shall make us a praise and glory, that men shall say of succeeding plantations [settlements]: the Lord make it like that of New England: for we must Consider that we shall be as a City upon a Hill, the eyes of all people are upon us."[19] The myth of America as a city on a hill implies that America is a moral example to the rest of the world, a world that will presumably keep its attention riveted on us. It means that we are a Chosen People, each of whom, because of God's favor and presence, can smite one hundred of our heathen enemies hip and thigh.

The society Winthrop meant to establish in New England would do God's work, insofar as sinners could. America would become God's country. The Puritans would have understood this to mean that they were creating a nation of, by, and for the Lord. About two centuries later, the pioneers and the farmers who followed the Puritans translated God's country from civilization to the grandeur and nobility of nature, to virgin land, to the purple mountains' majesty. Relocating the country of God from civilization to nature was significant in many ways, but the conclusion that this New World is specially favored by the Lord not only endured but spread.

In countless ways Americans know in their gut—the only place myths can live—that we have been Chosen to lead the world in public morality and to instruct it in political virtue. We believe that our own domestic goodness results in strength adequate to destroy our opponents who, by definition, are enemies of virtue, freedom, and God. Over and over, the founding Puritans described their new settlement as a beacon in the darkness, a light whose radiance could keep Christian voyagers from crashing on the rocks, a light that could brighten the world. In his inaugural address John Kennedy said, "The energy, the faith, the devotion which we bring to this endeavor [defending freedom] will light our country and all who serve it—and the glow from that fire can truly light the world."[20] The city on a hill grew from its first tiny society to encompass the entire nation. As we will see, that is one of the reasons why we compelled ourselves to intervene in Vietnam.

An important part of the myth of America as the city on a hill has been lost as American power increased. John Winthrop intended that his tiny settlement should be only an example of rectitude to the cosmos. It could not have occurred to him that his small and weak band of saints should charge about the world to impose the One Right Way on others who were either too wicked, too stupid, or even too oppressed to follow his example. Because they also had domestic distractions, the early American Puritans could not even consider foreign adventures. In almost no time they had their hands full with a variety of local malefactors: Indians, witches, and, worst of all, shrewd Yankees who were more interested in catching fish than in catching the spirit of the Lord. Nathaniel Hawthorne, brooding about these Puritans, wrote that civilization begins by building a jail and a graveyard, but he was only two-thirds right. Within only two generations, the New England saints discovered that there was a brothel in Boston, the hub of the new and correct Christian order.

The New World settlement was puny, but the great ocean was a defensive moat that virtually prohibited an onslaught by foreign predators. The new Americans could therefore go about perfecting their society without distracting anxiety about alien and corrupting intrusions from Europe. This relative powerlessness coupled with defensive security meant that the city on a hill enjoyed a favorable "peculiar situation." It was peculiarly blessed because the decadent world could not come here, and we did not have to go there. The rest of the world, but especially Europe, with its frippery, pomp, and Catholicism, was thought to be morally leprous. This is what George Washington had in mind when he asked a series of rhetorical questions in his farewell address in 1796:

> Why forego the advantages of so peculiar a situation? Why quit our own to stand upon foreign ground? Why, by interweaving our destiny with that of any part of Europe, entangle our peace and prosperity in the toils of European ambition, rivalship, interest, humor, of caprice?[21]

This is also what Thomas Jefferson told his countrymen when he was inaugurated five years later. This enlightened and skeptical philosopher-President announced that this was a "chosen country" which had been "kindly separated by nature and a wide ocean from the exterminating havoc of one quarter of the globe." He said that the young nation could exult in its many blessings if it would only keep clear of foreign evil. His prescription was that America should have "entangling alliances with none."[22]

One final example of the unaggressive, unimperial interpretation of the myth is essential. The entire Adams family had a special affinity for old Winthrop. Perhaps it was that they grew up on the soil in which he was buried. On the Fourth of July, in 1821, John Quincy Adams gave a speech that captured every nuance of the already ancient myth. His speech could have been the text for the Vietnam War critics. He said that America's heart and prayers would always be extended to any free and independent part of the world. "But she goes not abroad in search of monsters to destroy." America, he said, hoped that freedom and independence would spread across the face of the earth. "She will recommend the general cause by the countenance of her voice, and by the benignant sympathy of her example." He said that the new nation understood that it should not actively intervene abroad even if such an adventure would be on the side of freedom because "she would involve herself beyond the power of extrication." It just might be possible for America to try to impose freedom elsewhere, to assist in the liberation of others. "She might," he said, "become the dictatress of the world. She would no longer be the ruler of her own spirit."[23]

In 1966, this speech was quoted by George F. Kennan, the thoughtful analyst of Soviet foreign affairs, to the Senate Foreign Relations Committee which was conducting hearings on the Vietnam War. Perhaps not knowing the myth, Mr. Kennan said that he was not sure what Mr. Adams had in mind when he spoke almost a century and a half earlier. But whatever it was, Mr. Kennan told the senators who were then worrying about Vietnam, "He spoke very directly and very pertinently to us here today."[24]

The myth of the city on a hill became the foundation for the ritualistic thinking of later generations of Americans. This myth helped to establish nationalistic orthodoxy in America. It began to set an American dogma, to fix the limits of thought for Americans about themselves and about the rest of the world, and offered a choice about the appropriate relationship between us and them.

The benevolence of our national motives, the absence of material gain in what we seek, the dedication to principle, and our inpenetrable ignorance were all related to the original myth of America. It is temptingly easy to dismiss this as some quaint idea that perhaps once had some significance, but lost it in this more sophisticated, tough-minded, modern America. Arthur Schlesinger, Jr., a close aide to President Kennedy, thought otherwise. He was concerned about President Johnson's vastly ambitious plans to create a "Great Society for Asia." Whatever the President meant, according to Professor Schlesinger, such an idea

> . . . demands the confrontation of an issue deep in the historical consciousness of the United States: whether this country is a chosen people, uniquely righteous and wise, with a moral mission to all mankind . . . The ultimate choice is between messianism and maturity.[25]

The city myth should have collapsed during the war. The war should have taught us that we could not continue to play the role of moral adviser and moral enforcer to the world. After the shock of the assassinations, after the shock of Tet, after President Johnson gave up the presidency, after the riots, demonstrations, burned neighborhoods, and the rebellion of the young, it should have been difficult to sustain John Winthrop's optimism. It was not difficult for Robert Kennedy who, after Senator Eugene McCarthy had demonstrated LBJ's vulnerability in New Hampshire, finally announced that he would run for the presidency himself. The language he used in his announcement speech proved that the myth was as alive and as virulent as it had ever been: "At stake," Senator Kennedy said, "is not simply the leadership of our party, and even our own country, it is our right to the moral leadership of this planet."[26] Members of his staff were horrified that he could use such language because they correctly believed that it reflected just the mind-set that had propelled us into Vietnam in the first place. He ignored their protests. This myth could survive in even the toughest of the contemporary, sophisticated, hard-driving politicians. Of course, he may have used this language only to persuade his listeners, to convince the gullible. But, even so, it showed that he believed that the myth was what they wanted to hear. In either case, the city on a hill continued to work its way.

In some ways American nationalism resembles that of other countries. Between God's Country and Holy Russia there is not much of a choice. Between ideas of moral superiority and racial superiority there is even less of a choice, since one invariably leads to the other. The Middle Kingdom of China, the Sacred Islands of Japan, the Holy Islamic Republic of Iran, all rest in some sense on being Chosen. Israel also knows about this. More secular bases for self-congratulation are nearly ubiquitous: the glory of France, dominion of Britain, power and racial purity of the Third Reich, the satisfaction of thinking of oneself as the "cradle of civilization," as claimed by Egypt, Syria, Greece, and virtually every other ancient country on the face of the earth, along with the *Pax Romana. Pro patria mori*, the willingness to die for one's uniquely favored country, has no national boundary. The longer such a list grows the more trivial it is. National myths become important to the rest of the world only when they are coupled to national power sufficient to impose one nation's will on another. The old Puritans were only interesting, not important, because they were so weak.

A whisper runs throughout our history that the people of the world really want to be like us, regardless of what they or their political leaders say. The evidence that this is true is very powerful. Immigration to this country was the largest movement of people ever. Our entire history is the history of a magnet. However, the slave runners were obliged to use a whip instead of a lure, and so the record is far from consistent. But, since the Civil War, the overwhelming majority of new immigrants came voluntarily. Many were forced to leave their old countries, but almost all chose to come here rather than to go elsewhere. We refused to admit additional millions who wanted to become Americans. For most of this century our standard of living was the world's highest, and Americans ate better, had more leisure, and suffered less political or religious oppression. The Statue of Liberty meant what it said. Its torch lights the way to a better life. Who could deny it?

In fact, almost anyone could. For all the accomplishments of the American nation, its promises so far outstrip its reality as to leave its many victims gasping in disbelief at the betrayal of their dreams. This culture detests poverty and fears the poor. The ladder of economic mobility is a conceit of the many who have climbed it and a reproach to the many who cannot get on it. To defend themselves against their new country, many of the immigrants maintained their own cultures, their own ways of speaking and of doing things, instead of integrating into what Americans in the mainstream of American life call the mainstream of American life.

Everyone naturally prefers their own language, diet, and funeral customs. The ancient Greeks defined a barbarian as one who did not speak Greek. The classical Chinese defined the civilized man as one who spoke Chinese and used chopsticks. Much of the rest of the world would surely like to be richer and more powerful. But an unknown number would not exchange the familiarity of their local horizon, ritual comforts of the family graveyard, or their daily competence for greater material strength. We all prefer who we are and what we know, sometimes at the expense of the chance to make it big. It is an old story to almost everyone, except that American nationalism in its purest form thinks of the world as populated by frustrated or potential Americans. This is unique among the world's nationalisms. Thus, we believe that we can know others reasonably easily because of our assumption that they want to become us.

The great ocean that defended us throughout our history also kept us from knowing others. The less one knows of the world, the more appalling the local customs of others may seem. The other side of that is also true: The less one knows of the world, the more one's own little daily rituals seem to have been decreed either by God or nature. People in other countries have different domestic customs. This may make them seem colorful, and for the most strident nationalists, even stupid or disgusting. For some of us it is hard to imagine that there are people for whom the day of rest, the day when the stores and banks are closed, is Friday, and for others it is Saturday. For some people, belching during a meal is a compliment to the chef. Some people wear white to funerals.

The cultural arrogance that comes from cultural isolation is not, of course, an American monopoly. Many South Vietnamese considered Americans as barbarians. For example, Bruce Lawlor, a CIA case officer in Vietnam during the war, said,

> they thought we were animals. A lot of little things that we took for granted offended them fiercely, such as putting your hand on a head. Sitting with your feet crossed, with your foot facing another person, is a high insult.[27]

We seem to think that people who have such strange ideas do not really mean them. We seem to believe that they do such things out of ignorance or poverty. They cannot help it. If they could, they would become more like us. It is apparently beyond reason to believe that anyone would follow these exotic customs for deep cultural reasons, as deep as the reasons that compel us to shake hands instead of bowing.

This way of thinking about the world has a name—solipsism —and means that someone believes that he is the world. In the foreign affairs of the nation, solipsistic thinking—they are us— has been dangerous. The advantage of imposing the imperial American self on the rest of humanity is that it serves as a justification of ignorance.

Solipsism supports American optimism. Because they are thought really to be us, we think that we know what we are doing, know what makes them tick, and know what we can do that will work. In Southeast Asia this optimism proved to be brutal in the sense that American power was believed sufficient to compensate for our ignorance, to make the detailed particularities of Vietnam's otherness beside the point. This combi-

nation of solipsism and optimism finally revealed its enabling
ignorance. Because we were ignorant, we could proceed. It is a
reasonably good guess that had we somehow repressed our
solipsism; had we as a result learned something of both North
and South Vietnam, we would not have intervened quite so
smugly. Our ignorance, in short, permitted us to trust our guns
in the first place and to fail in our stated national objectives in
the last place.

The myth of the city on a hill combined with solipsism in the
assumptions about Vietnam made by the American war planners. In other words, we assumed that we had a superior moral
claim to be in Vietnam, and because, despite their quite queer
ways of doing things, the Vietnamese shared our values, they
would applaud our intentions and embrace our physical presence. Thus, Vice-President Humphrey later acknowledged that
all along we had been ignorant of Vietnam. He said that "to LBJ,
the Mekong and the Pedernales were not that far apart."[28] Our
claim to virtue was based on the often announced purity of our
intentions. It was said, perhaps thousands of times, that all we
wanted was freedom for other people, not land, not resources,
and not domination.

Because we believed that our intentions were virtuous, we
could learn nothing from the French experience in Vietnam.
After all, they had fought only to maintain their Southeast
Asian colonies and as imperialists deserved to lose. We assumed
that this was why so mighty a European power lost the important battle of Dien Bien Phu to General Giap's ragged army.
America's moral authority was so clear to us that we assumed
that it also had to be clear to the Vietnamese. This self-righteousness was the clincher in the debate to intensify the conflict
in Vietnam, according to George W. Ball, an undersecretary of
state for Presidents Kennedy and Johnson. Washington's war
planners, Mr. Ball said in 1973, had been captives of their own
myths.[29] Another State Department official also hoped, after the
fact, that Americans "will be knocked out of our grandiosity
... [and] will see the self-righteous, illusory quality of that vision
of ourselves offered by the high Washington official who said
that while other nations have 'interests' the United States has 'a
sense of responsibility.' "[30] Our power, according to this mentality, gives us responsibility, even though we may be reluctant
to bear the burden. Other peoples' greed or selfishness gives

them interests, even though they may not be strong enough to grab all they want.

Our grandiosity will, however, not be diminished so easily. At least since World War II, America's foreign affairs have been the affairs of Pygmalion. We fall in love with what we create. We create a vision of the world made in what we think is our own image. We are proud of what we create because we are certain that our intentions are pure, our motives good, and our behavior virtuous. We know these things to be true because we believe that we are unique among the nations of the world in our collective idealism.

There are many authors of this myth of American idealism, but the supreme American political idealist of our century was Woodrow Wilson. He had grown up in the South during the Civil War, the son of a Presbyterian minister from whom he learned the meaning of Christian duty, charity, and discipline. He was sometimes criticized for being a cold fish. Mr. Wilson built his career as a professor of government, president of Princeton University, and President of the United States on his quite remarkable talents as a writer and a speaker.

A man of peace, it was his misfortune to lead the United States into World War I. He had a vision of how the world should organize itself after the killing stopped, and a vision of open diplomacy that would not be dictated by bullies, with interests and without responsibility, behind closed doors. He supported national self-determination in place of domination by more powerful nations. His central vision was of an international forum, the League of Nations, where debate would replace carnage. In 1919, the terms of the peace were to be negotiated in a conference of the victorious nations to be held at the Versailles Palace. Despite warnings that he should stay away from Paris, President Wilson sailed to the Old World to cleanse it of the murderous decadence that had kept it, and the world, in flames for so long.

It is clear that President Wilson was a resident of the city on a hill. As he expressed it: "America was born a Christian nation; America was born to exemplify that devotion to the elements of righteousness which are derived from the revelations of Holy Scripture."[31] But as Commander in Chief he wanted actually to convert the heathen Europeans, not merely to provide them with America's healing example. His Presbyterian zeal easily enough became enmeshed in his nationalistic fervor, and he sailed to the cynical Old World to extirpate its sinning ways in the names of God and America.

He was welcomed in Europe as no mortal had ever been received before or since. In France, England, and Italy, millions of people cheered his triumphal march, lighted candles in his name, and brightened the streets of a continent with flowers to show his way. He was the incarnation of the best hopes of a wounded world, and the bright young men who were assembling in Paris to begin the work of making a permanent peace were ecstatic under the President's guiding light. He was the prophet who had foreseen that this war would be the war to end war. John Maynard Keynes, the English economist, was there, and he expressed the excited hopes of the world: "With what curiosity, anxiety, and hope we sought a glimpse of the features and bearing of the man of destiny who, coming from the West, was to bring healing to the wounds of the ancient parent of his civilization and lay for us the foundations of the future."[32]

Thinking about the role he had assigned himself to play in the Hall of Mirrors at Versailles, the President explained his larger vision to his secretary: "Well . . . this trip will either be the greatest success or the supremest tragedy in all history; but I believe in a Divine Providence. If I did not have faith I should go crazy." He believed that his inspiration would overcome, no matter what. "No body of men, however they concert their power or their influence, can defeat this great world enterprise, which after all is the enterprise of Divine mercy, peace, and good will."[33] Clemenceau, representing France, who was called "the tiger," was rarely without his skullcap and suede gloves, and wore, as one observer said, "the half-smile of an irritated, sceptical and neurasthenic gorilla."[34] This tiger-gorilla complained that President Wilson thought he was the messiah returned. The stage was set.

When the President arrived, Paris was overflowing with the men who were there to plan the peace. The Big Five—France, Great Britain, Italy, Japan, and the United States—were joined by representatives of virtually every state, minority, and tribe of Eurasia. None of the weak representatives were seriously consulted about anything. The salesmen peddling rugs, oil wells, and assorted blueprints for Utopia, along with the pimps and prostitutes, scurried around the edges of the picturesque throngs in Paris, doing their business with bits of every European language. To round out the fantastic scene, Germany and the other Central Powers, as well as the new Soviets, were not there. But a young man later called Ho Chi Minh was, and he actually rented a formal morning suit to look his western best for a meeting with Woodrow Wilson that would not be granted. He had wanted to make a case for an independent Vietnam. Later in his life he changed into shorts and sandals as he abandoned the role of supplicant to the deaf.

The tragedy was that Mr. Wilson failed in Paris. He tried to persuade politicians who responded only to power. The President had the power to force compliance with his vision, but he was unwilling to use it. It would have been inconsistent with the purity of his motives and the humility of his Christian mission. He traded away much of what he believed to win acceptance of the League of Nations. Along with millions, Mr. Keynes was devastated. He discovered that the President "had no plan, no scheme, no constructive ideas whatever for clothing with the flesh of life the commandments he had thundered from the White House." But, Keynes went on, "he could have preached a sermon on any one of them or have addressed a stately prayer to the Almighty for their fulfillment; but he could not frame their concrete application to the actual state of Europe."[35] A brokenhearted attaché of the American peace commission wrote a letter of resignation to the President: "I am sorry that you did not fight our fight to the finish and that you had so little faith in the millions of men, like myself, in every nation who had faith in you."[36] Nonetheless, when President Wilson returned to America he was sufficiently satisfied with his accomplishment to announce, "At last the world knows America as the saviour of the world!"[37]

The League was described in a letter which Sigmund Freud wrote to Albert Einstein in 1932, just before Hitler was elected to power in Germany: It was, he wrote, "an attempt to base upon an appeal to certain idealistic attitudes of mind the authority which otherwise rests on the possession of power."[38] Freud was allergic to American idealism. For example, he explained that all of our dreams are motivated by pure egotism, and told this story: "One of my English friends put forward this proposition at a scientific meeting in America, whereupon a lady who was present remarked that that might be the case in Austria, but she could maintain for herself and for her friends that *they* were altruistic even in their dreams."[39]

President Wilson's idealism, read in the context of Vietnam, shows the consequences of American goodness. "When men take up arms," he said, "to set other men free, there is something sacred and holy in the warfare. I will not cry 'peace' as long as there is sin and wrong in the world."[40] Now the Christian soldiers could march onward, armed with M-16s and napalm, to free the world of evil. Dr. Kissinger understood that "our entry into the [Vietnam] war had been the product not of a militarist psychosis but of a naive idealism that wanted to set right all the world's ills and believed American good will supplied its own efficacy."[41]

President Wilson's failure shook the world's confidence in America's capacity to rejuvenate Europe, that "old bitch gone in the teeth."[42] That bitch, however, was soon enough to go into heat and produce a new generation of beasts to savage the world. In the process, America did not lose its own confidence in its intrinsic goodness and benignity. Its moral revulsion led it to withdraw from the sordid affairs of the world in the 1930s. Since Pearl Harbor, however, it has felt obliged to drive "sin and wrong" off the face of the planet.

Although the nationalists of the world all share a peoples' pride in who they are, a loyalty to place and language and culture, there are delicate but important differences. Because of its Puritan roots, it is not surprising that America's nationalism is more Protestant than that of other countries. It is more missionary in its impulses, more evangelical. It typically seeks to correct the way other people think rather than to establish its own physical dominion over them. It is, as it were, more committed to the Word, as befits serious Protestants, than other nationalisms.

One of the peculiarities of American Protestant nationalism, especially in its most aggressive mood, is its passion about ideas. What we want is to convert others to the truth as we understand it. We went to war in Vietnam in the name of ideas, of principles, of abstractions. Thus, President Johnson said in his inaugural, "We aspire to nothing that belongs to others."[43] And added in his important address at Johns Hopkins in April 1965: "Because we fight for values and we fight for principles, rather than territory or colonies, our patience and our determination are unending."[44] This is what we mean when we think of ourselves as idealists, magnanimous and moral. It is what cold warriors mean when they say over and over that we are engaged with the Soviet Union "in a competition of ideas."

This is the Protestant face of diplomacy and war. It is Protestant in its commitment to the Word, the Book, instead of to what the founding Protestants believed was the impious Catholic emphasis on persons, the person of the Pope, or the superstitions about the person of the Virgin. When they abolished Christmas and Easter, these radical Puritans showed that they were even suspicious about worshipers of the person of Jesus. America's political founding fathers rebelled against the person of the king and replaced him with written ideas and codes. The Word shall make you free. It is no wonder that America has the world's oldest written Constitution. When America attacks, it does so to protect an abstract principle. This may make it a little less concerned with the welfare of the individuals we are trying to help than with the abstractions that we believe justify war.

Graham Greene, in *The Quiet American,* fully understood this American obsession with the mind, not so much ours as others. Greene's central character, Pyle, an American in Vietnam in the middle fifties, had a "young and unused face," and "with his gangly legs and his crew-cut and his wide campus gaze he seemed incapable of harm." Pyle's head was filled with theories about the Far East. He wanted more than anything else to help the Vietnamese, not as individual people, but as a nation. Pyle could not regard them as people. Greene's narrator could, and he responded, for instance, to the Vietnamese women dressed in their *ao dais:*

> Up the street came the lovely flat figures—the white silk trousers, the long tight jackets in pink and mauve patterns slit up the thigh: I watched them with the nostalgia I knew I would feel when I left these regions for ever. "They are lovely, aren't they?" I said over my beer, and Pyle cast them a cursory glance as they went on up the rue Castinat. "Oh, sure," he said indifferently: he was a serious type.

The narrator wondered why he liked "to tease the innocent," like Pyle. The young man had only just arrived in this complex and ancient place:

> Perhaps only ten days ago he had been walking back across the Common in Boston, his arms full of the books he had been reading in advance on the Far East and the problems of China. He didn't even hear what I said: he was absorbed already in the dilemmas of Democracy and the responsibilities of the West: he was determined . . . to do good, not to any individual person but to a country, a continent, a world. Well, he was in his element now with the whole universe to improve.

Young, dedicated Pyle, and others like him, could not see the wounds on a dead body. What they responded to was a representative of an idea, "a Red menace, a soldier of democracy." The innocence of these defenders of the true faith made them "like a dumb leper who has lost his bell, wandering the world, meaning no harm." The innocent Americans could, with the best intentions, infect the world. Finally, Graham's narrator tried to explain something of the humanness of Vietnam to Pyle:

> "You and your like are trying to make a war with the help of people who just aren't interested."
> "They don't want Communism."
> "They want enough rice," I said. "They don't want to be shot at. They want one day to be much the same as another. They don't want our white skins around telling them what they want."
> "If Indo-China goes . . ."
> "I know that record. Siam goes. Malaya goes. Indonesia goes. What does 'go' mean? If I believed in your God and another life, I'd bet my future harp against your golden crown that in five hundred years there may be no New York or London, but they'll be growing paddy in these fields, they'll be carrying their produce to market on long poles wearing their pointed hats. The small boys will be sitting on the buffaloes. I like the buffaloes, they don't like our smell, the smell of Europeans. And remember—from a buffalo's point of view you are a European too."

"They'll be forced to believe what they are told, they won't be allowed to think for themselves."

"Thought's a luxury. Do you think the peasant sits and thinks of God and Democracy when he gets inside his mud hut at night?"

Pyle inevitably caused havoc at every turn.[45]

In an astonishing literary exchange during a hearing before the House of Representatives Select Committee on Intelligence in 1975, Congressman William Lehman of Florida asked William Colby, the head of the CIA, if he had read *The Quiet American*. Congressman Lehman was concerned about whether Americans could ever have understood Vietnamese culture: "I am just concerned about how can we possibly prevent the kinds of miscalculations, the misconceptualizing or lack of understanding of what is going on—the basic limitations of someone like this fellow Pyle . . . who is dealing from one culture into another culture without knowing what the hell he was doing." Mr. Colby acknowledged the difficulties in understanding another culture, but insisted that "the professional intelligence service," not "amateurs," had the best chance of success. Mr. Lehman was not convinced, because of the CIA's Vietnam record, and because he thought that we were "going to have to intuitively assess things—which is sometimes better than what the professionals can do."[46]

Some of the war's generals understood America's cultural rigidity, along with the military price that would ultimately be paid, as they said after, not during, the American war in Vietnam. In 1974, retired Brigadier General Douglas Kinnard mailed a questionnaire to 173 army generals who had served in Vietnam. Some of them commented about the problem of American ignorance. "We erroneously tried to impose the American system on a people who didn't want it, couldn't handle it and may lose because they tried it." Another said that "as in all our foreign wars, we never really established rapport." That was because of "our overinflated hypnosis with the myth of the American way." A third, using the same hindsight, said that "we never took into account the cultural differences." Another general officer reported that the South Vietnamese army never made any substantial progress because, he said, "most of us did not want to associate with them."[47]

* * *

How was it possible for the Vietnamese to fail to realize that the ideas of Democracy and God are more important than life? American nationalism, especially when its fist clenched, went forward not to pillage, but to instruct. That is what missionaries do. And, therefore, we did not need to bother about learning who it was we were saving. We knew, as both JFK and LBJ told us, that the South Vietnamese were uneducated and poor. We believed that this made them susceptible to bad ideas. To stiffen their resistance we undertook a program of "nation-building" that would provide a "stable" government in the South, provide more and better education for the children, and improve the economy. To protect them from their lunatic northern brothers, we would make them a new country. We would invent South Vietnam. They would be delighted, we assumed, because we believed their old country was a mess and was responsible for the ignorance, disease, and illiteracy. They must have hated it all along.

Tangled up in old myths, fearful of speaking plain English on the subject, the political conscience of many Americans must be troubled. There is bad faith in accepting the city myth of American uniqueness as if the myth can be freed from its integral Protestantism, almost always of a fundamentalist flavor. Conservatives have less need to launder the myth of its religion. Because liberals require a secular version of nationalism, and if they need or want to retain some sense of the unique republic, they are required to rest their case on a secular basis. Wilsonian idealism was the answer in the 1960s, as liberals argued that America was the only society capable of creating social justice and genuine democracy at home and abroad. These ideals merged with the cold war and persuaded the best of American liberals to bring us Vietnam.

In America, as elsewhere, elected officials are especially susceptible to the fundamental myths of nationalism because they must embody them to get elected and act on them to govern. The vision of the world that suffused Mr. Wilson's Fourteen Points and League of Nations was also the vision of John Kennedy and his circle. They were pained by the knowledge that a people anywhere in the world struggled toward freedom but was frustrated by the imposition of force. So it was that John

F. Kennedy's inspired inaugural address carried the burden of Woodrow Wilson's idealism, and also carried the deadly implication that America was again ready for war in the name of goodness.

President Kennedy's language must be understood in the light of what was just around the corner in Vietnam. He announced to the world, "We shall pay any price, bear any burden, meet any hardship, support any friend, oppose any foe to assure the survival and the success of liberty." He said that it was the rare destiny of his generation to defend freedom when it was at its greatest risk. "I do not shrink from this responsibility—I welcome it."[48]

The difference between the two sons of the Commonwealth of Massachusetts, John Quincy Adams and John Fitzgerald Kennedy, was the difference between good wishes and war, but also the difference between a tiny and isolated America and the world's most powerful nation. Presidents Wilson and Kennedy both fairly represented American liberalism at its most restless and energetic. This was a liberalism that wanted, as President Wilson put it, to make the world safe for democracy, or as President Kennedy said, to defend "those human rights to which this nation has always been committed, and to which we are committed today at home and around the world." JFK described this as "God's work."[49]

An important part of the reason we marched into Vietnam with our eyes fixed was liberalism's irrepressible need to be helpful to those less fortunate. But the decency of the impulse, as was the case with President Wilson, cannot hide the bloody eagerness to kill in the name of virtue. In 1981, James C. Thomson, an aide in the State Department and a member of the National Security Council under President Johnson, finally concluded that our Vietnamese intervention had been motivated by a national missionary impulse, a "need to do good to others." In a phrase that cannot be improved, he and others called this "sentimental imperialism."[50] The purity of intention and the horror of result is unfortunately the liberal's continuing burden.

American conservatives had it easier, largely because they believed in the actuality of evil. In his first public statement, President Eisenhower informed the American public, "The forces of good and evil are massed and armed and opposed as rarely before in history." For him the world struggle was not merely between conflicting ideologies. "Freedom is pitted against slavery; lightness against the dark."[51]

Conservatives in America are closer than liberals to the myth of the city on a hill because they are not embarrassed by public professions of religion. They are therefore somewhat less likely to ascribe American values and behavior to other cultures. This is so because of the conservatives' conviction that America is so much better—more moral, godly, wise, and especially rich—than other nations that they could not possibly resemble us. Thus, President Eisenhower announced that one of America's fixed principles was the refusal to "use our strength to try to impress upon another people our own cherished political and economic institutions."[52] The idea of uniqueness means, after all, that we are alone in the world.

Conservatives shared with liberals the conviction that America could act, and in Vietnam did act, with absolute altruism, as they believed only America could. Thinking of this war, President Nixon, another restless descendent of Mr. Wilson, declared that "never in history have men fought for less selfish motives —not for conquest, not for glory, but only for the right of a people far away to choose the kind of government they want."[53] This was especially attractive because in this case the kind of government presumably sought by this faraway people was opposed to Communism, our own enemy. It was therefore an integral part of the universal struggle between freedom and slavery, lightness and dark. As a result it was relatively easy for conservatives to think of Vietnam as a laboratory to test ways to block the spreading stain of political atheism.

Power is sometimes a problem for liberals and a solution for conservatives. When Senator Goldwater rattled America's many sabers in his presidential campaign of 1964, and when General Curtis LeMay wanted to bomb North Vietnam "back to the stone age,"[54] they both made liberals cringe, partly from embarrassment, and partly because the liberals were appalled at the apparent cruelty. In the 1950s, Dr. Kissinger cleverly argued that the liberal embarrassment over power made its use, when necessary, even worse than it had to be. "Our feeling of guilt with respect to power," he wrote, "has caused us to transform all wars into crusades, and then to apply our power in the most absolute ways."[55] Later, when he ran America's foreign policy, his own unambivalent endorsement of the use in Vietnam of enormous power inevitably raised the question of whether bloody crusades are caused only by the squeamishness of liberals or also by the callousness of conservatives.

Implicit in John Winthrop's formulation of the city myth was the idea that the new Americans could, because of their godliness, vanquish their numerically superior enemies. The idea that warriors, because of their virtue, could beat stronger opponents, is very ancient. Pericles spoke of it in his funeral oration to the Athenians. The Christian crusaders counted on it. *Jihad,* Islam's conception of a holy war, is based on it. The Samurai believed it. So did the Nazis.

In time, the history of America proved to Americans that we were militarily invincible. The Vietnam War Presidents naturally cringed at the thought that they could be the first to lose a war. After all, we had already beaten Indians, French, British (twice), Mexicans, Spaniards, Germans (twice), Italians, Japanese, Koreans, and Chinese. Until World War II, the nation necessarily had to rely on the presumed virtue, not the power, of American soldiers to carry the day, and the war. This was also the case in the South during our Civil War.

Starting in the eighteenth century, the nation of farmers began to industrialize. As the outcome of war increasingly came to depend on the ability to inject various forms of flying hardware into the enemy's body, victory increasingly depended on technology. The acceleration of industrialization in the late nineteenth century inevitably quickened the pace of technological evolution. By then no other power could match the Americans' ability to get organized, to commit resources to development, and to invent the gadgets that efficiently produced money in the marketplace, and, when necessary, death on the battlefield. The idea of Yankee ingenuity, American know-how, stretches back beyond the nineteenth century. Our admiration for the tinkerer whose new widget forms the basis of new industry is nowhere better shown than in our national reverence of Thomas Edison.

Joining the American sense of its moral superiority with its technological superiority was a marriage made in heaven, at least for American nationalists. We told ourselves that each advantage explained the other, that the success of our standard of living was a result of our virtue, and our virtue was a result of our wealth. Our riches, our technology, provided the strength that had earlier been missing, that once had forced us to rely only on our virtue. Now, as Hiroshima demonstrated conclusively, we could think of ourselves not only as morally superior, but as the most powerful nation in history. The inevitable offspring of this marriage of an idea with a weapon was the conviction that the United States could not be beaten in war—not by any nation, and not by any combination of nations. For that moment we thought that we could fight where, when, and how we wished, without risking failure. For that moment we thought that we could impose our will on the recalcitrant of the earth.

A great many Americans, in the period just before the war in Vietnam got hot, shared a circular belief that for most was probably not very well formed: America's technological supremacy was a symptom of its uniqueness, and technology made the nation militarily invincible. In 1983, the playwright Arthur Miller said, "I'm an American. I believe in technology. Until the mid-60s I never believed we could lose because we had technology."[56]

The memory of World War II concluding in a mushroom cloud was relatively fresh throughout the 1950s. It was unthinkable that America's military could ever fail to establish its supremacy on the battlefield, that the industrial, scientific, and technological strength of the nation would ever be insufficient for the purposes of war. It was almost as if Americans were technology. The American love affair with the automobile was at its most passionate in the 1950s, our well-equipped armies stopped the Chinese in Korea, for a moment our nuclear supremacy was taken for granted, and affluence for many white Americans seemed to be settling in as a way of life.

It is, of course, unfortunate that the forces of evil may be as strong as the forces of virtue. The Soviet Union exploded its first atomic bomb way ahead of what Americans thought was a likely schedule. This technology is not like others because even a weak bomb is devastating. Even if our bombs are better than theirs, they can still do us in. America's freedom of action after 1949 was not complete. President Eisenhower and John Foster Dulles, the Secretary of State, threatened "massive retaliation" against the Soviet Union if it stepped over the line. They knew, and we knew, that this threat was not entirely real, and that it freed the Soviets to engage in peripheral adventures because they correctly believed that we would not destroy the world over Korea, Berlin, Hungary, or Czechoslovakia.

Our policy had to become more flexible. We had to invent a theory that would allow us to fight on the edges without nuclear technology. This theory is called "limited war." Its premise is that we and the Soviets can wage little wars, and that each side will refrain from provoking the other to unlock the nuclear armory.

Ike threatened the Chinese, who at the time did not have the bomb, with nuclear war in Korea. JFK similarly threatened the Soviets, who had nuclear capability, over Cuba. But, although some military men thought about using nuclear weapons in Vietnam, the fundamental assumption of that war was to keep it limited, not to force either the Soviets or the Chinese, who now had their own sloppy bombs, to enter the war. Thus, we could impose our will on the recalcitrant of the earth if they did not have their own nuclear weapons, and if they could not compel the Soviets or the Chinese to force us to quit.

In Vietnam we had to find a technology to win without broadening the war. The nuclear stalemate reemphasized our need to find a more limited ground, to find, so to speak, a way to fight a domesticated war. We had to find a technology that would prevail locally, but not explode internationally. No assignment is too tough for the technological mentality. In fact, it was made to order for the technicians who were coming into their own throughout all of American life. This war gave them the opportunity to show what they could do. This was to be history's most technologically sophisticated war, most carefully analyzed and managed, using all of the latest wonders of managerial procedures and systems. It was made to order for bureaucracy.

James C. Thomson, who served both JFK and LBJ as an East Asia specialist, understood how the myths converged. He wrote of *"the rise of a new breed of American ideologues who see Vietnam as the ultimate test of their doctrine."* These new men were the new missionaries and had a trinitarian faith: in military power, technological superiority, and our altruistic idealism. They believed that the reality of American culture "provides us with the opportunity and obligation to ease the nations of the earth toward modernization and stability: toward a full-fledged *Pax Americana*

Technocratica."[57] For these parishioners in the church of the machine, Vietnam was the ideal laboratory.

One major by-product of technology is faith in technology. For example, after an enormously bright group of computer-science graduate students recently tried to explain their research to me, I asked them to tell me about the limits of computers. Several responded at the same time: "What limits?" Their excitement and certainty are almost contagious. They are obviously participating in a great intellectual adventure that they believe will have beneficial results. They can develop appropriate algorithms to "disaggregate" sloppy questions, produce probabilities for various "options," and create endless "scenarios" for assorted tactical contingencies. It is easy to understand the imperial technological optimism of the young initiates who are being introduced to the new mysteries.

The technological view of the world is broader than the application of science to industrial and informational procedures. At its root it is an attitude about the nature of reality. At a dinner with a group of sophisticated engineers I was told that "if it doesn't have a solution it isn't a problem." According to my dinner partners, if there is no solution to what is needed or wanted, the problem was either badly stated or was not a "real" problem in the first place. One computer engineer explained that unreal problems are usually invented by woolly-minded politicians or out-of-focus humanists. Another explained that technology now rules the entire world, and he said it with the quiet certainty of a fact so firmly established that it was not worth discussing.

These attitudes focus many of the tendencies within technology that have been there all along. The technological mentality designs standardized means to achieve predetermined results. It does this when it designs machinery, but the process is also applied to finding out what products the public will buy, to advertising and other forms of propaganda, to the organization of businesses and governmental agencies, and to the tactics appropriate to a particular war. This way of thinking has, in short, become characteristic of all advanced industrial societies. What distinguishes these societies from others is their acceptance of standardized procedures. In a technological society authority is located in the process itself. In a more traditional society, such as Vietnam, authority is always vested in a person who may grant a favor, bend a rule, and get something done.

Spontaneity and eccentricity are the enemies of technology. It demands methods that are foolproof, that even a fool cannot disrupt. It has no praise to give to folly. It is impatient with intuition, experience, and judgment. It has an irresistible tilt toward mathematical conclusions. Technology demands rationality in place of individuality. It is immune to charm. It is sober, tireless, and irresistible. It can be slowed but not stopped by external forces.

When the technological mind is turned to the problems of organizing human activity, the result is bureaucracy. This means that an office is created with a predefined function and then a person is sought who meets the specifications of the office. Standardization, technology, never rely on the talents or inspiration of officeholders for solutions. The result, again in its purest form, is impersonality, procedures rather than on-the-spot intelligence, authoritative regulations, not people with authority. Legitimacy resides in the office, not the officer.

Bureaucracy is democratic. It is a way to stifle autocracy by the imposition of a previously accepted and impersonal system. The goal is to achieve the predefined objectives of the organization with the least amount of energy and money. The offices were designed with that goal in mind. It never works that way.

Although efficiency is a means, not an end, there is an overwhelming likelihood that bureaucracies will sooner or later, usually sooner, confuse means and ends, or will simply lose sight of the organization's objectives in the continuous search for higher levels of efficiency. A French sociologist explained: "Our civilization is first and foremost a civilization of means: in the reality of modern life, the means, it would seem, are more important than the ends. Any other assessment of the situation is mere idealism."[58] This is the case whether the technological mind has produced a machine—a tool, a means—or an organization—another tool or means. Both a helicopter gunship and the Department of Defense are means to an end. America's enormous technology is marvelously adept at making the tool, and is incompetent at providing the purpose.

The national purpose is supplied by the myth of the city on a hill, technology provides the tools, and bureaucracy provides the procedures. The city myth is, however, soft-minded, while technology is hard-headed. The first is mushy while the second is tough, "realistic," and more often than not can actually deliver on its tactical assignments. It is more difficult to be specific and concrete about the "city" than about the technological means for either its defense or expansion. But it therefore follows that it is much more difficult to attack the city myth. It lies beneath the surface, more in the bloodstream than in the mind, in the national atmosphere rather than in specific policies. The city myth is unassailable while the technological mentality is irresistible.

The war in Vietnam caused an explosion in the research and development of the technology of war. The use of new technology in combat usually proved that American lives could in fact be saved, and that the enemy would suffer terrible losses. But the war also unleashed the technology addicts and pushers who more than occasionally revealed that their grip on the real world was not quite perfect. They had, for instance, the idea to train bomb-carrying pigeons to land on and explode Communist vehicles, but they had some difficulty in teaching the birds to tell the difference between bad trucks and good ones. They attempted, in the Lava Plan, to find a chemical compound to convert the mud of the Ho Chi Minh trail into grease so that North Vietnamese convoys would get stuck. They actually designed and placed a sensing device in the shape of a dog turd on the trail. When they learned that there were no dogs around, they reconfigured the turd to look like a piece of wood.

Despite the comedy, such sensing devices were effective, and helped save the marines at the battle of Khe Sanh. They were in use all over the battlefield after 1968. Colonel David Lownds, the commander at Khe Sanh, in testimony before the Electronic Battlefield Subcommittee of the Senate, in November 1970, predicted "a continuation of the evolutions stemming from . . . the sophisticated technology used at Khe Sanh and which are in keeping with the sophisticated technological society in which we live."[59] Colonel Lownds understood the importance of the relationship between a nation's style of war and its culture. The American way of war had to be congruent with the American way of life.

America's ability to use machines and systems to destroy the enemy and protect the GIs was deeply satisfying all around.

American culture valued technological killing, but was outraged by the enemy's atrocities that occurred face-to-face. This attitude made Senator Fulbright explode at Maxwell Taylor during the Vietnam hearings of 1966:

> Well, the only implication of this question was that we are the only good people, and I certainly don't think we are a bad people, but I don't see any great distinction between using the weapons that we happen to have and others don't, to kill innocent people, to burn them slowly . . . and disemboweling with a knife because a knife is all you have got. I mean, I don't see we should claim any great superiority because we happen to have nuclear bombs and fire bombs and the others don't.[60]

The actual accomplishments of American war technology once led General Westmoreland into an uncharacteristic revery about the shining promise of the future. In 1969, he told the Association of the American Army that "the Army has undergone in Vietnam a quiet revolution in ground warfare—tactics, techniques, and technology." He said that this revolution was not yet understood. He believed that America was "on the threshold of an entirely new battlefield concept." He foresaw the "automated battlefield."

"I see," the general said, "battlefields or combat areas that are under 24 hour real or near real time surveillance of all types." Retaining his prophetic mood, he continued: "I see battlefields on which we can destroy anything we locate through instant communications and the almost instantaneous application of highly lethal firepower." He based his forecast on the expansion of technology already at his command in the field, or else on the way. That included "hundreds of surveillance, target acquisition, night observation and information processing systems either in being, in development or in engineering." In summary he saw "an Army built into and around an integrated area control system that exploits the advanced technology of communications, sensors, fire direction, and the required automatic data processing." To succeed in extending the automated battlefield he needed the cooperation of the military, industry, science, and engineering. With such assistance the new battlefield would exist in "no more than 10 years."[61]

Major General George Keegan, the air force intelligence chief, understood that technology leads to more technology, that its pushers must become addicts. In 1974, at a conference on the lessons of Vietnam, he recalled that General Westmoreland once ordered his staff to prepare a plan to block the Ho Chi Minh trail by invading Laos. The bureaucratic staff needed six months to complete the plan which required some four divisions, four new airfields, and ninety miles of paved road. General Keegan was outraged by "this great piece of staff work. . . . I would trade all of that for a dozen Ranger battalions." He added, "We have forgotten or lost a great combat art,"[62] how to fight on foot.

As with other forms of addiction, a psychological and physical dependency is inevitable, even for the technology freaks. When this dependency occurs, the victim cannot function without increasingly larger doses. The technology habit is the most expensive of all, and is probably as destructive of clear thinking as the heroin plague that destroyed many of the American grunts in Vietnam. But the American way of war must be congruent with the American way of life.

American culture values performance. Performance means the ability to "deliver the goods." Technology always delivers, and functions as it was designed to do. When it creates problems the fault is with the operators, what the airlines call pilot error and computer specialists call user error. Of course the military understands that technology performs. It has the time and facilities to train its people in the care and use of new machines, as well as new technological systems of organization and communication. In its dependence on technology the military is reflecting wider cultural values.

The traditional American male, as John Wayne personified him in scores of movies, performs, delivers the goods, is a loner, has the equipment, usually a six-shooter or a superior rifle, to beat the bad guys, and he knows what he is doing. He does not need to depend on others because he can perform, can deliver, and can bring home the bacon. He is also very good.

It is astonishing how often American GIs in Vietnam approvingly referred to John Wayne, not as a movie star, but as a model and a standard. Everyone in Vietnam called dangerous areas Indian country. Paraphrasing a bit of Americana, some GIs painted on their flak jackets THE ONLY GOOD GOOK IS A DEAD ONE. They called their Vietnamese scouts who defected from the Communists Kit Carsons. These nineteen-year-old Americans, brought up on World War II movies and westerns, walking through the jungle, armed to the teeth, searching for an invisible enemy who knew the wilderness better than they did, could hardly miss these connections. One after another said, at some point, something like, "Hey, this is just like a movie." What they lacked in cartoon bravery, they made up in technology. Their deadly machines transformed at least some of them from boys into warriors, into dominating men, not "fags" like the South Vietnamese.

The power of technology to convert boys into men, to bestow potency on the weak, caused many young American males to think of machinery and sex as the same thing, or at least as causally related. The teenage boy cruising the streets in his tail-finned car in the 1950s, or on his roaring motorcycle in the '60s, was training himself to love machinery, and to use the internal combustion engine as a surrogate for sex or as the means to make himself more sexually attractive. The more powerful the machine, the stronger the connection. The most manifestly powerful machines are those that kill. Thus, the narrator of a novel about Vietnam was described as having a "Puritan middle-class mind" who gets "killing mixed up with screwing." Norman Mailer, in his own Vietnam novel, was clearer: "Every one of these bastards has the sexual peculiarities of red-blooded men, which is to say that one of them can't come unless he's squinting down a gunsight."[63] It was not unusual for GIs in Vietnam to be explicit about the sexual excitement their weapons induced. The war's leaders in Washington had similar, if vastly more sublimated, attitudes. It was partly the thrill of domination, but it was more than that. They loved weapons.

Some GIs had the opportunity in Vietnam occasionally to swim in the South China Sea. One squad leader told of his encounter with American technology as he was swimming naked one day:

I was jumping around in the waves one time, and I saw a speck way off shore. All of a sudden I was eye to eye with a Phantom jet pilot. He gave me a nod and I'm looking at tail pipes, a black speck and he's gone. Came and went in the wink of an eye, about five feet over the water.

I said, "Wow, that guy must be coming in his pants. What a fucking rush that's got to be. Kicking with some heavy horsepower. Give me one of those and I'll own the world."[64]

Another grunt tried to explain why decent American young men would sometimes rape. They did not want prostitutes, and did not have to pay for their sex because, as he explained, "You've got an M-16. A gun," he said, "is power. To some people carrying a gun constantly was like having a permanent hard on. It was a pure sexual trip every time you got to pull the trigger." Carlos Campbell, a former football player at Michigan State, was transformed into a pilot by the navy. Flying, he said, was just like playing football, the same "pregame ritual of just sort of strutting." He went on:

Step out to that airplane, and you might as well be getting into bed with Denise Nicholas or Pam Grier. Because you just go *Oooooo*. You just gotta get it off now. You are in the preorgasmic mindset of the military person. And when you're in the airplane, and you fire a rocket, and you hear that whoosh leave your wing, then all of a sudden it hits. POW. It's like an orgasm.[65]

Michael Herr, a writer who spent most of his time living with the men in Vietnam, concentrated on the helicopter, Vietnam's most characteristic technology. He was particularly taken with the Loaches, light observation choppers:

"Man, one Dink with a forty-five could put a hurtin' on those Loaches they'd never come back from," a young captain said. It was incredible, those little ships were the most beautiful things flying in Vietnam (you had to stop once in a while and admire the machinery), they just hung there above those bunkers like wasps outside a nest. "That's sex," the captain said. "That's pure sex."[66]

Not only did our weapons make some of the GIs feel like men who defined sex as dominating the weak, that is, the unarmed, but it made some of them feel clean in killing. Of course there were bureaucratic "rules of engagement" about how to kill correctly. Philip Caputo, a platoon leader in the marines, and one of the first in combat in Vietnam, said that these rules meant that

> it was morally right to shoot an unarmed Vietnamese who was running, but wrong to shoot one who was standing or walking; it was wrong to shoot an enemy prisoner at close range, but right for a sniper at long range to kill an enemy soldier who was no more able than a prisoner to defend himself; it was wrong for infantrymen to destroy a village with white-phosphorus grenades, but right for a fighter pilot to drop napalm on it. Ethics seemed to be a matter of distance and technology. You could never go wrong if you killed people at long range with sophisticated weapons.[67]

Distance and technology are the same thing, because it is the machinery that makes long-range and anonymous killing possible.

We had to find a technology to win in Vietnam because of our delusion that machinery allows us to fight a clean war, using tools instead of men, and the more complex and sophisticated the better. We thought we could bomb them into their senses with only limited human costs to ourselves. We seemed to believe that the mammoth federal hardware store would always stock just the right gadget to kill them and save us. It also permitted us not to get our hands too dirty. The B-52 crew never saw the results of pushing that button. The artillery squad's job was to get the numbers of the coordinates right and push the button. Only the grunts, the walking warriors, had to look death in the face. And they, despite the American faith in our mighty machinery, determined the outcome. Everyone knew this except the air force, the navy, and the men who plan our wars.

In summary, our national myth showed us that we were good, our technology made us strong, and our bureaucracy gave us standard operating procedures. It was not a winning combination.

PART II
FIRE

DECISIONS THAT MADE THE WAR

TWO

THE CHAIN
TO VIETNAM

After the 1945 meeting at Yalta, the site of the international
conference that organized the postwar world, President Roosevelt returned to America by sea, aboard the U.S.S. *Quincy*. In
February, while en route, he thought out loud about the situation in Indochina. For two years he had worried about that part
of the world. He was determined to prevent the reestablishment
of European colonialism in Asia. He had previously discussed
Indochina with both Chiang Kai-shek and Marshal Stalin. In the
end-of-war style of moving nations around as if they were playing a gigantic game of Monopoly, Mr. Roosevelt had asked
Chiang: "Do you want Indo-China?" The Generalissimo replied, "It's no help to us. We don't want it. They are not Chinese. They would not assimilate into the Chinese people." They
agreed that Indochina should not be given back to the French
who had lost it to the Japanese during the war.

FDR believed that for over a century France had failed to
educate the peoples of Cambodia, Laos, and Vietnam. He was
convinced that the French had milked Indochina: "For every
dollar they have put in, they have taken out ten." In fact, even
before Pearl Harbor, Mr. Roosevelt had threatened to force the
French out. He now suggested that Indochina should become
a trusteeship composed of "a Frenchman, one or two Indo-

Chinese, and a Chinese and a Russian because they are on the coast, and maybe a Filipino and an American" to educate the Indochinese for self-government. Both Stalin and Chiang approved the plan.

Winston Churchill did not. FDR explained why: "It might bust up their empire, because if the Indo-Chinese were to work together and eventually get their independence, the Burmese might do the same thing to England." Any arrangement that was designed to assist colonial independence from European imperialism "would only make the British mad. Chiang would go along. Stalin would go along. . . . Better to keep quiet just now." Mr. Churchill wanted all the Southeast Asian colonies returned to the European powers "just the way they were." This attitude had already created a standing quarrel between the two leaders; Mr. Roosevelt had pressured the British to grant independence to India as early as 1942. The President explained that Mr. Churchill was a "mid-Victorian on all things like that." A reporter said to the President, "You would think that some of that would be knocked out of him by now."[1] For the moment it was thought better "to keep quiet." Indochina was, after all, not at center stage during the closing year of World War II.

Naturally, the view from Hanoi was different. Under the leadership of Ho Chi Minh, among others, including non-Communists, Vietnamese hostility to imperialism became fierce during World War II. Ho Chi Minh was born in 1890 to a family that was passionately nationalistic. He became a scholarly young man whose hatred of the French presence in his country convinced him to become an exile. He spent some time in London as a pastry-cook's helper at the posh Carlton House, and in New York where he shoveled snow in Harlem to earn money; he also wrote a pamphlet about the wretched conditions there. He then settled in France, where he was a photographer and a developing revolutionary. During his life he must have escaped the guillotine ten times, and for about a year he was chained by a Chinese warlord in a prison at Yunnan, where he occupied himself by writing poetry. At different times he had been a member of the French Communist Party, the Russian Communist Party, and probably the Chinese as well. He had lived outside Vietnam for almost thirty years, learned to speak a half dozen languages, was not known to the Vietnamese, and returned to his country by sneaking across the border. Tran Van

Don, a future South Vietnamese general, remembered that he first heard of Ho Chi Minh in 1945. A French journalist believed, "He is the man who remains awake when everyone else is asleep."[2]

Ho Chi Minh organized the Vietnamese resistance to foreign control into a nationalistic political and military body called the Vietminh. By 1945, he had collected an army of some 3,000 men. In March, while a famine in northern Vietnam killed 25 percent of the people, the Japanese deposed their French collaborators and took over the administration of Indochina. After the Japanese beat the French, ending eighty years of the white man's control, Hiroshima and Japanese militarism exploded in a mushroom cloud. In a few weeks, the French puppet emperor of Vietnam, Bao Dai, abdicated. Both France and Japan, the foreign enemies of Vietnam, were now defeated, and the question was who would move into the vacuum. This virtual anarchy gave Ho Chi Minh his opportunity. The Communists were organized, armed, and ready to move. The Vietminh executed most of the leaders of the non-Communist Dai Viet nationalist political party. But while the Vietminh dreamed of an independent and unified nation, the French planned to return. Within a year, General Leclerc led 10,000 French troops back into Indochina.

Although the Japanese had been hated as simply another intruding foreign power, Ho Chi Minh had taken careful note that Asians had once again defeated Europeans, as the Japanese had beaten the Russians earlier in the century. Almost as soon as the Japanese installed themselves in Vietnam, the Vietminh mounted a guerrilla war against them as the new colonialists. They did this with the help of Major Archimedes L. A. Patti, an American intelligence officer attached to the Office of Strategic Services, the precursor of the CIA.

Major Patti was assigned to Indochina by "Wild Bill" Donovan, the founding director of OSS, for the purpose of obstructing the Japanese by organizing a network of secret operators in Vietnam. When he was told where he was going, he later recalled, "I wasn't very sure where Indo-China was at that particular moment. I had an idea it was out in Asia somewhere." The President instructed him "not to assist any French objective to re-enter Indo-China."[3] He was given six months to learn about Vietnam, presumably including its location, and it was then that he first heard about a man named Ho Chi Minh who might be a knowledgeable contact.

Immediately after Major Patti arrived he was approached by the Vietminh and told that "the General," as Ho Chi Minh was often called because he had too many aliases to remember, wanted to be recognized by America. Ho Chi Minh had been calling for cooperation with Washington since 1941. During the war he once offered to guide a downed American pilot to safety, and although he did not actually do so he was rewarded by an appointment to the OSS as Agent #19, code name Lucius, with the task of reporting Japanese troop movements to Washington. The OSS parachuted about five thousand weapons to the Vietminh to be used against the Japanese.

In April 1945, Major Patti agreed to a secret meeting with the General. They met in an obscure village near the Chinese border where Ho Chi Minh greeted the American in English: "Welcome, my good friend." After bumming the first of many Chesterfield cigarettes, the General discussed in English, because he "needed the practice," with the major the ways their two countries could cooperate. Ho Chi Minh said that he "was ready to align himself with the Americans whenever they were ready." Major Patti concluded that the strange meeting had been a success, and that some good might come from it.[4]

Major Patti later recalled that this meeting originally "began just as a feeler." He knew that Ho Chi Minh was a Communist, and that the Vietminh expressed a party line. But Ho Chi Minh did not seem to be "a starry-eyed revolutionary or flaming radical, given to cliches, mouthing a party line." Ho Chi Minh's ultimate goal, Major Patti was convinced, "was to attain American support for the cause of a free Vietnam."[5] This did not conflict with American policy, as Major Patti understood it at the time. He passed the information to the American embassy in Chungking with the comment that the Vietnamese leader was more of a nationalist than a Communist.

Perhaps because of the final push against the Germans in Europe and the intensifying American concentration in the war against Japan in the Pacific, Major Patti learned that the intelligence he was providing did not interest his superiors. He became annoyed: "All the information that people in the field passed to Washington ended in a dry well."[6] He apparently did not know that this was becoming something of a tradition. Earlier in the year, even before Major Patti arrived in Vietnam, for instance, Dean Rusk, then a deputy chief of staff for the Allied Command in Asia, had asked the Joint Chiefs for guidance about American policy for Indochina. The word had come back from Commander in Chief Roosevelt: "I don't want to hear any more about Indo-China."[7] Twenty-five years later, most Americans had come to share this attitude.

After the Japanese surrendered, the Vietminh began to take control of local offices, largely as a result of Ho Chi Minh's growing reputation as the American-backed liberator of his country. This reputation was to endure, as David Ross, a medic in the First Infantry, learned in Vietnam twenty years later. During his first indoctrination after he arrived in Vietnam, he said, "We *were told not* to bad-mouth Ho Chi Minh, since the Vietnamese mistakenly thought he was the George Washington of their country because he had thrown out the French."[8]

Ho Chi Minh founded the Democratic Republic of Vietnam, and in early September 1945, a celebration of the birth of the new nation and of the Allied victory was held in Hanoi. American planes, probably inadvertently, flew above the city to the cheers of the 400,000 people who had gathered. Next to Vietminh officers on the reviewing stand stood American military officers saluting the new flag of North Vietnam. The "Star Spangled Banner" was played by the Vietnamese band. In General Vo Nguyen Giap's speech he mentioned Vietnam's "special affection" for America.[9] Ho Chi Minh began his own speech by quoting from the Declaration of Independence, "this immortal statement." He was proud of what had been done: "Our people smashed the yoke which pressed hard upon us for nearly one hundred years, and finally made our Viet Nam an independent country. Our people at the same time overthrew the monarchical regime established tens of centuries ago, and founded the Republic."[10]

Immediately after the celebration of Vietnamese independence, Ho Chi Minh wrote eight letters to President Truman or to the Secretary of State, asking for assistance in Vietnam's new struggle against the French. In his last letter to the President, Ho Chi Minh rehearsed again the crime of the French which, he said, "is a challenge to the noble attitude shown before, during and after the war by the United States Government and People."[11] He asked President Truman to give Vietnam moral support for its independence on the model of America's grant of independence to the Philippines. There was no reply to any of his requests.

Chiang Kai-shek sent 150,000 troops to Hanoi—as had been arranged at the Potsdam Conference—to liberate the North from the Japanese, and the British arrived in Saigon to disarm the Japanese in the South. The Chinese troops engaged primarily in robbing the country blind; the government of China had great difficulty in getting its troops to return home, and most profitably stayed for about a year. The Vietnamese would never forget or forgive this pillage. Ultimately, the anti-Communist Chinese turned their control over to the Vietminh in the North, while in the South the British, under orders, relinquished their control to the French, not, as many Vietnamese had expected, to the Vietnamese. France then reinstated Bao Dai, sunning himself at his mansion on the French Riviera, as the "emperor."

Neither Ho Chi Minh nor the French could accept this result, and unless one side would capitulate to the other, war between them now was inescapable. There was no ambiguity about French aspirations because Charles De Gaulle had already issued a declaration to "restore" the nations of Indochina. French bureaucrats believed that the restoration of France's colonies was essential to the glory of France, and the French *colons* living in Vietnam were desperate for a return of the motherland to resecure the privileges and elegance of their former lives. Several brave attempts at finding a way to live together were attempted, including an agreement, signed in Paris by Ho Chi Minh and General Leclerc, which gave Vietnam "freedom within the French Union,"[12] whatever that meant.

Just weeks after Franklin Roosevelt's death, President Truman came to the troublesome conclusion that the Soviet Union was violating the terms of the dramatic wartime international agreements. In April 1945, the State Department sent him a memorandum that described the condition of the world's important nations: The United Kingdom was a good and cooperative ally, somewhat too rigid in its dealings with the USSR, and sensitive about its loss of power that made it a junior partner of the Big Three. France was obsessed with its military defeat of 1940 as well as with its occupation by the Nazis; the loss of prestige led De Gaulle to make outrageous demands. France's need to regain its role as a world power was finally to lead it and the United States into the Vietnamese wars. As William Bundy of the State Department concluded, as late as 1967, French humiliation in World War II raised the curtain on the entire Vietnam tragedy: "Restored control in Indochina was a badge, however mistaken, for a France that meant to be once again a world power."[13]

In a separate memo for President Truman, the Far East division of the State Department, in those days before McCarthyism terrified it into chronic timidity and waffling, predicted the future. It prophesied that America's defeat of Japan would liberate Indochina and that America would be responsible for maintaining its freedom. The U.S. should encourage and assist the people of the region to create "autonomous, democratic self-rule in close, willing association with major Western powers." Only this attitude would sustain peace in Indochina. The crystal ball on the Far East desk sparkled: "If this policy is not followed, the millions who live in that area may well embrace ideologies contrary to our own...."[14] It recommended that America resist the French intention to reclaim its Indochinese empire.

American political culture at the end of World War II was focused on the Soviet Union. The cold war was a result of a steady and deepening mutual suspicion between the two postwar world powers that each was planning to extend its sphere of influence to the endangerment of the other. There was more than enough evidence on both sides to justify paranoia. America's early threats to withhold economic aid to the Russians unless they would agree to European political settlements acceptable to us convinced Marshal Stalin that the United States was determined to bribe or starve his nation into compliance. It seemed obvious to the Soviets that the United States had relied on its own technology and on the Soviet's soldiers during the war: About sixty Russians had been killed for each American who died. The Soviet's brutal refusal to permit Eastern Europe to escape from the control of the Red Army convinced many Americans that the Nazi's imperial lust for land had now been replaced by that of the Russians. On September 22, 1949, the White House announced that the Russians had successfully tested their own atomic bomb. A crisis over Greece and Turkey, the blockade of Berlin, the Communist revolution in China, and the outbreak of war in Korea combined to solidify the American view of the geopolitics of the postwar world. Anti-Communism had become America's ideology, policy, and mission.

It was essential to fix Soviet behavior in some wider view of the world in a way that would explain how America should respond. Many people made such an attempt, but none succeeded as well as George F. Kennan. Early in 1946, when he was a chargé d'affaires at the American embassy in Moscow, he sent to the State Department what is now referred to as "the long telegram" in which he began his analysis of the nature and future of the Soviet Union, along with his recommendations about the appropriate American responses. In 1947, under the signature of "X," he made public a longer version of this telegram in *Foreign Affairs*. His basic argument was that Americans had misunderstood the Soviet Union, and that cooperation was not to be won through FDR's charm or through the harder bargaining of the new Truman administration. Soviet policy and attitudes, he said, were determined by the internal needs of the Soviet Union, and it would do what America wanted only when it was in its interest to do so. Hostility between the two nations was therefore inevitable. Still, the United States need not be passive.

The pivot of the "X" article was Mr. Kennan's assertion: "The United States has it in its power to increase enormously the strains under which Soviet policy must operate, to force upon the Kremlin a far greater degree of moderation and circumspection than it has had to observe in recent years, and in this way to promote tendencies which must eventually find their outlet in either the break-up or the gradual mellowing of Soviet power."[15] The tactic for increasing the pressure on the Soviets was for American policy and force to be applied carefully only in areas of the world that were vital to its own security. The strategy was to "contain" the Soviet Union within the borders of its then current empire. It was essential, he later elaborated, for American policy to become more sophisticated and supple, and more particular about the place and timing of American action. As an important example he said that the way other governments organize themselves, including Communist governments, was none of our business.

Containment became America's strategy. The reason that Mr. Kennan's early arguments took hold in the minds of the highest policymakers in Washington was that he reflected, as well as shaped, their own attitudes. Because nothing else had worked, Mr. Kennan's analysis was devoured by official Washington. He had explained that neither persuasion nor rationality would move the Soviets. Dozens of senior bureaucrats had tried to convince the Soviets of one thing or another and all had failed. They were now perhaps glad to learn that because it had been impossible all along, their failures had not been their fault. There would no longer be attempts to hide American disagreements with the Soviet Union, no more concessions, America's military strength would be increased, and future negotiations would only serve to compel the Russians either to accept American terms, or else to allow America to win propaganda points by publicizing Soviet stubbornness.[16]

The inspiration that provided the basis for Mr. Kennan's view of the world was contained in a single paragraph whose intention John Winthrop would have understood:

> . . . the thoughtful observer of Russian-American relations will find no cause for complaint in the Kremlin's challenge to American society. He will rather experience a certain gratitude to a Providence which, by providing the American people with this implacable challenge, has made their entire security as a nation dependent on their pulling themselves together and accepting the responsibilities of moral and political leadership that history plainly intended them to bear.[17]

Mr. Kennan rejected the idea that the Russian people were really just like us, and wrote in a later article that the example of America was the strongest possible influence that this country could bring to bear both on the Kremlin and on the people of the Soviet Union. Containment, even in Mr. Kennan's careful prose, was consistent with the myth of the city on a hill.[18]

The result of all this was the Truman Doctrine of March 1947, in which the United States promised the world that it would resist Soviet expansionism wherever it occurred. This universalism was not what Mr. Kennan had in mind. But the President said that "it must be the policy of the United States to support free peoples who are resisting attempted subjugation by armed minorities or outside pressure."[19] President Truman and his senior aides immediately began to explain that this doctrine did not mean automatic assistance to every country in the world, but they had unknowingly forged the first link in the chain that was ultimately to drag us into Vietnam.

This is so not because of the direct application of the Truman Doctrine, but because the American diplomatic and military mentality was now fixed. The doctrine helped to make its set of ideas more familiar, more institutionalized, and as a result increasingly easy to apply. The trigger for the Truman Doctrine was for us to perceive "armed minorities" and to define "outside pressure." As the political mind-set of high government officials became increasingly crude in the context of the cold war abroad and McCarthyism at home, it became progressively easy to smother local realities in the world with the pillow of the Truman Doctrine. Mr. Kennan's deep knowledge and intellectual agility were finally reduced to mere slogans. The ideas behind the Truman Doctrine were the same ideas that were used to justify our Vietnam intervention. What had once been careful thought had become a reflex, an involuntary curling of the toes.

In February 1950, America formally recognized France's puppet Bao Dai, the second link in our chain to Vietnam, and thereby became Ho Chi Minh's enemy. There was one man in the United States who understood what was happening, and said so in public and to the administration. Harold Isaacs, a *Newsweek* reporter, had covered Southeast Asia for years. He reacted to the recognition of Bao Dai: "The United States embarked upon another ill-conceived adventure doomed to end in another self-inflicted defeat. It will not help the United States in its struggle against Communism. It will help the Communists in their struggle against the United States."[20] Two months after the recognition, Mr. Isaacs discussed Vietnam for an hour and a half with Charlton Ogburn, the information officer with the Far East desk of the State Department, who took notes for a memorandum circulated for internal consumption in State. It must have been consumed for all the good it did. Mr. Isaacs said that the Vietnamese considered the emperor ridiculous and contemptible. Only the ignorant could believe that Bao Dai, or even the French, could be helpful to America. The official asked what Mr. Isaacs thought of reports of Ho Chi Minh's declining popularity and Bao Dai's growing support. Mr. Isaacs said that such reports "could have come only from the French or from our

Consul General in Saigon, in either of which case they were palpably lies. . . ." The State Department bureaucrat asked whether the Soviet's recognition of Ho Chi Minh proved that he was a Soviet puppet. Mr. Isaacs "threw up his hands and asked what we expected the results of our conduct to be."[21] Publicly expressed doubts about the Vietnamese emperor became increasingly unfashionable in the Washington of 1950.

The American mind-lock was revealed in what was arguably the most important strategic document prepared by the American government since World War II. Two months before the Korean War began, President Truman received a long study from a special group of people in both the State and Defense Departments. The study, which was chaired and largely written in three months by Paul Nitze, Mr. Kennan's successor as head of the State Department's policy planning staff, was a response to the President's earlier directive to provide him with an analysis of the implications of the surprisingly fast Soviet success in developing an atomic bomb, of Mao Tse-tung's success in China, and Mr. Truman's own earlier decision to build a hydrogen bomb. This study from the National Security Council was known as NSC 68, and in a few months it became the authoritative expression of how America would conduct itself in the world.

It was a top-secret document, not fully published until 1975. One of its underlying assumptions was that containing Russia was inadequate. It assumed that the Soviet Union was becoming more dangerous because it could already force other nations to fight its battles as proxies, and thus mere containment of the Soviets was no longer sufficient. In a direct repudiation of Mr. Kennan's earlier insistence that the United States had to discriminate between international annoyances and real danger, this new policy stressed that freedom was indivisible, and that therefore "a defeat of free institutions anywhere is a defeat everywhere."[22] As Secretary of State Acheson said in 1950, "We must consider Korea not in isolation but in the worldwide problem of confronting the Soviet Union as an antagonist."[23] The United States would no longer distinguish vital from peripheral interests. This fundamental and widely accepted conclusion was the third link in the chain to the future American war in Vietnam.

NSC 68 reported that the USSR was organized for international violence, while the U.S. was organized for persuasion: "The prime reliance of the free society is on the strength and appeal of its idea, and it feels no compulsion sooner or later to bring all societies into conformity with it." Compulsion was, in any case, not necessary because "the idea of freedom is the most contagious idea in history." Consequently, the idea of freedom was a permanent threat to the Kremlin. The struggle for the minds of men was necessarily worldwide. Because of the nature of the underlying conflict, war could not "definitively end the fundamental conflict in the realm of ideas."[24] If ideas matter, as Graham Greene showed they do to Americans, the most basic conflict with the Soviet Union was a struggle between truth and falsity.

According to NSC 68, the tools available to the Soviets in their drive to annex the world were psychological as well as military. They would therefore exploit every chance to humiliate the United States, to weaken its prestige and trustworthiness. When it served their purpose the Soviets invariably charged that the United States, because of its presumed decadence, lacked the will to prevail in international affairs. American leaders therefore thought it necessary to prove the strength of America's will whenever it was tested. This effectively handed over to the Soviet Union the definition of America's vital interests. When the Soviets acted, we had to react, or face the presumed calamity of displaying our alleged decadence. Every war President during the Vietnam era repeatedly emphasized that the war was a test of American resolve, of national will, and of American character. Every war President made passing that test a justification for our intervention.

The overall recommendation of this significant document was that the United States must begin "a more rapid building up of the political, economic, and military strength and therefore of confidence in the free world." It called for substantial increases in the defense budget. It supported intensified spying and sabotage. It recommended "overt psychological warfare calculated to encourage mass defections from Soviet allegiance . . . and operations by covert means in the field of economic warfare and political and psychological warfare with a view to fomenting and supporting unrest and revolt in selected strategic satellite countries."[25]

* * *

On June 25, 1950, North Korea invaded South Korea. The American response was shaped by the desire to contain what was then understood to be a monolithic international Communism directed from the Kremlin that swept from Czechoslovakia to China. President Truman explained to the nation what he was doing: "The attack upon Korea makes it plain beyond all doubt that communism has passed beyond the use of subversion to conquer independent nations and will now use armed invasion and war." In a little noticed paragraph in the same statement he added: "I have . . . directed acceleration in the furnishing of military assistance to the forces of France and the Associated States in Indochina and the dispatch of a military mission to provide close working relations with those forces."[26]

Mr. Truman's decision in both Korea and Indochina was based on two contradictory convictions: The United States was apparently strong enough to work its will in the world; but, the Soviets were so determined to spread revolution across the planet that any advantage they gained would inevitably result in further aggression either by subversion or war. He told a group of congressmen that the world was grim. "If we let Korea down the Soviet will keep right on going and swallow up one piece of Asia after another. We had to make a stand some time." He was beginning to formulate what was later to be known as the domino theory. "If we were to let Asia go, the Near East would collapse and no telling what would happen in Europe."[27]

The President and his senior staff, especially Secretary of State Dean Acheson, believed that the entire "free world" was watching to see whether America had the will actually to defend an ally to whom it was bound. The Secretary believed that the lesson other allies would learn from our response to the North Korean aggression would presumably instruct all of them in the reliability of Washington as a defender of freedom. The President and others in his administration did not believe that Korea represented a major American interest. But as an adviser reported to Mr. Truman, Korea was "an ideological battleground."[28] By then France was arguing that in reentering Vietnam, it too was fighting the Communists, not merely seeking to reclaim its empire. France insisted it was holding back the troops that Mao Tse-tung already had amassed on his southern border with Vietnam.

The events in Korea seemed to prove the validity of NSC 68's basic analysis, and President Truman routinely approved this study in September 1950. One of its most expansive conclusions was that the security of the United States could no longer be separated from the security of the world. With this new American global responsibility the cold war itself would be fought globally. In this connection Korea was as significant as any other proving ground in the world. What was at stake was not the territory or political form of South Korea; the question to be decided was whether America or Russia would prevail.

One problem was that the American high command was never clear about what would constitute a victory, especially after the Chinese entered the war in December. General MacArthur was fired by President Truman for making too much noise about his belief, despite contrary evidence his own intelligence staff had gathered, that China would not enter the war. The Commander in Chief had decided that this was to be a limited war, and General MacArthur was asked to testify about the plans for winning such a war. "There is no policy," he said. "There is nothing, I tell you, no plan, no anything." A senator asked the Chief of Staff, General Omar Bradley, what the United States was trying to do in Korea. The general thought this was "a very fair question" and one that had "bothered the people." General Bradley thought for a bit and went on. It was possible that the North Koreans were unpleasantly surprised that the Russians failed to intervene themselves, and would as a result now be willing to negotiate for peace. The senator asked what kind of peace the United States expected. General Bradley did not know,[29] but said that we were involved in "the wrong war, at the wrong place, at the wrong time, and with the wrong enemy."[30]

An important part of the context of the Korean War was political recriminations in America about who was responsible for the "loss" of China. Because American political culture assumed American omnipotence, it was widely believed that Mao Tse-tung's success was the fault of those who were then in power in America. The Republican party had a field day supporting General MacArthur and blaming the Democrats for failing to prevent the Chinese revolution. But not only the Republicans. In 1949, young Congressman John F. Kennedy apparently wished to separate himself from what he thought was the calamitous Democratic record in China. He said that it was important to find the right people to blame. He even connected the attack on Pearl Harbor with the failure of his own party to understand the Far East. He said that President Roosevelt was sick at Yalta and, with the concurrence of General Marshall, consequently gave so much away to the Russians that the integrity of China was permanently sacrificed. He thought that the President and the State Department had dealt shabbily with Madame Chiang Kai-shek, and that was the last straw. "What our young men had saved," he said, "our diplomats and our President have frittered away."[31]

The increasing rancor about who to blame for Mao's victory helped to draw a political boundary around Democratic policymakers. This was consistent with NSC 68, with the relatively new sense that America was directly responsible not only for the peace of the world, but its ideology as well. It was nothing less than the forces of truth arrayed against the forces of falsehood, inside America as well as across the face of the earth. A powerful right-wing "China Lobby" was formed as a combination truth squad and pressure group to ensure that America would never again be "soft on Communism" or wobbly in support of Chiang Kai-shek's island fortress of Taiwan. The Truman administration answered the accusation that it had been soft on China by being tough in Indochina.

A widespread agreement emerged in America about the shape and meaning of politics in the postwar world. It was based on two assumptions which met with overwhelming favor in the succession of governments of the time, as well as with a great majority of American people. The first assumption was that the American economy was working so well that a truly new age of affluence was eliminating poverty and, therefore, economic classes from the nation. The second assumption was that this economic miracle—the American way of life—was mortally threatened by a monolithic, atheistic, international Communist conspiracy that was bent on universal aggression. At specific moments dissent from this consensus was perceived to be treason, as Senator Joseph McCarthy was to demonstrate.

The political significance of McCarthyism, the fourth link in America's Vietnam chain, was that it made reason and skepticism dangerous to many people, but especially to the careers of public officials, and they never forgot it. McCarthyism accomplished this by making foaming anti-Communism integral to what the political center now called patriotism. The senator succeeded so well, while he lasted, because he had stumbled on an American truth. Like John Winthrop and Woodrow Wilson, the senator was making war on Evil. The energy for his crusade came from the American need to slay monsters in the name of virtue. His crusade, as he advertised it, was nothing less than an effort to purge America of the traitors who had brought the country to what he thought was its humiliating condition. In June 1951, the senator clarified for his fellow senators that he believed the nation was being subverted by traitors in very high places:

> How can we account for our present situation unless we believe that men high in this Government are concerting to deliver us to disaster? This must be the product of a great conspiracy, a conspiracy on a scale so immense as to dwarf any previous such venture in the history of man. A conspiracy of infamy so black that, when it is finally exposed, its principals shall be forever deserving of the maledictions of all honest men.
>
> Who constitutes the highest circles of this conspiracy? About that we cannot be sure. We are convinced that Dean Acheson, who steadfastly serves the interests of nations other than his own . . . must be high on the roster. The President? He is their captive.[32]

The panic of high government officials in both the Truman and Eisenhower adminstrations led to appeasement of the senator for several years. It was not the senator's behavior that forged this Vietnam link, but the panic. From his moment forward, it became an article of faith in American public life that the crackpot right was extraordinarily dangerous, and that it had to be placated lest a new version of McCarthyism would erupt. It was thought better for the nation to appease the right rather than to prod it into action.

For President Truman, Korea was the modern test of whether the free world had learned the lesson of Munich: Appeasement of aggression invariably leads to further aggression. Thus, he said, if appeasement had been avoided in the 1930s, "there probably would have been no World War II," regardless, apparently, of the death camps that were just around the corner. What we were doing in Korea was quite simple, as he understood and explained it to the American people: "We are trying to prevent a third world war." He stated, "The Communists in the Kremlin are engaged in a monstrous conspiracy to stamp out freedom all over the world." Because aggression anywhere was a threat to peace everywhere, President Truman argued that "the attack on Korea was part of a greater plan for conquering all of Asia."[33]

The involvement of the United States in Korea was closely linked in the President's mind to "the forces of freedom . . . fighting in Indochina."[34] Each conflict was part of the larger global struggle, whether in the Korean War or in the emerging conflict in Indochina. "This," he said, "means military aid . . . to Indochina."[35] This was the fifth link, a gold one, in the chain to Vietnam the United States unwittingly was constructing. It was forged on May 24, 1950, when President Truman allocated ten million dollars to France for its war to reclaim its Southeast Asian empire against the forces of former OSS agent Ho Chi Minh. America had decided that anti-Communism was more important than anticolonialism.

Dwight D. Eisenhower campaigned for the presidency in 1952 by promising to go to Korea to end the war. Apparently, he was uniquely suited to deal with war, and presumably equally competent to manage the domestic military establishment. It was thought that his political skill had been revealed in his management of America's wartime Allies, especially the British. President Truman never quite escaped questions about his competence, partly because of the inevitable comparison with the towering FDR, and partly because of his own relatively simple background. There was no question about Ike. He was competent.

Senator McCarthy thought otherwise, as he told the Senate:

> Those of us who have confidence in General Eisenhower as a great soldier should realize that Eisenhower's hands are also tied by the same crowd that has tied the hands of MacArthur in the east; and if good-natured Ike is not careful, he is going to be taken for an awful ride. A good soldier such as Eisenhower does not have time to learn the ways of crooked, backroom diplomacy . . . he is not equipped by

experience to cope with unprincipled, crooked, clever diplomats. It is difficult for a soldier of integrity who has not
had time off to study ways of traitors to bring himself to
believe that people in high positions in this Government
could be actually disloyal to the Nation.[36]

By the time of the campaign, America's right wing had repudiated the policy of containment. It argued that containment
was an American guarantee that present slaves would never
become free. From this perspective the cold war would be won
only when the Soviet Union was beaten, not contained. During
the campaign the code word for this attitude on the part of
conservatives was "liberation." Their intention, at least rhetori-
cally, was to liberate the nations behind the iron curtain. They
wanted the United States to retake the initiative from the Soviet
Union, and not merely to continue to react to Soviet initiatives.
They believed that the Korean War had demonstrated the futility of engaging international Communism in limited actions
that could not have definitive conclusions advantageous to the
United States. For example, Ike's running mate, Richard Nixon,
attacked Adlai Stevenson, the Democratic candidate, as a graduate of Dean Acheson's "Cowardly College of Communist Containment."[37] Mr. Nixon was playing to the galleries that
supported Senator McCarthy.

During the campaign John Foster Dulles, the future Secretary of State, said that America must be prepared by all means
to liberate the satellite nations of Eastern Europe. Ike phoned
Mr. Dulles to complain that the two of them had earlier agreed
to maintain that liberation should be accomplished only "by all
peaceful means." Mr. Dulles explained that it was "just a complete oversight."[38] They never spoke about this again.

John Foster Dulles seemed to be one of the most powerful
Secretaries of State in the nation's history. His presence was
commanding, and he was enormously knowledgeable, having,
for instance, participated in drafting the Japanese peace treaty
under President Truman. He had a certainty of his convictions
that made him seem surefooted, optimistic, and clear. But his
boss actually made his own foreign policy and used Mr. Dulles
as a point man. In fact, Secretary Dulles often was reduced by
events to uncertainty and gloom. His public personality was
crafted to convey moral certitude. When he was in doubt he

could always retreat for guidance to his Presbyterian pantry of moral sustenance. More than anyone since President Wilson, John Foster Dulles approached the political struggles of the twentieth century from the vantage point of the Christian moralist. More than anyone since Mr. Wilson, he perfected the art of the sermon as a tool of political leverage. The President approved.

Ike believed that NSC 68 was unusable as an instrument of American policy, mostly because of the enormous expense it required. This does not mean that he was a lukewarm cold warrior. In his inaugural address he displayed his credentials for full membership in that club. He asserted his Manichaean view as plainly as possible: "Freedom is pitted against slavery; lightness against the dark." Destiny had laid on America the responsibility for leading the free world. The nation was equal to the job because of its moral strength, and because we were "not helpless prisoners of history." This American faith belonged to free men all over the world. This faith "confers a common dignity upon the French soldier who dies in Indo-China, the British soldier killed in Malaya, the American life given in Korea."[39] He implied that if America did not save the world, it would not be saved.

A few weeks later, in his first State of the Union address, President Eisenhower said that the only way to avoid a universal conflagration was "to win the cold war."[40] Secretary Dulles testified before the Congress: "[The President] proposes that our nation should reaffirm its awareness that the struggle in the world today is, above all, a moral conflict."[41] The President did take this view, but believed that this global moral conflict must not be allowed to break the bank. Ike's deeply conservative fiscal instincts led him to conclude that irresponsible spending, including defense spending, would weaken the nation from within as surely as a Communist victory would impair it from without. Financial integrity at home was the second front in the global struggle against international Communism.

His campaign promise to end the Korean War coupled with his decision to limit spending meant that he could not contemplate a wider and even more expensive war. He had to find a way to accept a stalemate, even though his rhetoric would not necessarily be similarly restrained. He believed that an armistice in Korea "that merely released aggressive armies to attack elsewhere would be a fraud."[42] America could not afford "so rapid a military buildup that we seriously dislocate our economies."[43] The Korean War was linked in his mind to the total Soviet effort across the earth as well as to America's capacity to resist.

When Ike went to Korea, the American military presented him with plans to achieve a conclusive military victory over the Chinese and the North Koreans. He refused to endorse the proposals because he thought they endangered the world. He sought an end to the war rather than a more satisfying victory over the Communists. He accepted "containment" rather than "liberation," as he consistently did in action if not in rhetoric. An armistice was signed in July 1953, but recriminations about what it all meant were to continue for a very long time.

The way to support a free Indochina was clear to him from early on. It would be more economic to hire the French than to mount our own effort in Indochina. President Eisenhower explained that voting millions of dollars for the French was "the cheapest way . . . to prevent" damage to American security while protecting our "ability to get certain things we need from the riches of the Indonesian territory, and from Southeast Asia."[44] Underwriting the French war against the Vietminh was a bargain.

In May 1953, he clarified his approach to Indochina: "We are proposing to make substantial additional resources available to assist the French and the Associated States in their military efforts to defeat the Communist Viet Minh aggression."[45] He increased French aid from President Truman's $10 million to $400 million a year, and before he was finished he promised to raise that figure to $785 million. By now America was paying for almost the entire French war effort, 78.25 percent, the sixth Vietnam link, another one made of gold. In effect, the French had become mercenaries in America's conflict with the Soviet Union. This was acceptable to a minority within France in the name of recapturing the colonial splendor of the old empire.

The "New Look" in America's defense policy, as described by the President and the Secretary of State, was closely associated with the conviction that the strength of the domestic economy was a key weapon in the cold war. This New Look, a term borrowed from the women's high fashion industry, concentrated on America's comparative strengths, on technology rather than manpower, and emphasized that the United States should resist the Soviet Union with weapons and tactics of our own choice, including the possibility of using atomic weapons, and not seek to match it man for man, or bomb for bomb. The New Look was supposed to benefit America's economy in two ways: It continued to provide fat contracts to key industries, and it prevented additional ballooning of the Defense Department's payrolls.

The technological focus of this attempted revision of basic policy emphasized atomic weaponry. Secretary Dulles began to threaten "massive retaliation" against Soviet depredations. This "doctrine," as it was grandly called, was so rigid, so overblown, that it began to unravel almost from the time it was announced. Beneath all the bluster, the doctrine simply promised the world an atomic holocaust virtually every time the Soviet Union committed another outrage. Such a doctrine, and such a promise, reflected the frustrations of the cold war in America.

Because of the perception of a moral struggle with the Soviet Union, it was widely believed that there simply had to be a way for the forces of good to win. A continuous struggle of limited engagements, usually on ground selected by the enemy, was not good enough because it was not decisive, took too long, and left the enemy still dangerous. Many years later, after the Vietnam War was over for Americans, Senator John G. Tower, a conservative Republican from Texas and enthusiastic advocate for the Pentagon, expressed this frustration for all of the American right wing: "The vast portion of American military experts and the majority of conservative elected officials have become disenchanted with the concept of both limited war and gradualism."[46] Ever since the end of World War II, American conservatives have been restless about the restraints the nation imposed on itself in its engagements with the Kremlin and its proxies. The restraints were most galling in the use of American technological superiority, including but not limited to atomic weapons.

The promise of liberation, like that of massive retaliation, was emptied of meaning virtually from the time it was first announced. When the Soviet Union rolled its tanks into Budapest to suppress the Hungarian uprising of 1956, the United States took no action. Although some conservatives grumbled about the contradiction between the Secretary's campaign promises and the apparent American paralysis, Mr. Dulles was not troubled. He privately said that the only way America could have aided the Hungarians was by nuclear war. "Does anyone in his senses want us to start a nuclear war over Hungary?"[47] In this single rhetorical question the concepts of liberation as well as of massive retaliation were shown to be meaningless even to their most passionate advocate.

Whatever difficulties or complexities the Secretary might have suffered in the actual world of international affairs, his moral perspective was bedrock. He stood on that with certainty. He believed that everyone had to choose between virtue and vice, so he announced that neutrality was immoral. The rest, the formulation of concrete policy or the specific reaction to a specific event, might be mere sound and fury. But morality endures. He told the National War College that " morality cannot prevail in exclusion of religious principles."[48] American military power was the shield to protect the traditional, inspirational, and fundamentally religious morality of the nation. It was inescapably true for Mr. Dulles that the cause of Soviet misconduct was "irreligion."

His father, like Woodrow Wilson's father, had been a Presbyterian minister. Mr. Dulles's worldview, like Woodrow Wilson's, was inseparable from the personal religion in which they both grew up and which nourished them as adults. Mr. Dulles had been part of President Wilson's mission to Versailles after World War I. His uncle was President Wilson's Secretary of State. Mr. Dulles was Woodrow Wilson's most direct and natural heir.

Mr. Dulles thought that force was the means to protect virtue. This agitated George Kennan, along with many other people, who wrote to Mr. Dulles in an attempt to persuade the Secretary to lower the flame under his moral stewpot:

> Let us keep our morality to ourselves. With regard to other nations let us not judge, that we not be judged. Let us not attempt to constitute ourselves the guardians of everyone else's virtue; we have enough trouble to guard our own.[49]

Mr. Kennan did not understand the depth of Secretary Dulles's piety. The Secretary was proud of his faith and proud of his nation. He could not distinguish between one and the other.

Preaching in his father's church in Watertown, New York, Secretary Dulles rehearsed for the congregation the religious and political faith of the fathers. America, he said, had not been designed only for Americans. It had always been intended for the world:

> We sought through conduct, example, and influence to promote everywhere the cause of human freedom. Through missionaries, physicians, educators, and merchants, the American people carried their ideas and ideals to others. They availed of every opportunity to spread the gospel of freedom, their good news, throughout the world.
>
> That performance so caught the imagination of the peoples of the world that everywhere men wanted for themselves a political freedom which could bear such fruits.
>
> The despotisms of the last century faded away largely under the influence of that conduct and example. There is no despotism in the world which can stand up against the impact of such a gospel. That needs to be remembered today. Our best reliance is not more and bigger bombs but a way of life which reflects religious faith.[50]

He believed that the Soviets only respected material force, so America needed to be materially forceful. He thought that atheistic aggression would ultimately fail in its contest with Christian morality, but meanwhile there would be "immense misery and loss." Because the Soviet Union had forcibly imposed its will on one third of the world's people, most of whom he considered religious and patriotic, in time the Kremlin despots would fail. For Americans, faith would prevail. "Our American history, like Hebrew history, is also rich in the story of men who through faith wrought mightily."[51]

It is clear that these sentiments were not obligatory ornaments hung on a political career. Mr. Dulles was a passionate and serious Christian. His celebration of faith was an authentic expression of who he was, how he defined the truth, and what he thought would help his nation.

For President Eisenhower the war in Indochina was a classic example of what he christened the domino theory, the seventh link in the chain that was to shackle us to Vietnam. At a press conference he explained, "You have a row of dominoes set up, you knock over the first one, and what will happen to the last one is a certainty that it will go over very quickly."[52] He believed that if France did not succeed in its struggle against Communism, against Ho Chi Minh's Vietminh, the entire world would be endangered. The 350 million non-Communist people of India and Pakistan would be outflanked. The Malayan peninsula could not be defended, "and tin and tungsten that we so greatly value from that area would cease coming." Burma would fall. Iran was already threatened by what were thought to be Communist forces at work (until the CIA contributed to the overthrow of the government and installed the Shah). Because the President believed that all those nations would collapse if the French failed in Vietnam, it would be ominous for the United States because "how would the free world hold the rich empire of Indonesia?"[53]

Later, the domino theory was essential to make Vietnam seem vital to the national interest of the United States, not by itself, but by its symbolic significance to Moscow and Peking. A peripheral problem was redefined as the flaming fuse on an explosive that could obliterate freedom in the world. This was a concept the American public could understand and support. President Eisenhower told a National Governors' Conference, "Somewhere along the line, this must be blocked. It must be blocked now. That is what the French are doing."[54] The President had accepted the French argument that they were in Vietnam not merely to retake their empire, but to stem Communism.

After he returned from an extended trip to Asia, Richard Nixon, the Vice-President, was asked by President Eisenhower to give a television report to the nation. Mr. Nixon made the now customary bow in the direction of the domino theory, pointed out the overall importance of a free Asia, and reported that he shook 100,000 hands, including some hands attached to Communists, to show Asians that the Communists' description of Americans was false. The Communists had engaged in a "vicious smear" of Americans by creating "in the minds of the people that we are arrogant, that we are mean, that we are prejudiced, that we are superior, that we are bent on war rather than on a program that will lead to peace." Deeds, not words, were necessary to counter this description of the ugly American, so Mr. Nixon shook as many hands as he could. In the process he discovered, despite the advice he had been given by experts, that beneath some obvious surface peculiarities, Asians were really like Americans. A classic solipsist, Mr. Nixon said, "We found the great majority of the people there were like the majority of the people here in their beliefs."[55] A more traveled and experienced man, the President did not believe that we are the world, and described this attitude as "one of the greatest errors that ignorance can make."[56]

Mr. Nixon told the television audience that the entire free world owed an enormous debt of gratitude to France. What France was doing was nothing less than restraining China, "the basic cause of all our troubles in Asia." Because of the Korean War, future conventional war was unlikely on the Asian mainland. The Vice-President's opinion was that subversion and revolution would become the favored techniques for further Communist expansion in Asia. But, not to worry: "Communism in practice goes against all the fundamental desires of the people of Asia."[57]

In 1954, France fought its last significant battle in a remote valley in the northwest corner of Vietnam. Ho Chi Minh's capacity to fight had grown dramatically in the previous decade. He now had about 100,000 regular army troops, about 50,000 regional troops, and some 225,000 guerrillas. The regular army was well equipped with American weapons the Chinese captured in Korea and gave to the North Vietnamese.

The area of Dien Bien Phu, including the T'ai valley, annually produced about two thousand tons of rice, so it was valuable to the Vietminh. More important, it was one of the most productive areas in Indochina for collecting and processing opium, which was worth about one million dollars annually in 1954 prices. Meo tribesmen grew the poppies in their mountain hamlets and the T'ai people of the valley acted as the distributors. The Vietminh had long used opium to buy American weapons in the black markets of Southeast Asia. *Le Monde*, the distinguished French newspaper, in its story about the French move into Dien Bien Phu, described this traffic:

> The whole area . . . is a major opium-producing area, from which the Viet-Minh draws many of its resources and par-

ticularly the means of paying the deliveries in materiel, arms and ammunition from Communist China. Ho Chi Minh also uses the clandestine sales of opium in all of Indochina to finance his intelligence services and his propaganda and to pay his troops.[58]

The French had expert knowledge of all this because the opium traffic in colonial French Indochina had been a state monopoly. The Vietminh could not allow the French to occupy so valuable a piece of real estate. In fact, that was what the French strategists were counting on.

The idea was to use the massing French troops as bait. Relying heavily on control of the air, the French commander hoped to lure General Giap into a conventional battle. The French built a garrison and improved the old grass airstrip. They ringed the garrison with barbed wire and bunkers to protect the 13,000 elite troops, all of whom had been parachuted in. The Foreign Legion carried the burden and every unit included substantial numbers of Vietnamese soldiers. *Time* magazine was delighted with the French prospects: "A year ago none of us could see victory. There wasn't a prayer. Now we can see it clearly—like light at the end of a tunnel."[59] Lieutenant General John "Iron Mike" O'Daniel inspected Dien Bien Phu and informed President Eisenhower that the battle prospects were even more encouraging than the French believed.

Ho Chi Minh and General Giap carefully studied the situation that was unfolding at Dien Bien Phu. The general, a former history professor, was essentially a self-taught strategist who "totally outguessed the French generals and colonels with their general-staff school diplomas."[60] General Giap concluded that this was the first time that the Vietminh could engage the French without danger of being destroyed. Seizing the initiative would be difficult, however, because of the French control of the air. General Giap told Ho Chi Minh that a force of 50,000 troops could be formed around the garrison, that victory would take months, and that they "would have to count every bullet."[61]

Every available Vietminh soldier—peasants, women, and children included—began to converge on the village. At their rear, hundreds of civilian teams moved on assorted animals and bicycles across the rivers and the mountains that presumably barred access to the valley. The French lost because the Vietminh supplied its soldiers in what for westerners was an unimaginable effort. Ant labor defeated western technology, including air power. Supplies had to be moved five hundred miles from the Chinese border, and for the last fifty miles there was no road through the jungle. The French strafed and bombed the entire supply route. General Giap described the decisive battle of logistics:

> Our troops opened the road and hauled the artillery pieces into our lines . . . our troops razed hills, cut roads into the mountainsides and opened the road to the artillery in the prescribed time. The secret was well kept thanks to excellent camouflage, and the roads were kept open until the end of the battle. . . .
>
> Night and day, the enemy bombed these very difficult roads and nonetheless our transports got through on the whole. Hundreds of thousands of *dan cong* [civilian coolies], women as well as men, surmounted perils and difficulties and spent more than three million work days in the service of the front, in an indescribable enthusiasm.[62]

The French shared the American conviction that bombing could destroy a line of supply in jungles or mountains. The Americans did not advise the French that such an attempt had not been successful two years earlier during Operation Strangle in Korea.

General Giap's first move was to prevent a French evacuation. After that he simply waited for a while. The French were now under siege, did not know the size of the Vietminh forces, and did not know that General Giap was moving heavy Chinese and Russian guns to the surrounding hills. French intelligence concluded that the Vietnamese had 50 medium howitzers that could fire 50,000 rounds; the actual figures were 120 guns that fired 200,000 rounds. Yet, French intelligence was not incompetent. The trouble was that the more accurate it was, the less the military command believed it. Perhaps they did not know about the guns because they had decided that the terrain was too difficult for moving heavy artillery. It took three months for men on foot to move the guns an inch at a time over the jungled mountains. The French were finally outgunned three to one, and the Vietminh held the high ground. The French had 10 American light tanks that had been dropped in by parachute.

On March 12, 1954, the Vietminh finally opened fire. The

artillery barrage lasted for about one hour and was a massacre. The French and the American advisers in the garrison were astonished at how close General Giap's artillery had been placed. The Vietminh, it turned out, could watch every move the French made in the valley below; they knew where every French gun was placed, which building was the headquarters, and where the ammunition was piled. The defense was such a shambles that the artillery commander, Colonel Charles Piroth, in shame used a grenade to commit suicide.

After paratroop reinforcements arrived, the French successfully countercharged a Vietminh position, with losses on both sides, but the bloody fact could not longer be denied. For the French, Dien Bien Phu was hopeless. With the airstrip demolished, the garrison was cut off from the world except for parachuted supplies. The wounded could not be evacuated.

General Giap now ordered his troops to dig miles of trenches leading right up to the French main force. This protected the Vietminh from both artillery and napalm. Of 800 French paratroopers who had reinforced the garrison, there were 80 left at the end. General Marcel Bigeard told his men, "We must hold out one more day. The Americans will not let us down; the free world will not let us down. They may come."[63]

While Dien Bien Phu was besieged, the Eisenhower administration grew increasingly concerned that the French might simply quit, might negotiate an unacceptable settlement at the forthcoming Geneva Conference, or even might lose. It was believed that any one of these alternatives would hand Indochina over to China to the benefit of international Communism. President Nixon recalled the significance of this as he had understood it at the time: "A French withdrawal from Vietnam would have placed us in a very difficult position because American policy was predicated upon the vital importance of maintaining an independent Vietnam."[64]

The French requested additional American aircraft, but the Chairman of the Joint Chiefs of Staff, Admiral Arthur Radford, did not believe that giving the French more planes would make the difference. He seriously began to consider a plan, codenamed Vulture, that had been prepared by American and French officers stationed in Saigon. It prescribed huge bombing runs by land-based and carrier planes to destroy the areas around the garrison where General Giap had his heavy artillery.

President Nixon later remembered that Admiral Radford's Vulture plan called "for using three small tactical atomic bombs to destroy Vietminh positions and relieve the garrison."[65]

President Eisenhower was worried about the French capacity to win this chapter of the cold war for the United States. In February 1954, he had sent some two hundred technical advisers, mostly army mechanics, to assist the French in Vietnam. The Congress forced him to promise that these men would be home by June. As the news from Dien Bien Phu began to reach Washington, it became clear that advisers would not serve the purpose. At the end of March he called in the congressional leadership to warn that "at any time within the space of forty-eight hours, it might be necessary to move into the battle of Dien Bien Phu."[66] But within a week the President had cooled down and told a meeting of the National Security Council that it was essential to persuade the British and the French to participate in united action in Vietnam, and to persuade the Congress to support an intervention.

A major reason for Ike's reversal was that Winston Churchill refused to cooperate because he did not believe that the loss of Vietnam would start the dominoes falling. He added that since the British people would not fight to "save" India for Britain, they would not fight to save Vietnam for the French. Mr. Nixon and the Chairman of the Joint Chiefs were "astonished" that a man who understood Communism so well did not believe in President Eisenhower's dominoes.[67]

The French response was infuriating, not astonishing. In a meeting with French General Paul Ely, Admiral Radford insisted that the United States take over the training of Vietnamese troops. General Ely delivered a catalog of complaints about the American national character which he thought made cooperation between the two nations difficult. He said that "Americans acted as if the United States sought to control and operate everything of importance," that "the United States appears to have an invading nature as they undertake everything in such great numbers of people," that "McCarthyism is *prevalent* in the U.S. and actually is akin to Hitlerism," and that Americans favored Germany over France, did not appreciate how difficult it had been for France to have fought two terrible wars, that American procedures were "enormously wasteful, irritating and paper heavy," and that Americans "appeared to lack confidence in the French in the manufacture of most modern weapons and equipment."[68] Finally, the French government seemed unable to say clearly that it would grant the three Associated States of Indochina real independence should the French actually beat the Communists. Mr. Eisenhower described French promises about the future of Vietnam, Laos, and Cambodia as "weasel words."[69]

Despite the French distaste for cooperating with Americans on American terms, the siege was endangering French troops and aspirations. In early April France asked the United States to bomb General Giap's positions. Without British support, without French acceptance of American terms, President Eisenhower was unwilling to let Vulture fly. Key members of the Congress were opposed to unilateral American intervention. For example, Senator Kennedy warned that military aid alone could never defeat a native political organization that has "the support and covert appeal of the people."[70] He also said that so long as France was in Indochina Ho Chi Minh would win.

Vice-President Nixon created a storm, either as a trial balloon for the administration or because of carelessness. During the question period following a speech, he said that if the French withdrew from Vietnam the United States would send its own troops to fight the Communists. This was headline news all over the country. In his memoirs he wrote that President Eisenhower was not upset and a few days later actually supported the Vice-President's assertion. But President Eisenhower made his own position clear: "If we were to put one combat soldier into Indo China, then our entire prestige would be at stake, not only in that area but throughout the world." He thought that the United States might provide training, and could use the American navy and air force to support local forces, but, he said, "I don't see any reason for American ground troops to be committed in Indo China."[71] Lyndon Johnson, the Senate's Democratic leader, rejected the "Nixon War" and would not support "sending American G.I.s into the mud and muck of Indochina on a bloodletting spree to perpetuate colonialism and white man's exploitation in Asia."[72]

By May 7, the end had come. Fifty-five days after the siege of Dien Bien Phu began, the French were forced to stop fighting, but would not fly a white flag. The Vietminh walked into the garrison. The French had 13,000 men in the garrison at any one time, but altogether 16,500 fought there. All the survivors were marched to one of two prisons, both 500 miles away. It was a march of death, as 10,000 of the 13,000 died within three months. They had been fed on fourteen ounces of rice a day, plus ten peanuts every ten days. The French colonial enterprise in Southeast Asia was finished because Dien Bien Phu destroyed military morale in Vietnam and public support in France. The following day, the Geneva Conference was ready to turn to the question of settling the conflict in Indochina.

One of the heroes of American nonintervention in Dien Bien Phu was the Army Chief of Staff, General Matthew B. Ridgway, then probably the most reputable military man in the country. He had led parachuting troops in World War II and had replaced General MacArthur in Korea. To add a bit of dash he always wore two live grenades dangling from his chest. He believed that both Admiral Radford and Secretary Dulles wanted to find a reason to get into the fight. He also knew that the President was a cautious politician. Without waiting to be asked, General Ridgway sent a team to Vietnam to survey what would be needed to win. He did not actually oppose intervention, but set the cost for doing so: a slogging foot soldiers' war requiring between 500,000 and 1,000,000 troops, draft calls of 100,000 a month, and the seizure of a Chinese island in the Gulf of Tonkin, with the risks obviously entailed. He said that there could not be a shiny, expensive, but antiseptic, technological solution. After briefing the President, General Ridgway later wrote that his report "played a considerable, perhaps a decisive, part in persuading our Government not to embark on that tragic adventure."[73]

The administration hated even the idea of holding an international conference about Southeast Asia. The Soviets and the British took the lead in the conference, and the Communist Chinese attended. The French arrived with an empty holster. On the first day of debate, Secretary Dulles told an American television audience that the administration was worried that the conference might ease the way for a Communist takeover. He later told American reporters that America would not accept elections as the way by which Ho Chi Minh would take over Vietnam. When he arrived in Geneva he acted like a "puritan in a house of ill-repute."[74] The Secretary would not soil his hands in such a place and so refused to shake hands with China's premier, Chou En-lai.

In the middle of June the French government fell and the new prime minister, Pierre Mendès-France, promised the French electorate that he would resign in one month if a Vietnam settlement had not been reached. The Americans were enraged that Mendès-France would guarantee success to Communist stalling at Geneva, and that he showed how desperate he was to strike any sort of a settlement that would allow him to keep his domestic bargain. By then it was clear that the French people had heard too much about Indochina, and the French imperialistic struggle was no longer supported by French voters.

After prowling the hallways at Geneva for a few days, Secretary Dulles returned home. It grew increasingly clear that some sort of a partition of Vietnam would be necessary, something along the lines of the Korean settlement. The Secretary was preparing himself to learn about a settlement that "we would have to gag about."[75] The administration turned its attention to the idea of letting Ho Chi Minh have something, but taking over the role of the French in defending the rest of Southeast Asia. The American negotiators were instructed to play only a passive role during the discussions at Geneva, in order for the United States to stay aloof from the distasteful compromises when they were finally reached. The key players turned out to be Mendès-France and Chou En-lai. No matter the outcome, America would not endorse a document that gave additional territory to Communists. Both the Soviets and the Chinese pressured the Vietminh to moderate its demands.

The Geneva Conference divided Vietnam along what was supposed to be a temporary military, not political, line along the 17th parallel. The political question was to be decided by internationally supervised elections within two years, in 1956. No new military forces or bases were to be introduced into Vietnam. Neither the northern nor the southern parts of Vietnam were to enter into military alliances. There was to be a ceasefire for Laos and Cambodia. The United States did not like these agreements and promised only that it would not disrupt them by force. What remained to be done, as the President understood it, was to take all steps necessary to ensure that Ho Chi Minh now had all the territory he was ever to get. There was a strong presumption that if America acted intelligently, Ho Chi Minh might not be able to hold on to what he was given as a gift at what the administration believed was the unfortunate conference in Geneva.

It was not sufficiently understood at the time that the dividing line would deprive northern Vietnam of food. It had always depended on southern surpluses of rice. This provided the northerners with something other than ideology as a reason behind their "fanatical" demands for reunification. The other partitioned nations, Germany and Korea, had not divided a population from its food supply. This single fact meant that increasingly the North would have to depend on its Socialist allies for aid. The line delivered North Vietnam's belly into the hands of the People's Republic of China, while its head remained in Moscow. Yet, it was a line first suggested by the North Vietnamese. They did this partly as a desire finally to get the French out, and partly as a reaction against increasing American involvement in the South. They were afraid that the Americans in the South would eventually push for a permanent partition of their country. They accepted partition in the hope that the promised elections would soon make the country whole again.

On June 17, 1954, the same day Mendès-France was installed in Paris, Emperor Bao Dai appointed Ngo Dinh Diem as prime minister of South Vietnam, thereby setting in motion a force that was to shape Vietnam, and America's response to it, for almost the entire next decade. Ngo Dinh Diem was to become an institution, his family a sovereign force.

He was a devout Catholic from a Buddhist country who had, in 1950, lived at Maryknoll seminaries in New Jersey and New York, and was sponsored by Francis Cardinal Spellman. His Catholic anti-Communism appealed to Senators John Kennedy and Mike Mansfield. His ancestors converted to Catholicism in the seventeenth century, and his father had been the chief mandarin at the emperor's court. Diem's Catholicism did not prevent him from being a thorough Vietnamese. Raised as a mandarin, spiritually wedded to the ancient culture of Hue, he was celibate, austere, stubborn, somewhat debonair, and elegant in a disciplined sort of way. He was a zealot about reviving the old, traditional Vietnamese morality, especially in public life. None of the Americans who were to have regular contact with him seemed to have understood that Diem was a "Catholic in the Spanish manner . . . a puritanical conservative."[76] Diem was a conservative cultural nationalist, while the Americans consistently demanded that he become a politician in their image: secular, innovating, and liberal.

To the dismay of the Americans, Diem installed his family throughout his government. He ruled not as a single personality, although his portrait decorated all of Saigon, but as the head of the Ngo family, as the patriarch of Vietnam. One of his problems was that the Americans seemed not to comprehend that he was Vietnamese. They were offended by what they considered his nepotism, by his appointment of his own relatives, including his younger brother and his wife, her father and mother, four other brothers, cousins, and assorted in-laws.

Ngo Dinh Nhu, Diem's younger brother, was more cosmopolitan and widely educated, and more brittle than Diem. He was appointed simply as "political adviser," and ruled Saigon and the southern part of South Vietnam. Another brother, Ngo Dinh Can, was of the old ways, did not wear western clothes, slept on the floor, was stern, uncultured, and was the boss of Hue and the northern part of South Vietnam. Ngo Dinh Can became a frenzied moral judge, determined to cleanse Vietnam of Communism and foreigners; he is supposed to have told his followers: "My hand will never tire of killing communists. . . . Everyone among you should offer the life of *one* Red to your country. As for me, millions. . . ."[77] In the South, Nhu and his beautiful, hissing wife became cultural and political arbiters who could rule because, like Can, they had the power of life and death over the people of South Vietnam.

In an interview with M. Jean Lacouture, a French journalist, Ngo Dinh Nhu explained that "in political action one is occasionally forced to dirty one's hands. There is a difference between what one wants to do and what one does." He knew that westerners believed his brother's regime was reactionary. M. Lacouture asked him whether he and Diem could ease up, could tolerate political opposition. Nhu tried to explain:

> Restore freedom, give free speech to the opposition, create conditions of coexistence with communism? First of all, you do not coexist with those who want to exterminate you. Moreover, the opposition is not so badly treated by us. It cannot speak up? Wait a minute. We do not permit our-

selves to be incited or destroyed, but these restrictions of liberty we also apply to ourselves. Are you aware of that?[78]

Madame Nhu devoted herself to eliminating vice, especially dancing, especially the tango, and believed that all modern music was prostitution.

The Americans would have to cross an immense bridge to comprehend the Ngo family. Yet, it was a fair test because the Ngos were culturally more accessible to the American mind than the infinitely more opaque culture of the villagers who made up about 85 percent of the population. However strange Diem might seem, he was more familiar to the Americans, partly because he was a Catholic, and largely because he was more westernized than the millions who were either active or passive Buddhists, who lived their lives in the close spaces of their hamlets, wanted only to harvest their rice, and were not exercised about the grand abstractions of international geopolitics. They were always more interested in who ruled the village than in who ruled in faraway Saigon. They were always less interested in Washington, Moscow, or Saigon than in their water buffaloes.

The American intelligence agencies believed the Geneva agreements made it likely that the Vietminh would consolidate its military position, and that Diem's government would probably have increasing difficulty maintaining itself. Ho Chi Minh demanded that elections be held on the schedule set by the Geneva agreement, but Diem refused to risk certain defeat. President Eisenhower accepted Diem's conclusion, believing that Ho Chi Minh would have won 80 percent of the vote. The elections were never held. Shortly, a guerrilla movement called by Diem the Vietcong, an insulting abbreviation of Vietnamese Communist, began in the South with increasing assistance from the North.

After Geneva, America concentrated on creating a nation out of the southern military zone in Vietnam. This nation was to be a showcase of anti-Communist democracy in Asia. An American scholar described the American effort: "Originating out of the exigencies of the Cold War, the experiment in nation-building tapped the wellsprings of American idealism and took on many of the trappings of a crusade."[79]

One dimension of this idealistic crusade was for the CIA to

send Colonel Edward G. Lansdale on a sabotage mission to Hanoi. This was consistent with the Eisenhower administration's New Look, an important part of which was covert activity. One legacy of the Korean War, according to a CIA agent in the Far East, was that it established the "CIA's jurisdiction in the Far East and created the basic paramilitary capability that the Agency employed for twenty years."[80] Under the directorship of Allen Dulles, the brother of the Secretary of State, the CIA was the only major agency Senator McCarthy backed away from. Allen Dulles warned the senator to keep his hands off, unlike John Foster Dulles who threw one victim after another to the senator. Allen Dulles's conception of intelligence work was essentially paramilitary action. The 1950s was the CIA's great era of overthrowing and creating governments, of international sabotage. The President was troubled by this, but not too troubled. He wrote in a private letter in 1955:

> I have come to the conclusion that some of our traditional ideas of international sportsmanship are scarcely applicable in the morass in which the world now flounders. Truth, honor, justice, consideration for others, liberty for all—the problem is how to preserve them, nurture them and keep the peace—if this last is possible—when we are opposed by people who scorn . . . these values. I believe we can do it, but *we must not confuse these values with mere procedures, even though these last may have at one time held almost the status of moral concepts.* [81]

Colonel Lansdale was the man who had helped repress a left-leaning guerrilla rebellion in the Philippines in the late 1940s. He was sent to Vietnam in 1954 to assist in establishing the Diem regime. When Diem arrived in Saigon, Colonel Lansdale was in the small crowd lining the streets to cheer the motorcade. He was appalled that the limousine sped past the people. Having just arrived in Vietnam himself, Colonel Lansdale concluded, "[Diem] had no instincts at all of politics. . . . So I jotted down some notes on how to be a Prime Minister of Vietnam at that moment."[82] He took his notes to the palace, found the newly installed Diem to whom he gave a lesson in how to be a successful Vietnamese prime minister, and the two men became friends. The colonel was the model for the central character in Graham Greene's *The Quiet American.*

One of Colonel Lansdale's first impressions when he arrived in Saigon was of the generosity of American aid to the French. "It seemed to me," he wrote in his memoirs, "that every last French officer and enlisted man was driving around town in his own American jeep."[83] He did not like the French, mostly because they were in his way. Nonetheless, his description of them immediately after Dien Bien Phu was accurate:

> ... the French living in Vietnam seemed not to have heard of the granting of independence. Their possessive attitude toward the Vietnamese remained as strong as ever, evoking strong French emotional responses whenever an American came near one of "their" Vietnamese. The French High Command, still directing a war against the Vietminh, continued in tight control of Vietnamese nationalist military forces. There still were French officials throughout the Vietnamese government, giving advice in tones that sounded strangely like orders. A Swiss journalist said, "The French are like a man giving up his mistress. He knows the affair is over, but he hates it when he sees his mistress ride by in the big car of a rich man she has just met." I gathered that we Americans were the rich newcomers.[84]

Colonel Lansdale's team was called the Saigon Military Mission, and began its work in August 1954, one month after the Geneva agreement was completed. The team's mission was to engage in paramilitary operations and psychological warfare, what the initiates called psywar, against the enemy. On the colonel's first night in Saigon, the Vietminh blew up an ammunition dump at the airport. The resident Americans in Saigon told Colonel Lansdale that the time had arrived for "positive action." His first operation was to start rumors in Hanoi, as he described it:

> The first rumor campaign was to be a carefully planted story of a Chinese Communist regiment in Tonkin taking reprisals against a Vietminh village whose girls the Chinese had raped, recalling Chinese Nationalist troop behavior in 1945 and confirming Vietnamese fears of Chinese occupation under Vietminh rule; the story was to be planted by soldiers of the Vietnamese Armed Psywar Company in Hanoi dressed in civilian clothes. The troops received their

instructions silently, dressed in civilian clothes, went on the mission, and failed to return. They had deserted to the Vietminh.[85]

When the French, who were now engaged in another colonial war in Algeria, evacuated Hanoi in October 1954, parts of Colonel Lansdale's team left with them. They were "disturbed by what they had seen of the grim efficiency of the Vietminh in their takeover, the contrast between the silent march of the victorious Vietminh troops in their tennis shoes and the clanking armor of the well-equipped French whose Western tactics and equipment had failed against the Communist military-political-economic campaign."[86] The northern team was in Hanoi to contaminate the oil of the city's buses, to sabotage the railroad, and to study potential targets for future operations. The oil-contaminating team had a close call when the fumes from the contaminant almost knocked them out. But they finished the job. Colonel Lansdale's men also taught English to the mistresses of important South Vietnamese officials. He personally played a crucial role in helping Diem survive opposition from an assortment of armed religious sects, including one that worshipped a statute of Victor Hugo in the jungle.

Despite elements of comic opera in some of his activities, Colonel Lansdale understood the nature of the conflict. He knew what made the guerrillas strong and therefore what had to be done:

> When the troops unite with the people, the war starts being won. Asian Communists understand this. Too few on our side do. People still get trampled under as our soldiers strive for the tactical goals given them. As long as this happens, we cannot win.[87]

Using whatever techniques were available to it, the Eisenhower administration bonded itself to Premier Diem, sought to build a nation for him to run, and violated the Geneva agreement. This was done to protect the world from the Kremlin acting through Hanoi. Diem was, however, not a good American politician. As premier, one of his first actions was to reject a land-reform program that was essential if the great mass of the population was ever to understand that the southern politicians had something to offer in opposition to the promises being made in the North. In fact, land reform in the North involved mass terror, with thousands of peasants executed by the Vietminh, an action for which Ho later apologized. Diem's viewpoint was traditional in Indochina, but it was not a policy with which Washington could become publicly cozy.

Diem announced that God had come South. In a letter to him in October 1954, President Eisenhower said that he was glad to respond favorably to the request for financial aid to assist in relocating the hundreds of thousands of Vietnamese, mostly Catholics, who were moving from North to South Vietnam. About 80,000 guerrillas and their families moved to the North; about 5,000 guerrillas stayed in the South to fight again another day. President Eisenhower informed Diem that the United States would like to begin "an intelligent program of American aid" if a way could be found to assure "the standards of performance" of Diem's government. The President wanted Diem to understand that America expected the Vietnamese to invent a nation that would fit into its intended slot in the cold war. He expected that Diem would undertake "needed reforms." The deeper purpose of the offer was made clear: "to assist the Government of Viet-Nam in developing and maintaining a strong, viable state, capable of resisting attempted subversion or aggression through military means." After this strong state came into being, the President hoped that its government would be wise, responsive to the people's nationalism, and effective in administration to the end that "it will be respected both at home and abroad and discourage any who might wish to impose a foreign ideology on your free people."[88] This letter was the eighth link in America's Vietnam chain.

The Catholic Vietnamese thrived under Diem's systematic discrimination against the Buddhists. The Catholics were preferred in the civil service, while those who lived in the villages were not always required to do the hard labor of building roads or other public works. The Catholic Church, unlike the Buddhist pagodas, had special rights to acquire and own property, as had been the case under the French. In time, this discrimination against the vast majority of the country would lead to politically lethal protests against Diem by the Buddhist bonzes.

As a step toward creating a strong, viable nation, per instructions, Diem called for an election in 1955 to determine whether the southern Vietnamese wanted a monarchy under Bao Dai or a republic under his own presidency. He did this because Bao Dai had ordered him to resign. Bao Dai had already lost support, as a young officer in the South Vietnamese army said: "How do you think it feels getting oneself killed in the jungles for that man who comes up here to swear us in wearing a Riviera suit, a polka-dot tie, and inch-thick crepe soles?"[89] According to Colonel Lansdale, Bao Dai needed additional funds "for his fun and games on the Riviera and had sold the position of chief of police for Saigon-Cholon to the boss of the underworld . . . for $1.25 million U.S."[90] This information was widely known at the time.

Of the 6,000,000 people who voted, 99 percent supported Diem, a result that might have concerned anyone who cared about Vietnam. In fact, Diem received 200,000 more votes in Saigon than there were registered voters in that city.[91] Colonel Lansdale had earlier advised his friend Diem not to rig the election: "All you need is a fairly large majority . . . not 99.99 per cent of the vote."[92] Diem repudiated the Geneva agreement provision for unifying Vietnam by a national election because of his fear that the Communists would not tolerate a fair election. On the other hand, when Ho Chi Minh later held an election in North Vietnam, the Communists won 99.8 percent of the vote.

The Eisenhower administration always believed that what was missing in Vietnam was a strong man like Syngman Rhee in Korea. Since so fevered an anti-Communist was not available, the administration sought to pay for the creation of one by transforming Diem and South Vietnam into what could then become, as Senator Kennedy put it in 1956, "the cornerstone of the Free world in Southeast Asia, the keystone in the arch, the finger in the dike."[93] For American leaders, both South and North Vietnam had no existence outside of the context of the cold war.

Being a finger in the dike, an ideological proving ground, or a cold war pawn, Vietnam never truly became a real and particular place for Americans. It was always a symbol, a detail that was sublimated into an abstraction. America's ignorance was a result. For example, General Maxwell Taylor, a major war planner in the future, met with Diem in 1957 to urge that the government be made more representative by including more people. Diem asked who General Taylor had in mind, and the general, briefed by the American ambassador, mentioned three likely choices for inclusion in the Cabinet. Diem "ticked them off gravely: the first had been involved in the recent coup plot; the second had a French wife; and the third was too prosperous to be honest." The American general was relieved when they then changed the subject to discuss matters on which he "felt better qualified."[94]

The American myth of technology as applied to government necessarily emphasizes process and organization, regulation and law. It is the technique that is relevant to Americans. The Americans had enjoyed deep satisfaction in the fact that Diem had been elected. This approval led Bernard Fall, an expert about Vietnam, to conclude that "this overemphasis on process rather than political facts can . . . be attributed to the application of an American scale of values to an alien situation."[95] The Vietnamese naturally retained their traditional interest in the people who ruled them, not in the system. As one American journalist said, the Americans complained that Vietnamese politics were "underdeveloped" as, in a sense, they were. The Vietnamese were unable to understand American talk about "the machinery of government," as Americans were unable to understand Vietnamese talk about the importance of finding leaders who displayed the "correct Confucian way of life." Frances Fitzgerald, an American journalist who was studying Vietnam, described this impasse: "In Vietnam it was simply embarrassing that gossip about the Vietnamese generals described the workings of the government better than all their organization charts."[96]

Diem annoyed Americans not only because of his personal way of doing things. He was an enthusiast when it came to repressing his political opponents, of whom he arrested upwards of 40,000. In early 1959, Diem legalized his brutality by creating special military courts to try political opponents and to pass sentences of death in no more than three days. These courts made the arrests, conducted the inquiries, and sentenced the guilty. The official newspaper explained the new law:

> To hide a communist, or permit oneself to become involved in anything with a communist, is to risk the death penalty. In connection with the crime there usually is a distant

97

instigator who has only given orders, an immediate instigator and a certain number of those who committed the crime, and all those who have directly or indirectly been of assistance. All must suffer execution. . . .[97]

Diem closed newspapers that did not support him with the requisite fervor. Worst of all, he destroyed the leadership in the villages and replaced it with his own appointees. He had become a dictator.

He forced the 300,000 Chinese, who were central to the commercial life of the nation, to choose between becoming Vietnamese citizens or losing their rights to do business. After asking Chiang Kai-shek what they should do, and after realizing that he would not answer, the Chinese gave up their nationality to Diem's demand. Their loyalty to Diem (and to Chiang) was probably not strengthened. North Vietnam also nationalized its Chinese residents, but it did so with the approval of the People's Republic of China. That made a difference.

Diem had become an enormously expensive puppet whose strings were manipulated in Washington. As would become clear in a few years, both the puppet and the puppet master were tied to each other, and the question of who had greater freedom is too metaphysical for the world of tough-minded international politics. The fact is that, being tied together, each may pull the strings of the other and each may refuse to dance as expected. Diem understood perfectly well that the American cold warriors needed him as much as he needed them. In the next American administration, when it was finally realized that Diem would not dance to our tune, President Kennedy did not prevent Diem's murder.

When President Eisenhower left office, there were some one thousand Americans in South Vietnam, the ninth link in the Vietnam chain which was not long enough to wrap around our national neck. About one billion dollars had created a Saigon economy that looked good, with well-stocked stores, available Coca-Cola, automobiles on the streets, and expensive houses going up in the expensive neighborhoods. Finally, the United States grew somewhat concerned about some of the obvious luxury items that Diem insisted were necessary to prevent local unrest, so it refused to continue the shipment of water skis and high-fidelity equipment, among other goods. The other 85 percent of the people of South Vietnam, the peasants living in countryside villages, were barely touched by this new, shiny dreamworld of expensive American objects. If it were possible with American advice and cash to build a nation that we could recognize because it would be like ours, it was to be attempted in what was arguably the least promising place on earth. This was a society dominated by the traditional values of family, land, and village, with a people who were engaged not in the large affairs of the world, but in the more significant activities of growing enough rice to feed the family and accommodating to the will of Heaven.

It was frequently said that this enormous infusion of money into South Vietnam made the South Vietnamese dependent on America. This missed the point of America's growing dependence on South Vietnam. Frances Fitzgerald wrote that "the idea that the mission of the United States was to build democracy around the world had become a convention of American politics in the 1950's."[98] This was what had become of the myth of the city on a hill. "Democracy" was offered to the Third World as a means of positioning America on the right side of the moral divide. Presumably, this would result in freeing the world from poverty and oppression, and consequently America would win the cold war. South Vietnam, as Senator Kennedy pointed out, was "the finger in the dike."

As a matter of course, opposition to Diem's repression, especially opposition by the 95 percent of Vietnam that was not Catholic, began to rise. Nhu's control of his CIA-trained police ensured that the repression would not be tepid. As a result of closing off more tranquil means of dissent, terror became daily news. The southern guerrillas, especially the five thousand or so who stayed behind in the South when populations were exchanged after the Geneva Conference, began their struggle against a tyrant who embarrassed the Americans. M. Lacouture estimated that about 25 percent of the guerrillas were Communists.

In September 1960, shortly before the American presidential election, bloody fighting erupted in Kontum, a province in the central highlands. The Diem government announced that it had captured some North Vietnamese who had infiltrated through Laos. This was not an invasion of a foreign power. It was not even a civil war between contending factions inside South Vietnam. It was a domestic uprising of people who would have been executed for their political beliefs by their own government if it could catch them. It tried very hard to do that. The true believers in the resistance to Diem had only two choices: betray their convictions or become guerrillas. Diem had outlawed the middle choice of permissible dissent. However, because of the appearance of a handful of men from the North, Ngo Dinh Nhu told a Paris newspaperman, "The second Indochinese war has begun."[99] Obviously, the Ngos knew what they were doing, and knew what bells to ring to make the Americans salivate. The Ngos had already been trained by Americans to understand that when the rich round-eyes got excited, they sent cash. By then, 70 percent of South Vietnam's budget deficit, along with all the expenses for the police and the military, was paid by the United States, the tenth link in our chain to Vietnam.

In one sense, American aid to Diem did not displease the North Vietnamese. Premier Pham Van Dong, Ho Chi Minh's closest colleague, said, "Monsieur Diem's position is quite difficult." The reason for his difficulties was the support America was providing to keep him out of difficulties. As the premier put it: "He is unpopular, and the more unpopular he is the more American aid he will require to stay in power. And the more American aid he receives, the more he will look like a puppet of the Americans and the less likely he is to win popular support for his side." An American responded that this sounded like a "vicious circle." The premier answered that it was worse than vicious, "more like a descending spiral."[100]

The National Liberation Front was organized during the Third Congress of the Lao Dong, the Vietnamese Communist Party, in Hanoi, in early September 1960. Representatives of the Communist world attended, along with representatives from Canada, France, India, Indonesia, Italy, Japan, and Morocco. The Third Congress emphasized the continuing importance of national reunification. Its last action called for revolution in South Vietnam against the Diem dictatorship. "Liberation of South Vietnam from American imperialism" was formally endorsed by the Congress, a step that was taken as a result of increasing criticism of North Vietnam's passivity by the guerrillas in the South.

Three months later, a group of about one hundred guerrillas

in the South announced the birth of the "National Liberation Front of South Vietnam," and published a program that Radio Hanoi read over the air. The NLF in South Vietnam was a local revolutionary movement only in part directed by the North. It resembled Fidel Castro's rise in Cuba. Beginning as domestic opposition to the local strong man, Fidel Castro was only later to seek Soviet help. If the NLF was created by anyone outside of its ranks, that person was President Diem.

One month after the announcement of the NLF's birth in the South, John Kennedy took the presidential oath. Now the ragged guerrillas would have to engage the enormous wealth, limitless power, and universal glamour of Camelot.

THREE

THE INVENTION OF SOUTH VIETNAM

President Kennedy brought some new attitudes to Washington. The members of his team were tough, unsentimental, and embarrassed by idealism, do-goodism, and other forms of what they called empty rhetoric. Although JFK made the myth of the city on a hill throb between the lines of his inaugural, none of the New Frontiersmen would ever like to be found guilty of talking out loud about that ancient poem. The memory of John Foster Dulles made them cringe. They thought of themselves as muscular realists, disciplined, potent, demanding hard facts, never pieties, connected with the way the world actually works, decisive, never vacillating or timorous, vigorous, and never tedious. They thought of themselves as above narrow or petty interests of mere politics in their dedication to the larger national interest. They believed that they knew what was good for the country. They were cool and confident, and did not trust emotion. They preferred intellectual speed, agility, and precision. They were rationalists. And they embraced power as if it bestowed immortality.

There were, however, some unsettling crosswinds. Years later, John Kenneth Galbraith, who had been President Kennedy's ambassador to India, recalled the halo that surrounded the inner circle at Camelot's round table. He said that many who had worked for JFK's election were tolerated in the administration, but that foreign policy belonged to the President and his closest advisers. "We knew," Professor Galbraith said, "that their expertise was nothing, and that it was mostly a product of social background and a certain kind of education, and that they were men who had not traveled around the world and knew nothing of this country and the world. All they knew was the difference between a Communist and an anti-Communist." A few doubters, including Professors Galbraith and Schlesinger, among others, who, however, were as bewitched as the rest, "were like Indians firing occasional arrows into the campsite from the outside."[1]

JFK's earlier record showed how deadly serious he was about the cold war. He had always known about the Communists. They were tough and we had to be tougher; they responded only to force so we had to have more force than they. Reminiscent of Theodore Roosevelt, President Kennedy called for Americans to get into geopolitical shape, to adopt a sort of athletic patriotism to meet the future's challenges.

Although JFK publicized what he quickly learned was a phony missile gap to beat Richard Nixon in the 1960 election, the fiction contained a truth: America, for him, had a right and a duty to arm to the teeth. Only then would we be respected where it counts, in Moscow. He jabbed Mr. Nixon by suggesting that he would be even tougher on Communism than the Republicans had been: "I wasn't the Vice President who presided over the Communization of Cuba."[2] He beat the Republicans with Cuba the way they had beaten the Democrats with China.

During the transition, JFK met with Ike several times. A memorandum of their last conference records that President Eisenhower replayed his falling dominoes. He then said "with considerable emotion" that Laos was the key to Southeast Asia and beyond, that the United States should try to get its allies to act in concert if possible, but should act "alone if we could not." He added, "Our unilateral intervention would be our last desperate hope." Apparently to shore up the courage of the younger man, Ike said, "I think you are going to have to send troops and if you do I will come up from Gettysburg and stand beside you and support you."[3] President Kennedy respected Ike's military judgment, and was afraid of his continuing political influence in the country should something in the world begin to smoke during the new administration. JFK later complained that Ike had not mentioned Vietnam.

Probably because of President Eisenhower's warning, the Kennedy administration tried to focus on the problem of Southeast Asia. The National Liberation Front of South Vietnam had already been created, and now war between the Royalists and the Communists broke out in Laos. Toward the end of April of their first year in power, Robert McNamara, the Defense Secretary, convened many of the senior officers of the government to plan what to do. Robert Kennedy, the Attorney General, asked where the best place was to draw the line, to stand and fight. Mr. McNamara replied that Thailand and South Vietnam were better places than Laos. The navy agreed. Secretary McNamara worried out loud about the collapse of the world's respect for American strength if the most powerful nation sat on its hands while the Communists nibbled away at the entire region. He said that he "would not give a cent for what the Persians would think of us if we did not defend Laos." General George Decker, the Army Chief of Staff, apparently remembering Korea, said that the United States could not win a conventional land war in Southeast Asia. But, he said, "If we go in, we should go in to win, and that means bombing Hanoi, China, and maybe even using nuclear bombs." Robert Kennedy asked whether airpower alone could defeat guerrillas, and General Curtis LeMay, Chief of the Air Force, said that it could. Mr. McNamara agreed, "But you would have to use nuclear weapons."[4] The Defense Secretary then adjourned the meeting to think more about what had been said.

President Kennedy's first display of strength regarding Vietnam was a secret. On May 11, 1961, he made two decisions: to add four hundred Green Berets to the Special Forces President Eisenhower had sent in 1957 and to send one hundred additional military advisers to Vietnam; and, to begin an undercover program of espionage and sabotage by the South Vietnamese against North Vietnam. These decisions violated the terms of the 1954 Geneva agreements, and the new President was already caught in the use of "only limited means to achieve excessive ends."[5]

In his last year in office, President Eisenhower had authorized the CIA to begin training eager Cuban exiles to overthrow Fidel

Castro. The first plan was to insert them into Cuba as guerrillas, but was soon changed to an invasion of the country. A corollary scheme was to assassinate Castro and some of his close associates. Because it was pressed for time by the transition, the Eisenhower administration left the execution of the plan to the Kennedy team.

What followed was a classic case of bureaucratic autocannibalism. Secretary of State Rusk did not approve of the invasion plan at all, but for some reason felt constrained not to make his objections too clear or too public. The CIA permitted its section in charge of covert activities to monopolize the invasion, and did not ask its own intelligence section for an estimate of likely consequences. No one informed Adlai Stevenson, ambassador to the U.N., about what was going on, so he unwittingly lied to the world about America's innocence. The Joint Chiefs of Staff had not been seriously involved in the planning.

The President was prevented from calling off the entire escapade because of its strong support within his own bureaucracy. It was certain that if he cancelled the invasion, someone in either the Pentagon or the CIA "would promptly leak to the Republicans—and his administration, plastered with a label of 'weakness,' would never get off the ground...."[6] JFK's fear of seeming weak led him to join the adventure weakly, which made its success even less likely.

The President switched the actual landing site, picked an impossible location, and cancelled an air strike that might have protected some of those he called the Cuban freedom fighters. He later said, "The advice of every member of the Executive Branch brought in to advise was unanimous—and the advice was wrong."[7] After the most elaborate vacillations, the President ordered the "invasion fleet" to sail on Sunday, April 16, 1961. He authorized one hour of U.S. navy air cover for the invasion, but for mysterious reasons the navy's planes were an hour early and had no one to protect. The 1,400 Cubans were decimated on the beach. Members of the Kennedy administration continued whispering to each other about the advantages of having Castro assassinated, including one CIA scheme to give him a gift of a poisoned wet suit, and another to take out a Mafia contract on him.

The interested officials of the CIA, especially Allen Dulles and Richard Bissell (both were fired because of this national embarrassment), may have understood perfectly well that they were planning a failure. It is not true that they expected a popular uprising to support the Cuban brigade. The basic difficulty was that the entire plan was foolish. The landing force of 1,400 men was thrown against 200,000 men in Castro's army and militia. It is probably not true that if the President had authorized a second air strike the invasion would have succeeded. It seems reasonable to assume that the CIA planners at least had a suspicion that the plan had gotten away from them, that a "covert" action of 1,400 men was too big to hide and too small to succeed.

A few weeks after this folly, Chester Bowles, the Undersecretary of State, an old-time Stevenson and Humphrey liberal, much given to long-winded and occasionally moralistic expositions about world politics, and therefore not liked by the hard-nosed Kennedy pragmatists, worried in his diary whether the President knew the difference between right and wrong. He was concerned about a President and his advisers who during a crisis could depend only on their analytical abilities because they had no solid convictions on which to rely. Mr. Bowles thought that adding up the advantages and disadvantages of a proposed action generally works well enough in most routine decisions. What troubled him was the quality of decisions such people would make when they were under stress, tired, or emotionally involved. He wrote, "The Cuban fiasco demonstrates how far astray a man as brilliant and well-intentioned as Kennedy can go who lacks a basic moral reference point."[8]

While the Bay of Pigs was unfolding, the Laotian war began to wind down, as another Geneva Conference was called to deal with it. A ceasefire was arranged early in May, and the dangerous flash point that had worried President Eisenhower receded from the primary attention of the New Frontiersmen. Within a year the Geneva Conference declared Laos to be neutral. Although Southeast Asia continued to worry President Kennedy, the tragicomedy of the Bay of Pigs had diverted his attention from Indochina. He told an adviser, "If it hadn't been for Cuba we might be about to intervene in Laos."[9] JFK later said that the botched invasion taught him never again to trust either the generals or the CIA, although he had not seriously consulted "the generals."

In January 1961, Premier Khrushchev announced that the Soviet Union would support wars of national liberation which he predicted would break out more often. His speech came only weeks after the creation of the National Liberation Front in Vietnam. Members of the Kennedy team were fascinated and terrified by guerrilla war. They were fascinated because it was just the sort of supposedly technical problem they believed they could solve, and they were terrified because they were not so sure that events in the world or in the nation would allow them to solve it.

A few days after the destruction of the Cuban invasion, President Kennedy spoke to a meeting of newspaper editors to explain that Cuba was "not an island unto itself." He wanted to make the "useful lessons" of the debacle clear, of which the most important, in the context of the Vietnam War, was that guerrilla warfare was a new and powerful threat the United States would have to learn to defeat:

> We dare not fail to see the insidious nature of this new and deeper struggle. We dare not fail to grasp the new concepts, the new tools, the new sense of urgency we will need to combat it—whether in Cuba or South Viet-Nam. And we dare not fail to realize that this struggle is taking place every day, without fanfare, in thousands of villages and markets —day and night—and in classrooms all over the globe.[10]

The lesson of the Bay of Pigs was that "the complacent, the self-indulgent, the soft societies are about to be swept away with the debris of history." America had to abandon its exclusive reliance "on armies prepared to cross borders, on missiles poised for flight." He believed that America's security could be lost bit by bit without armies moving or missiles flying. He was determined to resist this "regardless of the cost and regardless of the peril!"[11]

"What are we doing about guerrilla warfare?"[12] President Kennedy asked his aides almost immediately after he moved into the Oval Office. His interest in this was a result of his fear that the mice were quietly nibbling all over the world, and that the longer subversion, terrorism, and what he called the subterranean war went on without an American response, the more difficult it would finally be. Premier Khrushchev's speech dramatically emphasized the risks of ignoring scratching and chewing sounds in the night.

The question of how to fight guerrillas was the "most divisive issue" within the Kennedy administration. In fact, Roger Hilsman, then the State Department's director of intelligence and research, and a former commando with OSS in World War II, wrote, "The story of Vietnam is the story of the struggle over what that strategy should be."[13] McGeorge Bundy, the former Harvard dean and now the President's national security adviser, agreed. The struggle was caused by the President's clear strategic preferences colliding with traditional vested interests within his own bureaucracy. In such a contest it is likely that any President will lose, or fail to win as much as he wants to, unless he is a master administrator with skilled bureaucratic aides who can focus and sustain their attention. The New Frontier was not particularly skilled in such mundane managerial details.

The new administration was obsessed with the shadow tactics of the guerrillas for the good reason that it was not clear how to defeat them. In the earliest stages of his struggle, the guerrilla may live at home, go about his normal activities during the day, and fight only after sundown. His most important task is to win the support of people close to him, in his own village. He must have their help if he is forced to hide. They must provide him with food and with intelligence about government activities, and must not betray him. By becoming a terrorist, he is capable of proving to his neighbors that the government cannot provide security in the countryside. By murdering one village chief he can intimidate many others. Because the guerrilla is on his home ground, supported and protected by the people, he retains the initiative, fights only when he decides to, and occupies many government troops while he only occasionally fires a single bullet. JFK said that an established government needed ten or eleven soldiers for each guerrilla; this ratio was the conventional wisdom of the time. So long as the guerrilla is supported by either sympathetic or frightened people, he can continue to build his strength. Mao Tse-tung's maxim was correct: "Guerrillas are fish, and the people are the water in which they swim. If the temperature of the water is right, the fish will thrive and multiply."[14]

President Kennedy had read Mao Tse-tung and others on guerrilla war. In 1962, he told both the Congress and the graduating cadets at West Point that the guerrilla, although ancient in origin, was a new and present danger to the freedom of the world. He told the cadets that what he wanted was "a whole new kind of strategy, a wholly different kind of force, and therefore a new and wholly different kind of military training."[15] A few members of the military were delighted: "Seldom, if ever, in the history of our Nation has our political leader exerted such a direct and vibrant role as Commander in Chief of the Armed Forces."[16] But at that point the President had only blown his bugle. The battle had not yet begun.

He directed the Pentagon to get on with this new force, and when that did not proceed fast enough he personally met with the military Chiefs. That led to a crash training program for Special Forces at Fort Bragg. He insisted that these Special Forces wear a green beret as a symbol of their elite status. The Joint Chiefs objected, of course, and the President was forced to override them in this matter of the color and shape of their hats. When a President forces his prestigious subordinates to get in line, the bureaucratic weapon of the press leak is never farther away than the nearest telephone. The press soon reported that the Chairman of the Joint Chiefs, General Lemnitzer, recently back from a trip to Vietnam, believed that the new administration was making too much of guerrilla warfare, and that this obsession would weaken the nation's ability to defeat a more dangerous conventional attack.

JFK believed that if the Joint Chiefs made their opposition to counterinsurgency public, strong congressional support for them would surely form. He was convinced that if the military and its congressional allies attacked him on this issue, the political right wing would be unleashed, with all the muck of McCarthyism oozing again. It was imperative to keep the Chiefs on his side if possible, but if not, at least quiet. He thus began the long and tortured process of appeasing the Chiefs and appeasing the right wing so as not to appease the Communists.

In the process, the President lost his elite antiguerrilla force which, although the Green Berets came noisily into being, was not taken seriously by the traditional military establishment. It was not that the Green Berets were beaten in this internecine bureaucratic struggle, but that they were never made central to the increasingly bloody struggle in Vietnam. Their primary job was to train the mountain people to fight the guerrillas. They did, however, excite the public's fancy, and even in Vietnam a small aura began to shine around them. A writer covering the war in Vietnam once noticed a sign hanging in a Special Forces

camp at Me Phuc Tay: IF YOU KILL FOR MONEY YOU'RE A MERCE-
NARY. IF YOU KILL FOR PLEASURE YOU'RE A SADIST. IF YOU KILL FOR
BOTH YOU'RE A GREEN BERET.[17]

It was important for President Kennedy to succeed in effectively moving his administration toward competence in guerrilla warfare because otherwise the struggle in Vietnam would
almost automatically fall into the hands of bureaucrats who
would convert it into a conventional war of bombing, artillery
fire, and massed troop engagements. The conventional military
view of the guerrilla war in Vietnam came most easily to the Air
Force. One Air Force general said it all: "The airplane is the
equalizer in Southeast Asia." Air power supposedly made
Americans potent, especially against the primitives who dared
to confront us: "The opposition . . . has consisted of poorly
armed although fiercely determined Communist-led guerrillas.
So long as the opposition remains fairly primitive, without a
genuine antiaircraft capability, to say nothing of any air capability, we can do pretty much as we please."[18] Apparently, the war
would be a lark.

It was certain that every service would resist "fighting down,"
that is, abandoning the marvelous technology for more primitive weapons. But the best antiguerrilla weapon is the most
focused and precise, such as a knife or a noose or, if necessary,
a rifle. It is essential to avoid turning civilian bystanders into
supporters of the insurgency because of their anger at indiscriminate killing. The most dangerous weapons for those who
use them in counterinsurgency are bombing and artillery because both inevitably kill civilians. Conventional military strategists would make matters worse by their conventional choice of
weapons, tactics, and strategy.

Moving the Washington bureaucracy to adopt intelligent, un-
conventional counterinsurgency tactics would strain the skills
of the most masterly bureaucratic ringmaster, but President
Kennedy was not more than usually competent in this arena. By
its nature, guerrilla war must be managed across virtually the
entire range of the government. It is as much political as military as economic. It requires cooperation between such enormous and calcified agencies as the State and Defense
Departments, the CIA, and the White House itself. The President created an interdepartmental committee on counterinsurgency, and thought it important enough to appoint Robert

Kennedy as his representative. The State Department began providing instruction about insurgency to all officials, even ambassadors, who were assigned to the zone of guerrillas. The President understood that the threat of the guerrilla required that the American political and administrative bureaucracies, in Washington, Saigon, and the rest of the world, would have to work together. This was a challenge that might have sobered even the New Frontiersmen.

Controlling the bureaucracy was not the work for which Camelot had been assembled. No one at the State Department knew what the Secretary was thinking or doing because Dean Rusk defined his job as a private senior adviser to the President. After Cuba, the CIA was in a bureaucratic shambles. Only Robert McNamara at Defense understood why and how to manage a bureaucracy, the biggest and toughest in Washington. His success made the problem of coping with the Vietnamese guerrilla even worse. Only the Defense Department was organized, had answers, and had manpower. Inevitably, it would resist novel theories about political warfare.

Maxwell Taylor believed that part of the bureaucratic trouble was that the Pentagon and the CIA were both accustomed actually to running operations, while the State Department was notoriously content simply to observe and analyze. Military men, he said, were ready to act, and the President could not "hold them back to the pace of the slowest civil program." Looking back on this early bureaucratic collapse, the general concluded that "unequal progress among our programs plagued our efforts in South Vietnam for years and gave some ground for the charges of later years that the United States tended to neglect the political and social aspects of the situation and fatuously sought an impossible military victory."[19]

Roger Hilsman, among others, understood the unique bureaucratic strains caused by guerrilla war. After a trip to Vietnam, he reported to JFK: "The real trouble . . . is that the rather large U.S. effort in South Vietnam is managed by a multitude of independent U.S. agencies and people with little or no overall direction. . . . What coordination there is results mainly from the sort of treaty arrangements that are arrived at in the country team meetings. . . . There are formidable political and bureaucratic problems. . . ."[20]

The Kennedy administration never even came close to solving

such problems, except when the President intervened personally, as in the matter of the Green Berets. But such intervention is not usually successful in a resistant bureaucracy, as the career of the Green Berets in Vietnam was to show. The President made personal calls to desk officers in the State Department because he was unhappy with the department's rhythm and Dean Rusk's mushiness. The President's style was personal intervention, that is, muscle, rather than leadership.

When the bureaucracy fought back, or threatened to do so, the President was ready to yield. For instance, he decided to appoint General Lansdale, for so long associated with the CIA and President Diem, an old hand at guerrilla war, as ambassador to Vietnam, but the Pentagon had a collective seizure because it considered General Lansdale "too political,"[21] which presumably was the point, and JFK dropped the idea. He was intrigued by the suggestion that he appoint someone with guerrilla experience as the commanding officer in Vietnam, but the expectation of a noisy Pentagon reaction was enough to influence the most conventional appointment of General Harkins.

JFK sometimes ordered his subordinates to run risks he was unwilling to face. When, for example, Roger Hilsman was promoted to the sensitive post as assistant secretary for Far Eastern affairs, he was instructed by Secretary Rusk not to "intrude" into military matters. That single order was enough to sabotage the President's decision to cope with the guerrillas. Then Mr. Hilsman received a phone call from the White House. A voice, probably the President's, said, "You will . . . have been told to refrain from intruding into military and strategic matters." Mr. Hilsman said that he had. The voice then said, "Well, the President wants you to understand that it was precisely because you have stood up to the Defense Department that you were chosen, and that he expects you to continue."[22] The President expected a subordinate under secret instructions to betray his own immediate boss and to throw himself on the President's sword.

In June 1961, the President met with Premier Khrushchev at a summit meeting in Vienna. JFK was determined to convince the Soviets that, despite the Bay of Pigs, he was a strong and resolute American leader. He was concerned that Premier Khrushchev would think him weak and immature because the Russians might then seek to exploit these misperceptions by risky adventures. Mr. Kennedy went to Vienna to persuade the Soviets that they must take him seriously. It did not work.

Premier Khrushchev was in good voice, had his bag of maniacal threats ready at hand, and shook the President into a conviction that the world was an even more dangerous place than this well-trained cold warrior had believed. They did agree that Laos should remain neutral, approved a ceasefire there, and agreed on procedures for the forthcoming Geneva Conference. But Premier Khrushchev insisted on discussing Berlin, about which there could be no agreement, and the President wanted to discuss the Soviets' intervention in wars of national liberation around the world, about which there could be even less agreement. In a few months the Berlin wall started to go up. Premier Khrushchev believed that Berlin was "the testicles of the West. Every time I give them a yank they holler."[23] He yanked in Vienna, and the President called up the reserves soon after. He told a reporter, "If Khrushchev wants to rub my nose in the dirt, it's all over."[24]

While in Vienna the President told James Reston of *The New York Times* that he had been beaten up by Khrushchev, who probably concluded that the young American President was spineless. That was a problem because it would permit the Soviets to think they could get away with murder. The only thing that would convince Khrushchev was action. "So we have to act." President Kennedy believed he had to do something that would make his courage and his will believable. He said, "Vietnam looks like the place."[25]

As events continued to crash upon President Kennedy, the political and psychological forces working on him required that he find a way to prove he was a strong adult. He had been defeated in Cuba and Vienna, and for political and personal reasons he concluded that neither he nor his country could take much more of this. General S.L.A. Marshall, the military historian, believed that "our ever-deepening involvement in Vietnam . . . came about because of Mr. Kennedy's disappointment over Laos, his chagrin and political embarrassment over the Bay of Pigs failure, and his outrage over the taunting over Vietnam to which Khrushchev subjected him at Vienna. Chiefs do react to personal emotions and confuse them with reasons of state."[26] The right wing in America was already describing the new administration as too weak to stand up to the Soviets. When he learned that the Soviets had begun again to test nuclear weapons in the atmosphere, his response revealed both anger and frustration: "Fucked again."[27]

Without a sense of crisis, the administration continued to discuss Indochina. A reluctant Vice-President Johnson was sent to review conditions in South Vietnam. While abroad he informed the world that Diem was the "Winston Churchill of Southeast Asia." When a reporter asked LBJ if he meant what he had said, he answered: "Shit, Diem's the only boy we got out there."[28] In his report to the President, Mr. Johnson concluded that the struggle against Communism in Southeast Asia had to be won or else the Pacific Ocean would become a "Red Sea" requiring America to "take up our defenses on our own shores." He said that the time was not right to introduce American troops into the area because "at this time" they were not wanted by Asian leaders. "Possibly," he said, "Americans fail to appreciate fully the subtlety that recently-colonial peoples would not look with favor upon governments which invited or accepted the return this soon of Western troops." Waving the American magic wand, Mr. Johnson recommended that the United States make "imaginative use of our scientific and technological capability" in attacking hunger, poverty, ignorance, and disease because the Communists would continue to exploit misery for political gain.

Lyndon Johnson advised the President that although Diem had become "remote from the people" and was surrounded by individuals who were neither admirable nor capable, Diem was irreplaceable. "We must decide whether to support Diem—or let Vietnam fall." Finally, it was time to make a "fundamental decision" about whether we were going to stand up to the Communists in Indochina "or throw in the towel." He acknowledged that this decision might in the future require sending American troops. "We must remain master in this decision." Characteristically, he urged a "strong program of action."[29]

President Diem understood—he seems always to have understood—how deep the American need was for him to make, or appear to make, political and economic "progress" in South Vietnam. After Vice-President Johnson's visit, Diem sent President Kennedy a long memorandum in which he expressed his pride in the progress he was making, especially in education and health care. He knew exactly how to use American desires for the purpose of courteous diplomatic extortion. He requested a substantial increase in military aid; "otherwise we will be forced to make the tragic decision to abruptly cease all our social and economic programs."[30] President Kennedy agreed to some increased military assistance, but now insisted that Diem reform South Vietnam's tax structure and begin long-range planning. Thinking back on the war, one military strategist wrote, "We presumed that we knew what was best for the world in terms of social, political, and economic development and saw it as our duty to force the world into the American mold—to act not so much the World Policeman as the World's Nanny."[31] This was the distillation of American arrogance in general, and JFK's in particular. Washington did not understand that every demand made on Diem could become his justification for requesting more military aid. He may have been a recluse in his own country, but he was closely in touch with the psychology of Americans.

In the autumn of 1961, the intelligence community in Washington prepared an estimate of the NLF in South Vietnam. It was described as an arm of the North Vietnamese Communist Party, increasingly so since early 1960. The NLF had learned its guerrilla tactics from Mao Tse-tung and, although it was an extension of Hanoi, the NLF did its own recruiting and found its supplies within South Vietnam. The estimate concluded that the guerrillas' strength was then about 16,000, an increase of 12,000 in the last year, and that there was no evidence of Soviet, East European, or Chinese military equipment. The guerrillas were armed with captured French and American weapons.

The Joint Chiefs of Staff urged Secretary McNamara to approve joint military intervention with America's allies in Southeast Asia. William P. Bundy, acting assistant secretary of defense, was becoming tense about the growth of the guerrillas, and he wrote to his boss: "It *is* really now or never." He thought the NLF was about to "bloom." Warming to the crisis he perceived, Mr. Bundy spelled it out in plain language for Secretary McNamara:

> An early and hard-hitting operation has a good chance (70% would be my guess) of *arresting* things and giving Diem a chance to do better and clean up. Even if we follow up hard,

on the lines the JCS are working out . . . however, the chances are not much better that we will in fact be able to *clean up* the situation. It *all* depends on Diem's effectiveness, which is very problematical. The 30% chance is that we would wind up like the French in 1954; white men can't win this kind of fight.[32]

Mr. Bundy argued that if another month went by the chance of an American military intervention succeeding would drop to 60–40, and in sixty days would be only 50–50. It was already widely known that Secretary McNamara responded to quantification.

Robert McNamara was a phenomenon. The President was delighted with his energy, take-charge attitude, and passion for real facts instead of the usual goo. The Defense Secretary seemed to be accomplishing the impossible, seemed to have lured the Pentagon brass into a cage and, armed only with a kitchen chair, a whip, and a computer, he seemed to be taming the beasts. He and the young civilian "Whiz Kid" systems analysts he had brought into his office wanted and demanded facts, "objective analyses," and explicit assumptions and agendas that could be argued and tested.

Of course they drove the Joint Chiefs crazy. When, for instance, the President appointed General Maxwell Taylor to be Chairman of the JCS, the general, before accepting, talked to Secretary McNamara about the Kids: "I explained that during my year in the White House I had got the impression that the so-called Whiz Kids . . . had been allowed to swamp the Joint Chiefs with requests for studies to the point that their effectiveness had become seriously impaired."[33] They agreed that the new Chairman could block any request for data unless, of course, the request came from the Secretary or his deputy. This required a minor change in the technique used by the bright systems analysts.

The Secretary's apparent numbers fetish seemed to amuse some people, while it made others want to chew the carpet. He simply believed that problems that could be quantified should be. After he returned from his first inspection of Vietnam, he concluded, "Every quantitative measurement we have shows we're winning this war." Because he had no independent means to accumulate the essential data, he was forced to rely on the

South Vietnamese to provide the "facts." One Vietnamese general said, *"Ah, less statistiques!* Your Secretary of Defense loves statistics. We Vietnamese can give him all he wants. If you want them to go up, they will go up. If you want them to go down, they will go down."[34]

The Kennedy administration's much advertised rejection of rhetoric in favor of tough-minded facts was, as it developed in Vietnam, merely rhetoric. The administration tied itself to a "reality" the South Vietnamese wanted it to have. General Taylor acknowledged that the government of South Vietnam gave in to "the temptation . . . to doctor the information before releasing it." He came to the only possible conclusion: "It was not surprising that Washington plans and programs often did not correspond to the realities of the situation in Vietnam."[35] Despite JFK's rejection of "myth," he was in fact basing his presidency on and involving America in myths that were useful to him. He was living an illusion about Vietnam while parading the unsentimental, tough-minded realism of his presidency.

To get a firsthand report of conditions in Vietnam, President Kennedy sent General Taylor and a national security aide, Walt Whitman Rostow, on an inspection trip. General Taylor cabled the President that events were on a "downward trend" and that American military force had to be introduced in Vietnam to raise the dangerously low level of Vietnamese morale and effectiveness. The purpose of sending American troops, he said, was not to defeat the NLF, because "that should be the primary task of the Armed Forces of Vietnam," but to provide logistical support and training to "stiffen" South Vietnamese capabilities. Although he acknowledged that Americans might be forced into combat to defend themselves, he observed that Vietnam was "not an excessively difficult or unpleasant place to operate."

The possibility of sliding into a major land war in Asia was on General Taylor's mind. He informed the President that such risks were "present but are not impressive." This was true because the North was vulnerable to conventional bombing and could therefore be persuaded "to lay off SVN." He advised that the Chinese, called "Chicoms," would find it too difficult to intervene and would not do so.[36] In any case, he said, an American military force could be disguised as a humanitarian effort to assist the Vietnamese in recovering from a bad flood. To accomplish all this, General Taylor urged that the U.S. military advisory mission in Saigon "must be shifted from an advisory group to something nearer—but not quite—an operational headquarters in a theater of war."[37] Secretary of Defense McNamara wrote the President that he supported General Taylor's recommendations.

Although Secretary of State Rusk had been consistently content to let Secretary McNamara and the Department of Defense take the lead in Vietnamese matters, the State Department did not care for this new emphasis on military force. By now, however, President Kennedy did not like the State Department. For example, he told *Time* magazine: "The State Department is a bowl of jelly. It's got all those people over there who are constantly smiling. I think we need to smile less and be tougher."[38] Secretary Rusk was in Japan when General Taylor sent his first cable, and was concerned that the general would get to the President before State could make its case. Mr. Rusk sent a cable to his department questioning whether Diem was "prepared [to] take necessary measures to give us something worth supporting." Although he did not endorse the kind of force advocated by General Taylor, Secretary Rusk was prepared to "be tougher." He instructed his staff to remember that he did not want to commit American prestige "to a losing horse."[39]

The President rejected the flood-relief ruse, but was unwilling to think of negotiating a Vietnamese settlement for fear of seeming weak to the Republicans and the Russians. He tried to find a way somewhere between the Departments of Defense and State. He ordered more assistance and more advisers to Vietnam, but also came down uncharacteristically hard on President Diem. Mr. Kennedy demanded that South Vietnam's government be reorganized and made more rational according to American views of such matters, and insisted that the United States have a larger voice in South Vietnam's decisions. President Diem responded that South Vietnam would never become "a protectorate"[40] of America and complained about how little President Kennedy was doing for Vietnam. President Kennedy backed down from his demands and sent more aid and advisers.

The events in the fall of 1961 led to a different relationship between the United States and Vietnam. It was now clearer than it had been that America was trapped by its fear that Diem would do something we thought insane, such as telling us to get out or even negotiating on his own with the North, as in fact he and Nhu later considered. American leaders were trapped by their belief that the friendly world depended on the United States for protection against Soviet aggression, but that many of the weaker friendly nations would go to "the other side" if they lost confidence in America's willingness to stand and fight.

Domestically, American leaders were trapped by the fear that they would be accused by the right wing of being soft in general and soft on Communism in particular. That, after all, had been the accusation that created McCarthyism. This memory stuck to the Democrats like bad-smelling glue. As Mr. Kennedy said in 1963: "If I tried to pull out completely now from Vietnam we would have another Joe McCarthy red scare on our hands."[41] (Ten years earlier, the younger Senator Kennedy, while his father helped to finance Tailgunner Joe, had taken no public stand against Senator McCarthy.) The continuing fear of a right-wing backlash now also inhibited centrist Republicans who believed they needed the votes of their own fringe. It was already obvious that the young President believed he had to throw red meat to the right wing rather than risk acting wisely.

By 1962, President Kennedy was feeling better about his presidency. By threatening a nuclear holocaust he had successfully made the Soviets back off in the Cuban missile crisis. He had proved that he was tough enough to stare into the flames of the world and, as Dean Rusk said, the other guy blinked. Earlier, the President said about Khrushchev: "That son of a bitch won't pay any attention to worlds. He has to see you move."[42] The President moved on the Soviet missiles in Cuba and it was Khrushchev who was not tough enough to incinerate the world. The American public agreed that this was a Kennedy success. For the first time the young President could take pride in shaping world events rather than being buffeted by them.

Needing to be or seem tough, believing in the justice of the cause, unable to find protection against domestic pressures, all the Kennedy cold warriors learned that there was very little they could do about Vietnam other than to do as little as possible without losing. But they were vulnerable to doing more than they wanted if some external force, such as either Diem or Ho, threatened to change the odds by changing the war. Then American behavior would be significantly shaped by others.

Every increase, however small, in American involvement in

Vietnam made a change in course more difficult. Every American death made it more important to win, whatever that meant to the succession of war planners in Washington, to avoid the accusation that American soldiers had died for nothing. When President Kennedy took office he inherited an American force in Vietnam of about 1,000 advisers; one year later he had increased it to 3,200; another year brought it to 9,000; and by the time the President was killed in Dallas, the Vietnam force was about 16,000. In the light of what was yet to come this force was tiny, but the Kennedy administration did not know what was to come, had no more foresight than anyone else, and for the men who were making policy at the time this was an enormous commitment of American lives, cash, and prestige. They believed that this investment, risky as they knew it to be, had to be protected. The best way they knew to protect this investment was to invest more. And then hope.

The Kennedy team liked the idea of crisis management, of forcing world events to conform to their undoubted intelligence and determination. They were hostile to the Diem infection that inflamed our Vietnam connection. They resented his stubborn refusal to do what they believed was obviously the right thing, to delegate authority, and to make his government more representative, systematic, and rational. They were embarrassed by having to defend his dictatorial regime in the name of the freedom. They feared that he was unpredictable. Diem, in short, was in the way of the conscience, aspirations, and ambitions of the Kennedy administration. On his part, Diem was convinced "that Americans were impatient, naïve, and childlike, to be humored but never to be heeded."[43]

The scheming to overthrow Diem was, according to the conventions of Hollywood movies, as involuted as a good Asian conspiracy was supposed to be. The plot was on and off so many times, it is doubtful that even the major players were always able to keep track. Its beginning was buried in the long resentment against Diem's tyranny, and twice before elements of his own army had tried to depose him. The final phase began in May 1963, when in Hué Diem's troops fired into a crowd which was protesting a government order outlawing a display of religious banners on Buddha's birthday. Nine people were killed and others were hurt. The Buddhists accused the Catholic Diem of religious persecution, a charge that obviously would not play well in the American press. Some monks and priests went on hunger strikes and public protests spread.

For the first time, the American public learned that there was local trouble within South Vietnam, that Diem was not supported by numbers of his own people. Jan Berry, a radioman with the army's 18th Aviation Company, described his own reaction: "It became very clear to most Americans there who probably hadn't been paying attention that we were supporting a police state which, against its own people who were peaceably having demonstrations, would turn loose tanks and machine guns and barbed wire all over the country."[44]

In June, a Buddhist monk touched a match to the gasoline that another monk had poured over his head; the martyr burned to death on a street in downtown Saigon. A photograph of the burning, aged monk, Thich Quang Duc, was shown on American television. Madame Nhu, Diem's sister-in-law, dismissed it as a "barbecue" and offered to supply the gasoline for future volunteers. She especially hoped that David Halberstam would be next. She was sometimes called the Dragon Lady. Diem dismissed the immolation as street theater directed either by NBC or by the NLF, denying that it was a genuine expression of resistance to his regime by a sincere Buddhist. Thich Quang Duc's death fixed itself in the horrified imagination of America and the world, including the men in the Kennedy team. The bonzes announced that the Venerable Quang Duc's heart would not burn and placed it in a glass container in the Xa Loi pagoda where the people of Saigon could view it and pay their respects to a new martyr.

Six more monks burned themselves to death in public as the Buddhist protest grew into a widely based demonstration of dissatisfaction with Diem's autocracy. Key administration officials in Washington said many times that they had no clear idea what the protests were about or what the Buddhists wanted. Diem's secret police raided many urban Buddhist pagodas, arrested 1,400 Buddhists, mostly monks, and thousands of high-school students, and then thousands of grade-school students.

Frederick E. Nolting, Jr., the American ambassador in Saigon, agreed with Diem. He was an amiable Virginian, fluent in

French, and Diem's friend. In a 1974 interview he still blamed the animus against Diem on distorted reporting in the American press. He criticized *The New York Times* for creating the slogan "Sink or swim with Ngo Dinh Diem."[45] Not surprisingly, the ambassador carried on a war with the American press which the reporters were quite prepared to reciprocate. David Halberstam, for instance, wrote that the embassy had become a handmaiden to dictatorship: "In trying to protect Diem from criticism, the Ambassador became Diem's agent."[46] President Kennedy was so irritated by Mr. Halberstam's reporting that he tried unsuccessfully to pressure the publisher to send Mr. Halberstam away from Vietnam.

Ambassador Nolting believed that democratic progress was being made by Diem, although he admitted that it was too slow for the impatient men in Washington. The ambassador was now moving against the Washington currents, as he understood at the time: "There was a dump Diem movement which I could feel in the atmosphere coming from Averell Harriman, Roger Hilsman, and others—in the White House."[47] He pointed out that the CIA did not approve of dumping Diem. Mr. Hilsman responded, "We could not sit still and be the puppets of Diem's anti-Buddhist policies."[48] To the very great displeasure of Madame Nhu, President Kennedy replaced Mr. Nolting with the distinguished Republican Henry Cabot Lodge (thereby implicating the Republicans in the President's Vietnam "policy").

Shortly after his arrival in Saigon, Ambassador Lodge took some reporters on a walk through the city zoo. As a writer who was covering the war told it, a rude tiger pissed through its cage bars on the ambassador. The elegant ambassador tried through his wit to rise above the occasion by saying something like, "He who wears the pee of a tiger is assured of success in the coming year." Michael Herr knew better: "Maybe nothing's so unfunny as an omen read wrong."[49]

Ambassador Lodge's enormous confidence did not reach to Washington. The Kennedy political establishment was deeply split over what to do next: whether to keep Diem, and who would be a more cooperative replacement. General Taylor, now the Chairman of the Joint Chiefs, was opposed: "Maybe we can't win with Diem, but if not Diem—who? And the answer was complete silence." He described the President's attitude: "President Kennedy was hoping that it would work itself out, and became sympathetic to the idea of a coup if the Americans were not responsible, and not involved in it."[50]

In the midst of this tentativeness and disagreement, it was inevitable that the North Vietnamese would conclude that the United States did not know what it was doing. A member of the political bureau of the Communist party of the North concluded that America was getting stuck in Vietnam, just as the French had, that the U.S. was out of control, a paper tiger: "It can hardly be found in the annals of U.S. imperialism where its political and military leaders committed such serious blunders and long-standing errors as they did in appraising the situation in south Viet Nam."[51]

Ambassador Lodge, with the State Department bureaucracy supporting him, was a major force behind the idea of overthrowing Diem, and of maintaining close contact with the Vietnamese generals who were themselves to execute the coup. Within two days of his arrival in Saigon the ambassador reported to Washington that a coup was in the air. His most essential contribution was to argue against the typical vacillation within the Kennedy administration, and to resist General Paul D. Harkins, the chief of the U.S. military mission in Saigon, who disapproved of the conspiracy and made everyone in Washington aware of it.

Mr. Lodge was a skilled, smooth political operator who had run for the vice-presidency on Richard Nixon's ticket in 1960, had an independent political base, and was from the President's home state of Massachusetts, where John Kennedy beat him for the Senate in 1952. The record makes it obvious that President Kennedy treated Ambassador Lodge with exquisite tenderness, once explaining that he was himself the son of a former ambassador and therefore understood how important it was to allow a good ambassador to make decisions on the spot.

General Harkins was of the Frederick Nolting school of patting Diem on the back for the good job he would probably begin tomorrow. He was not quite in Lodge's league of bureaucratic maneuvering, but he was not a pushover. He was prepared to fight bureaucratic battles over turf by pitting the Pentagon tough guys against the State Department and White House sissies. His reports of military progress were consistently wrong in favor of Diem, and only superiors who wanted to be soothed could have put up with them. His military bosses never complained about his lullabies. He accepted Diem's political assurances and battle reports that supposedly proved the population of South Vietnam supported Diem's regime, and that supposedly proved that the army of South Vietnam was methodically destroying the NLF. The Vietnam he described was increasingly surrealistic, just inches or minutes away from achieving great victories.

Although Mr. Lodge won every round in this dispute, General Harkin's unhappiness made Washington nervous. This argument in Saigon reflected what was now the characteristic ambivalence in Washington about how to proceed. No one was less certain than the President, whose yo-yo performance, at least in the sordid Diem coup, accurately reflected the fact that the cool, confident, rationalist in the Oval Office was finally reduced to hoping against hope that somehow things would work themselves out in Saigon without dragging him into a war, and without his enemies having grounds to attack him for losing a precious nation to the Kremlin.

The United States took its first step on Saturday, August 24, 1963. Roger Hilsman drafted a cablegram to Mr. Lodge. JFK reviewed it at his house in Hyannisport and made no changes. Michael Forrestal, the President's senior adviser on the Far East, was given the task of keeping the President informed over the weekend. Secretary McNamara and CIA Director John McCone were out of town and were not contacted. When the government reconvened on Monday, the President was surprised to hear passionate objections to the cable, which had already been sent, from both Defense and the CIA. He was enraged that Mr. Forrestal had not delayed transmitting the cable until Mr. McNamara and especially Mr. McCone could be consulted. Mr. Forrestal offered to resign, but JFK snapped: "You're not worth firing. You owe me something, so you stick around."[52] No one, however, repudiated the cable.

According to the cable, Ambassador Lodge "should urgently examine all possible alternative leadership and make detailed plans as to how we might bring about Diem's replacement if this should become necessary."[53] Five days later, Mr. Lodge cabled Secretary of State Rusk: "We are launched on a course from which there is no respectable turning back: the overthrow of the Diem government." He added that the success of the coup depended on the generals, "But it depends at least as much on us."[54] The lead in the dump Diem adventure was taken by the

State Department, which now insisted that it was important to persuade the Vietnamese generals to make their move quickly. But, as General Harkins warned his boss, General Taylor, everyone was suspicious of everyone else and "you can't hurry the East."[55]

To help Walter Cronkite inaugurate the expanded thirty-minute evening news on television, the President agreed to be interviewed on September 2, 1963. He said that Diem had lost touch with the people, that the war could not be won unless the government of South Vietnam had popular support, and that the repression of the Buddhists was "very unwise." Mr. Cronkite asked whether Diem had time to "regain" popular support, and the President suddenly introduced a new element in public discussions. He said there was still time, and "with changes in policy and perhaps with personnel"[56] the South Vietnamese government could survive. It was not clear whether the reference to a change in personnel was a signal to the conspirators to get on with the coup, or a signal to Diem to dump Nhu, or something else. To General Tran Van Don, one of the leaders of the coup, JFK's language meant that the President "would support any change, any change."[57]

The South Vietnamese generals insisted on knowing whether America would support them after the coup. When they were not satisfied with the American response, they called the whole thing off. Then American officials stroked them and it was on again. At the end of August, the President informed Ambassador Lodge that he was giving the coup his "full support" and promised to help him "conclude this operation successfully."[58] On October 5, 1963, President Kennedy sent another cable to Ambassador Lodge. Total secrecy was so important that it was sent through the CIA's channel. Now the President said:

> [I have] today approved recommendation that no initiative should now be taken to give any active covert encouragement to a coup. There should, however, be urgent covert effort with closest security, under broad guidance of Ambassador to identify and build contacts with possible alternative leadership as and when it appears. Essential that this effort be totally secure and fully deniable. . . .[59]

"We have backed Diem for eight long hard years," General Harkins told the Chairman of the Joint Chiefs. "To me it seems incongruous now to get him down, kick him around and get rid of him."[60] The President's overriding concern was that if there was to be a coup it had to succeed, that indecision would be preferable to failure. He should have relied more on the incompetence of the Diem entourage, especially that of his brother Nhu, who was now taking perhaps too much opium, to ensure that a coup would succeed.

Lieutenant Colonel Lucien Conein of the CIA was an important connection between America and the Vietnamese conspirators. He was an old Vietnam hand and was friendly with several of the plotters. In fact, they refused to deal with anyone else, especially General Harkins who they feared was a stool pigeon. On the day of the coup, the Lieutenant Colonel brought about fifty thousand dollars of CIA money to the rebels' headquarters to pay the troops and provide death benefits to their families. One of the conspirators was the Catholic Colonel Nguyen Van Thieu, the future President, who was ordered to command the rebel troops who were to assault the presidential palace. Another was Colonel Pham Ngoc Thao, a spy for the North Vietnamese.

Mr. Nhu heard of the conspiracy and organized a fake coup that was supposed to lure the real conspirators out into the open where they could be captured by troops loyal to Diem. But the general with whom Nhu made his plans immediately warned the mutinous generals of Nhu's countercoup. The plotters could not be certain that this information was reliable, so they recruited the informer's chief aides to their side. General Don was aware that Nhu "was planning to make a false coup for arresting the supposed protestors."[61] The coup actually started, at 1:30 P.M., November 1, 1963.

President Diem and Nhu escaped from the palace, hid in a Catholic Church in the Chinese section of Saigon, and within hours were found. They were both killed, shot and stabbed, in an armored car that was taking them back to the headquarters of the successful conspirators. The people of Saigon rejoiced at the news. Nguyen Cao Ky, a future air marshal, prime minister, and vice-president, was a junior air force officer at the time. He later told a television interviewer:

> What was wrong was that you eliminate Diem and replace him by a bunch of generals who were more dumb than Mr.

Diem himself. I still believe that at least Mr. Diem had some ideal to serve, but the group of general officers who replaced him had no ideals at all. I think they were old, corrupted and not capable. . . .[62]

For Mr. Ky, the main result of the coup was to make all future leaders, except himself, afraid of the Americans who might arrange to kill them if they ever displeased the round-eyes.

General Taylor was in the room when the news of Diem's death was relayed to Mr. Kennedy: "The President was obviously shaken, sprang to his feet and walked out of the room saying nothing to anybody—and stayed out of the room for some minutes."[63] A senior aide concluded that the President "realized that Vietnam was his great failure in foreign policy, and that he had never really given it his full attention."[64] Early in the Kennedy administration, a reporter told Robert Kennedy that Vietnam might become the nation's most serious problem. He dismissed this idea: "We have thirty Vietnams a day here."[65]

Many members of Camelot's inner circle rightly insisted that the administration had not initiated the coup against Diem, nor had it been involved in the execution of the plot. But senior officers of the government encouraged and supported the conspirators. The President made it clear that he would welcome a successful coup. In any case, the President had the power to stop the conspiracy and did not do so. He was indirectly responsible for Diem's murder.

To this point no American administration had had its heart in Asia, about which General MacArthur earlier complained. The Far East finally became significant ground because it became a joining place for the U.S. and the USSR. The cold war turned Asia into an ideological battleground, but the real political center of gravity for Washington always remained in Russia and Europe.

A few days after Diem's death, Ambassador Lodge sent a cable to the State Department predicting that the Diem overthrow would shorten the war against the NLF. It is not often that such towering self-confidence and self-satisfaction so quickly proved to be so wrong. Within ninety days there was another coup when Major General Khanh took power for himself. In the next two years there were a half dozen more coups in Saigon.

* * *

Three weeks after Diem was shot, President Kennedy was killed in Dallas. As Vice-President, Lyndon Johnson had never been treated seriously, especially in foreign affairs, by the Kennedy team. He had argued against American complicity in the coup, and was certain that the President himself had been much too deeply involved. During the coup planning, when Secretary Rusk asked LBJ for his opinion, the VP responded: "We should stop playing cops and robbers."[66] A few months after the Dallas assassination, he told a friend that President Kennedy's assassination was punishment for Diem's assassination.

Lyndon Johnson's inheritance from John Kennedy was more than 16,000 military advisers in Vietnam and more than a tradition of American self-deception. He inherited the idea that South Vietnam was a nation, the idea that there was a South Vietnam that required vast American help to protect it from Communism. This was not merely cold-war paranoia about the Kremlin, or mere machismo, whether in the style of Boston or Austin. It was the conviction that South Vietnam was a "viable" nation state in some reasonable sense connected to this century.

South Vietnam was an American invention, conceived by Dwight Eisenhower but delivered by John Kennedy. What was invented was not the place called South Vietnam, obviously, but the idea about the place. South Vietnam never emerged as a coherent society during Diem's long regime. George Ball later remarked that "South Vietnam was never a nation but an improvisation. . . ." He believed that South Vietnam was "a country with an army and no government."[67] Ambassador Lodge told LBJ, "There is no tradition of a national government in Saigon. There are no roots in the country."[68] Bernard Fall, an expert on Vietnam, described the Buddhist uprisings as a "clear symptom of disintegration of the South Vietnamese social fabric."[69] The internal disintegration coupled with the ruler's dictatorial brutality did not permit the evolution of what the Geneva agreement of 1954 called the southern military zone into a nation whose people shared a common purpose, religion, or culture.

The manner of Diem's death deepened America's obligation to this place. The U.S. had to bear some responsibility for the political chaos that followed. We had permitted the assassination of a stubborn and brutal man and had jeopardized the existence of the nation we had invented. His complicity in the coup was President Kennedy's patent on the idea of that place.

There were men who knew better but usually would not say so. Henry Cabot Lodge, for one, did speak out, in an oblique and dull way, about the uncertainties of nation-building in the South. While the preparations for the coup were underway, he sent the White House a cable which said that the United States was attempting "to bring this medieval country into the 20th Century."[70] It was in fact medieval, with a feudal army whose loyalty was only to individuals. Diem was a despot who believed that God was Catholic and would provide the useful miracle when necessary. The deepest convictions of the South's rulers had nothing to do with building the nation that was in the minds of the policymakers in Washington.

On a simpler level, President Kennedy's bequest to Lyndon Johnson was no different from the "policy" he had inherited from Dwight Eisenhower. The men of the Kennedy team had not changed a thing, not even a nuance, from the perspective on Vietnam that had been held by President Eisenhower and John Foster Dulles. They accepted the need to contain either Communism or the Soviet Union, they were not sure which, and they accepted the validity of the idea of the falling dominoes. The result was that the New Frontier, for all of its amused sniffishness about the somnolence of the Eisenhower years, for all of its recoil from the overheated, moralistic rhetoric of Secretary Dulles, shared a world view similar to the one they ridiculed. The New Frontiersmen were only connecting the dots Ike left them. The difference between the two administrations was that the Kennedy team was more ambitious. The difference was, and it was a great difference, that the Kennedy administration converted its world view into action. The stream of youthful energy was creating a disaster.

The Kennedy administration had accepted "a universal obligation to maintain a status quo which, if it did not precisely resemble the United States, was at least one that familiarity had made comfortable."[71] To provide justification for its position, it reached back to the Truman years, to the Truman Doctrine which Dean Rusk once said was applicable universally, but especially in Southeast Asia, and to NSC 68 which had argued that containment of the Soviet Union required a response all over the globe regardless of the costs. The reliance on a world view that was some fifteen years old may say something about the brilliance of the Kennedy team. That administration had no ideas about foreign policy, and no organized way to think about the world. It lived off anti-Communism. The New Frontier relied on process rather than substance, and on illusions about both Washington and Saigon. This was Lyndon Johnson's political inheritance.

President Johnson inherited the idea of South Vietnam as a place where America could build a nation that Americans would like. It could accomplish this by doing two things: winning the war against the NLF, and "winning the hearts and minds" of the Vietnamese people. This anticipated conversion of the Vietnamese was irresistibly appealing to President Johnson's Texas populism. Winning over the people of Vietnam was precisely the right response to guerrilla warfare, but it was already clear that this would remain an afterthought, a diversion from the military's determination to fight this new war in the old, conventional, bloody, and futile way.

As the new President, Lyndon Johnson was overwhelmed by anxiety about whether he could do the job. Despite his prior reputation as the magician of the Senate, he had no national experience and no national following. As Vice-President he was on the outside of the government desperately wanting to be let in. He hated being the Vice-President, hated being made to feel like a crude Texas red-neck, all elbows and knees, in the heady atmosphere of the Kennedy White House. Most of all he hated the fact that he had nothing to do. The inherent function of the Vice-President is to keep the idea of the President's own mortality fixed in the President's mind. As LBJ put it, "Every time I came into John Kennedy's presence, I felt like a god-damn raven hovering over his shoulder."[72]

LBJ admired President Kennedy and was a loyal and astonishingly disciplined and subordinate member of the team. He kept his few serious disagreements quiet, not only in public but in private, did not usually speak at official meetings unless asked to do so, and may have been uncomfortable, as the President surely was at least for a while, with the memory of Senator Kennedy having come to him, hat in hand, when they were both in the Senate. His first impression of the young senator from

Massachusetts had been that he was "weak and pallid . . . a scrawny man with a bad back, a weak and indecisive politician, a nice man, a gentle man, but not a man's man."[73]

The shots in Dallas propelled Lyndon Johnson into an emotional whirlpool and a political crisis. He caught the tone of both pressures as he later reminisced:

> I took the oath. I became President. But for millions of Americans I was still illegitimate, a naked man with no presidential covering, a pretender to the throne, an illegal usurper. And then there was Texas, my home, the home of both the murder and the murder of the murderer. And then there were the bigots and the dividers and the Eastern intellectuals, who were waiting to knock me down before I could even begin to stand up. The whole thing was almost unbearable.[74]

His language is more restrained in his memoirs, and the way out of the personal and political vise was found. It must have occurred to him absolutely at once. He would be the executor of President Kennedy's political will:

> As *Air Force One* carried us swiftly back to Washington after the tragedy in Dallas, I made a solemn private vow: I would devote every hour of every day during the remainder of John Kennedy's unfulfilled term to achieving the goals he had set. That meant seeing things through in Vietnam as well as coping with the many other international and domestic problems he had faced. I made this promise not out of blind loyalty but because I was convinced that the broad lines of his policy, in Southeast Asia and elsewhere, had been right. They were consistent with the goals the United States had been trying to accomplish in the world since 1945.[75]

Thinking of himself as JFK's agent was expected, conventional, and politically essential. It was also courteous and self-protective. "I constantly had before me the picture that Kennedy had selected me as executor of his will, it was my duty to carry on and this meant his people as well as his programs. They were part of his legacy."[76] Lyndon Johnson had built his career out of seeming to make his word a solemn contract that could be put in the bank. He had taken a solemn private vow that he would be a faithful executor of the dead hero's political estate and retainers. The nation would remain steady on course in Vietnam. President Kennedy's war advisers would be President Johnson's war advisers.

The new and inexperienced President believed that he was obliged to retain all of President Kennedy's White House staff because he needed their experience and their skills. With a national election coming up in less than a year, he also could not afford resignations by these visible and articulate people. Significant defections of key aides would be interpreted as President Johnson's inability to work with the "best and the brightest," or as his failure to continue JFK's policies. He met individually with each of them, explained that President Kennedy had needed them, and asked if they understood how much more he needed them now, when the entire world was watching to see if the United States could hold together during this national trauma. Only Ted Sorenson, JFK's alter ego, and the Attorney General were immune, although Robert Kennedy shortly asked President Johnson to appoint him ambassador to Vietnam. LBJ refused because he thought it was too dangerous, and he might also have had other reasons. President Johnson lived to regret his decision to retain the team.

There was a welcome lull in foreign affairs during LBJ's transition. But in less than a week after taking the oath of office he ordered new planning from State, Defense, and the CIA for increased secret operations against North Vietnam. He also called for plans to increase military activity within Laos. These orders were given in National Security Memorandum #273, and the brand new President's touch was already apparent. The memo stated that American efforts in South Vietnam must include political, economic, social, educational, and informational, as well as military, efforts. "We should seek to turn the tide not only of battle but of belief," a typically Protestant goal of American imperialism. According to the memo, LBJ expected all "senior officers of the Government will move energetically to insure the full unity of support for established U.S. policy in South Vietnam." Probably thinking of the chronic squabbling between Ambassador Lodge and General Harkins, the memo added: "It is of particular importance that express or implied criticism of officers of other branches be scrupulously avoided in all contacts with the Vietnamese Government and with the press."[77] The fact of the disunity within the administration was to be swept under the rug of imposed bureaucratic harmony.

Having addressed the control of thought in the government, in the American press, and of the South Vietnamese, what remained was to change the way the American and world public regarded our involvement in Vietnam. Memo #273 was explicit: "We should develop as strong and persuasive a case as possible to demonstrate to the world the degree to which the Viet Cong is controlled, sustained and supplied from Hanoi, through Laos and other channels."[78] This was vital because our "case" absolutely depended on convincing everyone, including ourselves, that a foreign power was invading South Vietnam, that the struggle was therefore not a civil war, and that our intervention was therefore justified.

Our case depended on our belief that South Vietnam was an actual and independent national state, as President Kennedy taught. Then it could be invaded by "foreigners." Then we could intervene. Then we could change the way the South Vietnamese think, and then we could assist them in their new desire to destroy the guerrillas who were perceived as the local fist on the long arm of the Kremlin.

There was nothing new in Memo #273. It was intended to clear the throat and the mind of the government. Ten days later, Secretary Rusk sent Ambassador Lodge a telegram advising that President Johnson desired that "our effort in Viet-Nam be stepped up to the highest pitch." He passed along the President's instruction that "each day we ask ourselves what more we can do to further the struggle." Continuing to worry about our case, the Secretary said, "There is ground for concern that infiltration of materiel has increased, but little hard proof. This is a prime intelligence deficiency. It affects not only military tactics but our over-all Southeast Asia strategy."[79] At this time, the United States was still the prime arms supplier to the NLF; we supplied arms in the temporary care of the army of South Vietnam, to be forwarded to the enemy by capture, surrender, or sale.

Secretary of Defense McNamara made the third of his many trips to Vietnam in late 1963. He was disturbed by the indecisiveness and drift of the new local government. The continuing clash between the U.S. military and the embassy created confused leadership, bad information, and fragmented planning. In addition to our own self-imposed difficulties, the NLF had made great progress since Diem's overthrow, and this came as a surprise "because of our undue dependence on distorted Vietnamese reporting."[80] Mr. McNamara's conclusion, written in a memorandum for the file, was that "the coup came when there was a downward trend which was much more serious than was reported and, therefore, more serious than realized."[81]

After the coup, in other words, Secretary McNamara, the head of the military establishment, concluded that the military side of the Saigon squabble had been wrong, while the civilians had been right. He wrote, "The military government may be an improvement over the Diem-Nhu regime, but this is not as yet established and the future of the war remains in doubt."[82] Having argued that the coup would shorten the war, Ambassador Lodge was now optimistic about Saigon's prospects, perhaps to justify his support for the coup. Before the coup the military had been optimistic and the embassy pessimistic; now the positions were reversed.

The bureaucratic significance of Secretary McNamara's trip was that the State Department believed it was a mistake to send too many highly visible and senior Americans to Vietnam. It thought such trips signaled that we were worried and persuaded the world to think of Vietnam as America's war and America's problem. A State Department official concluded that JFK understood the dangers of such visits, and especially so many by Mr. McNamara, "but he felt he had to pay the price."[83] He felt this way because the military Chiefs were still opposed to limiting the war, or of being forced to fight on the guerrillas' terms. But they had not yet gone public with their unhappiness. The JCS' position was explained in a memo in January 1964, as it had been in May 1961 and in January 1962, all calling for a wider and riskier war: "The United States must be prepared to put aside many of the self-imposed restrictions which now limit our efforts, and to undertake bolder actions which may embody greater risks."[84] JFK "indicated that he felt he had to keep the JCS on board, that the only way to keep them on board was to keep McNamara on board—and that the only way to do that, apparently, was to let him go to Vietnam himself."[85] In short, JFK's fear of the Pentagon's political clout was sufficient to force him to agree to what he knew were mistaken actions in Vietnam. It is likely that President Johnson did not yet fully realize the intensity of the Washington war he had inherited.

In February 1964, the Johnson administration intensified its planning for increased secret actions against North Vietnam. On its face this plan looked like more of the same, as practiced under the two previous administrations. But it was not. It was the unintended beginning of "Johnson's War," of committing American troops, of massive bombing, and of ultimate failure. None of this was understood at the time, as the administration went about its business of incremental planning, taking only one step at a time, exercising what it considered to be enormous restraint, and not knowing what else to do.

This plan was drafted by men who wanted to get out of Vietnam at the earliest possible moment, who believed that Americans could do what the South Vietnamese had obviously failed to do, and who were coming to believe finally that the way in was the only way out. But for now, in early 1964, these future events were perceived only as risks that had always been present. In their opinion they were planning nothing dramatically different from what other Presidents had already authorized. It was called Operation Plan 34A, a perfectly colorless bureaucratic designation of the unwanted beginning of a new war. It was a secret.

Secretary McNamara recommended 34A to the President on the assumption that "progressively escalating pressure" on the North would force it to call off the southern guerrillas. The CIA and the Chiefs of Staff thought the chances of success were remote. The Joint Chiefs were, as usual, hypnotized by the domino theory and the question of national credibility: "The failure of our programs in South Vietnam would have heavy influence on the judgments of Burma, India, Indonesia, Malaysia, Japan, Taiwan, the Republic of Korea, and the Republic of the Philippines with respect to U.S. durability, resolution, and trustworthiness." Because this was America's first genuine test of its ability "to defeat the communist wars of national liberation formula, it is not unreasonable to conclude that there would be a corresponding unfavorable effect upon our image in Africa and in Latin America."[86]

Maxwell Taylor, speaking for the Chiefs, endorsed their

views. The military establishment supported the secret actions against the North, but warned, "It would be idle to conclude that these efforts will have a decisive effect on the communist determination to support the insurgency." What the Joint Chiefs of Staff desired was an unlimited war that could cover as much of Southeast Asia as necessary. Meanwhile, they would not object to the covert war their boss was urging on the new President. What they really wanted, however, was to take over the shooting war. They argued that we should take over the tactical command from the South Vietnamese, that South Vietnam should be made to invade Laos, bomb the North, send commandos to raid key targets in the North, and that U.S. troops should be committed, "as necessary, in direct actions against North Vietnam."[87]

It is hard to imagine that anybody thought the secret sabotage war would diminish or finish the insurgency. But it was all that intelligent men could think to do under the circumstance of a virtually collapsed government in the South, of bad morale, and of continuing NLF progress. It seemed the only possible approach because the President insisted that planning should not irreversibly commit us to additional effort. It is one of the hideous ironies of the war that political restraint on the military's demand for a bigger war ultimately gave the military some of what it wanted all along. The failure of small steps led to big steps.

No one in the government any longer asked whether we should be in Vietnam in the first place. Paul Kattenburg, the State Department's director of Vietnam affairs, asked this question after the news of Diem's murder reached Washington. No one answered it. By now, a few months later, the escalator was moving, both in Vietnam and, more important, in Washington. By now each step that was taken gave the military bureaucracy that much more leverage on the next step. Having agreed to the secret war, the President was no longer in charge.

The planning bureaucracy in the Department of Defense was now in its powerful first gear. The Office of the Special Assistant for Counterinsurgency and Special Activities, within the organization of the Joint Chiefs of Staff, ran Plan 34A. General Harkins was in command in Saigon and he administered the operations through what was modestly called a Studies and

Observations Group. The South Vietnamese were included in the field planning, and they or mercenaries were actually to conduct the operations.

The plan had three prongs and was to increase in severity over three phases throughout 1964. Prong one focused on espionage and sabotage in the North, including commando raids to disrupt North Vietnam's transportation system, such as it was, and bombardment of coastal facilities by PT boats. Prong two was a secret air war in Laos, using American propeller planes with Laotian Air Force markings, some of whose pilots worked for Air America, the CIA's airline in the area. U.S. Air Force jets performed the reconnaissance for bombing runs authorized by the plan. The third prong consisted of patrols, code-named DeSoto, by American destroyers in the Gulf of Tonkin. Part of the mission of the destroyers was to obtain information about coastal facilities that would help the South Vietnamese commandos of 34A.

An analyst of *The Pentagon Papers* said that the DeSoto patrols were not intended to provoke North Vietnam into an open attack on American warships.[88] This was plausible because the war planners could not imagine that the short, primitive North Vietnamese would have the nerve to attack battle-ready American destroyers. What would they attack with? What reason could they have directly to engage the world's strongest nation in a test of arms when America had all the arms?

Obviously the quaint natives in their black pajamas would not attack American warships. We could send our technology wherever we pleased. Our men and machines would be safe. Therefore, the DeSoto patrols were not intended to lure the North into an act of war. Whatever else might be true of the North Vietnamese, the war planners did not believe that they were crazy.

The Americans' ignorance of the North, of the mixture of nationalism and Communism, of Vietnamese history, culture, and language was limitless. In late 1962, Ho Chi Minh said, "The Americans are much stronger than the French, though they know us less well."[89] It was as if Americans believed that they did not need to understand the enemy because it was self-evident that they were wrong and we were right, that they were weak and we were strong, and that if they ever really went too far we could punish them severely at little human cost to ourselves. This dismissal of the enemy formed a reasonably good basis for predicting that our policy was on the way to becoming suicidal.

The complacency that permitted Washington's policymakers to remain ignorant about the North Vietnamese also allowed the permanent bureaucratic government, along with the President, to keep the American public and the Congress ignorant of their plans. The administration simply took two assumptions for granted: Whenever it became necessary the enemy could be beaten; and, so long as it was desirable the public could be manipulated. The administration seems to have had more faith in the ability of the North Vietnamese to behave wisely (by succumbing, however grudgingly), than it had in the American public to support its actions. The fear that the public and the Congress might become irrational if either were informed led the administration to its second front in the secret war: the war against what had in earlier wars been called "the home front." It is perhaps not surprising that in time the home front would declare war against the administration.

On May 25, William Bundy, McGeorge Bundy's brother, now head of the Far East section of the State Department, wrote a draft resolution that sought congressional approval for fighting Communism in Vietnam. The President could submit it to Congress when he felt the timing was right. He wanted some reason, some demonstrable aggression by the North, to justify the resolution.

One week later, the senior planners gathered in Honolulu to discuss the next steps. General William C. Westmoreland attended as the Saigon replacement for General Harkins. Ambassador Lodge said that he was now worried about the instability of the political leadership in South Vietnam and counseled bombing the North as a way to fight the NLF. This reflected a growing pattern in the minds of the war's engineers: Frustrated by the guerrillas' progress in the South, they increasingly favored bombing the North.

Shortly after the conference, the administration began leaking information to the press about its intentions in Vietnam, part of an intensified public-relations campaign, advocated by Mr. Bundy, to persuade Americans to support the Vietnam effort. In search of convincing arguments he might provide to the public, the President asked the CIA whether the "fall" of

South Vietnam and Laos would start the dominoes falling. The CIA's written response was no: "With the possible exception of Cambodia, it is likely that no nation in the area would quickly succumb to Communism as a result of the fall of Laos and South Vietnam."[90] The policymakers could not incorporate this conclusion into their mind-lock. The CIA, which a little earlier had argued that the NLF was not dependent on supplies or fighters from the North, was on the way to making itself irrelevant to the planning process. As it challenged basic elements in the developing American theology about Vietnam, it ran the risk of being ignored by the war's clergymen.

If the CIA was risking obscurity, the entire administration was as yet unable to declare what it wished to accomplish in Vietnam. Mr. Rostow, like almost everyone else, believed that "victory," however defined, could be won if we remembered who we were. It was obvious to him that the United States does not lose, an opinion he believed the rest of the world shared. What we had to do, therefore, was to take seriously our national reputation which alone would have "a real margin of influence on the outcome that flows from the simple fact that we are the greatest power in the world—if we behave like it."[91] If our national conduct could be made to conform to our self-esteem, we would win.

Throughout early June the policymakers continued to debate Mr. Bundy's draft congressional resolution. He believed that the coming national election might lead other nations to conclude that our war might be postponed. The proposed resolution was necessary to stop such dangerous speculation. He advised the foreign policy bureaucracies that the resolution would create "complete flexibility in the hands of the executive."[92] But the President now decided that the submission of the resolution might give Americans the idea that he favored war in Vietnam, and could therefore have the wrong impact on the election. He ordered a postponement.

July 1964 was a wild month. Several leading South Vietnamese officials, including Mr. Ky, leaked information to the press about the secret war in Laos and North Vietnam. The Chairman of the Joint Chiefs, General Maxwell Taylor, was selected to replace Henry Cabot Lodge as ambassador, an appointment that perhaps signified the growing role of the military. The secret Plan 34A raids against the North were in full swing, including a commando raid against two North Vietnamese islands in the Gulf of Tonkin.

On August 2, the *Maddox*, one of the destroyers assigned to the DeSoto patrols, was attacked by North Vietnamese high-speed torpedo boats. The North Vietnamese might have thought that the *Maddox* was a South Vietnamese escort vessel supporting the commandos who had assaulted the islands a few days before. President Johnson ordered another destroyer to join the *Maddox*.

The 34A raids began again on the next day, when South Vietnamese boats attacked coastal facilities in the North. This time the captains of the two American destroyers were informed about the attacks. The navy had wanted to keep the ships away from the area of the 34A raids. After dark on August 4, it was reported that the small torpedo boats of the North attacked both of the U.S. destroyers.

Within minutes of learning about the "attack," Secretary McNamara called the Joint Chiefs to his conference room at the Pentagon, where they were joined by Secretary Rusk and McGeorge Bundy. They agreed to recommend to the President reprisals, which had been planned several months earlier, against the North. Aircraft from carriers would bomb the bases of the North's torpedo boats, as well as an oil storage depot. That afternoon, President Johnson ordered the reprisals. He now decided to seek congressional approval of the resolution that he had been sitting on for weeks. The air strikes were on the verge of being ordered when Secretary McNamara heard from Admiral Sharp in Honolulu that the report of the second attack might have been false.

After some hours of confusion, Admiral Sharp phoned again to say that now he was satisfied that the second attack had occurred. To this day there is no persuasive evidence that the second attack actually took place. In a few days, the President himself doubted it. Disgusted, he said to George Ball: "Hell, those dumb, stupid sailors were just shooting at flying fish."[93] The sixty-four planes of the U.S. air strike successfully bombed their targets.

On the same day, the President told congressional leaders about the reprisal attacks, and informed them he would submit a resolution to Congress for approval of his actions. He asked each man sitting around the Cabinet table whether he would vote with him. Each said he would. LBJ now could not lose because he was on the side of patriotism. He did not tell them about the United States' command of the secret 34A raids immediately preceding the attack by the North, and still described the attacks as unprovoked. Close to midnight of the same day, LBJ went on television to inform the public of the reprisal strikes, to say that the United States did not want a bigger war, and that the reprisals were restrained and appropriate under the circumstances. He assumed that the Chinese would pick up the telecast and would get the message that the planes then in the air were not a threat to them.

In his special message to the Congress, LBJ said that the resolution was needed "to protect our armed forces."[94] The congressional resolution was sponsored in the Senate by William Fulbright (an action he would regret forever). After a forty-minute "debate," it was passed unanimously in the House (416 to 0), and in the Senate only Wayne Morse of Oregon and Ernest Gruening of Alaska voted against it (88 to 2). During the floor debate, one senator after another raised serious doubts about passing such an ambiguous and perhaps even unconstitutional resolution, and then voted for it.

The key language of the resolution granted the President extraordinary latitude. Most of the members of Congress seemed not to understand what they were voting for. According to the joint resolution, "The Congress approves and supports the determination of the President, as Commander in Chief, to take all necessary measures to repel any armed attack against the forces of the United States and to prevent further aggression."[95] It was this last phrase that gave the President his blank check. It went on to assert that peace and security in Southeast Asia was "vital" to the national interest.

In secret testimony held on August 6, Senator Morse said he knew about the 34A raids in which, he added, the U.S. destroyers had participated. (He learned this from an anonymous tip from the Pentagon.) Mr. McNamara denied that the navy was involved in any way with the South Vietnamese commando raids, "if there were any." He was emphatic that there was "no connection between this patrol and any action by South Vietnam,"[96] and he denied that the navy even had any knowledge that the 34A raids were taking place. Secretary Rusk followed the same general line. Neither was telling the truth.

Senator Morse summarized his position during the final Senate debate: "We are in effect giving the President . . . warmaking powers in the absence of a declaration of war. I believe that to be a historic mistake."[97] He never forgave Senator Fulbright for fronting for Lyndon Johnson's open-field running. Senator Fulbright's later justification for his key role in getting the Tonkin Gulf Resolution passed was that the President had lied to him. In a short while Senator Fulbright's Foreign Affairs Committee would become one of the early centers of opposition both to the President and to the creeping war.

The North was told, "[If it] persists in its present course, it can expect to continue to suffer the consequences." Premier Pham Van Dong "showed himself utterly unintimidated."[98] In the South, Ambassador Taylor cabled that the current political leadership in Saigon had an even chance of not lasting out the year. In America, the public was being prepared for more war, and overwhelmingly supported (85 percent in a Harris poll) the actions in Vietnam as well as the Tonkin Gulf Resolution. In the Pentagon and in the White House, the men who were planning the war had crossed over the line that made direct American military involvement easier. In the Oval Office, the President had also crossed that line, placing him tighter in the military's grip. He had learned, he thought, that manipulation could work as well in foreign as in domestic affairs. He was also moving toward a political campaign and was running as a peace candidate against the warlike Senator Goldwater.

President Kennedy's bequest to the nation had been faithfully executed by his successor. There was no longer any acceptable doubt that South Vietnam was a nation, was even a reasonably coherent society. Lyndon Johnson understood probably better than anyone that the United States could not and would not be "humiliated" by primitive Asians inflamed by ideology. He knew this because he believed that our cause was honorable, that we sought no territory, and that we were therefore not imperialists; we only wished the South Vietnamese well, and simply wished that the North would cease and desist.

Although most of the Kennedy team had not been so crude as to allude to the myth of the city on a hill, their actions were consistent with it. Dean Rusk was the exception. Like Woodrow Wilson and John Foster Dulles, his father was a Presbyterian minister. Secretary Rusk's biographer said of him that "most of all he wanted the United States to serve as the model and beacon for democratic revolutions."[99] He apparently did not see the tension between an exemplary and a warring America. All the members of the Kennedy and Johnson administrations were willing to invoke American technological magic.

Having now invented the maiden in whose name we would slay the Asian dragon, what remained was the killing.

FOUR

WAR BY THE NUMBERS

Lyndon Johnson's landslide election of 1964 gave him the "mandate" that President Kennedy, because of his own narrow victory, never enjoyed. In America's political dictionary a *mandate* means that its owner is not only free to lead, but has a duty to do so. The election victory, LBJ wrote, was "a mandate for action, and I meant to use it that way."[1]

He swept the election for a variety of reasons, not the least of which was that Barry Goldwater unwittingly cooperated in the Democrats' description of him as a mad bomber. In early September the Democrats sponsored a sixty-second political ad on television, the only time it was shown. A little girl, plucking petals from a flower, dissolved into a countdown of an atomic explosion, slowly changing into a mushroom cloud for the finale. Senator Goldwater's primary solgan was: "In your heart you know he's right." The Democrats answered, "In your heart you know he might."

The President campaigned as the man of peace, much as President Wilson had in 1916. One of Barry Goldwater's better placards read BETTER BRINKSMANSHIP THAN CHICKENSHIP, while President Johnson was being presidential, insisting, six days before the election, "[The] first responsibility, the only real issue in this campaign, the only thing that you ought to be concerned about at all, is who can best keep the peace?"[2] One of his constant themes was that American boys should not fight a war that should be fought by Asian boys. He became the nation's thirty-sixth President by winning, in a landslide, 61 percent of the vote. There were then about 25,000 American troops in Vietnam.

For the first time Lyndon Johnson was his own man in national politics. He no longer stood in the shadow of the Kennedys. No longer was he the country hick from west Texas who could not stand in his own boots on the national stage. His campaign promises of peace had seemed thoughtful and deliberate, but then not many Americans had yet become deeply concerned about the distant thunder.

During the closing month of the campaign, a happy month for the increasingly confident President, the CIA analyzed South Vietnam in pessimistic terms. It advised that politics in the South were deteriorating, another coup was attempted, and there were more riots and strikes, along with an armed revolt by the Montagnards. The South's army was still unmotivated and unaggressive. It was possible that defections from the army might now occur by entire units. Anti-Americanism was growing everywhere.

Remembering all this from the perspective of 1970, LBJ said, "I knew from the start that I was bound to be crucified either way I moved." In a reflective mood, he said, "If I left the woman I really loved—the Great Society—in order to get involved with that bitch of a war on the other side of the world, then I would lose everything at home." But if he left that war and allowed the North to unify Vietnam under Communist rule,

> ... there would follow in this country an endless national debate—a mean and destructive debate—that would shatter my Presidency, kill my administration, and damage our democracy. I knew that Harry Truman and Dean Acheson had lost their effectiveness from the day that the Communists took over China. I believed that the loss of China had played a large role in the rise of Joe McCarthy. And I knew that all these problems, taken together, were chickenshit compared with what might happen if we lost Vietnam.

> For this time there would be Robert Kennedy out in front leading the fight against me, telling everyone that I had betrayed John Kennedy's commitment to South Vietnam.

That I had let a democracy fall into the hands of the Communists. That I was a coward. An unmanly man. A man without a spine. Oh, I could see it coming all right.[3]

It is probably not true that President Johnson saw it coming at the time he was making the decisions of war. Like the rest of us, his hindsight was better than his foresight, and his need to put himself in the best possible light was not less than average. More likely than his ability to forecast the future, and more likely than his keen analysis of the terrible trap that was closing, was the probability that he could not at the time conceive of America failing to work its will on a tiny, undeveloped, and defenseless nation. He believed that America could lead South Vietnam to become a respectable democratic society that would earn the support of the South Vietnamese, that we could force North Vietnam to stop assisting the National Liberation Front which would then collapse, and that we could compel the North to pay a continuingly rising price for its adventurism, to the point where it would be profitable to stop.

President Johnson analyzed the domestic political consequences of the growing war in exactly the terms President Kennedy had used. They both reacted to the political right, and either took the left for granted or else ignored it altogether. They both assumed that left-of-center Americans would have to support them for what seemed like the strong argument that the liberal left had nowhere else to go. This conclusion led both Presidents to a sort of free-floating anxiety about how the right would react to them and their policies. It led to a determination, especially in foreign affairs, to appease the right by never seeming "soft."

The fact of the Presidents' reflex to cave in to the right was so obvious that even the hawks acknowledged it. General Westmoreland, for instance, as good a representative of the hawks as anyone, later wrote:

> both the President and the congressional leaders were afraid of an open national debate. They were unsure of the political repercussions and more concerned about the "hawks" than the "doves" on the convenient theory that Red China might be provoked to enter the war. They took counsel of their fears.[4]

General Westmoreland's amazing "solution" to this problem was to give the military a much larger voice in future conflicts.

This fear of the right and complacency about the left made withdrawal from Vietnam unthinkable. Neither JFK nor LBJ could imagine withdrawal without being haunted by the ghost of Joe McCarthy. Both Presidents believed they had to stick it out in Vietnam to protect Americans from what they perhaps correctly believed would be the ravages of the certain witch-hunt that would follow a collapse of the national will regarding Southeast Asia. They apparently could not imagine the ravages that would follow from their appeasement of the political right, with the consequent collapse of political authority itself. For them, domestic paranoia coupled with international arrogance settled us in the quagmire. And President Johnson wanted very much to avoid being thought of as the first American President to fail in war.

It is not clear what the Presidents and the engineers of the war had in mind to do if the relatively small number of Americans they had sent to Vietnam were directly attacked and some killed. Presidents Eisenhower, Kennedy, and Johnson all proclaimed their determination "to avoid a wider war." Each sent Americans to the zone of war, yet none had specific plans about what to do when, inevitably, television showed pictures of dead Americans in that strange place. The American advisers in Vietnam were obviously a target, and consequently a source of danger to the United States. Perhaps some of the Presidents' men figured that no one would dare shoot an American.

The Americans in Vietnam represented the trap that could force decisions in Washington, and could override the will of the President for reasons of domestic public opinion, for reasons of national pride and of the worldwide reputation of the United States, as well as for reasons of the individual psychology of the chief war planners. Those Americans in Vietnam represented the quite good chance that events, rather than intelligence or choice, would shape decisions.

By the beginning of 1965, the President faced three courses of action in Vietnam. America could leave. Or America could take over the war from the bungling Vietnamese and finally end it by winning. Or it could do something in between. All the Presidents had sought that middle way, neither entering the war, as they understood it, nor abandoning it. They each desperately wanted the South Vietnamese to win what we insisted was really their war. By 1965, it was no longer possible to sustain the fiction that South Vietnam was able to win, and for a few free souls it was no longer possible to regard South Vietnam as a reasonably coherent and indentifiable society run by a government that represented a positive force to the majority of South Vietnamese.

But it was precisely the assumed ability of the South Vietnamese to fight their own battles that permitted American policymakers to imagine the middle way. Thus, because of their own myths, fears, ambitions, assumptions, and blinding nationalistic pieties, President Johnson and his senior aides—Secretaries McNamara and Rusk, National Security Adviser McGeorge Bundy, Ambassador Maxwell Taylor, and General Westmoreland—invented an alternative to the South Vietnamese. General Westmoreland concluded that before 1965, before combat troops were sent, LBJ could have withdrawn from Vietnam "with justification and honor, thought not without strong political reaction at home."[5]

President Johnson understood institutional domestic politics as well as any man, and already knew what he wanted to do. In December 1964, he sent a top-secret cable to Ambassador Taylor to inform him what was on the President's mind:

> Every time I get a military recommendation, it seems to me that it calls for a large scale bombing. I have never felt that this war will be won from the air, and it seems to me that what is much more needed and would be more effective is a larger and stronger use of rangers and special forces and marines, or other appropriate military strength on the ground and on the scene. I am ready to look with great favor on that kind of increased American effort, directed at the guerrillas and aimed to stiffen the aggressiveness of Vietnamese military units up and down the line. Any recommendation that you or General Westmoreland take in this sense will have immediate attention from me, although I know that it may involve the acceptance of larger American sacrifices.[6]

This cable to Ambassador Taylor shows that LBJ's mind was made up long before he later led his advisers to recommend actions he had wanted for more than half a year. He was already prepared to make the so-called momentous decisions that he would supposedly make only seven months later. The difference was that in December he was thinking about antiguerrilla forces, but in July he sent conventional troops. The reason for the switch was that the delay gave the bureaucracies time to assist the President in formulating policy.

At the beginning of 1965, the need to find a surrogate for South Vietnam was caused by a growing number of dead and wounded Americans in a growing number of places in Vietnam, including five dead and 56 hurt at Bien Hoa airfield, 2 dead and 63 wounded by a bomb thrown in daylight in downtown Saigon, and 8 dead and 108 wounded in a guerrilla attack on Pleiku. The Pleiku assault, in early February 1965, threw a switch in Washington. Waving the list of casualties, President Johnson strode into an emergency meeting of the National Security Council and announced: "I've had enough of this."[7] The immediate reaction was to order retaliatory bombing raids on the North. The intermediate reaction took only three weeks longer: initiation of what McGeorge Bundy called "sustained reprisal" bombing of the North. The long-range reaction took only sixteen weeks, after which American ground troops were directly engaged in war.

It is a frequent mistake to think of the Pleiku attack as the cause of the Americanization of the war. In fact, this attack was plainly the war planners' justification for what they wanted to do for a long time. Three weeks *before* Pleiku, the White House told Ambassador Taylor, "Immediately following the occurrence of a spectacular enemy action you would propose to us what reprisal action you considered desirable."[8] America already had its finger on the trigger and was waiting for "the other side" to shoot with a big enough bang to justify our counterfire. Pleiku was the occasion, not the cause, for abandoning the middle way that the planners decided they could no longer defend.

If the South Vietnamese could not fight and win their own war, if South Vietnam was still perceived as "vital" to America's national interest, and if the President's deeply intuitive reading of American public opinion was correct (and who was to argue this point with him?), there was no hope for it. The collapse of the middle way left the President and his senior aides with only two choices: in or out. In their terms, this meant that they had no choice at all. This mentality almost mechanically produced the third and bloodiest and most futile phase of the war.

In the same month, McGeorge Bundy and Robert McNamara decided to try to change American policy. They believed that the current "directives" were failing and would continue to do so. The fundamental problem was that U.S. action had been linked to the governments of South Vietnam. Mr. Bundy advised the President that America was clearly prepared to do even more in Vietnam if the leaders there "will only pull up their socks." Neither man thought they would do so, as Mr. Bundy wrote:

> . . . no one has much hope that there is going to be a stable government while we sit still. The result is that we are pinned into a policy of first aid to squabbling politicos and passive reaction to events we do not try to control. Or so it seems. Bob and I believe that the worst course of action is to continue in this essentially passive role which can only lead to eventual defeat and an invitation to get out in humiliating circumstances. We see two alternatives. The first is to use our military power in the Far East and to force a change of Communist policy. The second is to deploy all our resources along a track of negotiation, aimed at salvaging what little can be preserved with no major addition to our present military risks. Bob and I tend to favor the first course. . . .[9]

After discussing this memorandum, the President sent Mr. Bundy to Vietnam for a firsthand review. He led a military and civilian investigating team which concluded its work on the day Pleiku was attacked. Mr. Bundy's long report to the President was drafted the day before Pleiku was hit. The report was carefully crafted, clearly written, and occasionally eloquent. It is an important document in the history of the collapse of political imagination in Washington, and it reveals the emptiness of the good logic that he and others like him applied to the Vietnam "mess." What Mr. Bundy composed for President Johnson was a model of the rationalist's inability to understand reality. Because Mr. Bundy's peculiar inabilities meshed with Mr. Johnson's different but compatible inabilities, Mr. Bundy's view of the war and his recommendations for action were accepted and became policy, became war.

The first sentence of Mr. Bundy's report dismissed the middle way as no longer tenable: "The situation in Vietnam is deteriorating, and without new U.S. action defeat appears inevitable —probably not in a matter of weeks or perhaps even months, but within the next year or so." As a necessary conclusion to this premise, he argued, "There is no way of unloading the burden on the Vietnamese themselves, and there is no way of negotiating ourselves out of Vietnam which offers any serious promise at present." If America tried to negotiate in the context of a losing effort, it would simply amount to "surrender on the installment plan." The iron logic was plain (but not true). We could neither rely on the South Vietnamese nor get out. Therefore, "new U.S. action" was inescapably necessary.[10]

Mr. Bundy reported that the NLF was winning, that it controlled a growing sector of the countryside. Among the peasants in the South, he said, "[there was a] widespread belief that the Viet Cong are going to win in the long run."[11] Even the "few" places that were controlled by the government of the South were "shrinking." Thus, he reported, "The prospect in Vietnam is grim." Above all, the guerrillas were magnificent killers:

> The energy and persistence of the Viet Cong are astonishing. They can appear anywhere—and at almost any time. They have accepted extraordinary losses and they come back for more. They show skill in their sneak attacks and ferocity when cornered.[12]

Despite all the difficulties and uncertainties, despite the continued chaos within the government of the South, despite the doubts of Americans closest to the action, and despite the fact that the guerrillas were winning, Bundy reported, "Yet the weary country does not want them to win."[13]

According to the Bundy report there was one centrally important problem that American could solve by itself. The Vietnamese, North and South, believed that we, as a nation, did not "have the will and force and patience and determination to take the necessary action and stay the course." To correct this apparent misperception the President had to be prepared to do something that would demonstrate his will, force, patience, and determination. A one-shot reaction, such as the Tonkin Gulf retaliation bombing, would not do. This whetted the appetite of the South Vietnamese government, and, when nothing followed, led to disillusion.

All the logic and controlled language of Mr. Bundy's report led to his major recommendation: sustained reprisal bombing of the North. It had to be sustained to demonstrate both patience and determination; it had to be bombing to demonstrate will and force. But "reprisal" did not mean an American attack specifically tied to some identifiable outrage by the NLF. It meant "a policy in which air and naval action against the North is justified by and related to the whole Viet Cong campaign of violence and terror in the South." This policy should be executed "with as low a level of public noise as possible." The bombing should begin "at a low level" and be stepped up or down in response to the activities of the southern guerrillas on, say, a weekly basis. The objective of bombing the North was "to influence the course of the struggle in the South." This was an important point for Mr. Bundy. Apparently having finally understood that the struggle in the South could not be won by the South Vietnamese government, if indeed the whirligig of temporary rulers could be called a government, he urged President Johnson to win in the South by bombing the North. He explained:

We emphasize that our primary target in advocating a reprisal policy is the improvement of the situation in *South* Vietnam. Action against the North is usually urged as a means of affecting the will of Hanoi to direct and support the VC. We consider this an important but longer-range purpose. The immediate and critical targets are in the South—in the minds of the South Vietnamese and in the minds of the Viet Cong cadres.[14]

This was apparently the end of the long American history of nation-building in South Vietnam. President Johnson could not consistently suppress this impulse, but with sustained reprisal bombing, the United States committed itself to defend the South against the guerrillas by altering the psychology of both the South Vietnamese and the guerrillas by bombing North Vietnam. The South Vietnamese, at least nearly all "articulate" groups, would presumably respond to the gospel of freedom, become optimistic, and the guerrillas would presumably understand the inescapable and mortal danger of the sound and light show America would stage in the North.

This altered state of mind would presumably give the United States new prestige and increased influence in the South. We could continue to press for a more democratic government. We would undertake joint military planning with South Vietnam, but America's role would be "controlling."

In short, Mr. Bundy found many reasons to launch sustained bombing, and very desirable consequences might be enjoyed if his plan worked in the way he had anticipated. But he had now written himself out on a thin bureaucratic limb. He had promised too much, and had failed, in bureaucratic language, to "cover his ass." In an attachment to the main report, written by Assistant Secretary of Defense John McNaughton, a former law professor from Harvard, there was an attempt to correct the certainty of the tone of the rest of the report, to back away slightly from the brilliance of Mr. Bundy's crystal ball, to provide an excuse in case things did not work out as described, to avoid responsibility if the new policy was a bust:

> We cannot assert that a policy of sustained reprisal will succeed in changing the course of the contest in Vietnam. It may fail, and we cannot estimate the odds of success with any accuracy—they may be somewhere between 25% and 75%. What we can say is that even if it fails, the policy will be worth it. At a minimum it will drop down the charge that we did not do all that we could have done, and this charge will be important in many countries, including our own.[15]

The report concluded by informing the President that if he kept his focus on what the NLF was doing in the South as the cause of our bombing in the North, the world's criticism of the bombing could be dealt with. If the American players would continually emphasize the atrocities of the guerrillas, "the international pressures for negotiation should be quite manageable."[16] America must not get sucked into negotiations for peace except for what amounted to an unconditional surrender of the guerrillas.

The President rightly believed that this report and the circumstances surrounding it constituted "a turning point."[17] It was everything that a bureaucratic report should be: clearly written, brief (for its momentous subject), apparently dispassionate, supportive of the boss, and it recommended only what was already familiar. President Johnson said, "Though the Bundy report proposed a course of action we had considered and turned down only three months before, I was impressed by its logic and persuaded strongly by its arguments."[18]

When he returned to Washington, Mr. Bundy delivered his report to the President at about 11 P.M. and was then directed to provide copies "at once" to the Secretaries of State and Defense in preparation for a meeting the following morning. LBJ read it before going to sleep. He was anxious to learn how his "other advisers had reacted in light of altered circumstances and the Bundy report."[19] In the morning he met with an expanded National Security Council in the Cabinet Room. Everyone present had either read or been told about the report and, according to the President's memoirs, "there was unanimous support for its principal recommendation." There was some debate about the pace of the proposed bombing, with the military unsurprisingly arguing for "an intensive program of attacks from the outset."[20]

There were a few critics of the Bundy report within the administration. Three men especially did what they could to introduce better logic and more caution into the discussions. James Thomson of the National Security Council staff argued that we had lost our perspective in Vietnam, and that we should use our imagination to find a "face-saving avenue of retreat." He added that the public was right in its impression that the bombing was an act of desperation. He described the bombing as a way "to achieve stability through sustained euphoria in Saigon."[21] Vice-President Humphrey also opposed the bombing, so he was not invited to discussions of foreign policy in the White House for about one year.

Most important of any of the Washington critics was George Ball, undersecretary of state. He was one of the directors of the U.S. Strategic Bombing Survey after World War II, and had more reason than others to know that bombing would neither break Hanoi's will nor win the war. Unlike the Vice-President, who could not be fired and who had his own political base, Mr.

Ball's criticism was actively encouraged by the President. LBJ went to elaborate lengths to give Mr. Ball his day in court not because LBJ wanted to hear a different point of view, but because he needed others—influential elites, the press, foreign governments—to realize that he was receiving a broad range of advice.

The President always placed the burden of proof on Mr. Ball, not on the advocates of bombing. He had to prove that the bombing would fail; they did not have to prove that it would succeed. "It was a Catch 22," Mr. Ball said, "and the quintessence of black humor." Bureaucratic "logic" was at work: "As though to demonstrate how harassed but ingenious men can turn logic upside down, my colleagues interpreted the crumbling of the South Vietnam Government, the increasing success of the Viet Cong guerrillas, and a series of defeats of South Vietnamese units in the field not as one might expect—persuasive evidence that we should cut our losses and get out—but rather as proving that we must promptly begin bombing to stiffen the resolve of the South Vietnamese Government." His conclusion was blunt: "Dropping bombs was a pain-killing exercise that saved my colleagues from having to face the hard decision to withdraw."[22]

The President convened a special meeting to hear Mr. Ball out. Secretary McNamara countered Mr. Ball's arguments with his usual "spectacular display of facts and statistics."[23] Mr. Ball's boss, Secretary Rusk, agreed with the Secretary of Defense. Mr. Bundy advised LBJ to listen to Mr. Ball, reject his arguments, and get on with the war.

President Johnson had already made his own feelings clear in his own language:

> We have kept our gun over the mantel and our shells in the cupboard for a long time now. And what was the result? They are killing our men while they sleep in the night. I can't ask our American soldiers out there to continue to fight with one hand tied behind their backs.[24]

One week after the Bundy report was drafted, the President ordered the start of sustained bombing of the North, code-named Rolling Thunder, and the evacuation of all dependents from Vietnam.

While the President and his principal aides debated, needing all the accurate information they could get, the CIA was up to its neck, with LBJ's approval, in covert activities in Vietnam. One caper could not have fooled Hanoi, but may have deceived the American State Department. According to Ralph McGehee, a twenty-five year veteran of the Agency, the CIA wanted to help Washington prove its case that North Vietnam was an aggressor against the South. The CIA faked a capture of North Vietnamese arms. Mr. McGehee wrote: "The agency took tons of Communist-made weapons out of its warehouses, loaded them on a Vietnamese coastal vessel, faked a firefight, and then called in Western reporters . . . to 'prove' North Vietnamese aid to the Viet Cong."[25] A State Department White Paper, written to document the North's aggression, devoted seven pages to describing this "evidence," including photographs, to show that Hanoi was arming the NLF. It is not possible to know whether such bureaucratic chaos within the U.S. government actually misled decision makers. What is known is that the President authorized Rolling Thunder one week after State's White Paper was issued.

Rolling Thunder reverberated around the world and caused widespread criticism of the United States. It was hard to believe that the strongest and richest kid in the world was going to beat up one of the weakest and poorest kids. It was hard to believe that whites were again to drop bombs on Asians. And, at the time, it was hard to believe that either the Soviet Union or the People's Republic of China would accept the destruction of North Vietnam. It was hard to understand what American policymakers were thinking about.

President Johnson thought that the outcry was a consequence of a widespread failure to understand that the change in American policy was a direct result of a change in the now more aggressive policy of North Vietnam:

> From the time our planes hit the first military target in North Vietnam early in February, we were subjected to an increasingly heavy propaganda barrage from Hanoi, Peking, and Moscow. Every other Communist capital joined in. The propaganda message was short and sharp: Stop the Bombing. Soon voices in non-Communist countries joined

the chorus—Indian, French, Swedish, and others. Before long, some American public figures began to repeat the theme. They all ignored the vital fact that we were bombing the North because Hanoi was stepping up the war in the South.[26]

LBJ said that Rolling Thunder was necessary because he believed that "Hanoi was moving in for the kill." The North was receiving more help from Moscow. The President "now concluded that political life in the South would soon collapse unless the people there knew that the North was paying a price in its own territory for its aggression."[27] He needlessly added that the Pentagon supported his view.

The response in North Vietnam was not precisely what Mr. Bundy, Ambassador Taylor, and the other remaining Kennedy wizards had anticipated. The North's reaction was described in Hanoi by Colonel Ha Van Lau, a future ambassador from Vietnam to the United Nations. He claimed that Rolling Thunder meant that "the occasion was lost to end the war." Perhaps reflecting Vietnam's ancient and deep distrust of the Chinese, Colonel Ha distributed the blame for Rolling Thunder between China and America. He believed that the Chinese had informed the United States that "China would not make war with the U.S. if the U.S. didn't attack China—and with that, with the Chinese card in hand, Johnson pursued the war."[28]

The behavior of China had been a constant concern of the American war planners. They did not want a repeat of Korea. By now, however, the international politics of the big powers had dramatically changed. Beginning early in the 1960s, Russia and China began to diverge and finally to break apart. It was no longer possible for Americans to think in terms of an international monolithic Communism (although it took the State Department several years to adjust to the new realities) directed by the Kremlin. Just before LBJ's election, the Chinese exploded their first nuclear bomb. Mao seemed less predictable than Khrushchev, perhaps because the Soviets, for all their apparent madness, were more European. The Chinese then seemed more spastic and irrational than the Soviets.

Khrushchev had just been deposed, and it was not yet clear whether his successors would leave America to its own folly while providing some assistance to the North. He had not threatened a worldwide conflagration over Vietnam. What would Leonid Brezhnev and Aleksey Kosygin do? President Johnson said that he would have to start all over again, to meet the new men face-to-face to begin his sincere manipulation of them. In fact, Kosygin was in Hanoi during the White House debate on retaliation bombing of the North after Pleiku, and there was momentary anxiety about whether we should delay the bomb strike until he got out of Asia.

After sustained bombing became established American policy, General Westmoreland, as head of America's military mission in Vietnam, became increasingly important to the conduct of the war, the nature of thinking in the White House, and the next, most important decision that President Johnson and his aides had to make. LBJ called what was coming his "hardest decision." What lay just ahead was the choice to send American troops to fight the war that he had said "only Asian boys" should fight. There was a constricted logic to the decision. Many of the bombing runs took off from the air base at Danang, so the war planners, including the President, decided that the base would become "a high priority target" for the enemy. The South Vietnamese authorities agreed that this was likely. General Westmoreland requested two battalions of marines to protect the air base. They were sent. The President wrote that "this released for offensive action against the Viet Cong some of the Vietnamese troops who had been protecting the base."[29] Now America had moved from providing military advisers to providing combat troops. This was done because Americans were getting killed, because the guerrillas were winning, because we believed we had to bomb the North to improve the morale of the population in the South, and because now we had to protect the crews who would fly the bombers.

The decision to send in the marines was based on the assumption that they would serve only "security," not combat, objectives. The war planners did not yet have to admit to themselves that they were in an Asian ground war. The President did not inform the American public about the decision to send the marines when he had the opportunity to do so. America soon learned what was happening, and Secretary Rusk explained, if that is the right word, that the marines were ordered to avoid combat, only to return enemy fire.

At this moment it was imperative that the war planners

should have been clear about American objectives in Vietnam. John McNaughton, Secretary McNamara's assistant, attempted to clarify in his own mind why we were there:

> 70 pct.—To avoid a humiliating U.S. defeat (to our reputation as a guarantor).
>
> 20 pct.—To keep SVN (and then adjacent) territory from Chinese hands.
>
> 10 pct.—To permit the people of SVN to enjoy a better, freer way of life.
>
> Also—To emerge from crisis without unacceptable taint from methods used.
>
> NOT—To 'help a friend,' although it would be hard to stay in if asked out.[30]

To the degree to which the administration officials accepted this allocation of national purpose, the overwhelming American strategy in Vietnam was to avoid humiliation. That purpose apparently had very little to do with the people of South Vietnam, had a little more to do with the geopolitical fear of the People's Republic of China, and had almost everything to do with the perception of America by Americans and the rest of the world. We had to be there because we would be embarrassed to lose there. Finally, it was Americans, not Asians, who were motivated by a desire to save face.

General Westmoreland had at the time, he later said, serious doubts about some of the decisions coming out of Washington. An embodiment of what had become the Good Soldier, "Westy" had trained himself to constrain himself, to follow orders, and to expect that his orders would also be followed. That was the code, and personal honor and integrity were at stake. His choice was to do as he was told or to resign, probably in disgrace. There is virtually nothing in the American military tradition that would support a decision to walk away from an order, especially one from the President of the United States. He was a soldier, not a fool or a bloodthirsty monster. He was a bureaucratic soldier, not an evil man, and he naturally insisted that he was forced to be a bad soldier because of the militarily misguided and dangerous orders he was given by those he considered to be the arrogant amateurs who were trying to run his war from Washington.

He was born in South Carolina in 1914, was an Eagle Scout,

and attended a military college in his home state. A West Pointer, he had an active and distinguished career. He posed for the cover of *Cosmopolitan* in the 1930s and went on from there to become "the most photographed" army general.[31] He was in several campaigns in World War II, including command of an artillery battalion during the landing at Casablanca in 1942, and afterward saw action in Tunisia, Sicily, and the D-day landing in Normandy. He was impressed by General Patton whom he saw often and admired, but whose quirks put him off.

His code was composed by the rules of the enormous military bureaucracy. In addition to his combat experience, he was being trained as a manager, not a leader, of men. It was as if his training were preparing him to become America's chief personnel manager. In 1953, he was appointed to the Pentagon where he directed the army's manpower office. From there he went to the Harvard Business School to take the Advanced Management Program which gave him, he said, "a number of management ideas that I used in later years."[32] He then became secretary of the general staff. He was captivated by the fashionable emphasis on the techniques of management, along with its subspecialty of motivation. His interests and style had moved him away from the ethos of combat and toward the textbooks, toward the organization charts, and toward bureaucratic advancement. He believed in the given rules of the game, and the name of the game relevant to him was bureaucracy, not war. In June 1964, he was named head of the U.S. Military Assistance Command, Vietnam.

Some members of today's military elite have told me that they are bitter about General Westmoreland's command in Vietnam. They are now the colonels and generals who were his field commanders there. They blame him for failing to resign, or, in contradiction, for failing to influence what they consider to be the damaging civilian orders from the White House and from the Office of the Secretary of Defense. They blame him for what was in fact his mindless optimism during the war. In blaming him they obviously do not have to blame the military. These new elitists have their scapegoat. The theology that supports this bitterness offers the solace that with a better commander America might have been more successful. These officers now wish that General Westmoreland had done something spectacular. There is nothing that bureaucracies detest as much as spectacular personal behavior.

General Westmoreland was obsessed with the regular North Vietnamese military units and less interested in the guerrillas. He was afraid that the North would mount a conventional military invasion of the South before there were means to repel it. He believed that the guerrillas could not achieve a military victory in the South, but conventional armies could. He could not be blamed for the sapping attacks of the guerrillas, but a defeat by "proper" armies would, by his code, be his responsibility. He knew that the guerrillas' effectiveness was at least as much political as military, and that fact helped to exonerate him from responsibility for their progress.

As a result of the way General Westmoreland's mind was organized, he objected in 1964 to bombing the North, and, in early 1965, to the way the bombing was being carried out. He wrote that if anyone had asked him about the Tonkin Gulf reprisal bombing, for instance, he "would have disagreed." No one had asked him. He "was particularly concerned lest the North Vietnamese respond to bombing by committing major troop units in the South." He believed that a ground invasion by regular units was the only way the North could respond, and if it did so, "the fragile structure that South Vietnam was at the time might collapse." He senselessly argued that a strong and stable government in the South could eventually "supress the VC," but was under "no such illusions should North Vietnam openly intervene."[33] He was proud of what he believed was his knowledge of the Communists.

When he heard that American dependents were to be evacuated and that marines would land at Da Nang, he worried that "either or both would reflect lack of confidence in the Vietnamese and would seriously affect their morale."[34] For the war he feared he needed a stable government in the South. But the Washington planners were less fearful of a conventional engagement, probably because they thought it less likely, and probably because they continued to be more interested in the counterinsurgency that so excited the Kennedy administration. Each side was partly right, and so both sides were wrong.

Ambassador Taylor, former Chairman of the Joint Chiefs, and the civilian planners were deciding to increase the bombing gradually, as McGeorge Bundy had recommended. General Westmoreland described this as "one of the most lamentable mistakes of the war," because in his opinion a slow increase gave the enemy time to lick their wounds and regroup. His alternative to gradualism was "to hit surely, swiftly, and powerfully." He thought that the civilians had a "phobia" about dragging China into the war, a view he dismissed as "chimerical."[35] His attitude was an exact reflection of General MacArthur's mistakes during the Korean War.

True to the code, as always, General Westmoreland concluded that the basic errors of the war were caused by civilians, and he was sometimes right. Once the bombing began, he said, "interference from Washington seriously hampered the campaign." On this subject his language, even long after the fact, came surprisingly close to violating the bureaucratic imperative of dispassion:

> Washington had to approve all targets in North Vietnam, and even though the Joint Chiefs submitted long-range programs, the State Department constantly interfered with individual missions. This or that target was not to be hit for this or that nebulous nonmilitary reason. Missions for which planning and rehearsal had long proceeded might be cancelled at the last minute. President Johnson allegedly boasted on one occasion that 'they can't even bomb an outhouse without my approval.' Fortunately, as time passed, the interest of the self-appointed air marshals in Washington gradually lessened, and airmen gained greater leeway.[36]

His deepest scorn was reserved for the held-over Kennedy wizards. He judged them to be well-intentioned but naïve, and their advice had a disastrous effect on "a President so politically oriented that he tried to please everybody rather than bite the bullet and make the hard decisions." President Johnson, according to the general, soon came to his senses. LBJ apparently told General Westmoreland that "his greatest mistake" as President "was not to have fired, with the exception of Dean Rusk, the holdovers from the Kennedy administration, which he called the 'Kennedy gang,' a group whose loyalty to him as President he questioned."[37] To General Westmoreland the chief villains were, however, not in the White House or, except for Averell Harriman, in the State Department, but in the Office of the Secretary of Defense, in the very seat of military authority, and that made it all the more galling. The people in his sights were John McNaughton, his successor Paul Warnke, the head of Systems Analysis Alain Enthoven, and Townsend Hoopes.

He described his enemies in Washington as "clever civilian theorists." He hated their sniffish rejection of the experience of military men, their intellectual pedigree, and their arrogance. "Those officials and some White House and State Department advisers appeared to scorn professional military thinkers in a seeming belief that presumably superior Ivy League intellects could devise some political hocus-pocus or legerdemain to bring the enemy to terms without using force to destroy his war-making capability."[38] If it were not so serious, he said, it would have been funny.

General Westmoreland did not understand Vietnam as well as he understood the Washington bureaucracies. What he wanted from President Johnson was authority to use "shock action" against "lucrative targets" near Hanoi.[39] He wanted to step up the conventional war to bring the North to its knees. And he seems never to have understood that the guerrillas in the South, dependent as they were on the North, could have conducted their political campaign, along with their terrorism, probably forever.

The war was a case study of political conflict. It could not have been won with any of the weapons endlessly available from the great federal warehouse. Novelists sometimes understand these things better than others. In *Targets,* Donald E. McQuinn has the central character, an officer in Vietnam, tell his newly won Vietnamese lover: "I should go home. I've won a heart and a mind. I've made my quota." His lover did not think that was funny: "I know you joke, but there is much truth in it. This war will be won with words."[40]

General Westmoreland, speaking for many military officers then and later, believed that Washington refused to let him win the war. Washington planners believed that the automatic reflex of the military was always to demand more and more of everything and the freedom to use it as they wished. Neither group took seriously enough the most important questions of all: What were we doing in Vietnam? What did we wish to accomplish? Would bombing help us to achieve our unspecified goals? What was the objective of the war in the South? No one in the administration gave clear answers.

The decision to bomb the North was, as James Thomson observed, an act of desperation. It was made because of the growing conviction that the collapse of the government of the South was imminent, and because the war in the South was being lost. The most influential senior aides figured that there was a chance, perhaps remote, that the bombing would be effective. They could not see how it would hurt the American cause, whatever that was. It was, in short, a decision reached by the gradual elimination of other alternatives, save one. It was at least something that could be done. And it was an American sort of a decision.

It was American because, since World War II, we had enough of the right sort of technology to delude ourselves that we could defeat an enemy at bargain prices. Our machines, especially air power, could perform for us on the cheap. We could invest in machines, not men. Over and over again we have to learn the lesson that air power cannot win wars, and having learned it we immediately forget it. Myths do not yield to facts. Perhaps the dream of a clean war for our side, for a war that is safe for America, for an antiseptic adventure in the name of our conception of due process, is simply too alluring to abandon. The air force too often supports this myth, perhaps in the hope of bigger budgets, and civilian leaders, especially Presidents, are very tempted to rely on the air force to destroy the enemy and bring the boys home safe and sound and soon.

After World War II a survey was conducted of the effects of the strategic bombing of Germany. It was discovered that the massive carpet bombing impaired Germany's warmaking capacity, but did not destroy the enemy's willingness to fight. During the debate about whether the United States should send its bombers to help the French at Dien Bien Phu, the Chief of Staff of the army, General Matthew B. Ridgway, recalled that in Korea, where he had been in command, "We had learned that air and naval power alone cannot win a war. . . . It was incredible to me that we had forgotten that bitter lesson so soon—that we were on the verge of making that same tragic error."[41] The lesson we had learned in World War II was forgotten before it was relearned in Korea, and was forgotten again in Vietnam. Old myths apparently neither die nor fade away. Before America withdrew from Vietnam, we dropped four times more bombs on Vietnam than all the bombs we dropped all over the world during World War II. It did not work, as the CIA regularly said it would not.

As a matter of course, General Westmoreland, after his disagreement about the start of reprisal bombing, wanted as much tactical air support, mostly bombing, as he could get to assist the ground forces. He especially wanted the high-flying B-52s to spread their bombs over the guerrillas' base areas. In June 1965, the first such strike occurred, and the results, he said, were "impressive" and "invaluable." As was becoming habitual, the war critics got under his skin: "Contrary to the carping of critics who likened it to employing a hammer to kill a fly, the B-52s became the weapon the enemy feared most." No wonder: "Flying so high they were beyond sight or hearing from the ground, they wedded surprise with devastating power." The general was particularly careful to point out that the B-52s, during his entire Vietnam tour, hit only "populated areas," that is, civilians, twice. That was because the accuracy of the big bombers was almost incredible."[42] In fact, a B-52 miss of one thousand feet was usual, perhaps close enough for the nuclear bombs they were designed to carry, but in Vietnam the huge, clumsy machines caused random civilian deaths.

Because the start of the air war required ground troops to secure the air bases, President Johnson, perhaps unwittingly, authorized the start of the ground war simultaneously with Rolling Thunder. Ambassador Maxwell Taylor, who had earlier urged President Kennedy to send ground troops, now objected to sending the marines because he believed that once American soldiers appeared in Vietnam it would become increasingly difficult to "hold the line," to refuse new military demands for more and more men. LBJ had received the advice to start the air war to prevent the ground war. But the two wars were so closely linked that having started either, the President necessarily started the other. It is not clear whether he was entirely aware of this linkage, and if any of his key aides helped him to think this through it is not on the record. In any event, the President had wanted to introduce combat troops at least seven months earlier.

Assuring a properly surrealistic image, 3,500 marines waded ashore near the Danang air base to a welcoming reception by local bureaucrats along with pretty girls who presented them with orchid leis. Four American advisers held up a bed sheet on which they had painted WELCOME TO THE GALLANT MARINES. With a backdrop of palm trees it was a classic Hollywood set.

American grunts were never again to have it so good. And having put his toe in the water, the President was no longer in a position to avoid falling in. The marines were there to protect the air base; it was soon enough clear that they could not remain passive, would have to patrol farther away from the base, up to fifty miles, and engage in combat, if necessary, for their security mission. This secret change of orders, from security to combat, was quickly discovered by the press in Vietnam, and began what was then called LBJ's "credibility gap." In a short while the war critics would not have believed him if he described a rainy day as cloudy. General Westmoreland had always been restive about the security role because it was too passive and "inglorious."[43] It was soon enough clear that two battalions could not do the job and that additional troops were essential to protect the marines who were there to protect the air base.

As General Westmoreland requested and received more and more American troops, the administration's action demonstrated that it was hedging its bets by bringing the American war to the South even while it continued to escalate the bombing of the North. It showed that the attempt to win the hearts and minds of the people of the South would be supported by American firepower on the ground, against the guerrillas when possible, and against the regular army of the North if and when it appeared in the South.

The war was now entirely America's war, and the President intended to win it without a general mobilization, and without informing either the Congress or the public. It was as if he wanted to win without being noticed. By now he knew that the war would be long, expensive, and unpopular. If his memoirs are to be believed, he already realized that the war was going to destroy his presidency, his hopes for the Great Society, and, unless his health after a heart attack would hold out, perhaps it would also destroy him.

He did not propose a declaration of war to the Congress because he believed the Tonkin Gulf Resolution was all the authorization he needed, and because so overt and public an act might provoke some unwanted reaction in Moscow, Peking, or Berkeley, California. He also did not deal with the Congress because he scorned that institution's easy compliance with his requests; he was so much the master of the institution and of its deep reflexes that he did not take it as seriously as a novice might. The Congress delivered what he ordered, usually on time. The Congress disgraced itself in the Tonkin Resolution "debate," and would continue to disgrace itself in voting the funds LBJ needed to pursue "his" war.

His refusal to talk sense to the public was based on the same fears and assumptions. It has been true, at least throughout this century, that American Presidents come to believe that they own the nation's foreign policy. Some of what they do in foreign affairs is secret. It follows that the public cannot know enough to vote or even speak intelligently on foreign affairs. Obviously, the less the public is told, the less it knows. A too secretive President necessarily creates a public that is too uninformed. Additionally, much of foreign affairs is considered so compli- cated, requiring knowledge of different cultures and traditions, that the public is excluded once again. The attitude that results in Washington is that the people must and should simply trust the President and his administration. This paternalism charac- terized Presidents Wilson, Roosevelt, Truman, Eisenhower, Kennedy, Johnson, and, later, Nixon. President Johnson, out of his hard-won faith in his ability to manipulate people and insti- tutions, probably had the most virulent case of this paternalism. But he did not know best, and his own knowledge of foreign cultures and histories was as slim as the public's.

To make matters worse, President Johnson had a warm and giving nature. He genuinely believed that all the peoples of the earth were the same in their need for food, health, and educa- tion, as of course they are. He had no comprehension that differ- ent cultures search for the satisfaction of these essential needs in quite different ways. His understanding of the Vietnamese, North and South, was minimal. His textbook was his own expe- rience in west Texas; his textbook was his own life. That is what Vice-President Humphrey meant when he said that for LBJ the Pedernales and the Mekong were not so far apart. That is why the President could even think of offering a massive flood-con- trol project to the North Vietnamese if they would only please stop fighting. He could imagine trading an enormous TVA project in exchange for the ideology of the North. With typical enthusiasm, he said, "We're going to turn the Mekong into a Tennessee Valley." North Vietnam responded that this was a "bribe." Bill Moyers, LBJ's press aide, later smiled and said, "If Ho Chi Minh were like George Meany, LBJ could have made a deal."[44]

LBJ was the perfect example of the American solipsist in love with his country and certain that the American way was the best and only solution for everyone. He regarded his own life as equivalent to the American way. This means that he did not understand enough of America. He believed that his own personal history was the ideal model for the oppressed of the earth. This means that he did not understand oppression.

He believed that his was the voice of "the common people" because he thought he was one of them, and believed that he therefore understood their needs and dreams whether in America or Vietnam. While he was destroying the country with bombing, defoliation, and napalm, he could without cynicism speak of peace and progress. He believed that the destruction was unfortunately necessary before the construction could occur. That was Ho Chi Minh's fault.

In early 1966, the President, on two days notice, called a big meeting to be held in Hawaii. He summoned the chief officers of the now "stabilizing" government of South Vietnam, along with many of his own senior aides. As he stormed into the conference he informed the participants of his purpose: He wanted "a better pacification program that includes everything." He warned the participants that he was not going to accept empty assurances from them; he would not accept "phrases, high-sounding words" because he demanded "coonskins on the wall."[45] Within days the Saigonese spoke comfortably about their need to get the coonskins.

President Johnson would surely have preferred to win the war by good works for the people of Vietnam. The rush of Great Society programs at home was tiny compared to the countless schemes for doing good in Vietnam cooked up by what Ambassador Taylor called "the panacea peddlers in Washington." He said, "The result was that a feeble government was in constant danger of being overfed, overphysicked, or constipated by the excessive zeal of his American physicians."[46] The ambassador pointed out that most of the American Mission's programs and money in 1964 and the first half of 1965 were devoted to winning the hearts and minds of the people, and he was irritated that the American press refused to report this fact. The arrival of the marines reversed this relative allocation of the Mission's effort and money.

The civil programs in Vietnam always collided with the military effort and so they worked against each other. It was difficult to win hearts when villages were being destroyed, either by resettlement programs or bombs. It was difficult to win minds when the government of the South almost always proved to be incapable of protecting the villages from terror. The cultural ignorance of most Americans was highlighted by the guerrillas' intimate knowledge of the country. On her trip to Vietnam, Mary McCarthy observed that at bottom most of the civil programs were designed to teach the Vietnamese how to do things better than they had always done them.[47] Her point was persuasive because teaching—changing the way the world thinks—is what always comes easiest to Americans abroad. It is not clear that the Vietnamese appreciated the lessons Americans gave them, including lessons on how to grow rice.

One major problem with the many "pacification" programs was that because they had to function in the countryside, they were all vulnerable to attack by the guerrillas. The villagers always had to make a private bet on the outcome of the carnage, and if they thought the guerrillas would finally win, the civil programs could not work. In late 1966, Secretary McNamara repeated the required political catechism when he referred to pacification efforts as "the important war," but added that this war was "worse off" than in the previous year.[48] At the same time, Ambassador Lodge agreed that pacification was "not really rolling."[49] Unless Americans learned to concentrate on the threat of guerrilla war, the pacification effort, usually described by Washington bureaucrats as the heart of the matter, would always be futile. Foreign observers, not wedded to the American theology of containment, dominoes, moral superiority, technological invincibility, or panic over the power of the native hawks, could see this earlier and clearer than Americans. The Israeli general Moshe Dayan came to the following conclusion when he visited Vietnam:

> The Viet Cong army can, if it refrains from pitting regular units against regular units in frontal engagements and organizes guerrilla warfare, prevent the Americans and the Saigon government from pacifying the country. The Viet Cong cannot drive out the Americans, but they can, by adopting appropriate methods of warfare, avoid being driven out themselves.[50]

Some Americans understood. If one could get away from the technicians, it was possible to understand. Secretary McNamara was to learn this in time. But when he was in charge and charging, there had always been something missing. Even McGeorge Bundy, the slick extension of the President, perceived Mr. McNamara's nearsightedness even before the Tonkin Gulf crisis. He told LBJ, in June 1964, that the Defense Secretary "has rather mechanized the problem so that he misses some of its real political flavor."[51] If one could somehow get away from the military, it was also possible to understand that without pacification there would never be a victory, and that the military would always smilingly ensure that pacification would be submerged by what they believed to be their more important, if unspecifiable, mission. It is ironic that a man of the Pentagon finally had the clearest vision of all. Paul Warnke, the director of a political bureau in the Pentagon, explained that the American military in Vietnam was actually an army of occupation that could succeed only so long as it stayed there:

> There is no question of the fact that we can keep on winning the war forever. We always win and we always will, and it won't ever make any difference. Our wins won't make a clear dent because there is no way in which we can bring about political progress in South Vietnam. . . . The more of an American military occupation you engage in the longer you're going to stay.[52]

General Westmoreland's insistence on fighting a big unit war of attrition, the Pentagon's continuous demands for more and more conventional troops and more and more bombing, and the policymakers acquiescence in the military's sense of the war meant that the guerrilla war would be deemphasized. That meant that the programs to win the hearts and minds of the Vietnamese people would fail. As the Americans militarized the war, its political center was at least obscured. As LBJ came increasingly to rely on the military's traditional desire to overwhelm the enemy by force of numbers, we forfeited the political and psychological struggle to the North Vietnamese and the NLF. Because that is what they did best, and could afford, the American forfeit must have suited them just fine. As we decided to fight a war by the numbers, our enemy decided to fight a war against American culture. They relied on the assumption that Americans would get tired of the war, counted on our continued ignorance, and exploited our political rhythms as they did in important military actions in the election years of 1964, 1968, and 1972.

We attempted to match their knowledge of us with the weight of numbers that only America could amass. LBJ clearly wanted to scoop up the hardware and men by using only his left hand (the right was reserved for the Great Society), but even that was a mighty scoop. Throughout his presidency he consistently acknowledged that he would spend "whatever it takes" to win. Robert Komer, a presidential assistant who was to play a leading role in the pacification program, summarized: "Wastefully, expensively, but nonetheless indisputably, we are winning the war in the South. Few of our programs—civil or military—are very efficient, but we are grinding the enemy down by sheer weight and mass."[53] Mr. Komer was mistaken about the results, but he was right about the means America employed to work its confused will. It was as if LBJ's war slogan were We Shall Overwhelm.[54] We used mass to compensate for the absence of brains, somewhat reminiscent of the dinosaurs.

Lyndon Johnson, of all men, was unable to understand the values associated with social stability. He believed that the traditions of Vietnam's culture were impediments to social progress. Had he actually been able to impose his vision of the Great Society on the Vietnamese, an entire culture would have been utterly destroyed out of the goodness of the American heart. From the Washington viewpoint, for those afflicted with Potomac fever, it was evidently easy to recast our victims as beneficiaries. It was not so bizarre, as millions of Americans thought at the time, that an army officer could speak of destroying a town to save it. The President and his administration were destroying a nation to save us.

When the President ordered the marines to secure the Da Nang air base, the Pentagon recommended sending an additional forty-four battalions. The men and machines poured into Vietnam as only America could afford. The hope was that the machines would save the men, and the idea of the possibility of failure was as unfamiliar in Washington as it was in official Vietnamese circles in Saigon. The machines both fascinated and appalled the South Vietnamese. Bui Diem, Chief of Staff for Premier Quat, a Cabinet member, and a future ambassador to Washington, described this in 1983:

> In the eyes of the Vietnamese, the Americans made the war too expensive by the way they fought it. It was a kind of "affluent war" never seen before or even thought of by the Vietnamese. They opened their eyes in bewilderment when they looked at the helicopters bringing hot food to the fighting men. They saw the thousands of gadgets piled up in huge PXs for the use of the GIs, the hundreds of planes flying back and forth across the Pacific for the transport of US troops and supplies. They witnessed the more than generous use of bombs and ammunition by the US forces, hours and hours of bombing and strafing by planes and artillery barrages triggered in many instances by mere sniper fire.[55]

The machines set the country on fire. The pile of dead began to grow. The forests were poisoned, as were the rivers and lakes. The Rome plow uprooted a huge tree with one swipe of its spike. The stench of diesel fuel, burning human excrement, and scorched or rotting flesh mixed with the natural odors of jungle decomposition. Some GIs found the smell of Vietnamese cooking the worst of all. Adhesive fear and hatred were everywhere, although fear grew best in the jungles, while hatred thrived anywhere.

There had never been an American war on a scale like this. There were no literary conventions to organize the thinking of the soldier, as there had been in World War I. The references were all to movies, preferably starring John Wayne. He served as the soldierly conscience of many grunts and perhaps officers, although they would have lost caste to have said so. None of them could identify the enemy, called Charlie, who did not wear a uniform. Charlie could be anyone, so the old woman just passed on the road might be armed, might be an enemy, and might kill. Should she be killed before she could strike? It was not an easy question for an American kid on that road. There was no front and no lines. An invisible enemy could be anywhere and was probably everywhere. Getting out of there was the only certain way to stay alive.

July 1965 was when President Johnson lost control of the war in Vietnam and America. There were 75,000 American troops in Vietnam. It was then that he made the decision to raise the level of killing and committed America to what the most thoughtful military men had consistently warned against: a land war in Asia. He said, and I believe that he thought, that he did this to stop aggression and to give the South Vietnamese a chance to build their society in a way that he would recognize as free. He did it to avoid shame.

A few months earlier there had been another change of political leadership in South Vietnam. The "young Turks," Air Marshal Nguyen Cao Ky and General Nguyen Van Thieu, threw out Premier Quat and took over. The Americans, especially Ambassador Taylor, liked Thieu with his solidity and apparent experience. But Ky looked and sometimes acted as if he had just stepped out of an American comic book. He liked to dress in black or bright yellow silk fatigues decorated with a vivid purple scarf, and toted an ivory-handled pistol. He admired Adolf Hitler more than any other Western "statesman." He worked hard to earn a reputation as a gambler, boozer, and womanizer. General Westmoreland liked Ky because "he was a man of action, a swashbuckler, but at the same time he was highly intelligent."[56] There was no optimism about the staying power or competence of the new team either within the American mission in Saigon or in Washington. Although Thieu and Ky would last out the war, at the time they seized power it was feared that this was just another turn of the Saigon merry-go-round.

Prime Minister Ky was a problem not only for the Americans, but for the South Vietnamese. One respected local journalist told Daniel Ellsberg, then stationed in Saigon, that Ky's political power was an "insult to the people." "Why," he asked, "do you have to humiliate us by hiring a man of this caliber for us?" It was not merely that Ky was perceived as a puppet: "We could live with a puppet—we're on your side—we could work with you with much more self-respect if you had someone more representative of Vietnamese values."[57]

These two Vietnamese leaders, like their predecessors, were on the thin ice of American intentions. They rightly feared the Americans would some day simply pack up and leave, to their very great personal danger. America had for years tried to persuade the North of the seriousness and perseverance of America's Vietnam intentions. It failed in the North; it also failed in the South.

The much desired stability of leadership in the South was purchased at the price of some influential southerners believing that Thieu and Ky were foreign rulers, American surrogates, resulting in a new colonialism. But neither of these men were as malleable as Americans expected. They too were capable of digging in and refusing to endorse American actions. They finally would create great difficulties.

For the fifth time since Diem's assassination, the American planners concluded that the new regime would not succeed unless the American war effort was intensified. By July 1965, the moment of the deceptive "great debate," no one with real power in Washington could hear George Ball's long-held conclusion: "No one has yet shown that American troops can win a jungle war against an invisible enemy."[58] No one was even asked to show how this could be done. It had become an article of faith, especially for Robert McNamara, who had taken over the war. Supermac, the former president of the Ford Motor Company, the supreme systemsman and rationalist, the can-do star of the Kennedy administration, was finally in charge of winning "Johnson's war."

Preparing for the debate the President was about to stage, Secretary McNamara asked Ambassador Taylor a series of questions. He wanted to know this: "What assurances do we have that with the resulting force level we can prove to the Viet Cong they cannot win, and thereby force them to a settlement on our terms?"[59] This is breathtaking because it was known that guerrillas do not need to win; they simply must avoid losing. Conventional forces must win. Guerrillas can wait for the expense of foreign expeditionary forces to wear down the enemy's economy, and for the accumulating casualties to enrage the home front. Guerrillas are at home to start with. They never need to fight set battles unless they choose to. Because they can wait, time is on their side and is therefore a test of the enemy's patience and will in a distant land. It is difficult to know what Mr. McNamara had in mind when he asked that question. He must have known better.

The momentous administration "debate" began when Secretary McNamara gave the President a plan that called for sending 175,000 more American combat troops to Vietnam. The Secretary said that an additional deployment of about 100,000 men would be necessary within about six months. Depending on developments, even more men might be needed in the future. Mr. McNamara also urged calling up about 235,000 Reserves and National Guard. And he wanted to increase the regular armed forces by 375,000 men. The net increase in one year would total some 600,000 men. LBJ convened a series of meetings to consider these recommendations.

Several witnesses, including advisers friendly to the President, such as William Bundy, believed that the President was not agonizing over the recommendations but was staging the discussions, engaging in political theater, which he did so well. For instance, George Ball asked why the military simply assumed that the guerrillas would accommodate us and come out fighting. General Wheeler assured Mr. Ball that intensified search-and-destroy missions would force the guerrillas "to fight somewhere."[60] No one asked the general why he thought that, or what evidence he had. When Mr. Ball said, "Thieu spoke the other day and said the communists would win the election," the President announced, "I don't believe that."[61]

On the next day, July 22, the President had a separate meeting with the Joint Chiefs to learn their reaction to their boss's plan. They liked it. Secretary McNamara acknowledged that his plan would result in a new war for which Americans would be responsible. Admiral McDonald, Chief of Naval Operations, took the initiative in giving the President a simple choice: "Get out now or pour in more men." General Greene, Marine Commandant, estimated that the war would take five years and 500,000 troops. LBJ asked what their reaction was to Ho Chi Minh's assertion that he was prepared to fight for another twenty years, and General Johnson, Army Chief, said simply: "I believe it." When LBJ asked what Ho's biggest problem was, General Johnson, displaying the American attitude that our actions determine results, answered, "His biggest problem is doubt about what our next move will be." General McConnell, Air Force Chief, recommended bombing "all military targets available to us in North Vietnam." The President worried about how to describe all this to the American people and to the Congress. The Secretary of the Army, Stanley Resor, assured the President that the public opinion polls showed the people were behind the President.[62]

On July 28, President Johnson announced that he was ordering an increase to 125,000 men in Vietnam, with more to go if necessary. From that day until LBJ left office, 30,000 Americans were killed in Vietnam. He did not call up the Reserves or the National Guard. Every one of his advisers responded that this call-up would be necessary when LBJ asked them individually whether they agreed. One week later, after it was clear that the President did not want to order the call-up, all his advisers now individually agreed that the call-up was not necessary. Such is the bureaucratic way when the Chief shows his hand.

The flood of Americans into Vietnam overwhelmed that fragile country. By the end of 1965 there were 184,000 American troops in Vietnam; by the end of 1966 there were 385,000; by the end of 1967 there were 486,000. The ancient tension of cultures and traditions in that place could not survive the dominating American presence. The Americans did not set out to destroy the habits of centuries in South Vietnam. The difficulty was that we did not understand the implications of what we were doing.

From the American viewpoint, naturally enough, it was argued that if we were going to risk American lives, we had a right to insist that things be done our way. It was maddening to have to seek agreement with the South Vietnamese for either political or military action that was obviously in the interest of safety or victory, especially when the natives wanted to do it differently and, from our point of view, badly. It was always a cultural standoff that could not be resolved, until Thieu was elected President. At first, he and Ky eased the cultural conflict for the reason that they stopped resisting. That helped to accelerate the corruption of Vietnamese culture by the tidal wave of Americans into Vietnam.

President Johnson's decision to Americanize the war finally brought the long-sought stability to South Vietnam's government. Thieu and Ky, for different reasons, so admired the Americans that they virtually abandoned what the Americans described as the "stubbornness" of the earlier regimes, but what some Vietnamese described as the "authenticity" of the earlier regimes, including the worst ones, even Diem's.

The Vietnamese were not seduced by the advantages of American culture, were not drowning in Coca-Cola, were not dazzled into compliance by American affluence. They were outmuscled. America could win their war for them. All the prestige of this superpower, all the lethal technology, all the American generals, the dramatic international conferences, and the President of the United States reflected the world's most daunting power. What could the bedraggled guerrillas do, what could Ho Chi Minh's peasant army do, to withstand American political and military culture, to withstand American fire and steel?

Captain Brian Jenkins of the Special Forces served three tours of duty in Vietnam. He was a careful student of the cultural consequences of American intervention. His conclusion was, if anything, understated:

> The American presence was a major corrupting factor. A massive infusion of American culture came with the American military presence; also a tremendous intervention in the Vietnamese political system to the point that Americans —not the military advisors but American political advisors —were deciding what colors the lights in the fountains should be in downtown Saigon; whether the library and national museum in Saigon should adopt a decimal system; whether the trees in Saigon should be cut down to make way for parking meters. . . . Certainly there was a destruction of the Vietnamese identity; certainly this would have had a major adverse effect on the cause.[63]

As LBJ understood it, we were not cultural imperialists. We were simply trying to assist others to improve their lives and the lives of their children, and to enjoy the blessings of freedom.

Unsurprisingly, anti-Americanism was one result of America's ignorance and arrogance. The Buddhists especially resented the deformation of Vietnamese culture as the price of preserving the Vietnamese Catholics in power, what we called freedom. Their periodic riots and demonstrations against both the local government and the United States always struck the Americans as ominous, somehow affiliated with the Communists, and always subversive of the aims of the war. In several major cities placards were waved: END FOREIGN DOMINATION OF OUR COUNTRY,[64] inescapably relating the Americans to the colonial French. The library of the American consulate in Hué was set on fire and the local firemen refused to put it out. Most of the American leaders never understood the Buddhists' intentions, why they were unhappy, or why the bonzes, as men of some God or other, should get mixed up in politics. When Ky used military force to suppress a Buddhist riot in Da Nang, the Americans praised him for achieving a victory. Americans, in other words, perceived internal differences within Vietnam as a source of danger, and the more parochial the differences were, the more traditionally Vietnamese the dissenters were, the more we worried that they were enemies.

The Johnson administration was unable to decide on the war's strategy. It continually slid from "breaking Hanoi's will" to "propping up the government of the South," from "suppressing" the guerrillas in the South to destroying them, from "careful" bombing of the North to the destruction of its economy and military capabilities, from cutting supply routes to preventing infiltration.

Captain Jenkins was right when he said that no one could assess the progress of the war "toward an ultimate victory because that goal has never been defined."[65] Under such a handicap the characteristic bureaucratic imperative took over: The daily routine became the purpose and the objective. It was not that the goal justified the means. The means became the goal, and procedures replaced objectives. General Westmoreland's "strategy" was to fight a "war of attrition," to kill as many guerrillas and North Vietnamese troops as possible. Then they would quit. Then we would win. The killing became the objective. General Westmoreland did not know what else to do: "What alternative was there to a war of attrition?"[66] Captain Jenkins understood that this is what had become of America's military goals: "The *operations are the strategy.*"[67]

The evidence that at least some officers understood the war, and therefore recognized that General Westmoreland did not, is surprisingly clear. In 1969, Lieutenant Colonel D. R. Palmer, an instructor at West Point, published a textbook for the cadets. He taught them that "attrition is not a strategy," and that a commander who adopted it revealed that he was intellectually unprepared for command. Such a commander "turns from warfare as an art and accepts it on the most unprofessional terms imaginable. He uses blood instead of brains." He did not equivocate: "Saying that political considerations forced the employment of attrition warfare does not alter the hard truth that the United States was strategically bankrupt in Vietnam."[68]

Yet many of the means succeeded. American troops did not

lose a major battle. This gave rise to the mindless optimism reported both from Vietnam and Washington. General Westmoreland was accused of overusing a favorite metaphor; it was reported that he regularly saw "light at the end of the tunnel." As Michael Herr, a writer particularly interested in the experiences of the grunts, described it, a soldier near Tay Ninh City was a specialist in tunnels

> whose work kept him "up to fucking here" in tunnels, lobbing grenades into them, shooting his gun into them, popping CS smoke into them, crawling down into them himself to bring the bad guys out dead or alive, he almost smiled when he heard that [Westmoreland metaphor] and said, "What does that asshole know about tunnels?"[69]

No mistake cost the administration more than its constant assurances and reassurances that "progress" was being made in Vietnam, that "the boys" could come home by such and such a date, that the "price" the North was being forced to pay was finally becoming intolerable to Ho Chi Minh, that "pacification" of the South's countryside was moving along, that government reforms were finally working, that victory was not only achievable but was being achieved.

Then came Tet. The battle of Khe Sanh was already under way, recalling unsettling memories of Dien Bien Phu. At the start of the Vietnamese New Year celebration, during the early morning of January 30, 1968, about 80,000 regular troops and guerrillas assaulted more than one hundred cities, towns, and villages. A small group blasted their way into the grounds of the American embassy in Saigon and fought for hours in the courtyard until they were all killed or wounded. Others attacked the major Saigon airport, the President's palace, and the headquarters of the general staff of the South Vietnamese army. In less than two weeks they were repulsed everywhere but in the ancient capital of Hué.

Hué was special. It represented the long continuity of Vietnam's history and traditions, and it contained the citadel, an ancient fortress. In Hué, 12,000 men of the North's army finally fought the kind of battle that General Westmoreland had been waiting for, something familiar in America's military tradition.

The battle of Hué was fought street by street. It was what marines had been trained to do, but they had had no such experience in Vietnam. The Americans had been fighting in the rice paddies and jungles for so long that they were now inexperienced in this sort of murderous urban battle. One American physician, based near Hué, described a bitter conclusion that some Vietnamese were forced to reach as a result of Hué:

> The urban civilians were learning lessons about this war that the peasants had known for years. The most certain method of self-survival was to avoid involvement. Punishment for ties with the Americans was quick and final. Many of our interpreters and housemice were killed. Our Vietnamese barber was brought in with both hands cut off. There was no word from Sun, except for several rumors of her ceremonial rape and murder.[70]

The citadel was bombed into dust and much of the city was ruined. Close to 6,000 civilians were killed, many by execution squads of the North Vietnamese army. It took weeks of some of the toughest fighting of the war for American troops to retake the city.

When the Tet offensive was finally defeated, General Westmoreland announced that 37,000 of the enemy and 2,500 Americans had been killed. Probably an additional million South Vietnamese had become refugees. The battle of Tet was, as the military believed, a great American victory. The guerrillas were decimated because they finally had come out in the open to attack and fought not as guerrillas, but as conventional troops. At Hué the North's troops were more seriously hurt than in any other battle it fought. America was never to recover from this victory.

"What the hell is going on," Walter Cronkite asked when he first heard about Tet. "I thought we were winning this war."[71] Because of the President's reliance on manipulating people, language, and symbols, he had consistently lied to or withheld the truth from the public. The irony was his belief that the U.S. intervened in Vietnam in the first place to show the world that America keeps its word.

Throughout 1967, the year preceeding Tet, President Johnson and his senior aides had lowered what they expected would be a comforting smoke screen over the official reports of the war's "progress." The growing unwillingness of the public to believe the reports was merely a suspicion before Tet. With all the assurances, with all the statistics of success, with all the wildly inflated body counts of enemy fatalities, how was it possible that the enemy could mount a nationwide attack of such magnitude? The avenging angel of symbol manipulators was to have her due. The North won the battle of symbols, and LBJ and General Westmoreland were furious. They believed it was the fault of the American press.

Reporters on the scene were not unusually irresponsible. Always on the scent of something spectacular, always searching for scandal, always needing dramatic film footage, they merely did what they always do. They first reported that the guerrillas had entered and taken the American embassy. That was a better story than what had actually happened. But the press did not invent the fact that the enemy mounted a nationwide assault after the administration had been blowing on the pain for more than a year. After all the B-52 raids and all the search-and-destroy missions, the enemy was still able to mount so massive an assault. The fact of this ability, rather than the fact of their defeat, caught the imagination of the press, and of the American public.

Finally, however, the press was unwittingly correct. The illusions created by LBJ had led inevitably to public cynicism. He was responsible for the perception of failure during Tet. He had been playing a shell game with the public, and Tet revealed his deception, not his dexterity. The public turned against him, and against the war. For the first time, a majority of Americans over fifty years old were against the war, while the younger generation was slightly more hawkish. By way of comparison, the highest percentage of Americans who had opposed World War I was 64 percent, in World War II the peak was 31 percent, and in Korea it was 62 percent. By August 1968, 53 percent believed that it had been a mistake to intervene in Vietnam. (By 1972, two thirds of the public was opposed to the war, the same as the opposition to World War I and Korea.) The difference during the Vietnam War was not the number of Americans who disagreed with government policy, but the number who took to the streets.

After Tet, there was still no strategy for the American war.

For instance, LBJ invited General Ridgway to the White House to discuss Tet. The general, accompanied by Vice-President Humphrey, spent several hours with the President who was constantly interrupted by phone calls. General Ridgway commented to the Vice-President that he had "never known what General Westmoreland's mission was." Mr. Humphrey said, "That's a good question, General. Ask the President when he gets off the phone."[72] In 1974, Brigadier General Douglas Kinnard surveyed 110 generals who had served in Vietnam and learned that 70 percent had never been clear about America's military objectives.

Before Tet, Robert McNamara had undergone a deep change in his perception of the war, and apparently a personal crisis about his own role in it. The pressures on a Defense Secretary are killing, even without a war, and Mr. McNamara worked in that heat longer than anyone else. As early as mid-1964, McGeorge Bundy wrote to LBJ that Mr. McNamara already had been "trying to think of ways of dealing with this problem [Vietnam] for so long that he has gone a little stale."[73] By 1967 he was finished. He secretly authorized the compilation of the *Pentagon Papers*. He finally committed bureaucratic suicide by telling the President to stop bombing because negotiations were the only way out. The Joint Chiefs threatened to resign as a body if the President accepted their boss's recommendations, which they called "an aerial Dienbienphu."[74]

LBJ concluded that his chief war architect was close to a "nervous breakdown,"[75] and the two men worked out an arrangement that allowed Mr. McNamara to resign as Secretary of Defense and to preside over the World Bank. LBJ considered this new appointment his personal gift to Mr. McNamara, one that would help to preserve his sanity. Instead of stopping the bombs, LBJ expanded the target list "to placate the Joint Chiefs and Congressional hawks."[76] Only a few policymakers thought that continuing the bombing would do any good, but the right wing demanded more.

Mr. McNamara's resignation was effective on March 1, 1968. Clark Clifford, an old friend of the President, had earlier been named the new Secretary of Defense. For LBJ's purposes, Mr. Clifford, a hard-bitten and expensive corporation lawyer, seemed like an ideal choice because his judgment was sound, his personal loyalty had already been tested, and he was not a bleeding heart on the subject of the war. He was the consummate hawk. He was ordered, even before taking office, to review a new request for 206,000 more troops, not whether they were needed, but how they were to be provided.

In the previous year, LBJ had asked Mr. Clifford and Maxwell Taylor, then a special assistant to the President, to visit America's Pacific allies to persuade them to increase their troop levels in Vietnam. This trip was the beginning of Mr. Clifford's loss of some of his hawk feathers. An earlier believer in the dominoes of Presidents Eisenhower and Kennedy, Mr. Clifford found that the locations presumably in greatest danger—Thailand, the Philippines, South Korea, Australia, New Zealand, and, later, Singapore—did not share America's belief that Vietnam was the key to peace or security in Southeast Asia, and none of them would send more troops. Mr. Clifford must have known that President Johnson could be a bit sarcastic about his opponents' failure to take the dominoes seriously: "I realize that some Americans believe they have, through talking with one another, repealed the domino theory."[77] Mr. Clifford, however, returned from his trip "puzzled, troubled, concerned. . . . Was it possible that our assessment of the danger to the stability of Southeast Asia and the Western Pacific was exaggerated?"[78]

Mr. Clifford's first step as the designated chief of defense was to dig into the military bureaucracy. He kept peeling the onion until he found the tears. His briefings on the new troop request wandered off the subject as more fundamental issues kept cropping up. The answers he got were at first incomprehensible, then infuriating, and finally devastating. The more he tried to learn from the star-crossed Pentagon, the less he knew. He described his tough questioning of the top military brass as a "revelation" that there was no strategy for conducting, much less winning, the war. Their answers were either vague or ignorant. "Will 200,000 more men do the job?" No one knew. If the new troops were sent, could the North compensate with its own increases? Probably. "Can bombing stop the war?" Never. Should the bombing stop? No. Can bombing decrease American casualties? "Very little, if at all." Did any of the military experts foresee any decline in the North's will to continue after four years of terrible casualties? No. The final "startling" blow was his discovery that attrition was the "strategy." Killing was the "strategy." "And so," Secretary Clifford wrote in July 1969, "after these exhausting days, I was convinced that the military course we were pursuing was not only endless, but hopeless."[79]

Revelation led to conversion. In explaining themselves to their new boss, the Joint Chiefs transformed a perfect hawk into a determined dove. Mr. Clifford told the President that the only Vietnam plan that made any sense was to get out. LBJ could not believe that his new appointee, a colleague of twenty-five years, was also cracking up. It was, Mr. Clifford believed, the single most consequential event in Mr. Johnson's evolving view of the war. The President was increasingly fearful of political paralysis. Two born-again doves as Secretaries of Defense, increasing protest across the country, and increasing pressures from the military to send 206,000 more troops were crushing the President.

It was characteristic of this bureaucratic war that the 206,000 troop request was made, not because General Westmoreland needed so many more soldiers, but because General Wheeler, the JCS Chairman, was playing bureaucratic games. The troop request originated in Washington, not Saigon. General Westmoreland was pleased with the military consequences of the Tet offensive and as a result sent Washington his usual optimistic reports. The Chiefs of Staff saw Tet as the opportunity they had been waiting for. Not only could they use Tet to frighten the President and his principal aides, they were finally to be free of Secretary McNamara, their longtime keeper. Their new boss was a tough and hungry hawk. Perhaps now they could force the President to call up the Reserves and to raise enough additional troops to strengthen what General Wheeler believed was the dangerously low level of the nation's worldwide strategic reserve forces. The Joint Chiefs had tried to do this at least six times, but had been overruled each time. Perhaps they could use the public outcry over Tet as a lever with which to pry the President loose from his recalcitrance.

General Wheeler was permitted to go to Saigon to confer with General Westmoreland. He told General Westmoreland to prepare a new troop request based on every conceivable misfortune, including the withdrawal of 50,000 South Korean troops. General Westmoreland did have some ambitious plans that he could not put into practice, such as invading North Vietnam, Cambodia, and Laos, because he did not have the troops. General Wheeler, who obviously realized that General Westmoreland's plans would be rejected in Washington, advised him that it was a mistake to request troops for specific purposes. General Wheeler said, "It was, I felt, an inappropriate time to argue that far down the line. Westy couldn't do that until he got the troops, so why argue strategy then?"[80] The two generals entered into a private agreement that Westy would only be assigned about half the new troops if the total request were approved and the JCS would get the other half for the global strategic reserve.

Back in Washington, General Wheeler told the President that North Vietnam was likely to follow up on Tet with yet another offensive, and that if the troop request was denied, the North would likely drive us out of the northern provinces of South Vietnam. Mr. Clifford asked a series of questions which General Wheeler sent to General Westmoreland to answer. "Unaware of the crisis context in which the Chairman of the Joint Chiefs had presented the case for reinforcements," General Westmoreland later wrote, "unwilling to accept that a crisis existed . . . I was in no position to answer the questions. . . ." Then General Wheeler informed Westy that the JCS could not fulfill his request for new troops. General Westmoreland later said, "I made no request"[81] other than for one regiment and one brigade. Obviously, neither General Westmoreland nor the civilian government fully understood what General Wheeler was up to. Mr. Clifford remembered that General Wheeler's "report was so somber, so discouraging, to the point where it was really shocking. . . . President Johnson was as worried as I have ever seen him."[82]

Finally, Secretary McNamara argued that there should be no troop increase, as did Secretary-designate Clifford. They both believed that the American war effort had lost its point, if it had ever had one. The President, always in search of some way to please everyone a little, finally authorized an increase of 20,000 men, to a new ceiling of 550,000, and a constricted area of bombing in North Vietnam.

By now LBJ was thinking not about getting out of the war, but of getting out of the presidency. Some of the people closest to him believed that this decision was largely based on his concern about his health. There is also no doubt that he felt betrayed by the American people. He had devoted his life to public service, cared more about the poor, the ill, and the weak, he thought, than any other President. Yet, when he needed the public's support, when the country needed public support, they rioted, protested, prevented him from speaking, and in fact were giving aid and comfort to the enemy. He believed their refusal to support the war was causing brave American boys to die in that wretched, far-off country. He had lost the hearts and minds of his own people. During Tet the public's approval of LBJ's conduct of the war sank to 26 percent, the lowest level ever, while 78 percent now believed that the United States was not making progress in Vietnam.

The most difficult month of Mr. Johnson's public life was March 1968. Along with Secretary Clifford's astonishing recommendation, it seemed as if the political universe were conspiring against him. American soldiers murdered hundreds of civilians at an obscure village called My Lai. Senator Eugene McCarthy, a peace candidate, came very close to beating the President in New Hampshire's presidential primary. The most hateful news of all was the announcement that Robert Kennedy, LBJ's nemesis, wearing his dead brother's mantle, intended to challenge the President in the coming primaries. LBJ felt that he was being "stampeded." At the end of March he announced a number of decisions that were intended to persuade the North Vietnamese to agree to negotiations, and he declared, at the very end of his speech, "I shall not seek, and I will not accept, the nomination of my party for another term as your President."[83]

What remained for LBJ was a characteristically frustrating fiasco. The North had at last agreed to negotiations. Averell Harriman was appointed to lead the American team. The discussions collapsed before they started. The North insisted that the National Liberation Front be represented at the talks. The South Vietnamese would not recognize it as a legitimate negotiating participant. Weeks were consumed in designing the tables so that the groups could be in the same room but not recognize each other. Neither the North nor the U.S. were prepared to give anything away, and the South was frantic that it would be sold out by America. President Thieu believed that he would be better off with the Republicans than with LBJ, and he was obviously stalling. Many of President Johnson's advisers urged that America negotiate without the South Vietnamese, but he worried that their absence would destroy the "peace effort." After Mr. Nixon squeaked by Mr. Humphrey, Thieu finally agreed to be represented at the negotiations in Paris.

Lyndon Johnson sacrificed himself on the altar of that bitch of a war. He did so partly in obedience to his civic religion, partly because he was an amateur in foreign affairs, deeply ignorant of the world, fearful of seeming unmanly, haunted by John Kennedy, hunted by Robert Kennedy, badly advised, badly served, unable to slow down long enough to think, and stubborn as a Texas mule. Bill Moyers remembered that LBJ said Vietnam was like hitchhiking in a Texas hailstorm: "I can't run, I can't hide and I can't make it stop."[84]

Mr. Johnson was not a huge puppet dangling on the strings of fate. He had the power and the opportunity to exert his will on the war. The proof is that he did so. It is not that he lacked the opportunity to get out of Vietnam. He had chances and rejected them. What nailed him on his own political cross was not the conspiracy of destiny, or the conspiracy of his aides, or the conspiracy of either the left or the right at home. Because he learned only from his own experience, because his life was his bible, his own assumptions and myths became his cross. His presidency was a tragedy. What this tragedy did to the Vietnamese was a catastrophe. For them, the end was not yet.

FIVE
THE POLITICS OF EGO

Early in his 1968 campaign Richard Nixon thought the Vietnam War would be his way to power. He announced the number of dead Americans, described LBJ's paralysis in diplomacy, and called on Americans to accept his conclusion that it was time for a change. He allowed the idea to circulate that he had a secret plan to end the war. But in October, in the midst of the election campaign, President Johnson telephoned the candidates to inform them that secret peace negotiations had begun in Paris and that a settlement might be possible. The President asked them to be patriots, to avoid mentioning the war lest something they said might delay the peace every American wanted.

Until that phone call Mr. Nixon had the election in his pocket. His campaign had been a model of a greased organization with an abundant treasury. The Democrats were continuing to engage in intramural butchery. Hubert Humphrey was broke, disorganized, and wedded to LBJ at a time when vast numbers of Americans repudiated the President. George Wallace, a significant threat in terms of popular support, was still a wild card who might hurt both major candidates. But the political currents were blowing Mr. Nixon's way.

Five days before the election, LBJ had his last moment on the world stage. He phoned the candidates again to tell them he was going to announce a halt to the bombing in the belief that North Vietnam was ready to negotiate. Mr. Nixon recognized that a truce could deny him victory, and he was furious:

> The telephone call over, I could feel my anger and frustration welling up. Johnson was making the one move that I thought could determine the outcome of the election. Had I done all this work and come all this way only to be undermined by the powers of an incumbent who had decided against seeking reelection? . . . Announcing the halt so close to the election was utterly callous if politically calculated, and utterly naive if sincere.[1]

In fact, Mr. Nixon was not surprised by the President because he had been warned by Henry Kissinger of what was happening in Paris. The Harvard professor had earlier been used by LBJ as an emissary to the North Vietnamese, and had just returned from Paris. He secretly advised Mr. Nixon to avoid saying anything new about Vietnam. Then Dr. Kissinger expressed his political concern "about the moves Johnson may take . . . before the election."[2]

Dr. Kissinger's helpfulness made Mr. Nixon nervous. He worried that LBJ's people were feeding Dr. Kissinger "phony stories." "In such a tense political and diplomatic atmosphere," Mr. Nixon wrote, "I was no longer sure of anything."[3] Dr. Kissinger was simultaneously offering Nelson Rockefeller's "shit files"[4] on Mr. Nixon to the Humphrey campaign headquarters. Richard Allen, a key worker in the Nixon campaign, concluded that "it took some balls to give us those tips" because it was "a pretty dangerous thing for him to be screwing around with the national security."[5]

Hubert Humphrey knew that progress in Vietnam could persuade Americans to keep the boat steady at a critical moment. This time the rumors about impending negotiations were not a gimmick. The Soviets were usefully assisting the peace effort, and President Thieu finally agreed to be represented in Paris. But because President Johnson insisted on total secrecy, no one had consulted with the full government in Saigon. When the news finally leaked all the way there, President Thieu was forced to back off because the Vietnamese National Assembly was enraged and Vice-President Ky was threatening to overthrow the government. The following day President Thieu backpedaled: "The Government of South Vietnam deeply regrets not to be able to participate in the present exploratory talks."[6]

The prospect for peace collapsed, but LBJ proceeded with the Paris talks even if his puppet in Saigon now refused to march in step. Meanwhile, Anna Chennault, a private citizen deeply involved with the right-wing China lobby, was secretly advising the South Vietnamese to stall because the new Republican administration would not sell them down the river, as the Democrats would. This incident convinced LBJ that the Nixon camp had sabotaged peace in Vietnam to win the election.

After Richard Nixon's apparently secure lead in early September, the final vote on November 5 delivered to Mr. Nixon the office he had sought since his narrow loss to JFK eight years earlier. He won by the slightest plurality. Mr. Nixon had lost to John Kennedy by just over 100,000 votes; now he had beaten Hubert Humphrey by just under 500,000 votes of the 73,000,000 cast.

As Lyndon Johnson thought of himself a master of domestic affairs and not deeply informed about foreign affairs, Richard Nixon regarded himself as LBJ's opposite. The President-elect was familiar with and enjoyed the trivia of party politics, and believed that he knew the way of the world. He confessed to ignorance about urban affairs and environmental matters. His mind and his passion were directed outward to the great affairs that shaped the destiny of the globe.

Vietnam was significant to him only as a pawn in the larger international game. He was fascinated by the big picture, by the geopolitical tensions and opportunities of big-power maneuvering. He was therefore most interested in the Soviet Union and in the People's Republic of China. He was interested in history, and he believed that he could change it. If LBJ was an egomaniac about his Great Society, Richard Nixon's conviction that he could alter the course of historic international relationships by asserting his own ego makes LBJ, of all people, seem like a wallflower.

Three weeks after the election, Henry Kissinger was invited to the Pierre Hotel in Manhattan to talk to the President-elect. He did not know the purpose of the meeting and recalled, "I did not anticipate a conversation that would change my life."[7] But his highly secret briefings about LBJ's bombing halt had hit pay dirt. Mr. Nixon recalled, "During the last days of the campaign, when Kissinger was providing us with information about the bombing halt, I became more aware of both his knowledge and his influence."[8] According to Dr. Kissinger, Mr. Nixon fidgeted and fumbled until he began to talk about the problems he faced in organizing the government. Mr. Nixon said that "the Johnson Administration had ignored the military and that its decision-making procedures gave the President no real options."[9]

According to Mr. Nixon, the conversation at the Pierre was different, more focused, less personal, and less neurotic. He remembered that he did not have much hope for the Paris peace talks and that he wanted to rethink all of America's Vietnam policy. He was "determined to avoid the trap Johnson had fallen into, of devoting virtually all my foreign policy time and energy to Vietnam, which was really a short-term problem."[10] He wanted to restore NATO's vitality, and to concentrate on the Middle East, the Soviet Union, and Japan. He also wanted a new course regarding China. He remembered that Dr. Kissinger was delighted with so broad a vision of foreign affairs. Dr. Kissinger then suggested that the National Security Council be restructured to give the President the best possible advice.

Because of Dr. Kissinger's "previous image" of Mr. Nixon as an opportunist and mindless Red-baiter, because of his long association with Nelson Rockefeller as his patron, Dr. Kissinger was surprised by Mr. Nixon's "perceptiveness and knowledge" of foreign policy. In response to Mr. Nixon's question, Dr. Kissinger described what the new President's foreign policy goal should be: "The overriding problem was to free our foreign policy from its violent fluctuations between euphoria and panic, from the illusion that decisions depended largely on the idiosyncracies of decision-makers."[11]

Although Mr. Nixon was not specific about what he wanted Dr. Kissinger to do, he had "a strong intuition"[12] about him and had decided that he should be the President's national security adviser. It was also a chance to have his own Harvard intellectual, and to take over one of Governor Rockefeller's men. After the meeting, Dr. Kissinger assumed that he might be offered some position in foreign policy and sought the advice of McGeorge Bundy, who had been LBJ's security adviser and was now the president of the Ford Foundation. Because of their Harvard connection, the two men could talk to each other even though there was something of a social problem, at least as Dr. Kissinger perceived it: "He tended to treat me with the combination of politeness and subconscious condescension that upper-class Bostonians reserve for people of, by New England standards, exotic backgrounds and excessively intense personal style."[13] Mr. Bundy assumed that Dr. Kissinger might be offered a relatively low-level position, perhaps assistant secretary of state.

The next day, Dr. Kissinger met with John Mitchell, the future Attorney General, and the following conversation reveals that Mr. Nixon's closest staff confidants understood the boss. Mr. Mitchell, characteristically blunt, came right to the point and asked whether Dr. Kissinger would accept the job that the President had in mind:

> What have you decided about the National Security job?
> I did not know that I had been offered it.
> Oh, Jesus Christ, he has screwed it up again.[14]

Whereupon Mr. Mitchell went to see Mr. Nixon who agreed to see Dr. Kissinger again, to clarify what was on his mind. He offered him McGeorge Bundy's old job, the security adviser to the President. Mr. Nixon remembers that Dr. Kissinger said he would be honored to accept. Dr. Kissinger remembers that he played hard to get for a few days and then accepted.

While still at the Pierre, Mr. Nixon and Dr. Kissinger decided that the new administration should take office with a comprehensive review in hand of America's entire foreign policy. An enormous study was planned, to be controlled by Dr. Kissinger, that was to result in a series of "option papers" from which the President could then select a course of action. The unique aspect of this was that the appropriate agencies of government would be asked to answer specific questions, but they would not see each other's responses. Only Dr. Kissinger and his staff would see all the conclusions. The first study requested, on January 21, concerned Vietnam. (At the end of the first year of the new administration, eighty-five studies had been ordered.) Daniel Ellsberg, then a consultant with the Rand Corporation, prepared twenty-eight questions about Vietnam for the government to answer, and Dr. Kissinger added one of his own about the significance of Cambodia as Hanoi's supply route to South Vietnam.

The answers came in one month. According to the CIA, President Johnson's policy, especially the bombing, had not worked: "The air war did not seriously affect the flow of men and supplies to Communist forces in Laos and South Vietnam. Nor did it significantly erode North Vietnam's military defense capability or Hanoi's determination to persist in the war." The Office of the Secretary of Defense starkly concluded, "North Vietnam is better off today than it was in 1965," that is, before American troops were sent. The State Department warned that a new round of bombings would fail unless it was "conducted with much greater intensity and readiness to defy criticism and risk of escalation."[15] The Joint Chiefs of Staff, the military command in Saigon, and the American embassy in Saigon agreed that new bombing was needed in Vietnam, along with Laos and Cambodia. In short, there were two bureaucratic alliances within the administration: The optimistic side was manned by the military and the Saigon embassy; the pessimists included the CIA, the civilian head of the Defense Department, and the State Department in its fashion. The President was free to choose sides, and Dr. Kissinger, obviously anticipating the boss's wishes, aligned himself with the optimists, that is, the advocates of violence.

The elaborate study served several purposes. As Dr. Kissinger himself said, it kept the bureaucracy sufficiently busy so that it would not have time to interfere with him—or with the President. It also forced the agencies to state their positions with clarity and precision for the first time, thereby providing a roster of loyalty to the President. What it failed to do and was not intended to do was shape the President's policy.

Mr. Nixon wrote that America's foreign policy during the 1960s had been distorted by the fixations of the Democratic Presidents. He correctly asserted that the nation's foreign policy "had been held hostage, first under Kennedy to the cold war and then under Johnson to the Vietnam war."[16] He believed that the single-issue focus of his predecessors had led to a weakening of policy everywhere else. He wanted to do it differently, to avoid tunnel vision, and to keep his peripheral vision always on the horizon while he was concentrating on a constantly shifting center. He would start with the European alliance to strengthen America's hand in talking to the Communists. This would contribute to "peace with honor" in Vietnam, because "the key to a Vietnam settlement lay in Moscow and Peking rather than in Hanoi."[17]

For this reason, Dr. Henry Kissinger was an ideal adviser for the new President. Each man viewed himself as a strategist of a grand international design, understanding the enemy, free of typical American sloganeering about the rest of the world, tough-minded, and "realistic."

Henry Kissinger's approach to the Vietnam exit was essentially the same as the President's. In the mid-sixties, Dr. Kissinger was offended by the spectacle of what he described as a "fourth class Communist peasant state"[18] frustrating the military and political goals of the United States. His sense of his own nation, his pride, and his global ideology were deeply implicated in the conduct of war. Before he was appointed to office, Dr. Kissinger had been dubious about the possibility of a military victory in Vietnam. He had been reasonably sure that the way out of Vietnam would inevitably come through negotiations, not the defeat of the enemy. It is important to understand what he meant by negotiations, and how he believed that America could prevail at the conference table when it could not do so on the battlefield.

Just before he became the President's man, Dr. Kissinger published an article entitled "The Viet Nam Negotiations" in *Foreign Affairs*, a prestigious journal. The timing of the article was perfect for his new appointment. In the article he wrote that the fundamental flaw in American policy was that Americans had not known how to think about the war: "The basic problem has been conceptual." Therefore, we had achieved "military successes that could not be translated into permanent political advantage."[19] He concluded that American operations and plans had little relevance to the lives of the Vietnamese villagers in the South. From their viewpoint it was a fact of life that the government of Saigon could control the villages during the day, but the guerrillas took over at night (somewhat like areas of New York City). The only way out would be through extraordinarily difficult diplomacy. He argued that the South Vietnamese had developed sensitive antennae to the real facts of political power in their country. They would always yield to the winner rather than face extinction. Therefore, he concluded, "If negotiations give the impression of being a camouflaged surrender, there will be nothing left to negotiate."[20]

He concluded that the American withdrawal should occur "over a sufficiently long period." He wanted the war to last long enough to force the South Vietnamese to attend to the matters of government that had been fumbled ever since 1954. The United States should "for as long as possible" not negotiate the nature of the government of the South. He correctly predicted that "we are likely to wind up applying the greater part of our pressure against Saigon as the seeming obstacle to an accommodation."[21]

Dr. Kissinger shared the basic assumptions Mr. Nixon brought to office: The Russians had dominated much of the world because they had a "greater moral toughness" and were "iron-nerved."[22] They also had a general theory that permitted them to keep the side effects of their actions in mind. They knew what their purpose was and did not flit from one issue to another the way Americans did. He and the President both viewed international tensions, especially the contest with the Soviet Union, as a vital test of the determination and will of the leaders.

Both men insisted that the ultimate battleground with Moscow was psychological. Strategy should be aimed at victory over the perceptions of the enemy. An English journalist and scholar understood this about the new team: "The fight is more for myth than for reality, more for credibility than for territory, and the prospect of loss is therefore more disconcerting than the 'limited' nature of the war might be thought to imply."[23] The "prospect of loss" was whether or not the opponent believed us, would take our threats seriously, and understood how tough we could be. From early on, Dr. Kissinger felt that psychological manipulation was the key to statecraft: "What the potential aggressor believes is more crucial than what is objectively true."[24]

The obsession to be believed in Moscow led both the President and Dr. Kissinger to their own version of the domino theory. Neither would be so simpleminded as to believe that shopworn slogan, although the President would use it when it suited him. For example, during a discussion on television in mid-1970, he said: "I know there are those who say the domino theory is obsolete. They haven't talked to the dominoes."[25]

They both considered Vietnam as a test of will between

Washington and Moscow. Dr. Kissinger insisted, "We are no longer fighting in Vietnam only for the Vietnamese; we are also fighting for ourselves and for international stability," as he and his President understood "stability."[26] He believed that the government of South Vietnam was incompetent and corrupt, but that it had to be saved in our struggle for world leadership. Even though he thought that the Vietnamese were unworthy of our efforts, they had become an occasion for a clear demonstration of our geopolitical will.

If the leaders of the Soviet Union believed that the leaders of the United States would be restrained because they were rational men, some of the useful danger would be drained out of the relations between the two nations. It was important to both President Nixon and to Dr. Kissinger to sustain that sense of danger, else the Soviets would feel freer to disrupt the world's stability. If the Soviets believed in the rationality of Americans, and if that gave them comfort, President Nixon and Dr. Kissinger both believed that it would be constructive to persuade Moscow (and, while they were at it, also Hanoi) that we were not rational. The President said in public, "The real possibility of irrational U.S. action is essential to the U.S.-Soviet relationship."[27] Earlier, he had told his chief aide, H. R. Haldeman, that he had elevated the usefulness of seeming unbalanced to the level of a "theory":

> I call it the Madman Theory, Bob. I want the North Vietnamese to believe I've reached the point where I might do *anything* to stop the war. We'll just slip the word to them that "for God's sake, you know Nixon is obsessed about Communism. We can't restrain him when he's angry—and he has his hand on the nuclear button"—and Ho Chi Minh himself will be in Paris in two days begging for peace.[28]

The President was not alone in his conviction that some final cataclysm of death would be necessary to end the war. During his first year in office, Dr. Kissinger called his staff together to discuss what he described as a "very, very sensitive matter." He said, "I refuse to believe that a little fourth-rate power like North Vietnam doesn't have a breaking point." He ordered his staff to design an action that would surpass this point: "It shall be the assignment of this group to examine the option of a savage, decisive blow against North Vietnam, militarily. . . . You are to sit down and map out what would be a savage, decisive blow." Dr. Kissinger excluded nuclear weapons from the study, but, he said, "You are not to exclude the possibility of a nuclear *device* being used for purposes of a blockage in the pass to China, if that seems to be the only way to close the pass."[29] As usual, the CIA criticized the plan on the grounds that a savage blow would not be decisive. As usual, it was ignored. The idea of a savage blow at this time was finally rejected by "the mad bomber," a term President Nixon would later use to describe himself to the North Vietnamese.

Mr. Nixon moved into the White House with at least one firm idea about administration. He detested the bureaucracy and was determined to overrule it when possible and ignore it when not. His special targets were the State Department and the CIA. He was convinced that both were packed with Ivy League elitists and liberals who would exploit every opportunity to subvert his will. Thus, he was willing to accept Henry Kissinger's plan, written by his aide Morton Halperin, to reorganize the National Security Council in a fashion that would give Dr. Kissinger extraordinary powers to dominate the foreign policy and intelligence agencies of the new government. Instead of having to struggle with these enormous and ragged agencies of the bureaucracy, Mr. Nixon, by granting Dr. Kissinger vast backstage authority, had the much simpler task of simply controlling Dr. Kissinger. The boss's needs coincided with the aide's ambitions.

The President never intended to share his power to make decisions. Sometimes he wanted to hear the opinions of the members of the National Security Council. But, he said, "I'll decide. That's what I'm hired for, to make the big decisions, not them."[30] His staff, along with the rest of the bureaucracy, were to be subordinated to his own will. It was characteristic that, although he had criticized President Johnson for failing to consult the military experts, President Nixon consulted them less. His life had taught him to rely only on himself. The rest of the government would do it his way or it would be punished. No one would block his will. Including the public. Dr. Kissinger understood.

Dr. Kissinger's writings are decorated with many intelligent discussions of the federal bureaucracy. He had earlier analyzed the problems of exerting executive leadership within a bureaucracy. It was a brilliant forecast of how he was to be used in the Nixon White House. He was particularly concerned with the relationship between the leader and his advisers. He wrote that it is inevitable for senior staffs, on which the leader relies, to take on a life of their own. When this occurs the internal momentum of the staff complicates the questions it was created to answer. The problem is that the leader might not be able to absorb all the information his staff provides, and "this heightens the insecurity of the executive and may thus compound either rigidity or arbitrariness or both." As if drawing a blueprint for his own future role, he concluded that presidents who "find themselves the prisoners of their advisers"[31] should find ways to function outside of normal channels. They should appoint "personal envoys" who are free of bureaucratic constraints and who stand above institutional routine.

Henry Kissinger had a feel for bureaucracy. His analyses of this subject display not one but two conclusions: He understood bureaucracy, and he would be a clever bureaucrat. He would have to engage all his substantial skills to reassure a boss who could never be reassured, to destroy his competitors, to retain and enhance his position and prestige, and always to sidestep the President's loyalists. Dr. Kissinger's substantial abilities were probably shown to best advantage in the adroit and elegant minuet he performed to avoid their clutches.

Dr. Kissinger's noteworthy success was a result of the President's permission to turn himself into a sort of one-man intramural CIA whose mission was intelligence gathering and covert activities against his colleagues in the government. In time he had two high-level secret contacts in the State Department, a wiretap on the phone of the Defense Secretary's chief military assistant, special lines out to the FBI, secret deals with ambassadors all over the world, wiretaps on his own staff members, and special and privileged relationships with the military, most of which were kept secret from the Secretary of Defense. To be sure, some members of the Joint Chiefs of Staff also had a spy in Dr. Kissinger's office, who, in time, stole some five thousand documents, some from Dr. Kissinger's briefcase and luggage.

The President played to Dr. Kissinger's style. By trying to run the world in secret, he conspired with his national security adviser to keep major activities, such as negotiating peace in Vietnam, secret from the Secretary of State and the Defense Secretary, along with the ambassador in Vietnam and the government of South Vietnam, not to mention the American public. They requested a secret plan for falsifying military records so that Cambodia could be bombed without anyone knowing about it, at least in America. The two men were made for each other.

The President's control of Dr. Kissinger was an elementary exercise. He merely had to play Dr. Kissinger's ambition and ego, refuse to meet with him, or have a private dinner with the Secretary of State to reduce Dr. Kissinger to uncontrollable anxiety and a determination to behave better in the future. By the nature of their two positions it was naturally less easy for Dr. Kissinger to succeed, and so his achievement is more impressive. He had to discipline himself to hide his contempt of the President, to keep the oil of flattery flowing especially when the relationship was cold, constantly to guard every flank, and to organize his mind into that of the perfect bureaucratic subordinate.

Mr. Nixon's domination of the bureaucracy resulted in his solo performance, especially in foreign affairs, just as he intended. This freed both the President and his principal aide not only from the constraints of the bureaucracy, but also from its support. It resulted in Mr. Nixon's isolation, as he preferred, and turned him inward. This naturally diminished the administration's level of consultation with Congress, the allies, and the public. It also liberated Dr. Kissinger from having to worry about anything other than the boss and his moods. The defeat of the bureaucracy finally meant that policy would result from the intelligence, character, and ambitions of the two men, an exclusive relationship based on mutual need. It turned policy into a consequence of personality to what was probably an unprecedented degree. In time, it also therefore made the defects of personality decisive in decisions about war and peace.

When Mr. Nixon took office, a friend in Congress recommended that he pull out of Vietnam:

> You didn't get us into this war, so even if you end it with a bad peace, by doing it quickly you can put the blame on

Kennedy and Johnson and the Democrats. Just go on TV and remind people that it was Kennedy who sent the 16,000 Americans in there, and that it was Johnson who escalated it to 540,000. Then announce that you're bringing them all home, and you'll be a hero.[32]

Rejecting this advice, President Nixon, for the same reasons of national "credibility" that had kept President Johnson stuck, charged ahead. To place the "short-term problem" of Vietnam into its proper niche in the big picture of international geopolitics, another 20,550 Americans and an unknown number of Vietnamese were to be killed in Vietnam. This was justified on the grounds that such sacrifices would produce a lasting, just, and honorable peace—one that would assure the world of America's "credibility," and would guarantee to the South Vietnamese that they could progress toward an open and democratic society.

Mr. Nixon and Dr. Kissinger expected to end the war during their first year in office. The basis for their optimism was the presumed significance of four ideas Mr. Nixon brought to office: He would find a way to induce the Soviets to reduce their support for Hanoi; he would find a way to put his madman theory to work; he would offer North Vietnam better terms than the U.S. had ever offered; and, he would begin to withdraw American troops while trying to strengthen Thieu's army. Each idea was quickly put into operation, with Dr. Kissinger conscientiously following the President's lead at every turn. Dr. Kissinger asked several of his critics to "give us sixty days."[33] "The President was absolutely convinced he *would* end it in his first year." As they were walking on a beach, the President told H. R. Haldeman, "I'm the one man in this country who can do it, Bob."[34]

The President believed that he could convince the Soviet Union of the credibility of his threat, as he put it, "to act dramatically" if the Russians continued to support North Vietnam. There was no reason, he had earlier told delegates to the Republican Convention, for the Soviets to want an end to the war. It was, after all, going their way, with the United States expending thousands of lives, billions of dollars, and apparently stuck forever. The ominous threat would get the Russians' attention, but there also would have to be something in it for them. He would tell them, he said to one of his speech writers,

"If you are willing to give ground and help us out of this morass, it could mean lots of good things."[35] The good things he believed the Soviets wanted included more trade with the U.S. and an agreement to limit the arms race. If Mr. Nixon could strike a deal in Moscow, even going so far as the possibility of arms reduction, he thought he could get out of Vietnam and have "peace with honor." Everything depended on persuading the Soviets to step on Hanoi's supply hose.

Because Mr. Nixon and Dr. Kissinger both made a religion of power, they did not respect small nations and were contemptuous of weakness. As a result, they simply assumed that the mighty Kremlin could find a way to compel the North Vietnamese to call off their war. From the Soviet and Chinese perspective, however, what was at issue was the continuing leadership of the socialist world. The angry quarrel between Russia and China, cleverly exacerbated by the two Americans, made it more, not less, important for the Soviets to continue to lead in its remaining sphere of influence. Although the President's policy of relaxed tension with the Soviets did lead them to try to serve as a peacemaker with Hanoi from time to time, the Nixon-Kissinger hope that Moscow would bail us out of Vietnam was insubstantial.

The second idea required, if irrationality was to frighten the enemy, threats of a massive escalation of the war if serious negotiations did not begin. The President was an absolute master at issuing ominous, ambiguous warnings that could easily conjure up, even for a reasonable person, a vision of a mushroom cloud. For example, he warned, early in 1970: "[If the North took] advantage of our troop withdrawals to jeopardize the remainder of our forces by escalating the fighting, then we have the means—and I will be prepared to use those means strongly —to deal with that situation more strongly than we have dealt with it in the past."[36] What was stronger than history's heaviest bombing?

The desire to do something dramatic about Cambodia was present at the very start of the Nixon administration. In fact, on his first day in office the President asked the Joint Chiefs how to "quarantine" Cambodia.[37] The Pentagon, never at ease about a limited war that denied authorization to attack the enemy where he lived or where he hid, had always wanted to carry the war into the sanctuaries in Cambodia and Laos, where the North Vietnamese staged and launched attacks into the South.

Because LBJ had imposed a bombing halt over North Vietnam, the navy and air force bombers had been diverted over the Ho Chi Minh trail in Laos. The "secret war" in Laos was directed by the ambassador there, and was funded and organized by the CIA. Almost 5,600 bombing sorties were flown over Laos in 1969, 60 percent more than in the previous year, and about 160,000 tons of bombs were dropped. This was the model the Pentagon wanted to use elsewhere, all over Indochina.

On March 18, 1969, just weeks after his inauguration, the President ordered the secret bombing of Cambodia. (This did not become public until it was leaked to *The New York Times* four years later, during the Watergate furor. The bombing became the basis of an article of impeachment against the President, but was voted down.) The reasons for the bombing included a demand to "answer" hostilities by the North Vietnamese, the military's old wish to damage the Cambodian sanctuaries, the illusion (especially believed by Dr. Kissinger's new aide, Alexander Haig) that bombing could destroy North Vietnam's military headquarters, which was supposedly located just over the border, and the President's insistence on proving to the aged Ho Chi Minh and the Soviets that he was both unpredictable and dangerous. The reason to keep it secret, according to Dr. Kissinger, was diplomatic, while, according to the more candid President, it was to avoid antiwar protests after only two months in office.

Air force Colonel Ray B. Sitton was directed to plan the bombing as well as a deceptive reporting arrangement that made it appear that the huge B-52s had dropped their "payloads" only in South Vietnam. Dr. Kissinger even tried to persuade Colonel Sitton to keep the real location of the targets secret from the pilots and crews, but the colonel explained that they could figure it out anyway. Dr. Kissinger was so compulsive about the need for "total" secrecy that Colonel Sitton recalled that secrecy "was the concern—even above wanting to do it."[38] None of the facts of the bombing were entered into the normal and highly secret military command-and-control systems. The secret was so well kept that Colonel Sitton was promoted to brigadier general. His role was not discovered until "a senior Pentagon official" leaked it to Seymour Hersh in 1979.

The bombing continued for over a year. The President finally had authorized 3,600 flights, while the Pentagon calculated that 110,000 tons of bombs had been dropped on that neutral nation. The enemy's headquarters were not hit and not found, the sanctuaries were not "knocked out," but a metastatic rot had now infected the American government.

The Secretary of Defense, Melvin Laird, a former congressman from Wisconsin, opposed the secrecy and challenged the Joint Chiefs when they assured him that Cambodian civilians would not be killed, but he finally, as congressmen are trained to do, "went along." Mr. Laird was a shrewd, practical, manipulative political animal. He decided military questions against the measure of political expediency. Usually pleased with himself, understanding only the surface of things, if that, he had no particular difficulty in rating Vietnam in terms of how it would play in Peoria. His cynicism was vast, so he disliked the secrecy of the bombing only because he believed it would leak. Without imagination himself, Secretary Laird failed to appreciate the fact that both the President and Dr. Kissinger were much more creatively cynical than he could dream. The secret was kept by falsifying and destroying records, and by lying to the public, to the Congress, to the press, and to many officials within the administration.

The third idea was quietly announced by the President in a May 1969 televised speech devoted entirely to Vietnam. He did not admit that he was reversing President Johnson's demand that the North withdraw its troops first. But that was the significance of his proposition "for a simultaneous start on withdrawal by both sides, for agreement on a mutually acceptable timetable, and for the withdrawal to be accomplished quickly."[39] The State Department was unable to adjust to this abrupt change in policy, and pointlessly tried to argue against it, confirming in the President's mind something he had long suspected about foggy bottom.

The fourth idea was the most significant. While proposing to Hanoi that all troops in the South should go home at the same time, the President planned to begin withdrawing American troops first, without waiting for any agreement with North Vietnam. In June, the new President announced the first troop withdrawal of 25,000 men. This plan was quickly dressed up as the Nixon Doctrine, a significant reversal in American foreign policy, a repudiation of at least the spirit of the Truman Doctrine. Its most important element was that America would provide its allies with economic and military assistance, not manpower. This was how the Soviets and Chinese had dealt with Hanoi. The President intended to make Saigon as strong a proxy for us as Hanoi was for them. Mr. Nixon announced his intention in a curiously casual way on the island of Guam, in July. This doctrine (first called the Guam Doctrine until the President complained) led to the withdrawal of American troops from Vietnam, and the withdrawal led to the policy called Vietnamization.

It was not easy to keep the Pentagon quiet over the decision to withdraw the troops. General Creighton Abrams, the country commander now that General Westmoreland had been promoted to Army Chief of Staff, "oozed with distaste"[40] when he told the President that the scheme was too risky, and would look like surrender to Saigon. The JCS began a bureaucratic guerrilla war to change the President's mind. It was not much of a contest. In 1969, he ordered 65,500 troops home; in 1970, another 140,000; in 1971, another 160,000; and in 1972, a final 157,000, for a four-year total of 522,500.

However, it was slow, and more than 20,000 Americans died while waiting for the "freedom bird" to get them out of there. No one wanted to die in waiting, in a war that was now even more absurd than Johnson's. As a result of the decision to withdraw the troops, the discipline of the grunts collapsed, and much of the officer corps of the army, as we will see, degenerated into a vast self-serving bureaucratic organization dedicated to advancing the officers' careers at the expense of the safety of the GIs in their charge.

General Matthew Ridgway, so often accurate about Southeast Asia, wrote that Americans should "accept the judgment of . . . civilian authorities" about withdrawal for not more than six to nine months, "ample" time for training and supplying the South Vietnamese. After this period, America should leave "expeditiously."[41] The general failed to consider the fact seriously enough, as it finally became clear to almost everyone that the handicapped Saigon regime could never stand on its own feet.

Vietnamization had been an American aspiration from the very start, early in the 1960s. What was new was the decision actually to reduce the American presence to compel an improvement in South Vietnamese performance. Vietnamization was first intended to use the South Vietnamese as a shield to protect Americans, but later to train and equip them to the point when Americans could leave in confidence that the war would roll on. Vietnamization, however, could succeed only if the South Vietnamese wanted it and were capable of making it work. In planning Vietnamization, the war's engineers, especially in the Pentagon, made their by now characteristic error of focusing more on us and not enough on the Vietnamese.

Meanwhile, President Thieu's attitude simply hardened, if that was possible, as his anxiety grew that the Americans were still determined to get out of Vietnam, and that they would strike a deal that would force him to cooperate with the NLF, now organized as the Provisional Revolutionary Government, a government-in-waiting. Should that happen, Thieu believed that his entire war effort was pointless. He made a characteristic offer to members of the NLF that they would be allowed to participate in a free election if they repudiated Communism, turned over their arms to the government, and agreed to accept the current constitution of the South as legitimate and binding, that is, if they surrendered.

Mr. Nixon and Dr. Kissinger made a good bureaucratic team, despite Dr. Kissinger's obsequiousness in front of the President and hypocrisy behind his back. The boss knew that he could rely on his subordinate's loyalty, at least in public, because Dr. Kissinger's career was in the President's hands. Dr. Kissinger knew that he could count on the President to support him because he was sufficiently careful never to challenge Mr. Nixon's view of reality, or his tactics for changing the world, and because Dr. Kissinger knew what to do to protect himself. He understood the bureaucratic maxim that one gains credit by giving it away, especially to the boss. Elsewhere he might raise his eyebrows as he described yet another of the President's supposedly brilliant flashes of insight about the nature of the world. In his own office, Dr. Kissinger described the President as having "a meatball mind."[42] Seymour Hersh wrote:

> Kissinger's backbiting began almost immediately. Rogers was a corrupt "fag" who had some strange hold over Richard Nixon; Laird was a megalomaniac who constantly

leaked anti-Kissinger stories to the press; Richard Nixon was a secret drunk of dubious intelligence.[43]

Dr. Kissinger needed President Nixon most of all as protection in his bureaucratic battles. To maintain his ascendancy in foreign affairs, he had to beat William Rogers, the Secretary of State. He could accomplish this by stealth, by keeping the Secretary in the dark about foreign affairs, and by agreeing to wiretap or co-opt members of the Secretary's staff. He put Alexander Haig in charge of the wiretaps. But this was merely routine bureaucratic gamesmanship. He could never win an all-out struggle unless he fought as the proxy of the President. Armed with the President's safe-conduct pass, he could not lose. Later, President Nixon wrote: "Rogers felt that Kissinger was Machiavellian, deceitful, egotistical, arrogant, and insulting." He also described the other side: "Kissinger felt that Rogers was vain, uninformed, unable to keep a secret and hopelessly dominated by the State Department bureaucracy."[44] The President felt that each man was right about the other.

The relationship between President Nixon and Dr. Kissinger was mutually enriching and parasitic. It was a partnership of Dr. Kissinger's intelligence and knowledge and the President's superhuman determination to impose his will on the weak, such as Vietnam, and on the ignorant, such as the Congress and the public. Both men respected the Kremlin more than the Congress. Their relationship was consummated in a shared dedication to secrecy, which always tends toward a conspiratorial view of political and human affairs. It was a marriage, therefore, whose affairs were best conducted in private, in whispers, and in the dark.

A relationship between a master and his manservant is hardly based on equality, even though the subordinate may through guile and petty theft accumulate substantial means to protect himself. From the beginning of his service to the President, Dr. Kissinger regularly shipped documents for safekeeping to Nelson Rockefeller's New York estate. To keep a record of phone conversations, he often had one of his own staff listen in on calls to or from the President. For his part, the President's intricate taping system in the Oval Office in time automatically recorded everything that Dr. Kissinger or anyone else said. Dr. Kissinger kept a log of all his meetings with the President, and Mr. Nixon regretted that he did not have the time to keep his own. Both men were constantly building a record to be used against the other.

They learned to distrust each other with the restraint required by the secrets of the other. Dr. Kissinger, however, also had to use the weapons of the contemporary bureaucratic courtier. He endlessly and outrageously flattered the President, as the President required. He frequently charmed the compliant Washington press columnists, such as James Reston of *The New York Times,* into publishing articles that would help him to hold his job by demeaning his bureaucratic competitors for the President's favor, or by implicitly informing his boss to be careful because his notorious manipulation of the press might someday be dangerous.

At the end of April 1970, 32,000 Americans and 48,000 South Vietnamese invaded—the White House called it an incursion— Cambodia with three major results: Cambodia was shoved into a murderous war, North Vietnam widened its war throughout Indochina, and the President was besieged. He told the nation that the invasion was a success because vast amounts of supplies had been captured—as much ammunition as the guerrillas had fired in the previous year (how anyone could have this information is beyond speculation), and enough rice to feed the North's troops in the South for four months. He claimed 11,349 enemy killed. More important, he said, "We have ended the concept of Cambodian sanctuaries, immune from attack, upon which the enemy military had relied for 5 years." He reported that the invasion ensured continued safe withdrawal of American troops, and the valorous fighting of the South Vietnamese provided "visible proof of the success of Vietnamization."[45]

Dr. Kissinger actively supported the President's desire to invade. One of his NSC aides explained Dr. Kissinger's decision:

> I don't think that Kissinger would have dared at that stage in the game to appear in a posture which would have compromised him in the eyes of the president. It was very important that Henry establish at least one experience in which the president did something demonstratively unpopular, even unpopular in the bureaucracy, to which Laird and Rogers were opposed, which created a terrific

storm in the country, which confirmed all of Nixon's paranoia about the media and about the rest of the government,
all the things Nixon liked to talk about and to worry about
—*and that Henry was on his side.* And Henry was willing to
cut the ties as well with lots of his friends. I think that kind
of credibility with Nixon when the going got tough—and
Henry was there—was essential to everything else that
Kissinger pursued. The one constituency that he could not
afford to lose was Nixon. . . . He wasn't yet the superstar.
He needed Nixon desperately. This was not a matter of
principle, it was a demonstration of loyalty. . . . Cambodia
is explained very much in terms of the politics of the White
House. That was Kissinger's first triumph, the precondition of everything else he ever did; Cambodia was the turning point.[46]

When Dr. Kissinger reviewed the intention to use American
ground forces in an invasion of Cambodia, his own staff tried to
argue him out of it. He responded, "We are all the President's
men." Four of his close aides—Tony Lake, Roger Morris, William Watts from the Foreign Service, and Dr. Larry Lynn, a
former Whiz Kid in Mr. McNamara's Defense Department—
resigned in protest. Morton Halperin and others had resigned
earlier. Roger Morris said that he and Tony Lake had considered making public their reasons to resign: "to tell the public
about the wiretapping and Nixon's drinking." He thought his
failure to talk out loud was "the biggest failure of my life."[47] As
several witnesses reported it, when Mr. Watts informed Dr.
Kissinger that he was going to resign because he objected to the
invasion, Dr. Kissinger responded, "Your views represent the
cowardice of the Eastern Establishment." When Mr. Watts left
his boss's office to write his letter of resignation, Alexander Haig
shouted at Mr. Watts that he could not resign in the face of "an
order from your commander in chief." Mr. Watts responded:
"Fuck you, Al. I just did."[48]

Other staffers in the White House became anxious when they
learned about the invasion. Dr. Kissinger explained, "We're not
interested in Cambodia. . . . We're trying to shock the Soviets
into calling a Conference, and we can't do this by appearing to
be weak." William Safire, one of the President's speech writers,
asked whether the use of American troops would not violate the

Nixon Doctrine, which had proclaimed that the U.S. would aid Asians with equipment and advice but not with American ground forces. Dr. Kissinger answered, "We wrote the goddam doctrine, we can change it." But it remained for Alexander Haig to summarize the meeting, which he did by jumping to his feet and shouting: "The basic substance of all this is that we have to be tough."[49]

The Secretaries of State and of Defense were deliberately kept ignorant of the extent of the Cambodian invasion planning, and it was now undeniable that Dr. Kissinger on a strong leash to the President was running the nation's foreign policy. So long as the President continued to hold Dr. Kissinger's hand, it was no contest. Dr. Kissinger would win, the President and the Joint Chiefs could have their invasion, and Dr. Kissinger, as the good and loyal bureaucrat who served at the pleasure of the boss, would "follow-up," would make sure that the planning actually turned into operations.

The search for a military solution to the Vietnam War was always an expression of American cultural pride and frustration. This fact was not overlooked by the North. It always relied on the American public's unwillingness to struggle on in the rice paddies forever, especially as the casualties increased. They could fight a war of attrition and succeed, as General Westmoreland attempted to but could not. The Vietnam equation therefore could not be solved: The American military wanted to "win," while the North Vietnamese wanted to avoid losing long enough to force the American administration to pay an increasing domestic price. That is what happened to France in the early 1950s. There was every sign that it would happen to America. The military solution not only failed to comprehend the politics of the Vietnamese, it also failed to comprehend politics at home. But that is not strictly the business of the military. More to the point, the Nixon administration made the same mistakes. And its strict business was politics.

Mr. Nixon's announcement to the nation of the Cambodian "incursion" was based on the lie that we had respected Cambodian neutrality, but he did not mention the bombing. Neither did Dr. Kissinger in his press briefings. The President said the invasion was intended to destroy the North Vietnamese military headquarters that the Pentagon had long believed was located just over the Cambodian border, although all the intelligence reports showed that it was not there, and, as a fixed facility, never even existed. Secretary Laird told that to the President several times.

The invasion had several immediate consequences. The domestic protest reached its most passionate and widespread level. The Congress finally settled into determined opposition to the war. Students were killed at Kent State University and at Jackson State in Mississippi. Close to five hundred campuses were shut down in protest. The President referred to student antiwar critics as "bums." The President, and "all the President's men," nourished their deepening paranoia, dug in their heels, and prepared to "tough it out."

At a Pentagon briefing the day after the invasion was launched, the President was unable to follow the discussion and interrupted the meeting with a rambling monologue in which he kept repeating that he was "going to clean up those sanctuaries." The Joint Chiefs, the Secretary of Defense, and Dr. Kissinger sat quietly in embarrassment as the President shouted: "Let's go blow the hell out of them."[50] The President, responding to the wave of public and congressional protests, wanted to stiffen the spine of his own staff members. He told them: "Don't worry about divisiveness. Having drawn the sword, don't take it out—stick it in hard. . . . Hit 'em in the gut. No defensiveness."[51]

The consequence of the Cambodian invasion was primarily to force the North Vietnamese to abandon their border positions and to withdraw westward, fanning out all over the populated areas of Cambodia and therefore sucking the war in behind them. The President intended to move the North Vietnamese away from the border, and to minimize American casualties. American "strategists" were once again annoyed that the North Vietnamese refused to stand up and fight. They once again melted away from an engagement they did not want, and prepared to fight another day.

The day following the invasion, the Senate Foreign Relations Committee voted to repeal President Johnson's Tonkin Gulf Resolution, still the only arguably legal basis for America's intervention in Vietnam. It also recommended, and the Senate approved, a bill to prohibit the use of American troops in Cambodia after about six weeks. It was the first time the Senate imposed a limitation on the Vietnam War Presidents.

When the Senate's action forced Mr. Nixon to abandon the invasion, he told a television audience that the operation had been a thorough success. However, instead of convincing the world of American "credibility," it backfired. Instead of intimidating the Senate with the toughness of the administration, it finally moved that typically reluctant body into action. The President's announcement of the invasion's success was simply another manifestation of his toughness, an attribute that was increasingly separating him from the realities of political life.

The President told the American people that the invasion of Cambodia had provided "visible proof" of the success of the policy of strengthening the forces of the South, so that they could assume their own defense as Americans left. It is not possible to know whether the President or Dr. Kissinger actually believed that Vietnamization was working, but they decided to test it in a way that could not be kept secret. In February 1971, the President ordered an invasion of Laos to be conducted exclusively by the South Vietnamese army. Because of Senate prohibitions, Americans were now restricted to providing only airlift support. The invasion was designed to cut the Ho Chi Minh trail.

It was a military and human disaster. The South Vietnamese walked into a trap, confronted tanks which no one realized were there, were mutilated, and fled. Their rescue by Americans was shown on American television, with South Vietnamese dangling from the helicopter skids. Some pretended to be wounded to be evacuated early, and some American helicopter crews were so enraged by such conduct that they wounded or killed some of the fakers. Almost 10,000 South Vietnamese and about 300 Americans were killed or wounded.

This carnage finally did provide "visible proof" about Vietnamization, not, as Mr. Nixon asserted, of its success, but of its failure. From the start, the policy had been built on American desires, not on Vietnamese reality. Yet, this mentality had shaped the entire war, from John Kennedy forward. Facts were not wanted. The CIA, distrusted by the President, had not been asked for an intelligence estimate before the invasion was launched. For the American war managers, wishes always replaced facts. The South's army was rotten and all the equipment that America provided made little difference. Its soldiers, at least at one time, had to pay their officers to provide artillery support.

It was impossible for the Thieu government to plan or take a step without Hanoi finding out about it. Every detail of the Laotian invasion was known by the enemy, including the location of the helicopter landing zones, as was proved by captured North Vietnamese documents. Samuel Adams, an analyst working in the CIA who was in deep disfavor in the Agency because he had been right so many times in the past, said: "Hell, they had every goddamned order, every change of plans."[52] In time the CIA learned that Thieu's chief of counterespionage was a spy.

Thieu's increasing rigidity may have been a result of the arrest and conviction of forty members of his government as spies for North Vietnam, including his special assistant for political affairs, and the even more influential Vu Ngoc Nha, his friend and adviser on Catholic affairs. CIA field officers broke the case, to the great displeasure of CIA headquarters in Virginia which would have preferred to avoid embarrassing President Thieu. Or perhaps the CIA elders did not wish to advertise how easy it had been for the North to penetrate Thieu's government while the CIA never recruited a single important agent from within the NLF.

From the Tet offensive until early 1972, the North Vietnamese had not been especially aggressive on the battlefield. One reason was that the North had suffered so many losses during Tet 68 that it was forced to recover and regroup before mounting another attack. That was one reason for the Pentagon's optimism. The North's explanation was that it was merely waiting for the right time, for President Nixon's troop withdrawals, and for the impact of American war protests to be more fully felt throughout the American government. One Saigon correspondent estimated that by the end of 1971 there was not even one North Vietnamese main-force division in the South.[53]

At Easter 1972, South Vietnam exploded. The North's intention in this new offensive was to damage the South Vietnamese army badly enough so that Vietnamization could not work. It also intended to bring maximum pressure on the President in an election year. The offensive was based on two goals: to return main-force units to the South to engage the South's army, and to revive guerrilla activity in the areas where the South's army would be forced to leave. Both goals were partly achieved. The desertions of southerners to the North were unprecedented, including the defection of an entire regiment and its officers. The South's army lost 70,000 troops in three months, of which 20,000 were deserters; an additional 70,000 local militia were lost either through casualties, surrender, or desertion. The United States estimated that the North also lost 70,000, including guerrillas. Before the offensive, only 7 hamlets were controlled by organizations sympathetic to the North; immediately after it, the official figure rose to almost 1,400. General Abrams sent a cable to the White House reporting that the South Vietnamese had no will to fight, and that the entire war may have been lost. Nonetheless, the Easter offensive failed for the North as its forces were unable to hold what they won.

President Nixon responded with massive B-52 raids on North Vietnam, including the city of Haiphong, whose port was now mined. This sent Mr. Nixon's popularity soaring. He defended this on the grounds that it would save lives by denying resources to the North. It did not work. These raids showed that the war was not diminishing, and that President Nixon seemed, like his predecessors, stuck.

In America, the aftermath of the Easter invasion was pure presidential politics. It was the summer of the nominating conventions, and Mr. Nixon was already worried that he might win. Never in American history had there been such a sore winner. When this sulk befell him, his political instincts took over. Just before the Republican presidential nominating convention, the last American combat troops were withdrawn from Vietnam, and the President announced that the draft would end in July 1973. Both actions guaranteed that domestic protest would collapse and that candidate Nixon could present himself as the architect of peace.

Earlier, the President had sent Dr. Kissinger to Paris to begin secret peace negotiations. The opening position was that the United States would not negotiate a political settlement in Saigon until two conditions had been met: withdrawal of the North's army and a full exchange of prisoners. What this meant in practice was that we wanted to get out safely, but also wanted to avoid any backfire that would occur if, probably when, the final political settlement failed. Our opening position was to get out in a way that would place the blame for political failure on the incompetence of our allies in the South, or treachery in the North, or both.   .

As Dr. Kissinger predicted before he joined the administration, the great differences in diplomatic style between the North Vietnamese and the Americans drove the Americans crazy. It was designed to do so. According to Dr. Kissinger the Vietnamese negotiate on the model of guerrilla warfare—jabbing, running, hiding, ambushing. They plan. Americans are allergic to planning; we prefer the pragmatic give and take of on-the-spot bargaining. Our models seem to be labor negotiations, plea bargaining, and haggling over the price of a souvenir in a foreign flea market.

The result was that periodically, during the exquisitely painful fits and starts toward negotiation, the highest officers of our government did not understand what the North was talking about. For example, in a press conference early in 1968, President Johnson revealed his own bewilderment: "As near as I am able to detect, Hanoi has not changed its course of conduct since the very first response it made. Sometimes they will change 'will' to 'would' or 'shall' to 'should,' or something of the kind. But the answer is all the same."[54]

The North demanded and America refused to discuss the nature of the postwar government in Saigon. This kept the Paris talks dragging on through the summer of 1972. By then the North had made a series of concessions about the allocation of political power in the South, but Dr. Kissinger successfully deceived the western press by denying that there had been any change in the attitude of the North. President Nixon and Dr. Kissinger both were obviously willing for the war to continue rather than to become implicated in the political future of the South. This obviously made a shambles of Dr. Kissinger's earlier criticisms of the Johnson administration's failure to consider the politics of the war in its maniacal fixation on the military aspects. It was, however, a possible way out if only the North would forget politics long enough to allow Americans to congratulate themselves for achieving "peace with honor," at which point the North could continue the war on its own terms, unless the President had some way to continue fighting after the war.

Years later, Dr. Kissinger was still at it, congratulating America for beating the Communists on the battlefield during Tet and 1972, while continuing to acknowledge that the North was fighting a different kind of war. "As in 1968, Hanoi opted for psychological rather than military impact by launching a countrywide offensive, which, as then, led to its military defeat."[55] The premier advocate of international psychological manipulation was being manipulated and was not amused. He was unable to make his own knowledge about Hanoi's strategy operational in Paris. He knew what the North was doing, but had no defense. After he was appointed to office, he respected America's raw force too much. Before he was in office, he had known better.

Mr. Nixon's emphasis on big-power maneuvering had also produced an unintended consequence. His emphasis on détente may have denied more active military help to North Vietnam when it thought it needed it and had a right to it. The Chinese and Russian dispute, the Chinese reception of the President, and the increasing anxiety in the Kremlin, all dampened enthusiasm in both Peking and Moscow for Hanoi's war. But this finally proved that the earlier confidence on the part of both Mr. Nixon and Dr. Kissinger had been groundless. Now that détente had at least slowed down the Soviets, Hanoi continued to fight, and once again Americans underestimated North Vietnam.

Détente proved to Hanoi that the traditional Vietnamese hatred of the Chinese, as well as fear of the Soviets, were justifiable. It was willing to fight the war by itself, continuing, however, to receive supplies from its suspect socialist allies. The President's much heralded successes with big-power diplomacy simply revealed that the North could still mount the Easter offensive. It also revealed that the mind-set of the Nixon administration was at least as incompetent as its predecessors. For the fact was that if the war was ever to end, Washington would have to find some sort of an accommodation with "the fourth class Communist peasants" in Hanoi.

Dr. Kissinger never gave up his desire to weave "a complex web" of diplomacy and death to isolate Hanoi. His intelligence led him to plausible analyses of the Kremlin. His ability to make his case was impressive: "We had more to lose in Vietnam than Moscow stood to gain by our humiliation. Thus in an odd way our bargaining position was stronger; our threats were more plausible."[56] This interesting viewpoint ignored the fact that the Soviet Union, like any other nation, would prefer, as Napoleon once advised, not to interfere with an opponent when it is failing. Dr. Kissinger's perspective ignored the facts of power, an unusual omission for one of power's sweethearts. The Soviets would not risk their empire for better trade relations with the U.S. He overestimated Soviet flexibility and underestimated paranoia. He overestimated the significance of Mr. Nixon's trip to China, although it was important in raising the level of Soviet anxiety. Mr. Nixon and Dr. Kissinger almost succeeded in isolating Hanoi. That near success and Hanoi's continued struggle should have taught the Americans something.

In October 1972, just weeks before the presidential election, the North Vietnamese presented Dr. Kissinger with a complete draft of a peace settlement, the first complete version presented by either side during the five years of negotiations. They dropped their earlier insistence that Thieu had to go, and they agreed to elections within six months after peace had been established. The President permitted Dr. Kissinger to negotiate on the basis of these concessions. The CIA and the State Department learned the contents of the draft only because a North Vietnamese who was a CIA spy received a copy at a briefing in North Vietnam and gave it to the CIA in Saigon.

In virtually all details, the North Vietnamese draft became what all the negotiators, including Dr. Kissinger, believed would be the final agreement. This draft was successful because Dr. Kissinger had ordered his staff in Paris to throw out the tough counterproposal they had prepared. "You don't understand," he shouted, "I want to meet their terms. I want to reach an agreement. I want to end this war before the elections."[57] The draft was acceptable to Mr. Nixon who told the leaders of North Vietnam on October 21, "The text of the agreement could be considered complete."[58]

Peace became possible because the U.S. and North Vietnam each made a significant concession, however slowly. The U.S. agreed that the North Vietnamese troops could remain in the South after the peace was signed. Both sides agreed that the details of the government in the South could not be worked out in the agreement itself, and that, somehow, this would be negotiated after the peace was signed, after the Americans had left, and in the presence of the North's army in place in the South.

Everything seemed in order until President Thieu balked,

and President Nixon, just before the election, was unwilling to face the outcry that might develop if Thieu denounced the peace as an American surrender to Communism. Dr. Kissinger's most arrogant mistake was his assumption that he could persuade Thieu to cooperate. President Nixon had, in effect, given Thieu the power to veto the peace, as Dr. Kissinger had promised in the Paris negotiations would not happen. What Thieu wanted, according to Dr. Kissinger, was "unabated United States support until his enemy disintegrated,"[59] and that provided Dr. Kissinger with another lesson about the Vietnamese. He wrote, "In September 1972 a second Vietnamese party—our own ally —had managed to generate in me that impotent rage by which the Vietnamese have always tormented physically stronger opponents."[60] The lesson might not have been that he could be made to lose his temper, but that it was not enough to be merely physically stronger. Mr. Nixon was forced to choose between appeasing Thieu and demonstrating his bad faith to the North. He chose betrayal, the "lesser hazard."[61]

Six years earlier, Dr. Kissinger had written that the American style of negotiating often led the negotiators to support the "maximum range of concessions" while they usually ended up trying to mediate "between Washington and the country with which they are negotiating."[62] In his own present negotiations, however, he could not mediate between Mr. Nixon and Hanoi. He was afraid of getting sacked, and had evidence that he would have been.

This was the only time that the President lost control of Dr. Kissinger, who wanted to end the war before Mr. Nixon was ready. This bureaucratic lapse on Dr. Kissinger's part convinced the President to fire him. A closely related problem was that Mr. Nixon was worried about Dr. Kissinger's growing popularity. H. R. Haldeman tried to make it seem merely funny:

Henry's popularity was a problem on the 1972 campaign trail. We'd arrive at an airport, and when Henry came out of the plane a roar from the crowd would go up. Everyone recognized him. This was fine except Henry would play to the crowds. He'd go right over to the fence and start shaking hands down the line of people just as if he were the candidate. By the time Nixon emerged from the plane all eyes were on Henry far down the line.

217

Nixon told me to stop it, so I told Henry it was all right to respond to the cheers, but to leave the handshaking to the President. Henry smiled. "You're just jealous, Herr Haldeman." But we would only make it through a few more airport ceremonies before he would forget and plunge happily into the crowd again.[63]

There is no hint that Mr. Nixon was amused. When he asked his favorite pollster whether he was as popular as Dr. Kissinger, and heard that they were about equal, the President "gulped."[64] It was important to the President to have Dr. Kissinger fail in some spectacular way.

Dr. Kissinger not only got back into line, but instantly became holier than the Pope, more hawkish than the President. He was threatened, chastened, broken, and later promoted. Mr. Nixon's performance in that crisis in their relationship was masterly but, given Dr. Kissinger's ambitions, relatively easy. Dr. Kissinger's performance was equally impressive but, given his obligatory instantaneous conversion, probably not so easy. What he did was to subordinate his values and principles to his career, and it would be ungenerous to fail to recognize the magnitude of his achievement.

In Mr. Nixon's world, what was apparent was never real. Bad faith was perceived merely as the way adults carry out their business. He seemed to spend his life in the dark, surrounded by hidden hissing things that threatened to poison everything —his plans, hopes, career, probably even his life. He lived his nightmare by gritting his teeth, by trying to be tougher than his fears. Because of his deep belief that he was surrounded by enemies, he had no trust, no generosity, and no belief that things would turn out the way he wished. He expected to fail, but insisted that no one help him toward that end. One reason for his secretiveness was the fear that someone would find him out.

At first, when peace began to seem possible, the President was delighted. He wanted an agreement to secure his coming election so much that he was ready to fire off another of his famous threats to force the North Vietnamese to get on with it. Charles Colson, a close political aide of the President, remembered that Mr. Nixon instructed Dr. Kissinger: "Henry, you tell those sons of bitches that the President is a madman and you don't know how to deal with him. Once reelected I'll be a mad bomber."[65]

But then his popularity was rising in the opinion polls, and he began to wonder whether peace might not hurt him, whether the risk of peace was worth it.

Mr. Nixon lied to the North Vietnamese to delay signing the peace treaty until after the election, and until the airlift of supplies to the South could complete the resupply. If we could only stuff enough hardware into Thieu's warehouses, he could continue the fight to a victorious conclusion, or else lose on his own despite the fact that we had given him the means necessary to win. Either way, in this world of images and symbols, President Nixon thought he could be a hero, at least for a little while. It was a virtuoso's display of deceit.

What President Nixon accomplished by playing games with peace was to enrage both South and North Vietnam. Dr. Kissinger also shared this achievement: "So at the end of the war we managed to 'unite' the two Vietnamese parties after all—in their common alarm at American objectives and eventually their common dislike and distrust of the principal American negotiator."[66] Hanoi understood what the Americans were up to and it made public the terms of the peace agreement that the President had accepted and then sabotaged. Because Dr. Kissinger's acceptance of a pre-election deadline had created the mess, Mr. Nixon accepted Dr. Kissinger's suggestion that he should appear on television to defuse the crisis. In all his years of closeting the truth and manipulating the press to serve his own interests, it was perhaps Dr. Kissinger's most effective and dangerous performance. He declared that "peace is at hand,"[67] thereby creating a rush of anticipation across America and the world.

The details of the remaining difficulties simply got lost in the prospect of an end to America's longest agony. And the very point of his show, from the President's perspective, became sidetracked. He assured the nation that the negotiations had achieved all of America's basic goals, that the North had misunderstood the details about the deadline for signing the agreement, and that in all other ways he had negotiated a quite splendid conclusion to the war that had been inherited from the Democrats. None of it mattered in the context of a peace that could be wrapped up in one more round of negotiations with the tricky Communists. What Dr. Kissinger actually meant by saying that "peace is at hand," was that the President had decided that the war would continue.

One informed student of the peace negotiations analyzed Dr. Kissinger's performance:

> Kissinger's presentation of the problems remaining attempted to obscure the fact that the United States was reopening negotiations which had already been formally closed on October 22. To the North Vietnamese Kissinger's press conference could only be read as confirmation of their fears that they had been manipulated by Nixon and Kissinger in order to have the appearance of a peace agreement within sight just before the election, and that the American position would begin to harden as soon as Nixon was reelected. Significantly, Kissinger did not bother to cite Saigon's objections as the reason for requiring further negotiations. He made it clear that the United States would support only those objections with which it agreed and not those which it felt unnecessary, thus confirming Hanoi's view that the United States had merely used Saigon's opposition to the agreement to cover its *volte-face.*[68]

For all of Dr. Kissinger's cleverness at bending the facts at his press conference, he had now promised the American public too much. The President believed that Dr. Kissinger had weakened the bargaining position of the United States. If peace was at hand, the public and the Congress would no longer tolerate endless delays, verbal assurances, or patent duplicity. Dr. Kissinger was usually so much the master of self-serving ambiguity as to satisfy the most finicky connoisseur of such matters. But now he had failed. If peace was as near as he said, America wanted to have it in, not at, hand. After a meeting with the boss, as Mr. Nixon wrote, Dr. Kissinger "soon realized it was a mistake to have gone so far."[69] The security adviser was aware of his own insecurity.

The false expectation of peace worked against the President's determination to force more concessions in Thieu's favor from North Vietnam. Dr. Kissinger warned the North Vietnamese that if they did not yield to President's Nixon's will, they would be made to suffer the most terrible consequences, worse than anything the United States had yet done. Believing that an agreement had already been reached, offended by the American lies, and too proud to bow to threats, the North unsurprisingly refused to budge. So President Nixon authorized the Christmas bombing of North Vietnam's two cities, Hanoi and Haiphong. There is no uncertainty about what the President had in mind because his phoned instructions to the Chairman of the Joint Chiefs of Staff sparkled with clarity: "I don't want any more of this crap about the fact that we couldn't hit this target or that one. This is your chance to use military power effectively to win this war, and if you don't, I'll consider you responsible."[70]

The B-52 bombing was intense, with entire neighborhoods obliterated by 36,000 tons of bombs. About 2,000 civilians were killed, but thousands more were saved because the North anticipated the onslaught and had evacuated large sections of Hanoi. It was, like Tet, a successful military operation that the President of the United States lost. As usual, the American war Presidents seemed oblivious to the political repercussions of their military successes. The Christmas bombing did not change the negotiating position of Hanoi. What it did accomplish was to turn more pilots and crews into prisoners of war. Because Hanoi believed that the American POWs were its best negotiating issue, the increase in sorties and the consequent increase in POWs actually weakened the American position at the bargaining table, as well as across America.

The military success of the bombing also persuaded the Russians and the Chinese to close ranks with the North Vietnamese, thereby erasing whatever success there might have been in the President's policy of détente. Still, if the horror of the bombing terrified people all over the world, that would fit in with the President's negotiating strategy. On the day the bombing started, Mr. Nixon told a columnist, "The Russians and the Chinese might think they were dealing with a madman and so had better force North Vietnam into a settlement before the world was consumed by a larger war."[71] Whatever the Communist nations thought of Mr. Nixon, they came to the aid of Hanoi and were bitter in their denunciation of what Hanoi called "extermination bombing."[72]

The domestic response did not surprise the President. As he recounted in his memoirs, *The Washington Post* wrote that the bombing caused Americans "to cringe in shame and to wonder at their President's very sanity." Columnists for *The New York Times*, again as preserved by Mr. Nixon, concluded that this was "war by tantrum," and that he was acting "like a maddened tyrant."[73] The President believed that the national outburst was merely the liberal-left media's first opportunity to get back at him after his overwhelming reelection victory which they had tried to prevent. The Christmas bombing, however, reduced what he repeatedly referred to as "my mandate" to an overnight low in public approval of 39 percent.

Mr. Nixon wrote that the decision to hit the two cities was his "most difficult" decision of the Vietnam War, but it was "the tough decision."[74] In March 1973, he told the nation that his decision had been forced because "the North Vietnamese stone-walled us at the conference table."[75] He was fortunate to have the support of Dr. Kissinger: "Henry talked rather emotionally about the fact that this was a very courageous decision,"[76] the President noted in his diary. "Henry" did, however, vacillate from day to day, but the President never flinched. Many staff members could not understand why Mr. Nixon did not explain to the public his reasons to bomb. "I did not feel that the American people were ready to be rallied at this time."[77]

It was necessary to rally President Thieu. Mr. Nixon was now in a frothing rage about Thieu's foot dragging, as he said to Dr. Kissinger: "Brutality is nothing. You have never seen it if this son-of-a-bitch doesn't go along, believe me."[78] To ensure that Thieu would not again resist President Nixon's will, Alexander Haig was ordered to carry a letter, written by the President, to Saigon. "General Haig's mission," the President wrote to Thieu, "now represents my final effort to point out to you the necessity for joint action and to convey my irrevocable intention to proceed, preferably with your cooperation, but, if necessary alone."[79] Thieu concluded that this letter was not about peace, but about whether he would continue to get American aid. General Haig agreed with this interpretation. Thieu shocked Mr. Nixon by telling reporters that he had refused to knuckle under to an American ultimatum.

The North Vietnamese agreed to resume negotiations in early January 1973. After twelve days the bombing was stopped. It is uncertain whether the bombing caused Hanoi to resume negotiations. What is clear is that the effects of the bombing not only forced Mr. Nixon to resume the negotiations, but also forced him to instruct Dr. Kissinger to sign an agreement. Dr. Kissinger believed that the United States had two alternatives: to get a quick settlement on the best terms obtainable, or to abandon Thieu and continue bombing until Hanoi released the American POWs in a trade for complete American withdrawal. The President was now determined to get out as fast as possible, as he noted in his diary: "Adding it all up I put it to Henry quite directly that even if we could go back to the October 8 agreement that we should take it, having in mind . . . that we can claim some improvement over that agreement."[80]

His willingness to reaccept the October 8 agreement means that the December bombing had produced no significant negotiating results. President Nixon correctly assumed that once he had made up his mind to have peace, the war would end. Thus, at the end of the meeting in which he instructed Dr. Kissinger about the forthcoming negotiations, he said: "Well, one way or another, this is it!"[81] This assumption that peace was his decision shows that the earlier delays and frustrations in ending the war had not been the result of North Vietnamese stalling or frivolity. The world and the peace only had to wait for the American President.

One reason why President Nixon concluded that peace now had to be arranged was the terrible surprise that Hanoi had prepared during the bombing. The North Vietnamese had always assumed that Hanoi and Haiphong would be bombed. They had prepared antiaircraft defenses, mostly Soviet-built SAMs, in the months preceeding the decision to bomb, and had made dramatic improvements in the effectiveness of their radars. An air force general described what the American crews faced: "The most concentrated air defense system in the world."[82] Some pilots and crews refused to fly, and members of the highly secret 6990th Air Force Security Service refused to monitor the North's SAM activities to protect the B-52s. This was mutiny and many were court-martialed, although only one was convicted.

Before the Christmas bombing, the U.S. had lost only one B-52. After the bombing, Hanoi claimed that thirty-four B-52s were shot down, while America admitted to fifteen. Thirty-one more pilots became prisoners. It was an unacceptable cost. A historian concluded that such losses raised "fears among the Joint Chiefs that America's strategic air arm might be indefinitely crippled."[83] Mr. Nixon almost admitted as much: "My major concern during the first week of bombing was not the sharp wave of domestic and international criticism, which I had expected, but the high losses of B-52s."[84]

The concern about the loss of so many B-52s spread to the Congress. Daniel Flood, a member of the House Defense Appropriations Committee, expressed what was probably the typical sense of outrage to the Chairman of the Joint Chiefs:

> My, my, my . . . that the Pentagon, that they were going to be handcuffed by some little country called North Vietnam and completely knocked off balance, good gravy . . . here this little backward, these gooks . . . are knocking down your B-52s like clay-pigeons, with all the sophisticated hardware which was beyond our own ken, being run by 'gooks.' This is some kind of lesson.[85]

The President's decision to bomb the cities was the last such decision he would make concerning the war. The bombing failed on every count, including the unanticipated reconstitution of a common purpose in Hanoi, Peking, and Moscow. Mr. Nixon's earlier conviction, shared by Dr. Kissinger, that he could maneuver peace in Vietnam through the Kremlin was exploded by the decision to bomb. America was isolated in the world. The President ordered Dr. Kissinger to return to Paris and arrange whatever "deal" was still possible. But when the negotiators reconvened in Paris, the anger of the North Vietnamese was uncontrollable, which, for those intensely disciplined individuals, was rare. The Americans had to ask the leader of Hanoi's team to stop shouting for fear the press would overhear. The North, in short, went back to Paris determined not to give another inch to the duplicitous Americans.

What the Americans wanted was to get the prisoners back, to throw up a smokescreen about the disposition of the government in Saigon, and to get out in the fastest way possible. That is what Dr. Kissinger negotiated in the last round of talks in Paris. The final agreement was concluded on January 9, 1973, and Dr. Kissinger sent a cable to the President: "What has brought us to this point is the President's firmness. . . ."[86]

Dr. Kissinger and his opposite number on the North Vietnamese team were later awarded Nobel Peace Prizes. President

Nixon was envious because he thought he, not Dr. Kissinger, deserved the prize. Le Duc Tho refused his award. When Saigon was captured by the North Vietnamese in 1975, Dr. Kissinger sent his back, but the Nobel committee returned it to him.

President Thieu finally agreed to the peace because he had no choice, and because Mr. Nixon had personally and secretly assured him that America would protect the peace in South Vietnam by continuing to bomb after a peace agreement had been signed: "We will respond with full force should the settlement be violated by North Vietnam."[87] This was the final symptom of what had become ego diplomacy, not foreseen in the Constitution. The Pentagon completed plans for post-peace bombing on November 20, 1972. Actions by the Congress finally stopped that and forced America to get out all the way. The North Vietnamese believe that the President also promised them a massive amount of money if they would sign. Mr. Nixon then blamed the Congress for the failure of the peace. Dr. Kissinger blamed Watergate.

The seeds of Watergate were planted in Cambodia and in the secrecy of private deals and commitments made by both American leaders. That is why Mr. Kissinger cannot be taken seriously when he blames Watergate for the failure of the Vietnam "peace" he negotiated. The mentality that created Watergate had earlier ordered the secret Cambodian bombing, the secret delay of peace, and the secret assurances of postwar bombing. These war actions and Watergate sprang from these leaders' disdainful distance from the American public and from the American legal system. In this sense, Dr. Kissinger was as deeply involved as President Nixon. McGeorge Bundy was rightfully offended by Dr. Kissinger's finger-pointing; of the ego diplomacy he wrote, "They did it all in their own secretive and deceptive way, breaking the limits of Presidential power as defined even before mid-1973. Mr. Kissinger should not now pretend otherwise."[88] In blaming Watergate for the failure of peace, Dr. Kissinger pathetically tried to shift the blame to the President alone.

The 1968 election of Richard Nixon had presented a unique opportunity to stop the war. John Kennedy had a tragically brief opportunity after the assassination of Diem, and Lyndon Johnson's landslide election also gave him a chance. Both Democrats were obsessed with the backlash of the political right in domestic American politics; they both believed that the thump they heard in the night was the restless ghost of Joe McCarthy. But Richard Nixon was the enemy they had feared, an enthusiastic participant in the McCarthyism of the 1950s. No one in American politics had a more perfect record of antic anti-Communism than Richard Nixon. He was, as even he understood it, sufficiently insulated from the right that he alone could with political impunity open relations with the People's Republic of China.

Mr. Nixon understood this. When he was talking to Chairman Mao during his dramatic trip to the People's Republic of China, President Nixon said, "Those on the right can do what those on the left only talk about." Apparently understanding the peculiarly American convolutions behind Mr. Nixon's statement, the ancient leader of much of the world's left wing responded: "I like rightists."[89] Of the Vietnam War Presidents, Mr. Nixon had the least need to mollify the American right wing.

Dr. Kissinger, however, was more willing to threaten a revival of the hordes of the right as a way to inhibit his critics on the left. As late as 1977 he was still at it:

> The time has come to end the Vietnam war debate. It could backfire, you know. If it continues, sooner or later the right wing will be heard from, too. And then we could have a very nasty controversy.[90]

Despite their freedom to act, they both were psychologically immobilized by their fears and the secretiveness which followed. It may be the fact that the need to be secretive, perhaps especially about such matters as war and peace, is not fully compatible with sanity. A secret is, after all, a private truth, and that is an acceptable working definition of madness. C. P. Snow once said, "The euphoria of secrecy goes to the head. . . . I have known men, prudent in other respects, who became drunk with it. It induces an unbalancing sense of power." A secret is both a shield and a weapon against enemies. But Mr. Snow was thinking about the consequences of secrecy on the secretive individual: "It takes a very strong head to keep secrets for years, and not go slightly mad. It isn't wise to be advised by anyone slightly mad."[91] At one point in his secret negotiations in Paris, Dr. Kissinger continued to slink out of back doors, use remote airfields, change subway cars in Paris, after the fact of the talks were already public. He wondered to himself why he was continuing with such elaborate procedures and concluded that for him secrecy had become a habit.

When bureaucrats become accustomed to secrecy, they inevitably find that the secrets of others are intolerable. It threatens their control. When secretiveness and power are combined, the power will be used to attack the secrets of the less powerful, perhaps through wiretapping, using the CIA to investigate domestic war critics, breaking into the confidential files of the physician of an enemy, or by overreacting to the inevitable leaks in government by hiring "plumbers" to stop the dripping.

A particular problem with the intense secretiveness of the Nixon-Kissinger team was that the most important secrets were kept from the American public and Congress, not from the North Vietnamese, Chinese, or Russians. This attitude derived from the President's conviction that he had to make "credible threats" to the North Vietnamese, while persuading Americans that he was winding down the war. Both Mr. Nixon and Dr. Kissinger kept the truth from Americans because they wanted to buy time actually to get out of the war. They were both aware that an antiwar attitude was slowly building in the Senate, that more antiwar protests could be expected, and that an election was coming in 1972. When the POWs finally returned to America, the President welcomed them home with a celebration of his technique: "Had we not had secrecy . . . you men would still be in Hanoi rather than Washington today."[92] If the President and Dr. Kissinger had allowed Americans in on the secrets they shared with the North Vietnamese, their countrymen would have raised hell. To avoid this, they both became increasingly secretive, increasingly manipulative, and, perhaps, slightly mad.

Dr. Kissinger grew increasingly concerned about whether his office was secure, and often had different agencies make checks to verify that no listening devices had been installed. When an aide was asked why the boss did not simply assign the sweeps to the FBI, he answered, "Who trusts Hoover?"[93] The form of madness induced by secrecy is very likely to be paranoia, even though Mr. Hoover had long since proved that he was not trustworthy. One consequence of all this was the public's conviction that the President, and the rest of the government, was lying.

President Nixon and Dr. Kissinger consciously set out to destroy the myth of America as a city on a hill. They knew the myth (but shortened its history by about 150 years), as illustrated in the President's second foreign policy report to the Congress, written by Dr. Kissinger: "America has always had a belief in a purpose larger than itself. Two centuries ago our mission was to be a unique exemplar of free government."[94] Mr. Nixon went on to say, "We need to replace the impulses of the previous era: both our instinct that we knew what was best for others and their temptation to lean on our prescriptions."[95] That was the larger point of the Nixon Doctrine—that America would help allies with our wealth, not our men.

What they were trying to do was perhaps fitting because the mind-set that conceived of the United States as God's country had significantly contributed to our involvement in Vietnam in the first place. The tough conservatives tried to bury the myth because they were so "realistic," so unsentimental about politics, that they relied on power, not ideas, to force their way on the world. The hideous irony was that ideas, not power, were always the only solution in Vietnam. This is why they were unable to force their way to "an honorable peace." The forming ideas of the President and his chief aide all had to do with explosions and death. Like the grunts, they loved American weaponry. Unlike the grunts, they both probably believed in what they were doing. They abandoned idealism for military power. Neither could have achieved American purposes, as those had been stutteringly expressed by them and their predecessors.

Many thoughtful observers understood that something basic in American life had changed, not as a result of Mr. Nixon's successes, but of his failures. For example, Tom Wicker, *The New York Times* columnist, wrote about the impact of Vietnam on America's myth: "In the long run it means that we will much more clearly understand ourselves in the future as being human beings with human problems rather than as some kind of specially gifted race whose businesses, institutions, and ideas were supposed to have been handed down from Mount Sinai." He believed that "has been shaken in everybody's mind."[96] At the time, that seemed indisputably true. It would not last very long.

Once, Dr. Kissinger correctly remarked that one cannot rely on goodwill for protection on the docks of Marseilles. The hidden question was whether the world was identical with those docks. He apparently thought so and accused his opponents of being softheaded. The naïveté of America was buried somewhere in Vietnam, MIA. The tough-minded realists had deliberately set out to accomplish this. Dr. Kissinger once wrote that he hoped to cleanse America's foreign policy of its characteristic sentimentality. Such an objective could only be applauded if it focused on the American sentimentality of aggression, of reconfiguring the world, by force if necessary, to conform to our sense of a secure future.

Both President Nixon and Dr. Kissinger, but especially Dr. Kissinger, were so fixed on the future, on creating a "structure of peace," that they paid too little attention to America's meaning. In the name of security they polluted freedom. What was it that they wanted to secure? They were both correct in saying that it is dangerous to plant corn outside of the stockade, that security is obviously essential. However, it is trivial to say so.

Like their predecessors in this war, they misrepresented the relevance of Vietnam to our security. The proof, of course, is the fact that the ultimate unification of Vietnam in 1975 under the control of the North hardly caused a crisis, or even a perturbation, in the security of the United States. The security argument had been a sham since 1950, and was designed to keep the sitting Presidents in office, safe from the political storm that would have erupted if any had walked away from Vietnam. Yet, the unwillingness to stop the war destroyed the presidencies of Lyndon Johnson and Richard Nixon. The moral and political confusions of the administrations, from John Kennedy forward, etched almost 58,000 names of dead American soldiers on the Vietnam memorial in Washington. The number of dead Vietnamese comprised about 10 percent of their nation.

Dr. Kissinger had a deeper sense of history than any other high government official. But his failure was precisely a failure of historical imagination. Mr. Nixon and his aide failed to take America into their account of the world. Their secrecy led them both to lie, as one would sensibly do on Marseilles's docks, but the Constitution is not usually thought to be applicable there. Dr. Kissinger argued that international order was essential to achieve progress at home. He believed that a successful foreign policy was a necessary precondition to a successful domestic policy. These two aspects of a nation's existence are much too closely entwined for his simple-minded sequence, and a better argument can be made for the opposite conclusion.

As a result of their significant achievement—their momentarily successful assault on deep American values—America was now like the other nations of the world, its meaning, if it still had one, in shambles. What was left for America was power, technology, and bureaucracy. What was missing was purpose.

The nation could not celebrate the war's end, as President Nixon announced it in January 1973. Too much death, and too much absurdity. Too many lies. Too much hatred on all sides. There was no victory to celebrate. The wild and marvelous throngs cheering in Times Square after World War II had by now been reduced in size and in joy. This time, a handful of Vietnam veterans collected, some drunk, some on drugs, screaming in rage at the television cameras. This time, instead of hooting horns, confetti, and thousands of strangers embracing and kissing, one black veteran, thinking of the President's announcement of the peace, shouted: "You can tell that bastard the war isn't over."[97]

PART III
BACKFIRE
BUREAUCRACY AT WAR

SIX

ENABLING IGNORANCE

America fought the wrong war in Vietnam, and almost everyone in Washington knew it. The enemy fought a political and psychological war, a war against American culture, and we fought a conventional war whose purpose was killing. That is why our military successes did not produce the intended results. The pattern of the way we fought is unmistakable: When something failed to work, we did more of it. If a thousand troops failed, we used half a million; if grenades failed, we dropped 3,500,000 tons of bombs. To understand how the guerrillas and the North Vietnamese beat the world's most powerful nation, it is necessary to understand why intelligent and dedicated men in Washington knowingly made decisions that would not work.

Decisions based upon myths explain *why* we went to war in Vietnam. The internal procedures of the federal bureaucracy explain *how* we fought. The failures were not the results of the titillating abuses of power or official corruption in Saigon or Washington. All the war managers attempted to serve the nation as best as could be accomplished within the loops and coils of the federal bureaucracy. They were all good Americans, mostly well educated, and patriotic. All their fascinating personal and political deformations helped to keep us stuck in the war, but they are not what shaped the daily decisions about how to fight.

It was a war with two fronts, one in Vietnam and the other in Washington. The Washington war was bureaucratic, between the White House and the State Department, between State and Defense, between the air force and the navy, between the CIA and everyone else, and between junior employees and their bosses. The failures of the government of the United States during the period of the Vietnam War were the failures that are built into the very nature of the enormous federal bureaucracy. The war in Vietnam revealed how this bureaucracy functions, and fails to function.

The inauguration of a President means that a new team of policymakers is coming to town. Too often overlooked is the fact that the permanent government, the other 99 percent, remains at work. Dean Rusk, the Secretary of State under JFK and LBJ, explained the continuity of his mushy bureaucracy:

> A transition is not so earth-shaking. Of the thousand or so cables that go out of here every day, I see only five or six and the President only one or two. Those who send out the other 994 cables will still be here. It is a little bit like changing engineers on a train going steadily down the track. The new engineer has some switches he can make choices about —but 4,500 intergovernmental agreements don't change.[1]

The permanent bureaucracy is not usually delighted that a new policy team will make changes. It is a widespread belief that a President makes policy and the government carries it out. Everyone knows better, but for some reason this fact seems hard to remember. Every new administration arrives in Washington determined to do something about the bureaucracy, determined to find a way to make the system respond to its will. It usually does not take long for the newcomers, the bosses, to begin complaining about leaks, and about some agency's failure to carry out an order. President Truman felt a little sorry for President-elect Eisenhower: "He'll sit there and he'll say, 'Do this! Do that!' *And nothing will happen.* Poor Ike—it won't be a bit like the Army. He'll find it very frustrating."[2] President Kennedy was furious when he learned that his decision to remove missiles from Turkey had been ignored by the State Department. JFK also once wistfully observed that he had made a decision that day but was not sure whether the government would approve.

LBJ could not prevent bombing in areas of North Vietnam that he declared would not be bombed. Dr. Kissinger summarized: "The outsider believes a Presidential order is consistently followed out. Nonsense."[3]

Forcing the bureaucracy to accept a change requires constant attention, mastery of detail, constancy of will, and clarity of purpose. It does not allow for distraction, fatigue, a short attention span, or either conflicting or ambiguous instructions. Bureaucrats will always exploit such lapses in their own interests. It is a fundamental rule of all bureaucracies that nothing should ever be done for the first time.

From the vantage point of the thousands of people employed in the government, Presidents come and go, presidential appointees come and go even more often, and the work of the government endures. The bureaucrats believe it is they, not the glamorous policymakers who are mere politicians, who make the nation work. The Foreign Service in the State Department is viewed by its members as a worldly profession, resentful of and resistant to changes imposed from "outside," that is, from the White House. The technicians in the Department of Defense believe that they understand both armaments and disarmament, and are scared to death that some politician, such as the Secretary of Defense, will endanger the security of the nation by imposing some birdbrained scheme, politically inspired, to change something or fire someone.

The underlying attitude of the bureaucracy is that individuals who have the skills to get elected to the presidency necessarily do not have the talent to govern. The president won his office by making a successful appeal for public support, or by the public's relative distrust of his opponent, or both. He will now set policy. The bureaucrats believe they have detailed knowledge that he does not and cannot have. Their view is that he is a mere politician while they are experts. It is the job of the bureaucracy to make certain that politicians do not endanger the departments and agencies. They know dozens of bureaucratic tricks to protect the nation from the President, his Cabinet, and his aides. To fight back, the President has power and influence. But they have manipulation. If they become visible, they lose. If he is distracted, frightened, or a little dumb, he loses. It's a fair fight.

Richard Nixon was the perfect model for the typical presidential response to the bureaucracy. After his first election he was determined to break its power because to him it was composed of enemies who would frustrate his designs. He warned his Cabinet to fire "holdover bureaucrats" and to do it quickly or else "they would become captives of the bureaucracy they were trying to change." This was not merely a desire to reward friends with patronage positions. He thought that his policies depended on it. "If we don't get rid of those people, they will either sabotage us from within, or they'll just sit back on their well-paid asses and wait for the next election to bring back their old bosses."[4]

Because of his well-nourished hatreds, President Nixon was at war on the second front in Washington. He sent Dr. Kissinger a memorandum that made explicit the dual nature of his struggle, one with the enemy in Washington, and the other with the enemy in Vietnam:

> We have the power to destroy his war-making capacity. The only question is whether we have the *will* to use that power. What distinguishes me from Johnson is that I have the *will* in spades. If we now fail it will be because the bureaucrats and the bureaucracy and particularly those in the Defense Department, who will of course be vigorously assisted by their allies in State, will find ways to erode the strong, decisive action that I have indicated we are going to take.[5]

This leads to an important fact: It is not possible to understand Washington if only the declaratory policy of the President and his administration is heeded. To attempt to do so is like trying to understand the behavior of children by paying attention only to the instructions of the parents. Very often there is a remarkable divergence between policy and performance, and very often this divergence is a result of the different interests of the President and the agencies of government which he tries to direct. Usually, he can control his own team, the Cabinet and other appointees, but it is never clear whether they can pass that control down through their departments. The divergence of interest also affects information flowing upward. People look out for themselves and want things to come out right, as they understand it, whether they are Presidents or junior-grade technicians buried somewhere in an agency. This divergence explains how America fought its most agonizing war.

The outcome of the battles of the Potomac were always reflected on the other front. After the cease-fire had been settled and American troops were withdrawn, a new military attaché to America's embassy in Saigon was briefed about his position, and what he learned was shocking. It was not what his Washington experience had led him to believe about Vietnam. After the briefing, he exploded: "Jesus Christ, I feel like I've been shot at and hit." The outgoing attaché had heard this before. "It is the usual syndrome," he said. "The further you get away from Washington, the closer you get to reality."[6] But this conclusion was mistaken because the Washington reality was as genuine and more influential than the Saigon reality. Within both Saigon and Washington, however, there were many realities, frequently divergent or even contradictory, and none was so powerful as consistently to overwhelm the others.

The bureaucratic problem that faced all Presidents, at least since Franklin Roosevelt, was how to make the vast federal government do what it was told to do. A subsidiary problem was how to know whether it was following orders. These two problems have led to chronic dissatisfaction and acute frustration for Presidents. Several postwar Presidents, for instance, functioned as their own Secretary of State because of their anticipation or experience of the unresponsiveness of the State Department. "Damn it," President Kennedy growled, "Bundy and I get more done in one day in the White House than they do in six months in the State Department."[7] All the Presidents have gone on a rampage to discover who in State ignored an important presidential directive.

One of the State Department's problems was that McCarthyism had ravaged its Far Eastern specialists. Joe McCarthy successfully thundered about State's boys who were so far gone that they spoke Chinese, and charged them with treason. The "loss" of China was his proof that somebody had sold out the nation. The old China hands were purged from State and the bureaucrats learned their lesson. They would no longer "get out in front" of any hot international issue. They would keep quiet and not write memos that would expose them again to the vengeance and political frustrations of the nation's witch-hunters.

The path to job security and promotions came to depend on the ability to conform to the pieties of the cold war. This rewarded the least thoughtful, most pliant, but least flexible, bureaucrats.

Mr. Kennedy and Dean Rusk, his Secretary of State, assumed that the State Department, under the President's direction, would run foreign policy. Perhaps because Mr. Kennedy's father had served as an ambassador he had some respect for the Foreign Service. But the Service was jealous, sensitive, and tough. A Kennedy aide said, "The White House could always win any battle it chose over the Service; but the prestige and proficiency of the Service limited the number of battles any White House would find it profitable to fight."[8] It is never clear what the outcome will be when a President requests something from the Service that it finds disagreeable to deliver. The Service's most powerful weapon is inertia. The President's weapon is power. Yet, his power is moderated by his need for the loyalty and even the enthusiasm of the Service.

The Service traditionally venerated the generalist abroad, had little patience with the Kennedy administration's demand for expert knowledge, language training, and effective participation, rather than gentlemanly observation, of the doings and undoings of foreign governments. The Service resisted the kind of deep knowledge and passionate advocacy that had landed the old China hands in the political soup. JFK's team was going to change all that. And yet every ambassador sent to Vietnam, by every administration, fit the old mold. None of them knew Vietnam, except as it was filtered through the political needs of the administrations in Washington. It was always business as usual.

To complicate things further, the federal government is not located only in Washington. Of the four million employees of the Defense Department, the overwhelming majority are stationed out of town. Washington is the central headquarters, with millions of people in the field who almost always conclude that the Washington bureaucrats do not understand the complexities of the local scene. The Washington bureaucrats respond that the field officers do not comprehend the policies and politics of the central city.

There is a tendency for planners and policymakers to think the job is done when their plans and policies are approved. The important job is considered to be making declarations, drafting papers, and issuing instructions. Seeing to it that the bureaucracy in Washington or in the field performs as intended is someone else's job. However, there is no distinct office with this responsibility, so the departments must monitor themselves and decide whether they are effective or not, a procedure that does not always encourage objectivity.

The development of the M-16 rifle illustrated this bureaucratic autonomy—the strong tendency for an agency to value its internal rules more than its performance. The Army Ordnance Corps had developed standard specifications for rifles, including an arbitrary velocity requirement. As it was originally designed, outside of this Corps, the M-16 was a dramatic improvement over the M-14, then standard issue. Army Ordnance ordered that the prototype, which never jammed and was light and murderously effective, be redesigned to meet its slower velocity standard. It realized that this would substantially lower the gun's effectiveness, but rules apparently are rules, and it also wanted the Olin Mathieson Chemical Corporation to remain the sole contractor for the old, less effective gunpowder. In 1963, it therefore redesigned the M-16 so that it would be less reliable, and it rigged tests to hide the disadvantages it insisted on. Troops in Vietnam were often killed because the new rifle jammed. General Westmoreland blamed the notorious jamming on the GIs who, he said, refused to keep their weapons clean. The Vietnamese guerrillas thought so little of the M-16 that they did not always take the rifle from dead Americans. A defense analyst described this series of events as "the purest portrayal of the banality of evil in the records of modern American defense."[9]

General Maxwell Taylor, reflecting on the Vietnam experience, commented that "our failures have been mostly in the assignment of clear missions to executive departments to carry out a presidential decision once made, and in the establishment of an effective supervisory system to check on progress and performance in execution."[10]

The single most important strategic decision for the Washington bureaucracy about the Vietnam War was what significance to assign to the insurgency, the NLF, in the South, and what significance to assign to the conventional armies of North Vietnam. The results of this decision determined whether and how

239

America would fight, the role of the South's military force, whether U.S. troops should be used and for what purpose, how many U.S. troops would be needed, what kind of troops should be sent, and the purpose of bombing the South and the North. The answer to this strategic question would shape America's view of the government of South Vietnam. If the allegience of the people to its government was a key, as it always is in counterinsurgency, it becomes self-defeating to support a narrowly based regime whose chief claim on our support might otherwise be its mere stability. America's celebration of stability was an implicit confession that we had abandoned counterinsurgency for something else.

This fundamental question about the importance of the guerrillas was never answered in a definitive way, as declaratory policy vacillated over time. To say this differently, the American war managers slipped into decisions that were based on their inability or unwillingness to make the necessary assignments of significance. This strategic forfeit became intolerable after American ground troops were committed to Vietnam for the simple reason that they had to be given a mission to perform.

One contributing factor to the inability to make the strategic decision about the importance of the NLF was the original justification for our presence in Vietnam in the first place: The problem, we said at the time, was external aggression, not civil war. We would apparently not intervene in a civil war. This led to a persistent view in Washington that the insurgency was less important than the North Vietnamese army, the external aggressors. This insistence on the greater significance of the "external" threat was ideological and less important in shaping the actual tactics of the war than the bureaucratic imperatives that immediately swamped everything else.

President Kennedy's enthusiasm for "counterinsurgency" was his response to the Soviets' support for wars of national liberation. The problem of the struggle within South Vietnam was not so complex as to be beyond the intellectual capacity of the American government. The goal was to find a way to prevent the guerrillas from prospering because of the support of the villagers. As the Americans learned how to talk about this problem, the guerrillas' support system became known as the VCI, "Vietcong Infrastructure." If the base could be pulled out from under the guerrillas, they could not continue to fight. Conventional military tactics, designed to fight Soviet armies on the fields of Poland, could not achieve this goal, and could make the problem worse if heavy technology were brought to bear because bombing, artillery, napalm, and Agent Orange would terrify, wound, and kill the very people whose support we needed.

This was widely acknowledged from the start. There were about 2,000 men, mostly East Europeans working against the Soviet Union, in the Special Forces before JFK became President. A group in the State Department argued that regular forces were neither trained nor equipped to fight guerrillas. That was why JFK was so excited about the possibilities of the Green Berets, a special force that would be trained to integrate military and political tactics. The President told the graduating cadets at West Point that guerrilla warfare required "a new and wholly different"[11] approach to the war.

The Joint Chiefs of Staff were less than enthusiastic about "a new and wholly different" way of taking care of business. Someone leaked to the press that General Lemnitzer believed Americans were being "oversold" on counterguerrilla programs. Somebody was throwing down the gauntlet, and the bureaucratic guerrilla war on the Potomac was heating up.

The Pentagon would not be guilty of disobeying the President. If he wanted an elite special force, he would have it, despite his implicit criticism that the military establishment was otherwise not able to serve the nation's interests. At first the marines insisted they were already a special force. The air force argued that bombing was the key to counteracting guerrillas. None of the services assigned real, that is budgetary, significance to the President's peculiar enthusiasm. The struggle over the beret itself was not enlightening. General Maxwell Taylor had eliminated it in the 1950s, but reinstated it when JFK requested some symbol of the "elite" nature of his expanded force. It was the elitism that made the Pentagon's teeth ache. In 1963, one young marine intelligence officer reported that "not only the colonels, but also the generals and admirals were fundamentally bored by the complexities of Vietnam."[12]

The Green Berets were usually assigned the task of training a counterpart organization of the South Vietnamese, or other training duties. None of the Special Forces, including the navy's Seals, ever received adequate funding. More important, it became obvious that the road to promotions remained with the conventional combat forces. As one scholar put it, "Special forces were known to be a dead end for anyone who aspired to high rank."[13] One general, responding to the demand that the army adapt itself to new conditions in Vietnam, exploded: "I'll be damned if I permit the United States Army, its institutions, its doctrine, and its traditions, to be destroyed just to win this lousy war."[14] The President could issue orders, but the bureaucratic definition of the kind of experience that warranted promotion would always be decided by the traditional military command structures, not by the President. Although the Green Berets performed well in Vietnam, the President's confident expectation of these forces was undercut by the Pentagon from the very start.

In JFK's administration a steering committee was set up, according to its chairman, General Maxwell Taylor, "to develop an integrated governmental effort behind the counterinsurgency program." Its purpose was to "assure recognition throughout the U.S. government that subversive insurgency was a political-military conflict equal in importance to conventional warfare; [and to] verify that this recognition was reflected in the organization and training of the Armed Forces and in appropriate programs of . . . other participating departments. . . ."[15] Robert Kennedy was the President's personal representative on what came to be called the Special Group Counterinsurgency. The group started off in high spirits and deep dedication, but began to subside after 1962, according to General Taylor, because the "counterinsurgency program got under way."[16]

The very fact that such an interdepartmental group had to be assembled is evidence that there was no agency within the bureaucracy to lead the effort. No agency had a vested interest in Vietnam's political struggle, and no agency could be held accountable for failure or success. No one was responsible, and counterinsurgency, as a result, was always someone else's problem. During JFK's administration, only the President could keep the meaning and importance of insurgency alive, but the presidency is not an operating agency (although JFK turned it into one during the Cuban missile crisis).

In 1962, as intelligence reports revealed that the strength of the guerrillas had increased from 5,000 to 23,000, mostly by recruitment in the South, General Earle Wheeler, a future chairman of the JCS, confidently declared, "It is fashionable in some quarters to say that the problems in Southeast Asia are primarily political and economic rather than military. I do not agree. The essence of the problem in Vietnam is military."[17] A new field commander had to be appointed for Vietnam, and the opportunity to appoint someone with either experience of or a commitment to counterinsurgency was missed because the Pentagon would have started to smoke—again. General Paul Harkins, whose formative experience was the conventional war in Korea, was selected, largely in a futile attempt to gain a cease-fire among the contending bureaucracies in Washington.

Enthusiasm for assigning appropriate weight to the insurgency did develop in selected pockets of the Washington bureaucracy as well as among some officers serving in Vietnam. But the generals, the JCS, and the Office of the Secretary of Defense had other fish to fry. Even the senior military brass, such as General Harkins, agreed it was important to win the support of the people of the South, but did not believe that the conventional war should be subordinated to political tactics. They all were convinced that the "big war" could be fought alongside the political struggle. Some of them recognized that the two efforts were at least in tension, and more often were directly contradictory, but they acted as if they did not.

The standard argument of the military was that someone else should attend to the insurgency, but there was no one else. One State Department officer asserted, "The real blame rests with the Secretary of State and his department . . . [who] failed to stand up and make the case for the political side of the equation with the strength, vigor, and determination with which Secretary McNamara and the military chiefs made the case for the military side."[18] Senator Wayne Morse once congratulated Secretary McNamara for his "brilliant and masterful support of an unsound policy."[19] The result was that the President's specific order to concentrate American efforts on the insurgency was not translated into action.

One reason for the failure of insurgency policy was the understandably different attitude of soldiers in the field about the importance of political activity. For the men whose lives were at risk the policy of counterinsurgency as a political tactic was unrealistic. Veterans still smile knowingly about the assumed naïveté of the advocates of civil action, political programs, and what was finally called winning hearts and minds.

The rejection of politics and acceptance of conventional military tactics went far beyond mere disapproval. For example, a marine colonel was ordered to "pacify" a village so that the forces of the government of South Vietnam (GVN) could take over:

> Before we begin our discussion on Phong Bac, it should be noted that the course of action selected was and is contrary to the spirit and intent of every directive, regulation, or order issued . . . all of which require U.S. forces to serve as a forerunner of GVN control. For this breach of discipline the responsibility is mine. The men who participated in Phong Bac's pacification carried out my orders and plans because they were good Marines and because they believed in and understood what they were doing. My primary purpose was to protect American lives and property—pacification was the means. The secondary goal was to enable the people of Phong Bac to become strong enough to resist the predatory incursions of both the GVN and the Vietcong.[20]

It was pointless to argue that soldiers should increase their danger by organizing themselves for political activity when they were being attacked, or when they were ordered to attack.

The "other war" was ideological, and too few Americans were equipped with education or inclination to engage in it. In any case, the Vietnamese were so suspicious of foreigners that we would have entered this struggle with a fatal handicap, one that even the most doctrinaire North Vietnamese would not share. We also forced the people whose support we claimed to want to detest us. We accomplished this by supporting Vietnamese bureaucrats, city elites, mandarins, and some intellectuals, all of whom had a lot to lose if we lost, and by disregarding the rest (about 85 percent) of the people.

We earned hatred by the effects of our inappropriate weaponry, but also by what was termed resettlement. That is, we moved peasants away from their homes, land, and the graves of their ancestors to a new and strange place where their security would be improved. Major General S. H. Matheson, 101st Airmobile Division, unwittingly described what resettlement actually meant:

On 10 June 1967 the brigade began the evacuation of people and livestock from Song Ve Valley. There were approximately 8465 people and 1149 animals. The people were told that they could take whatever they could carry.... ARVN [South Vietnam's army] was to have driven the livestock, however, they considered the job degrading and began to shoot the cattle so they had to be replaced by Americans. ... On leaving the village, crops were burned to prevent enemy use and to discourage the return of the villagers. The Song Ve Valley was the largest civil affairs project ever undertaken by the 1st Brigade. It was an overwhelming success and a model for future operations.[21]

As usual, the GIs knew better. David Ross was a medic who described one old woman who was being resettled away from her village of Ben Suc. When she and her family, along with some pigs and chickens, were loaded on a Chinook helicopter, he said, "She ran up and put her arms around me and wanted me to do something about it. There wasn't anything I could do. And that's when I started having second thoughts about the war. ... Most of us were never able to see the Vietnamese as real people."[22] David Ross was then nineteen years old.

As Robert McNamara pointed out, the Department of Defense was the third largest planned economy in the world, following only China and the Soviet Union. It is the largest single bureaucracy anywhere. To understand its role in Vietnam, and especially its attitude about counterinsurgency, it is essential to consider the internal bureaucratic pressures and battles that go on behind its normally closed doors. Whatever else DoD was during Vietnam, it was never a harmonious fraternal agency. Despite the fact that the Pentagon never fully appreciated guerrilla warfare in Vietnam, it was masterly at bureaucratic guerrilla warfare within DoD. The problem, from its viewpoint, was that it had to contend with the most powerful Defense Secretary ever.

Aside from his own intelligence and energy, Secretary McNamara's weapon against the Joint Chiefs of Staff was the Office of Systems Analysis he created as part of his own office. The office was staffed by bright young men from around the country, all aggressively expert at economic reasoning about war. Their job was to unearth the assumptions hidden in policy recommendations, to make them explicit and subject to debate. They were expert at breaking large issues into smaller ones, at assigning numerical values to issues that could sensibly be quantified, and at thinking in terms of the new planning, programming, and budgeting system that the Secretary had ordered installed throughout his enormous department. This led them to tease out all the alternative courses of action, quantified if possible, to assist Mr. McNamara in making decisions. This new system also required these quick analysts to consider the relationship between the costs and the benefits of every proposal, including plans to bomb the North and plans to increase the number of American troops on the ground. An English observer said, "Vietnam policy and the rationalist defense theories developed at the same time in response to the same national security problems, and they are thus interconnected."[23]

The analysts conducted a number of informal and unofficial studies of the war. One study showed that in 1967, General Westmoreland's intelligence chief overstated a particular body count by "at least 30 percent."[24] Another exercise concluded that in engagement against guerrillas, Americans lost as many men as the NLF lost, and that about 25 percent of American deaths were caused by mines and booby traps. The analysts discovered that the North could replace its losses for years into the future, at the very time that U.S. commanders claimed that victory was assured because of the irreplaceable losses the North was suffering. The analysts knew that General Westmoreland's "attrition strategy" could not succeed.

The war's planners could have learned the facts. The analysts explained that the enemy lost men only when he decided to fight, that he could choose the time and place "in over 85 percent of the firefights in Vietnam,"[25] and that if he did not want to be found, he would not be found. Another of these unsolicited studies showed that shortly after Rolling Thunder began, about "65 percent of the total tonnage of bombs and artillery rounds used in Vietnam was expended against places where the enemy *might* be, but without reliable information that he *was* there."[26]

What ensued within the Defense Department was a sometimes comic philosophical debate over epistemology, over the nature and source of knowledge. It was reason versus experience. As the military inevitably celebrated the philosophical school of hard knocks, the systems analysts replied that the military's arguments were ambiguous, its terms sloppily defined, while systems analysis was mathematically correct, assuming, as the analysts did not, that the military was sufficiently educated to understand the numbers in the first place. It was like a classic standoff between foreigners who do not share a common language and believe that shouting will aid the other's comprehension. The military failed to see the humor. When it found a way to fight back, the analysts lost their cheerfulness.

Reacting to something like a law of nature, the Joint Chiefs hated all this, and they responded with every bureaucratic weapon they had. What was at issue was whether their judgment and experience would count in the struggle with the unanswerable computations of the systems analysts. It was demonstrable that in a conflict between the Chiefs and the systems people, the Whiz Kids, the Secretary of Defense sided with the Kids more often than with the Chiefs. This drove the military into what may moderately be called a frenzy. General Westmoreland was particularly outraged: "What special audacity prompted civilian bureaucrats to deem they knew better how to run a military campaign than did military professionals? Is no special knowledge or experience necessary?" He often referred to them as "the self-appointed field marshals."[27] General Thomas S. Powers, the commander of the Strategic Air Force, carefully explained, "Computer types who were making defense policy don't know their ass from a hole in the ground."[28]

It is another law of nature that when the military becomes frenzied, it is only a matter of time before its congressional allies become frenzied. In 1968, the House of Representatives Committee on Armed Services held hearings on the function of the systems analysis office. Congressman Porter Hardy, Jr., of Virginia, told Alain Enthoven, the head of the office, that he was "the most dangerous man we have in government."[29] This committee's chairman, L. Mendell Rivers of South Carolina, proposed the abolition of the systems office through legislation, which the House of Representatives passed, but the Senate did not. The analysts were saved, but warned. Admiral Hyman G. Rickover, in his annual love-fest before the House Committee on Appropriations, put it somewhat more elegantly: "At one time the Pagan Gods ruled the world. Later the Kings. Then the Warriors, followed by the Lawyers. Now it is the Cost Accountants."[30]

One way the JCS fought back was by installing a systems

analysis capability within each of the services. Maxwell Taylor, as JCS chairman, decided that "the strategic analysis approach and the cost analysis technique of Dr. Enthoven's analysts should not be rivals but allies of the Chiefs,"[31] provided, of course, that the analysts kept out of matters of strategy. As usual, word of the change spread throughout the services in a flash. By 1966, an air force major showed how quickly the military can adapt to a bureaucratic challenge: "Military people concerned with the problems of counterinsurgency should be aware of what systems analysis can do for them and should make use of it."[32] By the late sixties, the navy employed seventy-five professional analysts, the air force had about two hundred, the army had fifty-seven, and the staff of the JCS employed fifty.

Because of the enthusiasm for and fear of the analysts, the limits of what they could do were obscured. There was too much noise for careful thought. The analysts could analyze a question, but could not pose the question in the first place and could not ask a different question. They were trapped by their useful technique into accepting the given framework. Like other bureaucrats, they wanted to please the boss, their only audience, and did not want to offer him recommendations which they knew he would reject. They were therefore trapped by considerations of power and influence. They could analyze what the U.S. could do better than they could analyze what the enemy could do. One critic said that systems analysis "discourages the study of one's opponents, his language, politics, culture, tactics, and leadership."[33] By now, this is a familiar point. Systems analysis reinforced the traditional American assumption that the enemy, or anyone else, is just like us. This ignorance made it even more difficult to take the insurgency seriously, a point that James Schlesinger, then at the RAND Corporation, made in 1967.[34]

This American solipsism, now supported by the most sophisticated analytical tools, produced a crazy inversion in Vietnam, a kind of macabre case of mistaken identity familiar in Marx Brothers movies. Because the number of American casualties was overwhelmingly important to us, we kept a body count of the enemy. But, being a poor country, not because they valued life less than the rest of the world, North Vietnam was forced to rely on manpower, not on technology which they did not have. Not immune to their very own peculiarities, the North valued equipment and technology so highly that it kept a count of our machines it had wrecked, not a body count but a broken-tool count. It also maintained a comparative cost estimate of how much money we were spending and losing compared to their own tiny investment. Each side counted the losses of the other in terms that were most important to each, but not to the other.

The systems office did not become fully operational until 1963. At that time the effects of the new planning and budgeting system were obvious, especially the greater centralization of authority in the Secretary's office. The new system produced a steady flow of data and information upward to the Secretary, and not only made it possible for him to exercise operational control, but required him to do so. This led DoD to present its views on the war in Vietnam in what seemed like a clear, force-ful, substantiated fashion, in contrast to the waffling of the State Department. The increased power of Mr. McNamara was lead-ing to the conclusion that counterinsurgency was important, but the real answer to the muddle in Vietnam was American military power. The military Chiefs and the Secretary seemed to agree.

However, the policy of gradual and measured escalation, un-waveringly supported by the analysts, divided them again. The JCS preferred a fast escalation that could be "decisive." The analysts and the Secretary favored the level of violence that would convince the North Vietnamese to mend their ways. The civilian side of DoD wanted to force the North to understand that the cost of the war was not worth whatever benefits it might enjoy. The Chiefs intended to beat the North according to a conventional military script. The political war was sinking into the bureaucratic swamp for the good reason that there was no one within DoD whose career depended on rescuing it.

The increase in U.S. combat troops and the air war against the North were both managed by the Defense Department, and both were shaped by the systems group and the budgeting sys-tem. The Secretary, who did not believe that the massive bomb-ing of the North would significantly reduce the flow of men and supplies to the South, selected the targets in the North. He aimed to force the North Vietnamese to think like the rational-ists in the systems group.

Although the Secretary could select the targets, he could not compel the navy or the air force actually to bomb them. It was estimated that only between 5 and 10 percent of the "bombing resources" were used to hit authorized targets, while the rest were used for "armed reconnaissance," whose objective was what the JCS wanted all along, interdicting supply lines and destroying transportation facilities. When this failed to reduce the southward flow substantially, as the Secretary had predicted, the military blamed (and still blames) the imposition of restrictions by civilians. The air lobby was sufficiently powerful and closely linked to congressmen panting for defense contracts in their home districts to prod the Senate Preparedness Subcommittee to inquire into these assumed restrictions. As one scholar pointed out, "So vulnerable to the weight of military criticism was the Department of Defense that they conceded a large package of targets the night before the inquiry opened, including some in the prohibited areas around Hanoi and near the Chinese border."[35] The Secretary and his systems analysts were not the only power in town.

The apparently irresistible bias of the American military is to train other nations' military organizations as our clones. This typically includes the Americans insisting on the bureaucratic organization of other armies into divisions, dependent on technology and committed to enormous firepower. It was inevitable in Vietnam that we would train a local air force, supply the planes and bombs, establish military academies, institute annual performance reviews, and suffer daily disappointment that the Vietnamese seemed unable to do the job. The unanswered question was what was the job. Because we were unable to put our own counterinsurgency tactics into operation, we trained the South Vietnamese to be similarly incompetent. Counterinsurgency, political war, required discipline and clarity to avoid using artillery and bombs. The American brass would never relinquish its technological superiority.

The CIA was less strangled in red tape and hallowed conventionality than the military services, and as a result was more clever about the problems of insurgency. But it was not as powerful in a bureaucratic struggle. Peer De Silva was appointed the CIA's chief of station in Saigon in late 1963. The ambassador, Henry Cabot Lodge, was known everywhere as a grouch, a miserable manager, and was mistakenly thought to be unusually well informed about South Vietnam. The ambassador had not wanted a new CIA chief, but LBJ did. To start off on the right foot, Mr. Lodge immediately told Mr. De Silva: "You have in-herited from your predecessor a very large and long black Chev-rolet sedan. That car is newer and longer than my official car. Get rid of it."[36]

To his great credit, Mr. De Silva recognized, "I knew nothing of the nature of the war being fought in Vietnam," an unusual attitude for a senior American official. What he soon learned was that the NLF was the key to American success or failure, and that the newly arrived ambassador, Maxwell Taylor, and his newly arrived protégé, General Westmoreland, along with Sec-retary McNamara, had come "to the wrong war." What Mr. De Silva learned—it is difficult to say this—was that terrorism ter-rifies people who will respond by doing things to avoid more terror. "This simple reasoning," he wrote, "eluded us for a long while."[37] The CIA station in Saigon realized that Mao was right, that the guerrillas were dependent on the villagers, and that unless the peasants were defended against terrorism, the NLF would grow progressively stronger. Mr. De Silva knew that sympathy, as well as terror, induced some peasants to cooperate with the guerrillas.

One point was especially important: Only Vietnamese, under their own leadership, could successfully work with the peasants. "The key to the problem was the farmer and his family."[38] Because of this, even the role of the CIA was not clear. Mr. De Silva learned from a Vietnamese officer that small teams of lightly armed men could protect a village if they wore no uni-forms and were from the area in which they operated. The advantage was clear: These teams would stay put, unlike the Americans with the great mobility their helicopters provided. The villagers knew, as the Americans also knew but acted as if they did not, that the guerrillas would return as soon as the Americans flew away. These Vietnamese teams would be as-signed the defense of their own homes, and would therefore be a permanent presence. The CIA provided the resources to build a training camp for the members of these indigenous teams.

Americans must name every program, and this was one was christened by the CIA: People's Action Teams, PAT. Mr. De Silva had accurate information from the field that these teams accomplished the purpose for which they had been created, and he was excited. Perhaps the answer to the war had now been found. He briefed the ambassador and General Westmoreland about the nature and success of the operation. The general was

not happy: "Well, I can see we're going to have some problems."
He was worried about draining away Vietnamese manpower
from more conventional activities. General Westmoreland
asked Mr. De Silva to brief the senior members of the general's
staff, as Mr. De Silva called them: "several more general officers
and clouds of colonels." This briefing revealed the conventional
military mind in all its glory.[39]

First, the military brass was in "anguish" when it heard that
the members of the PAT teams elected their own leaders. They
were then informed that the teams wore typical peasant clothing, had no base, no barracks, and no flagpole. "Heads wagged
negatively and the room sounded like a barnyard of chickens,
while hands shot in the air." One officer asked: "If they don't
wear uniforms, how can you tell your own men from the farmers?" Answer: "You can't, but neither can the Vietcong." Question: "Don't you think that a special cap or an armband or some
kind of emblem would be good for unit morale?"[40] The briefers
explained that morale was so high, there had been no desertions,
a remarkable fact in Vietnam. The teams so far had lost four
weapons, but had captured more than four hundred.

Two generals told Mr. De Silva that the program was interesting and obviously effective, but it would grow beyond the ability of the CIA to manage and the military would have to take
it over. Mr. De Silva disagreed because if the program lost its
Vietnamese or its civilian character, it would no longer work.
One of the generals "exploded" in anger that the team members
were nothing but soldiers. "And they've got to be made to look
like soldiers and act like soldiers."[41]

The response of General Westmoreland's headquarters,
MACV, was relatively simple: "All right, that's all very well,
but we can do better." The general finally informed Mr. De
Silva that the bureaucratic imperative was working: "Which
American element is best suited to support the Vietnamese in
their development of the PAT program? CIA or MACV?" The
question was rhetorical. The military took it over, increased the
size and firepower of the teams, shortened the training period,
and eliminated the political part of the training. Desertions
from the teams rose and their effectiveness fell. Because of the
bureaucratic power of the commanding officer, and of the Pentagon over the CIA, Mr. De Silva had been initiated into the
mysteries of bureaucratic war: "My God, I thought, we are

finally finding the right solutions. In implementing them would our adversaries be the Vietcong or our own military establishment? It turned out to be both."[42]

It is a mistake to describe the Pentagon as a single and unified bureaucratic agency. The services are capable of conjuring up the image of unity when they are faced with a common foe not on a battlefield in war, but what is apparently more important, a bureaucratic threat, such as Secretary McNamara, at home. Mr. McNamara offended the Chiefs by trying to force the services into reasonable coordination. For example, he pointed out that the air force planned for short wars, while the army planned for long ones. He was at a loss about how to coordinate their plans. "We can imagine," he wrote, "many different kinds of wars the United States must be prepared to fight, but a war in which the Army fights independently of the Navy, or the Navy independently of the Air Force, is not one of them."[43]

Interservice rivalries, competitive scratching for a bigger slice of the budget, run long and deep in the United States. But the playing out of these emotions and self-interests in Vietnam was especially interesting because Mr. McNamara had frightened the services into surface unity in Washington. He was widely regarded as having finally annexed the Pentagon to the government of the United States. Perhaps it was the other way around. But the services in the field, in Vietnam, were not so easily domesticated.

The three most important and absurd interservice competitions were between the army and the marines, the army and the air force, and the aircraft carrier navy and the air force. The strategy of each of these battles was clear: to demonstrate the comparative effectiveness of one service against another, to translate that perceived effectiveness into a bigger budget, and, therefore, to secure a privileged position after the war.

The Marine Corps will apparently never forget that after World War II the army fought hard to take over its function. It is sensitive about its future and jealous of its distinction, which it must try to prove at every opportunity. At one point General Westmoreland sensibly wanted to impose a unified command over ground combat in Vietnam. Because this meant that the overall commander would be a general of the army, the marine corps had a fit. As a result the Commander in Chief of the

Pacific, an admiral, vetoed the proposal to fight in a more organized way.

The role of the marines is to fight amphibious warfare. They
did this often, attacking the Vietnamese coast. Three results
were obvious: The marines got good practice at their distinctive
mission; the splashy landings were not very effective in terms
of the real war; and, the army was angry. The army insisted that
the landings did not produce satisfactory results, and that, in
any case, the army itself could do whatever it was that the
marines did. The army also suggested that the marines had not
been effective during the Korean War.

What no one could argue with was the very high effectiveness
of the marines when they fought on the ground, just like army
grunts. But in the bureaucratic war for the marines that was a
problem, not a solution. Their tough assignments in the
northernmost military region of South Vietnam, and their murderous assignment at the battle of Khe Sanh, proved absolutely
that the marines were at least the equivalent of any other
fighting unit. Because they were performing as land-based
grunts, they were not upholding the unique Marine Corps function. Thus, the way the marines fought was thought useful to
the conduct of the Vietnam War, but not to the other war
between the marines and the army.

The tension between the army and air force also had deep
roots. The army wanted the air force to provide air support for
the army's troops in battle. The air force wanted to concentrate
on big bombers that could carry nuclear bombs to the Soviet
Union. That was where the glamour and the money was. The
army threatened to develop its own tactical air support if the air
force continued to be unreasonable. The air force argued that if
the army did this it would be duplicative and a waste of taxpay-
ers' money. The army said it could not be duplicative because
the air force was not doing it. And so on.

The answer was the helicopter, and it came from Secretary
McNamara's early conviction that the army's traditional doc-
trines were inappropriate in a guerrilla war. He argued that
speed and mobility were essential because a traditional army
could not be everywhere it needed to be in a contest with irregular fighters. Air mobility would compensate for the absence of
the huge numbers of regular soldiers thought to be required
against guerrillas. The army brass, of course, resisted the con-

cept of air mobility, and the Secretary simply forced it down the army's throat. The air force's claim to dominance was its owner-ship of fixed-wing, land-based aircraft. The helicopter flew away from that definition. In short, the weapon the army initially rejected became its instrument for its bureaucratic war with the air force, and the air force was furious. After Vietnam, the army had more pilots and planes than the air force.

In late 1964, the Air Force Chief of Staff, General Curtis LeMay, "upbraided" General Westmoreland for permitting the army to "usurp" the function of the air force. The problem was that the helicopter gunship, perhaps the most characteristic weapon of the war, was beginning to be used. It provided the army with the close air support it needed. General LeMay then called General Westmoreland to a meeting in Hong Kong where, as General Westmoreland described it, "He adminis-tered a tongue-lashing for what he called failure to uphold Air Force doctrine."[44] The real problem, as General Westmoreland knew, was that the helicopters were being armed and were thus capable of performing the necessary function that the air force had refused to perform. It is not easy to imagine what would have happened in the other war, the one being fought in Viet-nam, had General LeMay won the bureaucratic one. Because Secretary McNamara was the chief cheerleader for the army in this issue, the air force lost.

The most vital battle for the air force was with the navy. This battle was at the very heart of the two services, and so it was fought with a ferocity not present in any other interser-vice rivalry. This one shaped military operations in Vietnam, and neither service was ever willing to give an inch of ground or sky. The question was whether land-based (air force) or car-rier-based (navy) planes were more effective. The answer to that question would, the two services believed, determine their future budgets.

Before the big air war got off the ground, the navy, using its own systems analysis, studied the relative efficiency of land-based and sea-based air power. The navy discovered that its way was more effective at lower cost. The air force did not believe a word. The test of comparative effectiveness had to be in Viet-nam, not Washington. Many planners were aware that strategic bombing would not work on North Vietnam, and that its use in the South, against the guerrillas, would strengthen the guerrillas instead of weakening them. Nonetheless, the huge B-52s were wheeled out because they were at the center of the air force's most important function, strategic bombing of the USSR. If the air force had not been allowed to use these machines, it feared that its strategic-bombing role might be downgraded after the war. For the same reason, it insisted on using its highest performance jets in the South, as a historian concluded, "despite studies indicating that slower propeller-driven models would have been three times as accurate, from five to thirteen times less costly, but with roughly the same loss ratio."[45] Because the air force is the most technologically oriented of the services, it was incapable of using less than its best, even though less than the best would have been better.

The debate about whether to use propeller or jet planes was enormously important to the air force. Robert Komer explained:

> ... the Air Force kept saying that jets are better at close air support than these slow prop-driven planes. The Air Force did not believe that—what the Air Force really meant was that if we buy prop-driven planes for dealing with guerrillas in Vietnam, we will end the war with an inventory of prop-driven planes when what we need is jets! Because against the Russians prop planes are hardly the answer. ... The Air Force did not level with the civilians, particularly the systems analysts, who were all saying that the Air Force did not know what it was talking about.[46]

Because of the air force's bias toward short war, it may be that it did not want to distort its long-range supply because of a short-run problem. If so, it was wrong on two counts: underestimating the length of the Vietnam War, and failing to provide the ground troops with the most effective support.

The decisive form of the struggle between the air force and the navy was a competition to fly the most bombing missions. The contest was between the Seventh Air Force and the Seventh Fleet aircraft carriers sailing off the Vietnam coastline. It was apparently thought that the winner in this contest would prove its comparative effectiveness, so the stakes could not have been higher, and the principles could not have been lower.

Promotions and length of duty were determined by the number of sorties each pilot flew; the more sorties, the sooner they could leave Vietnam, probably with a higher grade. This set of incentives meant that the pilots wanted to fly as many sorties as possible, and had every reason to stay out of trouble by avoiding tough targets. Cumulatively, the budgets of the air force and navy were determined by the "sortie rate," so the services had the same bizarre incentive as the individual pilots. Everyone tried to be in the air as often as possible, so long as they could avoid dangerous targets.

The pilots generally flew two sorties a day, which the North Vietnamese timed and usually could anticipate. There was no good bureaucratic reason for the pilots actually to reach their target because they would get credit for a sortie even if, as many did, they dropped their bombs on fish in the sea, or on places already destroyed by bombs, or on places where there was nothing to bomb, except perhaps the rice paddies which fed the people. In 1966, a local distribution foul-up put fuses and bombs in different places, so CINCPAC, who controlled much of the air war in the North, rationed the complete bombs but did not curtail the sorties. In other words, the planes would fly at the same rate even though they did not have full bomb loads, or any bombs at all. An air force colonel was candid about this episode: "Our planes were flying with one-half a load, but bombs or no bombs, you've got to have more Air Force over the target than Navy."[47] In fact, both services came to prefer incomplete bomb loads because more sorties would be required to deliver the total tonnage.

Late in 1975, during a hearing of the Select Committee on Intelligence of the House of Representatives, Congressman Ronald Dellums of California asked a question of James Graham, who had worked for the CIA from 1948 to 1973: "Do you have enough knowledge to indicate to us whether or not you were given accurate figures by the 7th Air Force?" Mr. Graham responded: "I would say the briefings which the 7th Air Force gave on the effects of their aerial interdiction efforts were not accepted as accurate by the CIA after careful analysis."[48]

To ensure that each service received the credit it deserved, Vietnam was carved into separate preserves, called route packages, each owned by a different service. The Seventh Air Force owned Hanoi, some rail lines, and the area just north of the demilitarized zone. Haiphong and northeastern North Vietnam belonged to the Seventh Fleet. The commander in Saigon could control only targets in the extreme south of South Vietnam, where the Seventh Air Force reported to him. The flights of the B-52s were separate from all this because they were controlled by the Strategic Air Command. This crazy quilt of geography and command, said Dr. Kissinger, "told more about the Pentagon bureaucracy than about military realities; indeed, it showed that Washington's organizational requirements overrode strategy."[49] This incredible system was devised to guarantee that every bomb dropped would be credited to the appropriate service. President Nixon ordered the system changed, but Secretary Laird and the Chairman of the JCS refused.

More than three million fixed-wing sorties against South and North Vietnam, Laos, and Cambodia were flown by U.S. and South Vietnamese air forces during the war. Though bombing halts or other restrictions were occasionally imposed, the sortie rate did not diminish. If bombs could not be dropped on North Vietnam, they were dropped on Laos. When neither the North nor Laos could be bombed after the peace of 1973, the bombers changed course for Cambodia. During the war there were never restrictions on bombing South Vietnam, where most of the war's sorties had been aimed. But throughout the war, the guerrillas and the North obtained "about 70 percent of their supplies for operations in South Vietnam from sources *inside* the country."[50] It is difficult to credit the military's complaint that civilian restrictions impeded the bombing campaigns.

The rewards of scoring bureaucratic points, of serving individual and institutional interests, made a serious discussion of overall war strategy seem pointless. The widely held belief that air technology would necessarily destroy efforts to win the allegiance of the farmer and his family clearly could not prevail over the institutional preferences of these two services. There was at the same time a great debate in Washington about whether the continuing growth of the NLF was a result of recruitment and terrorism in the South or infiltration from the North. As usual in the Vietnam era, the problem was contained in the wrong question. The growth of the guerrillas was as much a result of the bureaucratic struggle between the air force and the navy. The results of that struggle, the random rain of bombs, terrified the entire population more than any actions of the guerrillas.

* * *

The strategic significance of the guerrillas in the South could not be decided unless the war's engineers had basic information about their number. This relatively low-level, but difficult, intelligence problem created an enormous bureaucratic storm that had not subsided by 1984, when lawsuits were still pending. The responsibility for this information was spread around several service intelligence operations, including the CIA. As it turned out, a young CIA analyst named Sam Adams did get some of the needed information. The military's rejection of his findings finally turned out to be a classic example of the war planners rejecting the truth that was available, but not useful to them. If they had accepted Mr. Adams's findings, they could not have continued to underestimate the NLF. If the military headquarters in Saigon would have tried to understand the meaning of a war of national liberation, it would have had serious problems with continuing the air war in the South and would otherwise have had to rethink its tactics.

If the bureaucrats had accepted Mr. Adams's conclusions, their freedom to preserve the status quo would have been jeopardized. Then they would have a lot of explaining to do. Ignoring Mr. Adams gave them freedom to do what they wanted to do. Some suspected that the CIA analyst might be right, but they continued to support plans they realized would fail. The Adams figures would have closed down some of the alternatives the United States was choosing. That is what "enabling ignorance" means, the freedom that comes from ignoring the truth. This is a freedom that will ultimately fail.

Sam Adams, a fourth cousin seven times removed of America's second President, joined the CIA in 1963, eight years after he graduated from Harvard. He was a perfect recruit because he loved rummaging around in documents, and was intelligent, indefatigable, persistent, and courageous, perhaps even foolhardy. Two years after he signed on, the CIA handed him a research plum: He should study the NLF.

He was delighted with his new assignment. No one supervised him: "Not knowing what else to do, I began to tinker with the VC defector statistics."[51] This was apparently mild enough, routine, bureaucratic busywork, the kind of paper shuffling that suits the green-eyeshaded old man who is trying to survive long enough to receive a pension. But Mr. Adams was young and vigorous.

He learned that the NLF was losing many more defectors

than anyone had imagined. In fact, the defection rate was so high that he began to worry about the accuracy of the official American estimate of the total size of the enemy's forces. It had already become a settled piece of received wisdom in Washington and Saigon that there were 270,000 guerrillas in the field. But if, as Mr. Adams learned, the guerrillas were losing perhaps as many as 100,000 defectors a year, and since we were killing, wounding, or capturing as many as 150,000 a year, we were winning and the war was almost over. Except it was not true.

In January 1966, Mr. Adams went to Saigon to dig deeper into what was becoming an obsessive puzzle. The CIA station chief learned that he was poking around in the embassy's statistics, and he gave Mr. Adams good advice: "Those statistics aren't worth a damn. No numbers in Vietnam are, and besides, you'll never learn anything sitting around in Saigon." Mr. Adams went into the field to read captured enemy documents. He learned that in one province, Binh Dinh, there were more than 50,000 guerrillas of all types; he then checked the "official" U.S. figure and found the guerrillas listed as 4,500. This was meat for the lion, and in what he described as "a state of nervous excitement" he turned to the figures for Phu Yen province where there were 11,000 guerrillas, but the U.S. listed 1,400. He yelled from his desk: "There goes the whole damn order of battle!"[52]

An order of battle, or as the military inevitably calls it, OB, is simply a listing of military units. Mr. Adams was learning that the American military was significantly underestimating the enemy's strength. The official figure was 270,000, but he concluded that the actual figure was 470,000. This was no longer a pointless exercise. His research showed that instead of an imminent collapse of the guerrillas, the U.S. was facing a more formidable foe than had been known.

He put his findings in a memorandum for "the seventh floor," the lair of the executives who ran the CIA. He anticipated a dramatic response consistent with the significance of his conclusions, including the probability that someone would tell him the President needed to be informed. He believed that "this was the biggest intelligence find of the war—by far."[53] Mr. Adams was not only a talented analyst, he also had some understanding of Washington. He explained why his research was significant:

It was important because the planners running the war in those days used statistics as a basis for everything they did, and the most important figure of all was the size of the enemy army—that order of battle number, 270,000. All our other intelligence estimates were tied to the order of battle: how much rice the VC ate, how much ammunition they shot. . . . If the Vietcong Army suddenly doubled in size, our whole statistical system would collapse. . . . Some experts maintained that in a guerrilla war our side had to outnumber the enemy by a ratio of 10 to 1; others said 5 to 1; the most optimistic said 3 to 1. But even if we used the 3 to 1 ratio, the addition of 200,000 men to the enemy order of battle meant that somebody had to find an extra 600,000 troops for our side. This would put President Johnson in a very tight fix—either quit the war or send more soldiers.[54]

Mr. Adams's phone did not ring, and he received no answering memo. After days of mounting anger he went to the seventh floor himself, and found his memo marked "Indefinite Hold" in a safe. He tried again with an even more complete memo, and personally carried it upstairs. According to Mr. Adams's version of what happened, an officer, Waldo Duberstein, said: "It's that Goddamn memo again. Adams, stop being such a prima donna." The official next in line was equally helpful. He explained that the order of battle was the exclusive concern of General Westmoreland, and the CIA had no right to interfere. Mr. Adams explained, "This is no joke. We're in a war with these guys."[55]

There were several categories in the official U.S. estimate of NLF strength, and the numbers in three of the categories had not changed at all for two years, so that, for instance, the size of guerrilla-militia had been put precisely at 103,573, and had remained exactly the same for twenty-four months of the war. Mr. Adams discovered that the idiotic number came from a South Vietnamese invention of 1964 which the Americans had accepted without verification. "Can you believe it? Here we are in the middle of a guerrilla war, and we haven't even bothered to count the guerrillas,"[56] Mr. Adams said to a colleague. By now he had learned that his first estimate of NLF strength of 470,000 was too low; it should have been 600,000.

In May 1967, the "official" CIA figure remained 270,000. Mr. Adams protested, and, according to him, after a little compromising, the figure was reset at 500,000. Then a conference was called in which the entire intelligence community participated. The representative from the Defense Intelligence Agency said he could not accept 500,000, that 300,000 was the best he could do.

In testimony before the House Select Committee on Intelligence in 1975, William Colby, the CIA's director, explained the figure of 500,000, which the agency had accepted as essentially accurate:

> . . . it is pretty clear that the CIA was very substantially influenced by Mr. Adams' original studies, but we didn't accept every dot [sic] and tittle of his presentation. There is no question about it: In some of his earlier studies of these documents and studies into these very busy forces, he put some very general numbers around them and we initially accepted, to some degree, those numbers. That is where the 500,000 figure comes from.[57]

At the same hearing, Paul V. Walsh, the CIA's associate deputy director, answered a little differently: "In December of 1966 Sam Adams said that the whole bag of whatever you want to call them was 600,000. Then we sent him out to Saigon . . . and he came back and said it was 500,000."[58] In any case, the CIA was generally in agreement that the number of guerrillas of various categories now added up to half a million, about double the military's estimate.

At a meeting in Saigon, Mr. Adams explained his conclusions. One of the colonels present thoroughly explained the military's conclusion: "Adams, you're full of shit." Privately, an army officer told him, "We've been told to keep our numbers under 300,000."[59] According to Mr. Adams, Richard Helms, the director of the CIA, sent a cable in effect instructing his employees to accept the military's figure which was now 299,000, but it was soon dropped to 248,000, even lower than the original official OB. But when George Carver, the CIA's deputy for national intelligence officers, was asked by a House committee whether the CIA people at the Saigon conference had received such instructions, he answered, "Absolutely not."[60] The military's view, as expressed in 1976 by Lieutenant Colonel Daniel Graham, director of the intelligence office in DoD, was that "Mr.

Adams' figures were not rejected because of a conspiracy; they were rejected because his analysis was bad. . . ."[61]

George Allen, a senior CIA officer, attended that Saigon conference where he made a pencilled note to himself: "I consider this to be essentially a contrived retrospect effort aimed at rationalizing a phony comparison between the old figures and the new; the guerrilla estimate was controlled by the desire to stay below 300,000. . . ." Seven years later, Mr. Allen told the select committee that this note "was an initial kneejerk reaction,"[62] and that he had accepted the official, that is, the military's figures that emerged from the conference.

The conflict between Mr. Adams and the military, with the CIA standing somewhere in the middle, was whether to include the irregular guerrillas in the count. Mr. Adams said yes, the military said no, and the CIA said yes but it was impossible to count them accurately. Yet, on several occasions in 1966 and 1967, the Agency informed the President's staff, and the Secretaries of State and Defense, that General Westmoreland's staff's estimate of the size "of Vietcong's irregular forces may have drastically understated their growth, possibly by as much as 200,000 persons."[63] Robert Komer, who was soon to be put in charge of America's first organized counterinsurgency effort, later wrote, "The U.S. and GVN military intelligence empires . . . were focused in classic style mostly on order of battle . . . to the neglect of such other key elements . . . as local guerrillas or the Viet Cong infrastructure." Consequently, the military underestimated the enemy. "Many military intelligence officers . . . seemed to have closed minds to such other facets of the war. It was not their job, after all."[64]

General Westmoreland's staff consistently refused to include the irregulars, the defense forces and others, of the NLF as part of the military threat. Mr. Colby tried to help the committee members understand the sort of guerrilla the military refused to count: "Take the occasional help you get from an individual who walks into a marketplace and throws a grenade. Is that a number or not?"[65] The military believed that it was not. Mr. Allen, under questioning, said that the military "were relatively conservative" and "tended to understate enemy's strength."[66]

The military command in Saigon was fixated on conventional, big-unit war, and therefore concentrated on the enemy's units that could engage the Americans in the sort of war the

Americans wished to fight. That is one reason why Saigon headquarters refused to count the individual grenade thrower. That is why the headquarters, according to Mr. Adams, but not according to others, was unprepared for the Tet offensive. The American military was deaf and blind to the insurgency. As Robert Komer put it, the intelligence agencies estimated the OB "to the total neglect of the guerrillas and the so-called Viet Cong infrastructure, the political-military apparatus that was really running the war."[67] The struggle over the order of battle was in fact not over the numbers, but over the very nature of the war, and none of the participants were clear about the underlying argument at the time.

Nonetheless, the Pentagon was winning the war, not the one in Vietnam, but the one in Washington. William Hyland, also with the CIA and in attendance at the Saigon conference, tried to be helpful: "Sam, don't take it so hard. You know what the political climate is. If you think they'd accept the higher numbers, you're living in a dream world."[68]

Mr. Adams told me that there was a computer programmer, an enlisted man, in General Westmoreland's headquarters, who was forced to play a key role in juggling the numbers, what Mr. Adams called the "nut bag operation." This "poor bastard" had to adjust field estimates about the guerrillas' strength to stay under the military's figure. Mr. Adams said that there was a direct order in writing from the head of the OB section, marked "Internal Use Only," that no new units or numbers could be counted if they increased the total.[69] If something new was added, something else had to be dropped.

Richard McArthur, a lieutenant who served in military intelligence in the order-of-battle section of General Westmoreland's headquarters, worked on the size of the guerrilla force. After a field study, he arrived at the figure of 80,000, but soon learned that someone had cut his figure back to 40,000. He complained to Lieutenant Colonel Paul Weiler, the chief of the OB section, who told him, and Lieutenant McArthur testified this was a direct quote: "Lie a little, Mac, lie a little."[70] He refused, was transferred out of intelligence, and, when he could, resigned from the army.

Back in Washington again, while this struggle was at full throat, one of Mr. Adams's Agency colleagues wanted to know whether the CIA had "gone beyond the bounds of reasonable dishonesty."[71] Mr. Adams judged that it had. Director Helms supported the military's fiddling with the numbers as he signed the CIA's estimate using the military's lower figures. But Mr. Helms indicated, as Mr. Adams did not acknowledge, that the figure did not include the irregulars.

The Tet offensive might have persuaded almost any rational person that Mr. Adams had been right. Mr. Adams reported to me that Mr. McNamara told the CIA, on February 5, 1968, that "half the enemy units in Tet were not in the order of battle."[72] Mr. Adams believes that during Tet, the Secretary discovered in field reports entire enemy units that the military had argued out of the OB. As head of the entire military establishment, he now accepted the CIA's estimate of the guerrillas, not that of his admirals and generals. He had long before lost his confidence in the war and was preparing to leave the administration. After Tet, the CIA continued to support the figure of 500,000, the military continued to argue for reduced numbers, and no one knows what the White House was thinking.

Before Tet, however, Walt Rostow, the President's security adviser, had been told of the controversy and had done nothing about it. Mr. Helms had argued with Mr. Rostow in the past, and apparently was not eager for another round. If the CIA loses the White House, after all, it loses its only audience. It was never clear, and still is not, whether the White House had pressured the military into manipulating the numbers.

Mr. Adams filed charges against the CIA's Research Department and against Richard Helms, the director of Central Intelligence. He did so in the bureaucratically correct manner, by staying within channels, so he could not easily be fired. Mr. Helms ordered the Inspector General of the CIA to proceed with an investigation of himself. Mr. Adams was warned that he was going to be fired if he kept it up.

After Richard Nixon was elected, Mr. Adams wanted one of his memos sent to the President-elect, via the White House. Director Helms requested the pleasure of Mr. Adams's company at a meeting, to inquire whether Mr. Adams's supervisors were behaving badly, or whether Mr. Adams thought he should be promoted faster, was that the problem? No, Mr. Adams said, "My problem was that you caved in on the numbers right before Tet."[73] He explained this for about ten minutes. Mr. Helms responded that he could not take on the entire military establishment, and that the numbers did not matter. Mr. Adams explained to the head of the CIA that it was not the CIA's business to worry about what would matter, only to provide accurate intelligence. Mr. Helms agreed to help Mr. Adams see the right people in the White House, but no meeting ever took place. Mr. Helms refused to allow Mr. Adams to send his memoranda, detailing his charges against Mr. Helms, to the Johnson administration or to the incoming Nixon team.

Mr. Adams now discovered that he was no longer invited to meetings within the CIA when "outsiders" were present, that he was not allowed to go to Vietnam, and that he was both ostracized and under a form of bureaucratic solitary confinement. After several years of additional skirmishes, Mr. Adams noticed a newspaper item that reported that the government was trying Daniel Ellsberg for revealing secrets, including the estimates of NLF strength. The secret Mr. Ellsberg revealed was the old military invention of 270,000. When Mr. Adams testified for the defense, the CIA again threatened to fire him, he complained, "and, as usual the Agency backed down."[74] After a short time, he quit.

There is no doubt that members of the military manipulated the truth in this controversy. They did so because they believed it was necessary to retain the support of the public and the administration. Some did so out of their political judgment that good news from the battlefield would persuade Americans, including the President and Congress, to "stay the course." When the depressing facts revealed by Mr. Adams and others were understood, as they were immediately, by the brass, a decision was made to cheat to maintain optimism. It is not necessary to predict the outcome of General Westmoreland's $120 million libel suit against CBS to conclude from the sworn depositions of his own senior staff members that the military cooked the books.

General Westmoreland now admits that the higher enemy figures which even his own intelligence officers provided him in 1967 were closer to the truth than the "official" figures he released at the time. But when he first heard the more accurate figures he said he was shocked and surprised. The truthful figures, he said then, would be "a political bombshell," and he asked his own intelligence officer, "What am I going to tell Congress? What is the press going to do with this?" His major concern seemed to be to report lower numbers "because the people in Washington were not sophisticated enough to understand and evaluate this thing, and neither was the media."[75]

Colonel John Williams had been the Defense Intelligence Agency's chief analyst on the subject of enemy strength. He now commands the group responsible for intelligence and counterintelligence in Europe. In a sworn deposition he testified: "I think the policymakers were misled by the numbers game and I think the American people were misled by the numbers game." Many, more senior, officers disagree.[76]

Colonel Gains Hawkins had been in charge of the OB estimates within General Westmoreland's headquarters. He was "Mr. OB," and was regarded as the military's foremost expert on the question of enemy strength. He wrote, "As the officer with primary responsibility for estimating the total enemy strength, I misused the available information to establish a figure on the irregular and political categories of enemy forces to meet what I had no doubt was the command requirement." In his sworn testimony Colonel Hawkins said that what he had done was a "coverup."[77] Other officers within General Westmoreland's command who in recent sworn statements agree that the books were cooked include Bernard Gattozzi, Richard McArthur, Russell Cooley, Kelly Robinson, Michael Dilley, Norman House, Marshall Lynn, David Morgan, John O'Donnell, Michael Fraboni, and Michael Hankins.[78]

Richard Kovar has been with the CIA for more than thirty years and now prepares President Reagan's daily intelligence report from the CIA. In 1967, he was a member of the executive staff of the CIA's deputy director of intelligence. In his recent affidavit he said, "Sam Adams had been right and I and Mr. Helms and Paul Walsh had been wrong. It was not just the CIA versus the Army, but ultimately a matter of truth or consequences, and the consequences had been military and political defeat and death and maiming for untold numbers of Americans and Vietnamese."[79] Other CIA officers who now swear that the numbers had been massaged include George Allen, John T. Moore, John Dickerson, Dwain Gatterdam, Thomas Becker, and Douglas Parry.[80]

Despite all the fiddling with the numbers, the more fundamental dispute was about the definition of the enemy. From General Westmoreland's perspective, the irregular forces were not a military threat and therefore should not have been counted, or, if they were, they were the responsibility of the South Vietnamese. Some of his officers, however, perceived that lower numbers were wanted and they juggled the truth. There was at least a massive breakdown of communication within the military headquarters in Saigon.

The military's conduct during this episode was not characteristic. Normally the military overestimates the size of the enemy to secure more troops and equipment, and bigger budgets. So why did it fight to reduce the estimate of the NLF's forces?

According to one observer familiar with the ways of Washington, "The high priests of Saigon decided that we were 'winning.' Then the paramount interest became to show the enemy's reduced capability to recruit and a slowdown in infiltration due to our bombing."[81]

By 1967, the military, sensing (or being told) that the White House needed evidence of progress, obliged by fighting with the CIA and Mr. Adams. George Carver told the staff of an investigating committee of the House of Representatives a tantalizing story:

> According to George Allen, pressure was put on CIA by Walt Rostow . . . to prepare positive indicators of progress in the pacification program. When Mr. Allen suggested that there were few, he received the reply, "I am amazed at your unwillingness to support your President in his time of need." Rostow then requested that the Office of Current Intelligence produce a compilation of extracts showing progress, which OCI did, while attaching a cover letter caveat. Rostow removed the cover letter and reported to the President "at last an objective appraisal from CIA."[82]

There were two bureaucratic impulses at work in this sorry tale of the numbers: Officials in the field manipulating the central office by engineering data to make the field look better than it is; and, lying to please the boss. The as yet unanswerable question is whether the boss or his agents ever implied or whispered to the military, as Professor Rostow did to the CIA, what sorts of deceptions the boss or his agents would most enjoy. It is therefore not clear whether the deceptions about the enemy's strength, probably contributing to the terrible surprise of the extent of Tet explosion, was the familiar divergence between men in the field and those in Washington, or whether Washington—the White House—was in secret collusion with the military manipulators. In either case it is obvious that the distorted data could not and did not lead to sensible decisions in Washington or in the field. It did contribute to the national shock over Tet, coming as it did in the atmosphere of the military's cheeriness about the declining strength of the enemy.

The deceit was not always practiced long distance. Ambassador Bunker and General Westmoreland briefed President Johnson in November 1967, shortly before Tet. They showed the President several charts, prepared in General Westmoreland's Saigon headquarters, that allegedly documented "progress" on the ground. Professor Rostow's cover memo said that "the evidence of progress these statistics demonstrate" was "confirmed" by other sources. One important chart, entitled "VC/NVA Strength," showed enemy strength in 1965 as 207,000, in 1966 as 285,000, and in 1967 as 242,000.[83] This "proved" that the war was progressing in the right direction. The problem, however, was that the guerrillas' self-defense forces were included in the first two years but not in the third. The military's own separate OB figures for these three years shows that this chart was composed only of hot air. David Boies, CBS's attorney in the case brought by General Westmoreland, told me that if the year 1967 on the chart had included the same groups as had been included in the other two years, the correct figure for 1967 would have been over 400,000, not 242,000. The difference was simple: Instead of winning the war, as the chart shown to the President indicated, the war was being lost. It is not possible to know what "confirmed . . . evidence of progress" Professor Rostow was talking about.

In a bureaucracy, the displeasure of the boss can destroy the integrity of information provided by intelligence agencies. Richard Helms was not a fool, and he did not resist Mr. Adams out of a desire to mislead the nation. He resisted him to obey the bureaucratic imperative to protect his organization. The question in his mind must have been whether accuracy about the size of the NLF was worth the isolation of the Agency, with the result, as had happened before, that the President considered its reports irrelevant. Mr. Rostow was already sending CIA studies to the President with little handwritten editorial comments:

"Usual CIA bias."[84] If truth could destroy the Agency's bureaucratic "effectiveness," it was apparently better to hide the truth on which its actual effectiveness depended. There is a biblical sentiment cut into the marble of the CIA's building: "And ye shall know the truth, and the truth shall make you free." Unless the boss objects.

One of the bureaucratic facts of life for an intelligence officer is that personal success frequently depends on being pessimistic. Intelligence officers who work in offices and can sniff the political winds are more attuned to this fact than the covert-operations types who conduct sabotage in the field. One intelligence analyst tried to explain reality to a hyperactive adventurer: "Look, the way to get ahead in this outfit is to be always opposed . . . about any operation that's suggested. Never be enthusiastic. Almost all operations end up failures finally. If you get known as having been opposed to the idea from the beginning, people think you are very shrewd and must be a good administrator."[85]

An intelligence expert would be dismissed as a fool if he predicted an easy operation that turned out to be hard, and would be dismissed as a national menace if his favorable prediction actually contributed to an operation that failed, as in the Bay of Pigs. Many astute bureaucrats outside of intelligence, including Henry Kissinger, were familiar with this reflex, with the result that policymakers did not generally rely on intelligence reports. In the context of the Vietnam War, this was a mistake. When intelligence officers "covered their ass" by being gloomy, they prepared the closest approximation of the truth that was available during the war. Their negative exaggerations caused by bureaucratic timidity and personal ambition often turned out to be unintentionally accurate.

Two weeks before President Nixon authorized the invasion of Cambodia, the CIA's analysts had given Mr. Helms a report on the likely outcome of such an operation. According to the report an invasion would not prevent the North Vietnamese from continuing the war. When the President asked Mr. Helms for his support of the invasion, the director gave it and suppressed his agency's report. The analysts within the CIA were furious, and began a petition to fire the boss. It was swept under the rug. Mr. Helms's fear of his boss deprived the boss of reality. In this case the problem was that the boss rejected reality. By 1970, as one scholar said, Dr. Kissinger had broken the CIA:

"The CIA no longer automatically analyzed intelligence data on critical issues, but immediately turned over the raw information to Kissinger and the NSC for them to analyze as they saw fit and draw whatever conclusion they chose."[86]

At the same time that the military successfully fought off the idea that the irregular guerrillas counted, the American government decided to do something about them and their supporters. On the surface it looked as if the Americans were preparing to understand and respond to the wide range of activities that constituted the insurgency. This would be difficult because it required persuading the people of South Vietnam who supported the NLF to align themselves with Thieu's government. Because we are practiced at devising new bureaucratic arrangements, the new program was launched with high hopes.

It began with the appointment of Robert Komer, a former CIA analyst, as an assistant to President Johnson. Mr. Komer understood that an effective bureaucratic approach to a people's war required making somebody responsible for its success. As he wrote, "Counterinsurgency fell between the stools; it was everybody's business and nobody's."[87] The declaratory policy of the war Presidents had always emphasized the importance of the NLF, but performance in the field consistently swung in the other direction, the "strategy" of attrition.

Mr. Komer predicted that bureaucratic resistance would develop against a new interdepartmental operating agency, and persuaded the President that the chief of the new program would require a title sufficient to persuade the bureaucrats and technocrats to get in line. In late 1966, LBJ appointed Mr. Komer as the head of the Civilian Operations and Revolutionary Development Support (CORDS), with the title of ambassador. He asked for and got William Colby, a former CIA chief of station in Saigon and future head of the CIA, as his deputy. Now, presumably, President Johnson was prepared to fight the "other war" he had emphasized at the Honolulu conference of that year.

Ambassador Komer, nicknamed "Blowtorch" by Henry Cabot Lodge, reported to the President, but he was placed within the military hierarchy of General Westmoreland's headquarters on the quaint idea that this would make the military responsible for the program. The insertion of high civilian authority into the military structure was extraordinary. About a dozen different programs formerly run by the State Department, Defense, and the CIA, among others, were all placed under the CORDS umbrella, and although this was not a CIA program, the CIA's men were in charge. By 1969, when CORDS was at its peak, it employed 1,100 civilians and 6,500 military men to advise 900,000 South Vietnamese in paramilitary units, the police, and in the civil service.

The CIA was determined to collect information about the "Vietcong infrastructure," the full sweep of activities that supported the guerrillas. Ambassador Komer, roughly translating from the Vietnamese *phung hoang,* called this program Phoenix. Its point was to "neutralize" those who were providing aid and comfort to the NLF. As General Westmoreland put it, the "project aimed at identifying and excising the VC political infrastructure."[88] The technique was to organize South Vietnamese police or paramilitary "reconnaissance" units to find and "detain" individuals within the "infrastructure" who would provide information about others to be detained, with the ballooning effect of a chain letter. "Interrogation centers" were set up in every province, three in Saigon, and more for each of the military zones. Ambassador Komer set prisoner quotas for each of the 242 districts in South Vietnam, assigned CIA personnel to "advise," and a carefully organized and well-financed campaign of fresh terror was laid on every city, every hamlet, wherever anyone held a grudge against anyone else.

Even before it was all over, according to Mr. Colby, who replaced Mr. Komer in 1968, Phoenix produced 17,000 Vietnamese who surrendered to the program to win "amnesty," 28,000 who were captured, and 20,587 (the South Vietnamese government said this figure should be doubled) who were killed. "But the word was 'killed,' " Mr. Colby later wrote, "not 'assassinated.' "[89] The killings did not become characteristic until the prisons were filled, including the infamous tiger cages, prefabricated in California under contract to the U.S. Navy. The intelligence estimate before Phoenix rose from the ashes was that the "infrastructure" contained about 70,000 people. Mr. Colby's figure of the number "neutralized" was already 65,000.

There are two questions about all this. How did it happen that the original decision to find a way to win the allegiance of the South Vietnamese turned into a program of bribery, arrest, and killing? Was Phoenix, as widely claimed by its critics, an assassination program?

The answer to the first question seems to be that not even the ingenuity of Americans was equal to the task of creating popular allegiance to President's Thieu's government. In that case, there was nothing that CORDS could do to "neutralize" the NLF in political terms. This was the time when Dr. Kissinger was meeting secretly in Paris to negotiate a peace on condition that President Thieu remain in office. Unable to win with Thieu, unable to act on the knowledge that he was a problem, not a solution, CORDS eliminated the insurgency by killing and detention, not by winning the allegiance of the villagers.

The senior CORDS administrators knew that every Phoenix target had to be identified with something close to absolute accuracy, as Mr. Colby agreed: "Action against an innocent person would produce hostility and sullen resistance throughout his village, causing a far greater loss to our campaign than any ten proper arrests could compensate for."[90] But because the intelligence net began with the confessions of prisoners, many of whom were tortured despite the CIA's conviction that torture produces bad intelligence, and because the CORDS apparatus paid cash to impoverished villagers who accused others, the likelihood of error was not zero.

According to several ex-CIA officials who were on the scene, Phoenix was not a precise operation. The CIA's chief strategy analyst in Saigon said the problem was that no one was clear about the definition of a suspect:

> Bureaucratically, the problem was definition. No one, neither Vietnamese nor American, had ever decided who was to be considered a Viet Cong cadreman. Was he a local village chief who served the North Vietnamese part time? Or did the definition extend only to hard-core Communists with full party membership? For lack of finite guidance the Phoenix strike teams opted for a scattershot approach, picking up anyone who might be a suspect, and eventually when the jails were filled to overflowing they began simply taking the law, such as it was, in to their own hands.[91]

There was no law to worry about because Phoenix operated outside of the courts, and depended on something called administrative detention. One CORDS directive (1970) clarified the requirements of proof for arrest. Among other acceptable proofs were statements of others "regarding the position or function of the accused" and "interrogation statements or confessions." That the Phoenix administrators were not overly fastidious is shown by their instruction to the field agents: "Intelligence reports are admissible in that there is no prohibition against hearsay." People were subject to administrative detention in cases where "sufficient evidence for a trial" was lacking.[92] The ultimate conclusion in this directive was clear: "A violation of the national security laws need not be proven; all that must be demonstrated is that a reasonable belief exists that the suspect threatens the national security."[93] It would be difficult to show that such orders contributed to the precision that Mr. Colby considered essential.

At a congressional hearing, Mr. Colby obviously could not deny that there had been assassinations under the wings of Phoenix. No one could know, despite the typhoon of rumors about police with silenced guns murdering sleeping people. No one could know because the program was nationwide, and the Phoenix squads were everywhere. Mr. Colby did insist that "over 85 percent" of the 20,587 official deaths occurred in "combat actions," and only 12 percent by police. "What's more," he added, "most of the latter deaths occurred in fights when the VCI cadre . . . resisted arrest, fled, or otherwise defended themselves." He believed assassinations were unlikely because he had issued specific instructions prohibiting them. This is the bureaucratic reflex: Issuing instructions solves the problem. "I specifically denied that Phoenix was a program to assassinate VCI," Mr. Colby wrote in his memoirs, "and pointed to the clear 1969 directive that I had issued on this point."[94] Why then did his office provide an exit for what a journalist called "the squeamish among Americans," an offer to excuse them from this duty? Although Mr. Colby later denied the horror stories, the CORDS directive was rather generous, as these things go: "If an individual finds the police type activities of the PHOENIX program repugnant to him . . . he can be reassigned from the program without prejudice."[95] No one will ever know what Phoenix actually did, and that includes the people who ran it.

As Phoenix learned, the insurgency was an intensely human

problem. That was why it was so bloody. All the technology and all the technocrats could not solve the equation between the guerrillas and their village support. The fundamental issue was always political, and neither detention nor killing were germane. By 1969, the CIA apparently had an attack of institutional squeamishness and pulled out of CORDS, ran for cover, as a former CIA analyst said. The CIA shifted its position largely because it concluded that Phoenix was inappropriate as a consequence of what it believed was an important shift in the North's tactics. It believed the North had moved away from military engagement to lacing the entire government of the South with spies, some said as many as 30,000, so that Thieu's government could be easily overthrown after the Americans left. The CIA therefore embarked on independent intelligence work, that is, stealing secrets from both the South and North Vietnamese. It is also reasonable to assume that, for some reason, Phoenix worried some of the bureaucrats within the CIA, especially those who never believed that covert operations were as important as gathering intelligence.

Nonetheless, the CIA now committed what was probably its most outrageous intelligence failure of the war. Again, this error was not a result of an inability to gather the facts, but an unwillingness to trust them. It had to do with the route by which supplies were provided to the NLF. The military had for a long time insisted that supplies were coming through the port of Sihanoukville in Cambodia. The CIA denied this, arguing that the Ho Chi Minh trail was the primary route. The Agency had almost always found that the military's bombing of the North was not having the desired effect, and that the men and supplies continued to flow to the South down the trail. Because the American navy had effectively blockaded the seas, the North could not ship matériel along the sea routes, so the trail had become essential to the North. But the army kept insisting that great quantities of supplies were moving through Sihanoukville.

Those who favored bombing and invading Cambodia argued that Sihanoukville was an important supply depot; those who did not preferred the Ho Chi Minh trail. The bureaucratic war over the significance of the port, according to a CIA officer, "raged all over town."[96] President Nixon, always suspicious about the CIA, liked what the military was saying. Yet, the CIA had a report in hand that about 6,000 tons of matériel was coming through Sihanoukville. The report came from one of the CIA's spies in Cambodia. Paul Walsh, a CIA intelligence analyst, disregarded this inside information. The military had been estimating that 18,000 tons were passing through the port. Enemy documents captured in Cambodia raised that figure to 23,000 tons. Director Helms wanted an explanation of this failure, so he appointed a committee of inquiry and named Mr. Walsh its chairman. Ultimately, the CIA's pride in itself was at stake. Sam Adams told me that the CIA, having argued its case for so long, could not contemplate the fact that the military had been right all along. "Bureaucratic pride was the cause of the breakdown."[97] The two men who had led the CIA's struggle to downgrade the importance of the port were soon promoted.

The Washington bureaucracy did not want to know enough to manage the American bureaucracies in Vietnam, as the case of John Paul Vann illustrates. In 1962, when Lieutenant Colonel Vann was thirty-seven years old, he was in the Delta region in South Vietnam to command a team of two hundred advisers. He worked closely with the Vietnamese, understood guerrilla war, and refused to report "progress" to Saigon headquarters when there was none to report. He became the "most informed American in the country."[98] In the autumn of 1963, he admitted in a news magazine that the war was being lost because the South Vietnamese senior officers obeying their government's orders would not fight the guerrillas. There were two reasons for this. Diem and Nhu were afraid that a successful army might turn against them, and they were afraid that American aid would be cut if the guerrillas were beaten. He said these views were "almost universal among military people who are not afraid to speak out."[99]

His superiors, General Harkins and General Maxwell Taylor, did everything possible to muzzle him. His reports were censored and suppressed. He returned to the States in the summer to discover they had ordered that he not give a report to Pentagon officials. He did brief a few friends, presenting hard data. Others heard about his presentation and asked to hear it in person. As the circle widened, the deputy chief of staff of the army heard it and prepared for the JCS to be briefed. Lieutenant Colonel Vann was warned not to be critical of General Harkins because Maxwell Taylor, now Chairman of the JCS, was protective of his protégé.

John Paul Vann showed up early for his presentation. While he was waiting, a phone rang on an aide's desk. The aide asked, *"Who* wants the item removed from the agenda?" He then asked whether the order came from the Secretary of Defense or the Chairman, Maxwell Taylor. The aide continued: "Let me get this right. The Chairman *requests* that the item be removed."[100] The Pentagon was spared from hearing what it did not want to hear and could continue to give the President encouraging news.

As soon as possible, John Paul Vann resigned from the army.[101] This pattern was repeated by other officers throughout the war. Shortly after Tet 68, thirty-three officers on the West Point faculty quietly resigned from the army, as some said for personal reasons, but it is too coincidental for so large a group to resign at about the same time for only personal reasons.

The Pentagon was content to learn about Vietnam from selected field reports and crash inspections by senior Washington officials. When the officers in the field did not know what was happening in their own operations, obviously something would get lost in the transmission, and decisions by the President would have to be based on something other than reality. Nevertheless, the military and its political allies complained then, and continue to complain, that the problem of Vietnam was too much interference by civilians over military matters. The systems analysts in DoD claimed the problem was just the opposite, not enough management by Washington, and in studies they conducted they were usually right.

Essentially, Washington left the conduct of the war to the military. The "conduct" of the war means the war's tactics, and because there was no strategy, the tactics were everything. What the Presidents did was define where the war was to be fought and set budgetary and manpower limits, although the military's role in such matters was usually decisive. Secretary McNamara said that he would leave the war to the generals because they were experts and he was not. The generals in the Pentagon deferred to their general in the field. Although the American ambassador in Saigon was the formal head of the entire American presence in Vietnam, the parade of ambassadors always deferred to the commanding officer. This delicate dance of bureaucratic deference was motivated by a desire to avoid responsibility for a military failure, by a recognition of incompetence, but mostly by the fact that this is the way bureaucracies work.

The divergence between policy and performance was made worse by the distance of 10,000 miles between the two. But even when attempts were made to coordinate operations, there were ways to resist. For instance, joint campaign plans were sometimes negotiated between the U.S. and South Vietnam. One corps-level commander was asked what he thought of a recent joint plan. He answered, "I never read them, it would only confuse me."[102] This sort of passive aggression was one way to maintain autonomy, but it was not the best way.

The greatest leeway was found by interpreting vague or ambiguous orders as one wished. Dr. Kissinger learned this lesson about the State Department: The Foreign Service "will carry out clear-cut instructions with great loyalty, but the typical Foreign Service officer is not easily persuaded that an instruction with which he disagrees is really clear-cut."[103] This reflex is compounded in the military.

McGeorge Bundy explained this process in the use of chemicals, especially herbicides, including Agent Orange. The original authorizations to spray, Mr. Bundy said, "were narrowly framed, at least as understood by civilians in Washington." He remembered that the first goal was to restrict herbicides to destroying foliage "along narrow jungle trails." There was no intention to destroy crops. A senior Pentagon officer testified before Congress in 1969 that by then the military had developed "five separate classes of military use of herbicides." Mr. Bundy correctly said that this was not a matter of outright insubordination. It was simply that "under the pressure of availability and battlefield urgency, the initial authorizations from Washington have been steadily widened."[104] It is probable that no single officer ever decided to subvert policy. It occurred partly in response to the military maxim that "if you've got it, use it." A sign hung in the ready room of the pilots who sprayed defoliants: "Only you can prevent forests."[105]

In a bureaucratic society, the military's most important task is to take responsibility for victory and defeat. That is why it is always reluctant to get involved, as it was reluctant about Vietnam in the 1950s, but wants an all-out commitment when it is ordered to fight. This responsibility for battlefield results is immense and carries the consequence of personal and organizational glory or humiliation. The military is understandably proud of its exclusive ownership of this accountability. The pressure on civilians to leave the military alone is enormous. Should a civilian order result in a military loss, the military would be freed of its burden, and the civilian authority would surely suffer. President Truman came close when he fired General MacArthur. Civilians are usually paralyzed with fear at the idea of sharing the military's unique capacity to face the possibility of blame and shame.

The Nixon administration abandoned counterinsurgency. Its attention was fixed on three other policies: withdrawing American troops, strengthening the South Vietnamese military establishment, and linking Vietnam to global geopolitics. One analyst wrote that by "the mid 1970s, very little if anything remained of the analytical structure which constituted the justification for the gravity with which, in the 1960s, the United States had viewed the threat of people's war and the urgency with which it sought to counter it."[106] So important a switch of strategy in so brief a period was historically extraordinary. Yet, this switch was not a result of a new team in Washington, but of different assumptions about the war.

The Nixon administration realized that the guerrillas no longer were a significant threat. The NLF was chewed to pieces during Tet, and the remainder was devoured by Phoenix. Some prominent Communists admitted as much. Dr. Duong Quynh Hoa said of Tet, "We lost our best people." A North Vietnamese officer reported that Phoenix resulted in "the loss of thousands of our cadres." Nguyen Co Thach, the foreign minister of Vietnam after the unification of the country in 1975, conceded that Phoenix "wiped out many of our bases."[107] The proof is that the North's remaining two offensives, in 1972 and when it achieved its final goal in 1975, did not rely on the guerrillas. Between the NLF's fatal mistake during Tet and America's terroristic attack on the terrorists, the guerrillas had been "neutralized."

This success, as usual in Vietnam, backfired. We had destroyed much of the NLF's military capability, but, as William Colby warned and did nothing about, we had created a nation of "sullen villagers." Robert Komer later agreed that CORDS, including Phoenix, did not result in "positive and active rural population support for the Government of Vietnam."[108] The Phoenix program, probably more than anything else, created a society, such as it was, that was waiting for us to go away so the killing would stop.

The virtual destruction of the insurgency in the South caused the North to change its strategy. It committed itself to a long war of big-unit engagement, just the kind of war America's generals had always hoped for. In early 1970, General Giap conceded that future progress could be made only through "*regular war* in which the main forces fight in a concentrated manner."[109] But now the North would not have to face Americans. From the minute Mr. Nixon announced that America's troops would be withdrawn, there was no reason for the North to continue the daily struggle. It responded in three ways: It had to survive Mr. Nixon's bombing campaigns; it had to avoid a decisive loss in the South; and it had to negotiate peace terms that would ensure its ultimate victory over President Thieu. Because it was capable of all three responses, North Vietnam won the war.

It is possible that President Nixon's policy of Vietnamization threw away a military victory in the Vietnam War. It is possible that after Tet and bloody Phoenix, another escalation of the war would have brought the results Americans had been hoping for since 1950.

However, it is not possible to imagine Mr. Nixon ratchetting the war up instead of down. The lies of the government before Tet led to the almost universal perception of Tet as an American disaster. It was not the distorted press reports of Tet that disillusioned the American people. It was the distorted official reports of the government itself. By then Americans had enough of that "lousy little war." President Nixon had not fought so hard to win the presidency merely to get stuck in Vietnam even for the sake of victory there. Accurately reading the strains in American culture he did what had to be done: end the draft, reduce casualties as elections neared, and rely on American technology. He thought he could end the war by manipulating the American people. He was mistaken. After so many lies, so much carnage, the myth of the city on a hill no longer provided the moral justification for American involvement in Vietnam. After so many disappointments, so much tested patience, the cultural faith in technology became weaker than the desire to cut our losses and run. The North's conviction that American culture would not be able to sustain the war proved to be correct.

President Reagan has claimed that our politicians withheld permission for the military to win. Some Americans wanted out more than a victory, and most Americans wanted out more than additional frustration. The military was not beaten in battle; American culture was beaten in the face of victories. The political and military leaders of the nation taught the people to distrust the legitimacy of governmental institutions, to become cynical, and to abandon the nation's war aims. The war and its official salesmen were finally judged as counterfeit. The war's casualties were considered as political victims. The hideous bureaucracy of the war made it all seem worse.

Because the North Vietnamese understood something of the culture of Americans, they believed they would win if they did not lose, if they could just hang on. The American war leaders believed they would lose if they did not win. Both sides were right. When military victory proved elusive both in fact and perception, the Americans—LBJ and Professor Rostow, RN and Professor Kissinger—were perhaps driven into manipulating mirrors as a substitute for substance. They thus joined with the North Vietnamese in the attempt to manipulate the Americans. But time was always on the enemy's side. Benjamin Franklin taught us that time is money. As we spent billions, they spent years. They paid a higher price in lives. Their investment succeeded.

SEVEN

THE
WARRIORS

The drafted grunts who humped the boonies came from all over America. Street-smart ghetto kids, raised in the basketball wars, became battlefield buddies with dewy farm kids from Minnesota, patriotic, wide-eyed innocents who choked up a little when they sang "God Bless America." Hispanics, passionately ambivalent about Anglo culture, fought and drank alongside their closest war pals, the steelworkers, gas station attendants, and high school dropouts who never had a steady job. The entire nation went or was sent to war, except for the rich, the middle class, the vast majority of college students, and individuals who objected to war, or who objected to that war.

After LBJ decided to send combat troops, and after the draftees were moved into combat, the Vietnam War was fought by working-class teenagers. The draft was designed to produce that result. The average age of the American soldiers in Vietnam was just over nineteen. In World War II, the average age of the GIs who were in for the duration was about twenty-six. It was said that the military brass understood that Vietnam was a teenage war, that the kids were unruly, and that there was not much that could be done about actually imposing discipline on these post-adolescents, strong boymen who were juicers and drank too much, or were smokers on skag or pot, and were too irreverent to obey by instinct or tradition. The youth of the Viet grunts, the popularity of black English, and the metastasis of military jargon help to explain why this was the slangiest war ever recorded.

As in Korea, the army, navy, and air force rotated individuals out in twelve months, and, until 1969, the marines in thirteen. They were almost always replaced one by one by new meat, or twinks, or cherries, or FNGs (fuckin' new guys) who were twelve or thirteen months younger than they were on their DEROS (date eligible for return from overseas).

When these kids enlisted or were drafted, at least after the American invasion in 1965, they knew that the so-called crazies were protesting the war, running away to Canada, hiding in colleges. Many of these soldiers had not thought much about the war, disliked the long hair of the hippies, and were offended by TV pictures of braless young women. Like most of the rest of the nation, they rejected the war protesters without thinking much about the war. Some men enlisted to get a better deal than the draft offered, or to get a new start in their young lives, or because a close friend signed up, or to escape the family, or to see the world, or to combat Communism. Some did not know why they enlisted. For some, it was an article of faith that the President knows best, and when he calls, you go.

George Ryan enlisted after he graduated from high school in Virginia. He had only read girlie magazines, sports magazines, and racing-car magazines. "If Vietnam was such a mistake," he asked, "how come the leaders of our country, the wisest men we have . . . how come they sent us in? None of the doves I ever met had any answers to *that*."[1]

A student of the army collected more of these reactions:

> I know one thing. Before I went in, my brother could kick my ass, but now he can't. . . . He ain't nothing no more.

> The only thing I used to read was sports. . . . So I didn't have any feelings one way or the other. I figured it was more or less right, because why would I be going if it wasn't right?

> I knew almost nothing about it. The war I thought was like they taught us in high school, you know, you're fighting communism, you know, it was just the good guys against the bad guys.[2]

A majority of the kids who were drafted thought of the draft as an event like measles, a graduation, the weather, something that happened to people. Young men got drafted as their fathers had in earlier wars. Sometimes brothers were already in. You had to do it because it had been done before, and probably would always be done, and you had to take your turn. It was usually more intimate and domestic than patriotism, although occasionally that too played a role. More often it was an unwillingness to let someone down, to hold up your end, and to do the right thing, as that was defined in the family and in the small circle of good friends. There is not much soul-searching required to honor so simple an obligation. Someday you have to earn a living, probably marry and have children, pay taxes, but first you get drafted.

There were more enlistees than conscripts, but the draftees were especially vulnerable. They were more likely than the enlistees to find themselves in the shooting war. The draftees made up 16 percent of the battle deaths in 1965; in 1969, they were 62 percent. Draftees represented 88 percent of infantry riflemen in 1970. The army apparently considered the draftees disposable—throw-away, nonreturnable men.

The Vietnam draft was an ideal model of discriminatory social policy. It kept the middle class from creating political pressure on the war administrations. So the draft was biased by level of income. The higher the income, the less chance of being drafted, importantly but not exclusively because of educational deferments. Poor young Americans, white as well as black and Hispanic, were twice as likely to be drafted and twice as likely to be assigned to combat as wealthier draft-aged youth. The draft rejected many blacks, but it was more likely to accept poor men than richer men with the same qualifications, or the same lack of qualifications. As a result, poor black Americans were swept into the fighting war in disproportionate numbers. Economic class, even more than race, except that people of color were more likely to be poor, was what determined who fought and who died. In 1980, the VA commissioned a survey of attitudes about the Viet vets and concluded that "while minority Americans may have suffered a disproportionate share of the exposure to combat and combat fatalities, their suffering was the product not of racial discrimination, but of discrimination against the poor, the uneducated, and the young. . . ."[3] General

Westmoreland reported that the state with the highest number of deaths in relation to population was West Virginia.

Alongside the deferred students was a large body of boys who could not meet the military's minimum physical or mental standards, the group Secretary McNamara called "part of America's subterranean poor" when he announced Project 100,000. This was to be a program to rehabilitate 100,000 poor men a year so they could be accepted into the military. Allegedly, they would be trained to improve their skills, earn higher incomes for the rest of their lives, and receive veterans' benefits. However, the useful training never amounted to much, although several hundred thousand of them, 40 percent black, did fight in the rice paddies. They were called the "moron corps" by other GIs. Instead of training these men to meet the military's standards, the military lowered its standards for admission, but not for the training necessary for the desirable military jobs. Senator Moynihan, then the official guru about the black family, hailed the program because he said it would teach black men some self-respect. One army officer told a plainer truth: "I'd prefer a company of riflemen with fifth-grade educations over a company of college men anytime."[4]

Education in this country is a badge of class. One study of Chicago neighborhoods found that kids from areas with low educational levels were four times as likely to be killed in Vietnam than those from more schooled neighborhoods. It was as if the war had been designed to digest America's victims, the men President Eisenhower called the "sitting ducks"[5] for the draft. Class and education also shaped the experience of the young men who enlisted. Two staff officials of President Ford's clemency board showed that a college graduate who enlisted had about a 40 percent chance of being sent to Vietnam, while a high school graduate's chance was about 65 percent, and that of a high-school dropout was 70 percent.[6]

Something of a price was also paid by the fortunate children —the future professionals—of the families who could afford to send their sons to college. After the war, James Fallows, a writer, described his own guilt in an article called "What Did You Do in the Class War, Daddy?" The draft lottery had assigned him a low number in 1969, when he was a senior at Harvard. To avoid the draft and the risks involved in draft resistance, he chose to get a physical deferment, "the thinking man's route." His physical exam was held at the Boston Navy Yard, and he and almost all his Harvard friends managed to flunk. As the students were delightedly leaving, another contingent of potential draftees arrived, this time from Chelsea: "thick dark-haired young men, the white proles of Boston." The new arrivals were fresh out of high school "and it had clearly never occurred to them that there might be a way around the draft." About four in five of the Harvard students were deferred; about four in five of the working-class men were sent to war. Mr. Fallows concluded, "We let the boys from Chelsea be sent off to die."[7]

One general described the troops to a journalist, as invented by James Webb in a novel that tells a truth. A general asked who are the foot soldiers, and answered: "They are the best we have. But they are not McNamara's sons, or Bundy's. I doubt they're yours. And they know they're at the end of the pipeline. That no one cares. They know."[8]

Combat troops in Vietnam were aware that the majority of their age group was beating the draft and they hated it. It made some of them feel like fools for being there while others stayed at home, in "the World," to prepare for careers, to party, or to struggle against the war the grunts were trying to fight. For instance, Steve Harper, a poor kid from Ohio, said, "The critics are pickin' on us, just 'cause we had to fight in this war. Where were their sons? In fancy colleges?"[9] Some campus protesters disliked this inequality, but justified their privilege on the grounds that the war was immoral. They must have assumed that less well-educated victims of the draft thought it was moral. Some of the privileged young men argued that they were so talented, and already so well educated, that they would serve the nation best if they were left alone to pursue their careers as physicians, lawyers, executives, or professors. When graduate-school deferments were ended in 1967, the Harvard *Crimson* editorialized that the new policy was "careless expediency" and "unfair to students."[10]

General Westmoreland admitted that the draft was "discriminatory, undemocratic and resulted in the war being fought by the poor man's son." He believed that the antiwar movement on the campuses was caused by a "guilt complex" suffered by the beneficiaries of injustice. He also argued that the army had to lower its standards and commission "some marginal types" because ROTC was closed down by protests on many of the best campuses. Finally, he said that when college deferments ran out, the army suffered "an education inversion," with thousands of new privates with college and graduate degrees taking orders from less well-educated officers.[11]

Of the 27,000,000 men who constituted the male half of the post-World War II baby boom and who were eligible for the draft during the war, 2,215,000 were actually drafted, while 8,700,000 enlisted. More than 500,000 more—the group Richard Nixon called "those few hundreds"—technically became criminals to evade or resist the draft. Approximately 16,000,000 had deferments, exemptions, or disqualifications. Of these two groups, millions had their lives changed because of the threat of the draft, the moral crisis of deciding what to do about it, and the terror that some experienced, or the isolation that many more experienced, in leaving the country or going underground to resist.

The set of circumstances the grunt could expect when he arrived in Vietnam is better understood now than it was at the time. The human risks of the war are clarified by the end-of-war figures: Altogether, about 58,000 men were killed, and about 300,000 were wounded, half badly enough to be hospitalized. Only the marines had more casualties in Vietnam (105,000) than in World War II (90,000). Of the 2,700,000 men who served in Vietnam, more than 500,000 received less than honorable discharges. That made jobs harder to find after they returned.

It was worse for American blacks. In earlier wars, black Americans had to struggle for the right to fight. Now, blacks comprised 11 percent of the population. One study showed that in 1966, only about 1 percent of draft-board members were black. Seven states had no blacks on draft boards.[12] American discrimination against blacks prevented them from getting Vietnam assignments that would improve their skills. They were assigned to combat in proportions far exceeding their numbers, and this is one of the reasons why Martin Luther King spoke against the war, against the "cruel manipulation of the poor."[13]

None of the foot soldiers could have been prepared for Vietnam, for the climate of the land or the climate of the war. When they climbed out of the chartered plane that sped them to Vietnam—unlike earlier wars when the slower troop ships allowed time for some adjustment to the coming realities—they were physically hit by the heat, by the sensation that here is where the war is. One Braniff pilot announced as he descended into Vietnam: "The temperature outside is one hundred and three degrees; groundfire is light to moderate."[14] They were processed, assigned a place, and went off to find the war, or to let the war find them.

Sometimes the process was not quite so routine. The novelist Tim O'Brien wrote about the reenlistment officer who would show up just before the fresh and petrified GIs were sent out to their first fight. This officer explained that some of them were about to be killed: "It's gotta happen. One or two of you men, your ass is grass." If they would reenlist for another three years, he would reassign them from combat to a safe job in the rear. "Then what?" the re-up NCO asked. "Well, I'll tell you what, it'll save your ass."[15] On that day, none of the men accepted his offer.

One of the patterns of the grunts' life in Vietnam, as in earlier wars, was the realization, always in a fire fight, that hey, this is real, that somebody is trying to kill me, really kill me, and I might never make it out of here. A combat sergeant: "The first time you were under fire, you thought, 'How the fuck can they do this to me? If only I could talk to the cocksuckers firing at me, we'd get along.' . . . We're just pawns in this fucking thing, throwing the shit at each other."[16] In the midst of it, in the terror of a fire fight, most of the GIs realized that one way to survive was to kill first, or kill more, not in the interest of the grand abstractions of patriotism, or freedom, or strategy, but to survive.

Survival was the strategy of the American GI, not different from soldiers in earlier wars. But, for the great majority of Vietnam grunts, there was no external purpose to the war—not defending national goals, not resisting an evil enemy, not defending motherhood and apple pie. As a result, there was no animating justification for combat or for risk. The best way to survive was to keep away from danger. This absence of external purpose made it difficult for some to develop a sense of shared enterprise with other GIs outside their own unit. Because the replacements were inserted into the war as individuals, not as members of a unit, these GIs were in fact movable parts, separate cogs in the war's machinery. Such separateness induced a sense of fragility, probably more intense and widespread than in other wars. The separate arrivals and departures, along with the absence of shared purpose, emphasized the individuality of the grunt, even while they formed the life-saving bonds of brotherhood in their small squads or platoons. It is touching and painful to hear how often the veterans felt alone.

The grunt was the instrument of General Westmoreland's "strategy" of attrition. For entirely different reasons, the grunts' war plan became identical with the general's. There was no real estate that had to be taken and held, there were no objectives to be seized. The plan was to kill the enemy, wherever and whoever he or she was. Because the body count was the scorecard, killing supposedly proved progress. This made war sense from the grunt's perspective because it was simply based on the desire to live, not necessarily callousness or moral collapse, but war through the eyes of the walking conscripts.

That is why the "other war," the ideological war, meant nothing to most of them. It did not seem, at least in the short run, the time that really mattered, to protect their lives. So they mocked the entire effort to "win the hearts and minds" of the Vietnamese by referring to it as WHAM and embroidering it even further: "Grab 'em by the balls and their hearts and minds will follow."[17]

Luis Martinez, a Puerto Rican marine, decided he would learn something about the Vietnamese and treat them with respect because "if the Viet Cong is going to do something, he remembers you and you have a better chance of surviving."[18] In this sense, winning hearts and minds might help him to return home in one piece. It was like money in the bank that could produce interest in the future. But in this war's twists, respect and friendship for the Vietnamese could backfire. For example, a sergeant became friends with a Vietnamese woman and her daughter. They were both killed by the NLF because they had associated with him. He decided that from then on he would leave them all alone. For most, the "other war" would take too long, was out of focus, and was therefore not a good shield for the vital or fatal 365 days they would be targets.

The grunts hated bloody fighting to take a fire base, perhaps losing buddies in the process, and then being ordered to abandon the base to fight or patrol somewhere else, and then having to endure another fire fight to recapture the first base. Some bases were retaken three or four or more times. One GI put it this way: "We don't take any land. We don't give it back. We just mutilate bodies. What the fuck are we doing here?"[19] It seemed senseless to risk everything over and over for the same piece of turf. There was no achievement to show for the mutilations and deaths. Except the numbers. They had to train themselves to think of achievement by the numbers. Many, probably most, could not do it. They could not think of what they were doing only in terms of the body count. Even in war, death was supposed to be for something, not a thing in itself.

They recognized that the body counts were being hyped to satisfy, or shut up, corrupt officers who kept demanding higher numbers. The men could deliver any number any REMF, "rear echelon mother fucker," wanted. Of course that made the killing even more pointless. If the brass would accept fake numbers, and if the whole point of the war was numbers, why risk your life to get real kills? The war could have been fought over the radio, with a squad or company reporting whatever number was wanted. That is what sometimes happened. The grunts knew it was fraudulent and they became contemptuous of their officers. For example, after one fire fight, Herb Mock, a rifle-squad leader, said: "General Westmoreland flew in. All the news outfits and everything. It was the most hilarious thing. As these son of a bitches came out there, the GIs started lying. The newsmen would walk up to just anybody and say, 'What did you do?' 'I singlehandedly killed three hundred thousand with my bowie knife.'"[20] Lieutenant Robert Santos spoke for many when he said, "You come home with the high body count, high kill ratios. What a fucking way to live your life."[21]

They thought it should have been done differently, and then we would have won. Some said that American power—tanks, planes, all the sophisticated equipment, and all the American men—should have been arranged in a line across Vietnam's southernmost rice paddies. Then they should walk north. One of the grunts said that whatever the GIs left behind them in this march would be something they *wanted* behind them. They should keep walking until there was nowhere left to walk within the country. Then the war would be over, and America would win. The trouble with this, of course, was that *they* would never let it happen, and the fighting around in circles, walking point through the same treeline over and over again, ambushing and being ambushed, hunting and being hunted, instead of real soldiering, would go on forever.

Real soldiering meant that you could capture a place and hold it. It meant a sense of progress, however slow and incremental, toward a known goal. After all, if you captured enough places, you could finally win the war. Many GIs were hugely unimpressed with complicated explanations about the fact that the NLF aimed to control people, not territory. The Vietnamese guerrillas were willing for the Americans to dominate the countryside during the day, approximately from nine to five, so long as they owned the night.

Some grunts were stunned by the open hostility of some South Vietnamese, the people they had come to defend. When they had to run up chicken wire to block the objects, including grenades, that some South Vietnamese threw at them, there was no way they could avoid wondering what they were doing there. It was maddening to discover that the food or medicine they gave to friendlies would be handed to the guerrillas after dark. It was a shock to march past an aged mama-san selling Coca-Cola on the road and notice her head nodding as each grunt passed; she was counting them. What for? What could you make of the fact that the friendlies who washed your clothes or cut your hair were found dead in your ambush of the NLF during the night? And what about the mama-san who brought you things right into your fire base and hung around a little while so she could memorize where your bunkers were so the guerrillas that night could zero in with their mortars? What about the local whores telling you where you were going next, before your own officers had announced it? This war was not like others. You could never identify the enemy. That created constant danger, not merely at the front—there was no front—but everywhere, and not merely during a battle, but anytime. Any Vietnamese could be the one. A T-shirt worn by the grunts displayed the message: KILL THEM ALL! LET GOD SORT THEM OUT!

Having no larger external purpose, there were also often no external constraints. The line beyond which an action would become a transgression was a matter of individual conscience, a Protestant formula. This was as true for the officers as for the troops. The moral formlessness of the bureaucratic war necessarily emphasized technique and means, not goals or purpose. Bureaucracies typically do not do as well at expressing where they wish to go as they do at expressing how to get there. "If you're lost, drive faster; that way you'll get it over with sooner." This left the teenage warriors to their own moral devices, such as they were. Group pressures formed one code of conduct; a watchful officer might sometimes form another. Unlike earlier wars, the Vietnam rule was the moral independence of the foot soldier and his officers.

The rapid turnover of their immediate officers—usually every six months, often less—led to the conviction that the grunts knew better than anyone else, especially better than the six-month wonders, the shake-'n'-bake lieutenants, how to stay alive. These teenage warriors were therefore thrown back into themselves in a way unusual in war. They had to take care of each other if they were to make it. After a while they could wear earrings, write almost anything they liked on their helmets and flak jackets, shoot up on drugs, get drunk, and more often than not get away with it, especially when they were in the field, which everyone called Indian country. They enjoyed getting away with it, and hated "chicken shit officers" who worried about shined shoes; but getting away with it also taught some of them that the brass did not care, and that they were on their own both as a unit and as individuals.

Because of the differences between place and time, Vietnam was not a shared experience for the men sent there. Fighting in the mountains was different from the jungles, which was different from the rice paddies, which was different from the cities. The combat grunts, however, did share the experience of danger, perhaps of killing, and of witnessing pain and death. Fighting, for the the relative few who actually faced the enemy was obviously far removed from the experiences of the majority, who sat out the war in the relative safety of the rear, with easy access to palatable food, the post exchanges, television, bars, and prostitutes. Among the amenities on American installations in 1971 were 90 service clubs, 71 swimming pools, 12 beaches, 160 craft shops, 159 basketball courts, 30 tennis courts, 55 softball diamonds, 85 volleyball courts, 2 bowling alleys, and 337 libraries.[22]

Fighting before and after 1969 was markedly different. In 1967, General Westmoreland, with his usual jut-jawed cheeriness, reported to Congress that the GIs in Vietnam were "the finest ever fielded by our nation."[23] He reported that the troops understood and believed in the war. When General Abrams took over, he could not share such optimism, partly because he was less of an overage boy scout, and partly because by then the GIs had changed. The college students now drafted, and black militants, were both capable of finding ways to do "their own thing" regardless of military "chicken regs." More important, however, Mr. Nixon's troop withdrawals drained any vestigal meaning from the war for those who believed in any meaning in the first place. The withdrawals signaled that there would be no American victory for the Americans still fighting. By the time Mr. Nixon became President, the new recruits had experienced the antiwar movement, the tougher phase of the civil-rights movement, as well as the antiauthoritarianism of the counterculture. Blacks had been deeply angered by the murder of Martin Luther King, Jr. The civilian lives of these new grunts had prepared them to be less docile than their predecessors, and the officers permitted such independence. By 1969, too much of the army officer corps had degenerated into a self-serving, dishonest, bureaucratic organization designed to exploit the troops for the personal advancement of the leaders. The result was chaos: drugs, desertions, mutinies, riots, atrocities, and murder.

My Lai 4 was a tiny village on the northeastern coast of South Vietnam, near the South China Sea. Shortly after 8:00, on the morning of March 16, 1968, Charlie Company of Task Force Barker, 11th Brigade of the Americal Division, entered the hamlet and massacred 347 civilian women, children, and old men. Some of the younger women were raped before they were murdered. At 11:00, the Americans took a lunch break. Charlie Company burned the entire village, killed the livestock, and destroyed the food and the wells. Lieutenant Colonel Frank Barker, Colonel Oran Henderson, and Major General Samuel Koster were in their separate helicopters watching some of the action on the ground. Later, these officers could not remember seeing anything wrong. One warrant officer, Hugh Thompson, Jr., threatened over his chopper radio that he would start shooting the GIs if he saw them "kill one more woman or child."[24] On the same day, Bravo Company of the same task force murdered civilians in another bloodbath at My Khe 4, a few miles away from My Lai. The officers and men of the Americal Division lied to each other about what had happened, expected to be rewarded for doing so, and tried to hide the truth from the world. (Seymour Hersh won the Pulitzer Prize for reporting about My Lai.)

The American was a hodgepodge division, with an incompetent and demoralized senior staff that was afraid of the commanding general who insisted on elegant meals, engraved china, and movies after dinner. The officers' mess, preceded by a daily cocktail hour, was almost as elegant, and drove some of the grunts to fantasize about blowing up the mess hall. A lieutenant colonel's driver had to get his boss to "the Club" in time for the daily happy hour: "It was just like they were in Washington. They would talk about promotions and all that stuff—just like a cocktail party back in the world."[25] There was nothing in the code of the bureaucracy that required the leaders of men to be uncomfortable. Following the example of the commanding general, all the senior staff officers air-conditioned their living quarters.

The division's procedures for fact-finding was a perfect example of bureaucratic self-protection. A field report of the death of a Vietnamese would not be investigated if it was reported as "combat-related." As Mr. Hersh described it, "The men who could declare such incidents as being combat-related were the officers in charge; in effect, their choice was between a higher body count or a war crime investigation."[26] All the bureaucratic incentives drove men to lie. Truth might make you free, but without a promotion or a pension.

In the far reaches of bureaucratic hardening of the arteries, paper becomes more important than function. Establishing the correct paper trail, ensuring that guidelines and procedures are published and filed, replaces a concern with performance. Thus, the commander of American, along with most of his senior aides, later testified that "directives," letters, and memos had been disseminated that specifically prohibited indiscriminate burning of people's houses, called hooches, and urged humane and friendly treatment of civilians. General Westmoreland later said that "orders were clear. Every soldier had a card on how to treat an enemy in his hands."[27] Having issued the appropriate paper, however, there was no attempt to enforce the rules.

The existence of the paper guidelines, along with the commander's introductory remarks to FNGs, was all that was considered necessary to satisfy the bureaucratic code of the army.

Lieutenant General William R. Peers, in charge of the My Lai investigating panel, understood this point. In 1970, he wrote a secret memo to General Westmoreland, then the Army Chief of Staff, to explain that paper was not the same as function: "Directives and regulations . . . are only pieces of paper unless they are enforced aggressively and firmly throughout the chain of command."[28] This was a direct challenge to the bureaucratic instinct, and as such could not be and was not a learnable lesson. Nothing happened.

The failure to enforce rules was always someone else's fault. The general had delegated enforcement responsibility to his executive, who did not follow through; the exec delegated it to the major who passed it on to the captains and lieutenants who, in turn, charged the sergeants with this responsibility. The result of this chain of delegation, buck-passing, was always the same: Finally the grunts became responsible for self-enforcement. General Peers acknowledged this routine by condemning it: "Commanders at all echelons are responsible for the actions and the welfare of all the men under them. A commander cannot delegate such responsibility. . . ."[29]

More concern for issuing guidelines than for ensuring compliance also typified the high military command in Saigon. General Westmoreland issued more than thirty rules of engagement that were intended to define how and when to use American firepower. But 76 percent of the 110 generals who responded to a survey conducted in 1974 said that these rules were only "fairly well adhered to" or "not particularly considered" at all.[30]

The massacres revealed a number of important facts. Frightened and frustrated adolescents who love their weapons are capable, if pressed hard enough, of going berserk. In the context of this war, it is astonishing that it did not happen more often. The investigations of the horrors also began to reveal that a part of the officer corps of the army had become corrupt, and that the army, knowing this, refused to face the facts, and failed, as they say in the bureaucratic trade, to take corrective action. When the Department of the Army investigated what had happened, when it began to learn the facts, it expanded the Americal Division's cover-up to include the entire officer corps. The army itself covered up, and still will not explain why it failed to press charges against all the officers who had been identified, and why it still will not release all of what it knows about that grisly day.

My Lai can be explained by the bloodlust of unsupervised boymen who could not tell the difference between friend and enemy, by the official demand for killing, sometimes indiscriminate as in the free-fire zones, and by cynical officers who intended to profit from high death reports. It had partly to do with the numbers racket. Keeping the war's score by the arithmetic of kill-ratios and body counts puts an irresistible premium on good numbers.

Many of the grunts understood what was happening, but did not care about the numbers. They would report whatever they had to report to keep the CO off their backs. They were often pressed into lying by greedy officers who had only a short time to make their mark, to be "blooded" in the only available war, and to get away from the fire field as soon as they had compiled an enviable record of kills.

The malfeasance of some senior officers, the hatred of the Vietnamese, the frustration of fighting an invisible enemy, the thwarted desire for vengeance or justice, released some individual GIs from whatever restraints, if any, they had brought to Vietnam. Some of these killers were encouraged, or were not discouraged, by their officers. One grunt, for example, not connected with My Lai, described himself:

> I had a sense of power. A sense of destruction. . . . In the Nam you realized that you had the power to take a life. You had the power to rape a woman and nobody could say nothing to you. That godlike feeling you had was in the field. It was like I was a god.[31]

The possession of exciting weaponry that converted late adolescents into potent, godlike men also changed their moral codes. It released them from whatever inhibitions they may have brought to the war. Perceiving the Vietnamese as subhuman completed the release. They sometimes would "get even" because they could. They became free, autonomous, and dangerous. Such soldiers can exist only if their officers allow them to get away with metaphorical and literal murder.

The panel the army created to inquire into the My Lai murders asked Lawrence Congleton, a radioman who was there, whether it was usual to report body counts when no one had counted the bodies. The question was asked because the military reports from the scene of the action indicated no civilian deaths, only recognizable guerrilla fighters. The soldier explained, "You can't really take too much stock in what was put on the log or something like that, because it seemed like sometimes the commanding officers were like trying to write a movie script and make it read a little more juicy for the people that were going to read it." After the massacre, the radioman said that Captain Earl R. Michles told him "to make it look good."[32] Richard F. Silva, also present at the command post on the My Lai morning, told the investigating panel that he did not care what numbers were reported over the radio. He took them all: "They could say two thousand were dead, you know. I could care less. . . . They can say whatever they want over their radios and everything else because from past experiences I knew it was a bunch of bull anyway."[33]

While the blood was up no officer even tried to stop the murders at My Lai or My Khe. A review of the findings of the army's investigating panel led to the conclusion that fourteen officers should be brought up on charges, including Major General Samuel W. Koster, the commander of the American Division at the time of My Lai, who was then the superintendent of West Point. He resigned to protect the academy and gave a speech to the cadets which concluded with an implicit warning about the bureaucracy: "Don't let the bastards grind you down."[34] The cadets honored him with a standing ovation, although several said they did not mean to support the general for his alleged crimes, merely to show solidarity, to show that they understood what it meant to get squeezed by the system. Yet one cadet, perhaps speaking for most, had the typical bureaucratic defensive reaction: "Such an outstanding career, all ruined to appease the media."[35]

The others who were charged include another general, two colonels, two lieutenant colonels, four majors, two captains, and two first lieutenants. As it finally turned out, only Lieutenant William L. Calley was convicted, to the dismay of much of the nation. President Nixon wanted to intervene on the lieutenant's behalf, an action that was probably illegal. General Westmoreland believed that the army had been forced to accept such substandard men as Lieutenant Calley because the student deferments kept better men out of reach. Most of the charges against the others were dismissed without a hearing, but Major

General Koster had to endure a long secret hearing before the charges against him were dropped. Several of the high-ranking officers, including Major General Koster, were demoted and stripped of selected decorations.

My Lai was investigated only because NCOs and grunts charged that something terrible had happened. First the officers in the field were forced by the men to stage an inquiry; then the Pentagon was forced to act for the same reason. Ronald Ridenhour, an ex-GI who had not been at My Lai, was the whistle-blower who forced the Pentagon to investigate. He testified before the investigating panel that the folklore of the army had changed: "That's the first thing that you learn when you go in the Army now. We didn't learn 'Don't volunteer,' we learned 'Cover your ass.' "[36]

The members of the prestigious panel convened to hear the cases were not corrupt. Rather, these panelists viewed their charge through the prism of their lifelong habits and allegiances. Members of the Nixon administration wanted to assist in the cover-up, but, as General Westmoreland said, "I threatened through a White House official" to go to the President "and object. . . . That," he said, "squelched any further pressure for whitewash."[37] The assumption of the panel was simply that what went wrong at My Lai was the result of the failures of marginal individuals who probably should not have been given command responsibility in the first place. They could not see, and probably should not have been expected to see, that the army as a bureaucratic institution was implicated.

When Sam Stratton, a pro-military congressman from upstate New York, heard that the charges had been dropped against Major General Koster, he made an angry speech to the House of Representatives: "I am afraid that this is a case where the ground rules of the mythical WPPA, the West Point Protective Association, have taken precedence over the welfare of the nation and the fundamental right of the American people to know the facts: never mind what happens to the Army or to the country, just make sure we keep our paid-up members out of embarrassment and hot water."[38]

The congressman had perhaps unwittingly stumbled onto an important truth revealed by the Vietnam War: In modern American bureaucratic organizations, military and others, the welfare of officers as individuals takes precedence over the objectives of the institution that pays their salaries, and that is the way the organization wants it, the way rewards and punishments are distributed. As thousands of grunts came to learn, this truth was an essential aspect of their Vietnam experience.

The foot soldiers learned that parts of the army officer corps as an institution had become corrupt in specific bureaucratic ways: Personal careerism collided with the army's own code of conduct. That code had become hollow, a source of bitter humor in thousands of foxholes. The corruption made some officers dangerous to their men, which helps to explain the mutinies, fraggings, and desertions. A lieutenant was told by his colonel: "I don't care what happens to your men, but I'm not losing any more God damn tanks."[39] Field-grade officers—majors and up— were the carriers of the pathology, generally not the company-grade officers—the captains and lieutenants—many of whom fought and lived with the men, and many of whom were good soldiers. Many GIs hated their sergeants, lieutenants, and captains, too, but this was the more normal hatred of the officers immediately in view. It was the senior brass that was tarnished. The behavior of senior officers was a significant reason why the war was so demoralizing, so crushingly absurd.

The moral decay and increasing incompetence of the army's senior officers in Vietnam was minimally caused by personal failures of individuals, despite General Westmoreland's use of Lieutenant Calley in this way. The corruption in Vietnam was systemic and was caused by procedures within the army that had been borrowed from other American bureaucratic institutions, primarily industry.

When the army adopted the "up or out" model of personnel management soon after World War II, it assumed that if an employee is not promotable, he is not employable. That meant that individuals with long and useful experience, who had found their right rung on the bureaucratic ladder, could not be retained. Up or out always devalues experience and always demands change at the price of stability. Americans seem unable to imagine an individual being satisfied by doing a job for which he is suited. We insist that job advancement must be perpetual. This constant upward swimming produced the bends, maybe not for the individuals concerned, but for the army as an institution.

Although the industrial bureaucratization of the army began in the 1940s, the extent of its corrosive damage was first made undeniable in Vietnam. What had happened was that a system of rewards was imposed on the military that changed the senior officer from a military leader into a bureaucratic manager. Many senior officers in other times and places led their men into battle, shared their risks, and were respected if not loved. Vietnam proved that men cannot be "managed" into battle.

Why should a bureaucrat risk his life to manage his men? When the code of the military was replaced with that of the bureaucracy, personal risk became not only meaningless, but stupid. If the point was promotion, not victory, risk was, as they say, counterproductive. The details of the army's definition of career management assaulted military logic, morale, and honor. The My Lai slaughter was a consequence of this deformation.

The bureaucratization of the army led to a definition of officers as personnel managers and troops as workers. It was not clear why the "workers" should have risked their lives to follow the orders of the "boss" who was not at risk himself. This sort of corruption invariably starts at the top, with the big boss. In 1966, General Westmoreland reported in unashamed industrial language and with apparent pride, "[My troops] work, and they work hard. It has been my policy that they're on the job seven days a week, working as many hours as required to get the job done."[40] Perhaps his bureaucratic instincts, as deep as any man's could be, had been reinforced by his stint at the Harvard Business School. Vice Admiral James B. Stockdale wrote that "our business school-oriented elite tried to manipulate rather than fight the Vietnam War."[41]

General Westmoreland was America's senior personnel manager in-country, and that is how he thought of himself. He reported to the National Press Club that by 1967 the armed forces of South Vietnam had made progress. The first reason for this good news was: "Career management for officers, particularly infantry officers, has been instituted." The second reason was: "Sound promotion procedures have been put into effect." As a consequence of these and other "improvements," he concluded, "the enemy's hopes are bankrupt."[42]

The peculiar swagger of Americans, as John Wayne personified it, had been changed from confidence born of competence and courage to confidence wrung from ignorance.

Bureaucrats are planners, and they must always believe, or pretend very hard to believe, or at least insist they believe, in the effectiveness and wisdom of their plans. The result is the sort of arrogance that drains the oxygen from a room, that makes the bureaucrat-in-chief light-headed. For example, General Westmoreland had not one doubt: "We're going to out-guerrilla the guerrilla and out-ambush the ambush . . . because we're smarter, we have greater mobility and firepower, we have endurance and more to fight for. . . . And we've got more guts."[43]

It is written that one should know one's enemy, that pride precedes failure. The general had insulated himself from reality, was unable to hear criticism, and seemed quite pleased with himself. He was America's perfect manager of a war. As a result he was more interested in procedures and public relations than content. He wanted to engineer appearances, not substance. Every reporter who listened to his Saigon briefings understood that it was a shell game. Evidently, he himself had no idea that this was so.

Under the leadership of General Westmoreland and the rotating Chiefs of Staff, the military bureaucracy became so top-heavy that it lost its balance. There was a higher percentage of officers in the field during the Vietnam War than in other American wars, and higher than in the armies of other nations. At its peak the percentage of officers in Vietnam was almost double what it had been in World War II. In 1968, there were 110 generals in the field in Vietnam. In absolute terms there were about as many generals, admirals, colonels, and navy captains in Vietnam as there were at the height of World War II. There was a lower ratio of officer deaths than was true earlier and elsewhere. Of the seven generals who died, five lost their lives in their helicopters. There was a higher ratio of medals distributed to officers, especially as the combat began to wind down, than ever before.

Colonel John Donaldson's Vietnam career is illustrative. In 1968, he was given command of the American Division's 11th Brigade, which a few months earlier had sent Lieutenant Calley's platoon into My Lai. The colonel replaced Colonel Oran Henderson, who would be acquitted of the charge of a My Lai cover-up. In his first six months of command, Colonel Donaldson "earned" an "average of about one medal a week: two Distinguished Flying Crosses, two Silver Stars, a Bronze Star

Medal for Valor, twenty Air Medals, a Soldier's Medal, and a Combat Infantryman Badge." He was soon promoted to brigadier general and won nine additional Air Medals and two Legions of Merit, and was transferred to the Pentagon as a strategist.[44] During the My Lai investigation it was thought that to protect his predecessors he had destroyed key documents needed by the investigators. He denied this. In 1971, he was the first American general charged with a war crime since about 1900. He was accused of "gook hunting," shooting Vietnamese from his helicopter. He was acquitted.

In 1962, military promotion decisions had been centralized under the Chiefs of Staff. Thereafter, the military became a bureaucratic promotion machine. Meanwhile, the grunts continued to slog through the paddies and jungles. Many of them knew that something was rotten. By 1967, combat troops made up 14 percent of the troops in Vietnam; in World War II it was 39 percent; 34 percent at the end of the Korean War; and, 29 percent in 1963.[45] Approximately 86 percent of the military in Vietnam was not assigned to combat. At the height of the build-up in 1968, when there were about 540,000 military personnel in Vietnam, 80,000 were assigned to combat. The rest, the other 460,000, constituted the grunts' enormous category of REMFs.

It is probably true that never before, in the military or anywhere, had bureaucratic officials so enthusiastically served their own interests to the detriment of the objective they were supposed to accomplish. The managerial corps finally lost to dedicated troops in black pajamas.

As the officers blamed the politicians, many grunts blamed the officers. Bruce Lawlor, a CIA case officer, knew what was happening: "The only thing the officers wanted to do was get their six months in command and then split back to the States and be promoted and go on to bigger and better things. It doesn't take long for the average guy out in the field to say, 'Fuck it!' "[46] Or, as another example, a colonel sent troops into action without telling them (to make sure they would not evade a fight) that they would encounter an enemy base camp. Herb Mock, an infantryman who walked point on that mission, later went to find the colonel: "You made us walk right into the ambush. That's a sorry goddamn thing to do. You ain't worth shit as an officer."[47] Herb Mock's best friend was killed in the ambush.

* * *

The army itself recognized that something was wrong. In 1970, General Westmoreland ordered the Army War College to conduct an analysis of the officer corps. The study was so damaging that he at first had it classified. What had happened, in the language of the Army War College study, was that, "careerism" in the officer corps had replaced the ethic of the officer. Careerism means that personal advancement replaces the desire to get the job done. In fact, the "job" *is* personal advancement. (This helps to explain the cheating scandals at the service academies.) Bureaucratic employees get paid to get promoted.

In April General Westmoreland ordered the commandant of the Army War College to study the moral and professional climate of the army. Although he did not believe that the army was suffering a "moral crisis," he directed the study to focus "on the state of discipline, integrity, morality, ethics, and professionalism in the Army."[48]

In the study's preface, Major General G. S. Eckhardt, Commandant, simply stated, "This study deals with the heart and soul of the Officer Corps of the Army."[49] The study involved interviewing about 420 above-average officers, an extensive questionnaire, and many group discussions. As a result, the study concluded that "prevailing institutional pressures" had created a divergence between the ideals and the current practices of the officers corps. "These pressures seem to stem from a combination of self-oriented, success-motivated actions, and a lack of professional skills on the part of middle and senior grade officers."[50] The officers participating in the study described the typical Vietnam commander: "an ambitious, transitory commander—marginally skilled in the complexities of his duties—engulfed in producing statistical results, fearful of personal failure, too busy to talk with or listen to his subordinates, and determined to submit acceptably optimistic reports which reflect faultless completion of a variety of tasks at the expense of the sweat and frustration of his subordinates."[51]

Many of the officers involved in the study agreed that the cause of this breakdown was that the army itself had "generated an environment"[52] that rewarded trivial and short-run accomplishments to the neglect of significant achievement and the longer-term health of the army. The cause was not the "permissive society"[53] at home, or the antiwar and antimilitary protests, but the army itself.

The study reported that junior officers were better officers than their own commanders, and that the younger men "were frustrated by the pressures of the system, disheartened by those seniors who sacrificed integrity on the altar of personal success, and impatient with what they perceived as preoccupation with insignificant statistics." A captain was quoted: "Many times a good soldier is treated unfairly by his superiors for maintaining high standards of professional military competence." A colonel said, "Across the board the Officer Corps is lacking in their responsibilities of looking out for the welfare of subordinates."[54]

An important conclusion of the study was that moral failure and technical incompetence were closely connected. Incompetence seemed to come first and the need to cover it up created the thousand techniques for lying, passing the buck, and avoiding responsibility. The study acknowledged that such behavior was army-wide: "signing of false certificates; falsification of flight records; condoning of the unit thief or scrounger; acceptance by middle and upper grade officers of obviously distorted reports; falsification of . . . trips for self gain and the attendant travel pay; hiding of costs under various programs; hiding AWOLs by placing them on leave to satisfy commander's desire for 'Zero Defect' statistics."[55]

The army's emphasis on quantification (a disease it caught when Secretary McNamara sneezed) meant that success was defined only by what could be measured. This was partly caused by the computer craze and resulted in the application to the army of "the commercial ethic."[56] This contributed to two unfortunate consequences: ignoring characteristics that could not easily be expressed in numbers, such as leadership, and emphasizing activities that could be measured, such as "savings bond scores and the reenlistment rate."[57] Officers were promoted for doing well in these "programs," while they were not reprimanded for failures in areas that the computers could not be programmed to measure, such as duty, honor, country. One captain complained: "The fact that my leadership ability is judged by how many people in my company sign up for bonds or give to the United Fund or Red Cross disturbs me."[58] (One noncom told me that his superior in Vietnam always forced him to buy bonds, but encouraged him to cancel as soon as the good report went out.)

This definition of what mattered to the army as an institution suited the careerist officers who were in "the business" to make a good living. One captain described his battalion commander as a man who "had always his mission in mind and he went about performing that mission with the utmost proficiency. His mission was getting promoted."[59] A major exploded: "The only current decorations I admire are the DSC and Medal of Honor, all others are tainted by too often being awarded to people who do not deserve them. . . . Duty, Honor, Country is becoming— me, my rater, my endorser, make do, to hell with it."[60] Another major was a little more relaxed: "My superior was a competent, professional, knowledgeable military officer that led by fear, would doublecross anyone to obtain a star, drank too much and lived openly by no moral code."[61] This "superior" was soon promoted and got his first star.

The Army War College study revealed how the officers derived bureaucratic lessons even from My Lai. Officers got into trouble at My Lai because they found no AK47s, Soviet-made rifles carried by both the guerrillas and by the North's army; that made it difficult to claim that all the villagers were combatants. "This exposure to My Lai . . . it has driven some of the units to carry AK47s around with them so that if they did kill someone they've got a weapon to produce with the body."[62]

When General Westmoreland read the study he proclaimed it a "masterpiece," and restricted its distribution to generals only. As a group they had quite substantial reservations about its conclusions. General Westmoreland did, however, write a number of letters to inform the officer corps that integrity was important. That was the most significant result of this remarkable study. Young Pentagon officers formed a group called GROWN: Get Rid of Westmoreland Now.

Vietnam was the only available war for upwardly mobile officers, and if they failed to get an assignment in Vietnam, called getting their ticket punched, their careers would be thwarted. This infected the officer corps from top to bottom, beginning even before the West Point cadets graduated. For example, James Lucian Truscott IV arrived at West Point in 1965, where he hoped to follow his family's tradition of soldiering:

> When I was 22 years old I was pretty well convinced from having officer after officer after officer—major, lieutenant colonel, full colonel—come and tell me, personally or in

front of a class, "You've got to go to Vietnam and get your fucking ticket punched. The war sucks. It's full of it. It's a suck-ass war. We're not going to win it. We're not fighting it right, but go and do it." You know, "Duty, Honor, Country" had suddenly become "Self-Duty, Honor, Country."[63]

A year after he graduated from West Point, Mr. Truscott resigned his commission rather than go to Vietnam.

For the office warriors, Vietnam was a marvelous opportunity to get ahead in the world. According to marine General David Shoup, some of the generals and admirals hoped to deepen America's involvement in Vietnam to speed promotions.[64] But such motivation was not a sufficient reason to risk getting hurt or killed, or even to suffer through the war in more discomfort than was absolutely necessary.

Among the Vietnam generals he surveyed, Brigadier General Kinnard found that 87 percent believed that careerism was "somewhat of a problem" or "a serious problem."[65] Careerist officers would not take risks in combat or in their relations with their superiors. Risk could lead to error, and a single mistake noted on an officer's efficiency report could ruin his career. This produced an equivalence of error, from incorrect table manners at "the Club" to a failure of judgment in combat. An instructor at the Command and General Staff College, said this of the rating procedure: "The system demands perfection at every level—from potatoes to strategy. It whittles away at one's ethics."[66]

When every glitch, however petty, might end up as a black mark on the rating sheet, officers of course trained themselves to be passive, to keep quiet, and to worry more about pleasing those above them than those below. Carried to an extreme in Vietnam, the rating system produced an even conformity of thought, a religion of pleasing superiors, a very high price on dissent, and a comfortable tour for the three- and four-star generals who were not rated. Careerism inevitably forced officers to think of their subordinates as their most important resource for making them look good, to protect their "image" on paper.

Career management and sound promotion procedures, as General Westmoreland described them, motivated the bureaucratic colonels and generals who observed the war, if they observed it at all, safe in their helicopter offices fifteen hundred feet above the danger. They claimed they needed to be in the air to see the bigger picture, so as not to lose perspective by the more limited horizons of the earthbound warriors. Sometimes this was true, but the grunts hated it. Whether it was necessary or not, the chopper always gave the officers an opportunity to have the desired combat experience without the risks of combat. The availability of helicopters meshed perfectly with the imperatives of ticket-punching. Field commanders, especially lieutenants and captains, resented it also, but for obvious reasons they were less outspoken. For the grunts, the appearance of the colonel's chopper was a reminder that they and not he might get blown away. He would not be late for the happy hour at the Club, while they would remain in the field with another meal of C-rats. It reinforced a class hatred that was, in its pervasiveness, probably unique to the Vietnam War. Mike Beamon, a navy antiguerrilla scout—he called himself a terrorist—said it all: "I was more at war with the officers there than I was with the Viet Cong."[67]

The length of time an officer in Vietnam served in a combat assignment was not a matter of established military doctrine. It was a rule of thumb of the commanders in the field. Although there were exceptions, and although some officers served more than one tour, the expectation of a twelve-month tour, even for officers, set the outer limit of a combat assignment. In 1968, the systems analysts in the Office of the Secretary of Defense studied the length of time officers served in combat. They found that the typical combat command of a maneuver battalion or a rifle company was "surprisingly short."[68] More than half the battalion commanders, usually lieutenant colonels, were rotated out of combat command in less than six months. More than half the company commanders, usually captains, were relieved before they completed four months. One of the reasons for so short a command tour was reported in a secret document prepared in the Office of the Deputy Chief of Staff for Personnel in 1970: "Career personnel have greater opportunity for career development and progression. . . ."[69] With short assignments more officers could get their tickets punched.

After 1970, 2,500 lieutenant colonels each hoped to command one of the 100 battalions, 6,000 colonels wanted a command of one of the 75 brigades, and 200 major generals wanted to get one of the 13 divisions.[70] The competition for one of these assignments was fierce, and the office politicking was everywhere. As they got the right punches, the right assignments, the officers' careers flourished. Of the men who were considered for promotion to major, 93 percent succeeded, as did 77 percent to lieutenant colonel, and 50 percent to colonel. Colonel David Hackworth understood what was happening:

> We had all the assets to win this war. We had half a million troops, unlimited amounts of money and the backing of the administration. No doubt we could have won if we'd had commanders who knew how to use these assets, instead of these amateurs, these ticket punchers, who run in for six months, a year, and don't even know what the hell it's all about.[71]

There were two important consequences of these short command assignments: Officers did get the "experience" required for their promotions; and the men under their command were killed in higher numbers because of their commanders' inexperience. The systems analysts discovered that a maneuver battalion under a commander with more than six months experience suffered only two thirds the battle deaths of battalions commanded by officers with less than six months of experience. The average command lasted 5.6 months. The analysts discovered that a battalion commander with less than six months experience lost an average of 2.5 men a month; those with more experience lost 1.6 men a month. In their technocratic, economistic, dehydrated view of the world, the analysts explained that "the rate of battle deaths is a measure of the cost of success." They wanted a "cheaper price."[72]

The analysts also found that the length of experience of a company commander reduced the battle deaths of his troops. The average command was just under four months. These officers were themselves killed at a higher rate than more experienced officers, a rate that rose in each of the first four months, and that dramatically dropped by two thirds in the fifth month, from which point it remained low and stable. In the first four months, about 4 percent of these officers were killed; afterward, 2.5 percent were killed. "This implies," the systems analysts concluded, "that a company commander could be left in office 6 more months, for a total of 10, without incurring an additional risk as great as that to which he was exposed during his first 4 months in command."[73] Nonetheless, they were "relieved" (perhaps in several senses of that word) in four months so that another green commander could step onto the promotion escalator, and two thirds of them were sent out of combat to staff positions. The typical captain in Vietnam had three different "jobs" during his twelve-month tour in Vietnam. The companies commanded by officers with less than five-months experience had an average of .8 killed in action each month; those with more than four months lost .6 KIA, a drop of 25 percent.

As usual, the military was not delighted by the work of the Whiz Kids. As usual, the military argued that the systems analysts did not understand war. The deputy chief of staff for operations concluded, "Our commanders in the field can best judge the length of time an officer should remain in command of a unit in combat."[74] The brass on the spot had not "arbitrarily" set the average command assignments at six months and four months. These periods of time were selected because "we know from experience that a commander begins to 'burn out' after a period in this hazardous and exacting environment." After the typical time in command, and after burnout, "the commander is not fighting his unit as hard as he did during the first few months of command when he was full of snap, zest and aggressiveness and eager to destroy the enemy."[75]

The analysts were unimpressed by the Pentagon's argument. They claimed there was "no data" to prove that commanders burn out. Their conclusion was ominous: "We cannot prove its existence and we suspect that the present rotation policy may be based more on considerations of providing a wide base of combat experience than on the 'burn out' factor."[76]

The military headquarters in Saigon obviously had to join this argument, to "rebut" the analysts. MACV acknowledged that there was a "learning curve" for battle commanders, contested the statistical reliability of the figures used, and insisted that the analysts had failed to understand that battles vary in intensity. The analysts agreed about varying intensity, but added that "regrettably, data are not available," presumably unavailable in Saigon as well as Washington. They did not believe this was a serious point because their study covered so many areas of combat that differences would cancel each other out. They agreed that more information would always be helpful and might have produced different results. "But we doubt it. It was our view (and MACV confirms this) that more experienced battalion commanders are more effective: on the average fewer of their men get killed in combat."[77]

The American military establishment took pride in its effective adoption of "sound business practices." But, on the question of the duration of command, the military borrowed from no one. There is no other institution that transfers its leaders before they can learn their jobs. There is also no other institution in which the price of ignorance is the death of other people. One scholar compared the time in office between military officers and business executives and found that military officers with less than one year's experience was 46 percent of all officers; the comparable figure for executives was 2 percent. Military officers with five or more years of experience were 6 percent of the total; 88 percent of business executives had that much experience.[78] There were reasons why the military moved its people so quickly, but the development of competence and the safety of the troops were not among them.

General Westmoreland uncharacteristically said, "It may be that I erred in Vietnam in insisting on a one-year tour of duty. . . ." But, as he reconsidered the possibility of an error, he concluded that longer tours would have been "discrimination against officers" and would have added to his difficulties in getting enough junior officers from OCS and ROTC. Perhaps, he said, an eighteen-month tour would have been "a workable compromise."[79] He did not mention the fate of the GIs.

Yet, every sane observer of the rotation system agreed that it interfered with conducting the war. The Army War College study of the careerism of officers cited the short tour as a major factor in the deformation of the code of officers. Careerism, it said, can be diminished "by building mutual trust and confidence, and loyalty that comes from being in one assignment long enough to be able to recover from mistakes; and to have genuine concern—as a practical matter—about the impact which expedient methods will have on the unit next year."[80] After questioning and interviewing hundreds of officers, this study pointed out that the army had not questioned its promotion policy "for some time," and had simply continued to make the assumption that moving officers through the wide variety of jobs required for promotion was a sound policy. "The implications of this assumption," the study said, "are so far-reaching that possibly no single personnel management concept—save that of the uninhibited quest for the unblemished record—has more impact on the future competence of the Officer Corps."[81]

Before a company commander learned his job he was sent elsewhere. Before an intelligence officer could establish all his contacts he was sent elsewhere. There was no way the military could learn from its experience. That is what John Paul Vann, a distinguished officer who had resigned in disgust from the military, meant when he said that America did not fight a ten-year war, but rather ten one-year wars. For the officers the spin was even faster. Experience obviously could not accumulate. Lessons could not be learned. It was not only a teenage war, but a war in which no one had time to become seasoned or wise. There was no institutional memory, and with every year's rotation, the war began anew, with staff trying to hold up "the old man" who always had the power of command.

It was thus a teenage war led by amateurs. The GIs did not complain, of course, about serving "only" one year, but some of them knew, as Thomas Bird, a grunt with the 1st Cavalry, admitted:

> Toward the end of my tour, when I started knowing what I was doing in the jungle and started knowing what to do under fire, it was just about time to go home. I'm going to be replaced by a guy who is as green as I was when I got here, and by the time he gets good at it he's going to be replaced by a guy who is green. It's no wonder we never got a foothold in the place.[82]

Keeping the war's score by counting bodies, an index imposed by Washington, was made to order for careerist officers. They could and did distinguish themselves by reporting more bodies than their competitors. One general later concluded that the body count was "gruesome—a ticket punching item."[83] Another said, "Many commanders resorted to false reports to prevent their own relief," that is, to prevent someone else from replacing them and getting ahead by filing more acceptable reports. Another general said, "I shudder to think how many of our soldiers were killed on a body-counting mission—what a waste."[84]

When a career depends on the reported height of a pile of bodies, several sorts of decay result. Once, when the men of Charlie Company engaged the enemy, their lieutenant called for a helicopter to evacuate the wounded. "To hell with the wounded, *get those gooks,* "[85] the lieutenant colonel radioed back from his helicopter above the action. The lieutenant turned to see his machine gunner firing at the commander's chopper.

Having instituted a process that rewarded cheating, the bureaucratic bosses simply denied that it could have happened. Most (61 percent) of the generals in Vietnam knew that the statistics were snake oil,[86] but none complained in public. They were wedded to the system. For example, in 1973, some of the majors at the army's Command and General Staff College at Leavenworth asked the commandant to permit a discussion of the ethics of officers in Vietnam. According to a reporter:

> One general was saying that he was right on top of things in his units, that no one would dare submit a falsified report there. A young major stood up and said, General, I was in your division, and I *routinely* submitted falsified reports. The General's response was, When you speak to a general officer, stand at attention.[87]

The most senior officers, "Old Bulls," then at Leavenworth rejected what they called this "moralistic streaking." It is an iron law of bureaucracy that the higher one is in the organization, the more optimistic one is. How could it be otherwise? If one is in charge, things must be working well. A corollary is that the more senior one is, the more one is subject to the disease of being hard-of-listening. This law and its corollary may also partly explain General Westmoreland's constant assurances that things were working out satisfactorily, and that a solution would come soon. It seems reasonably clear that he really believed his own crooning. It is extremely difficult for the chief administrative officer of an organization to think that someone else would have done a better job. The Old Bulls at Leavenworth were not different from senior supervisors in Saigon, Washington, or anywhere else where bureaucracy is a settled fact of life.

Some defenders of the bureaucratic army argue that the problem in Vietnam was caused by the disorganization of American society at the time. They say that the pool of men from which the military had to draw was inadequate for military purposes. The "permissive society," the availability and use of drugs, and, most of all, the collapse of respect for authority throughout American culture apparently produced some officers who were not up to the military's legitimate expectations of correct conduct. The conclusion to this argument is that something did go wrong in Vietnam, but it was the fault of American culture, not the military.

The most careful work on this subject was done by two former officers, Richard Gabriel and Paul Savage. They argue that it was the army itself, not permissive American society, that produced the Vietnam officers' conduct. They show that earlier armies had always enforced conduct separate from contemporary fashions. That is what the military must do, and formerly had done, because it is a unique institution. It cannot function if its style of command, leadership, and even management is responsive to changing social fashions. The necessary characteristics for an officer in combat has no useful civilian analogy. Combat is unique. The army must train soldiers to perform specific functions regardless of any set of social circumstances.

The Army War College study itself asserts that the failures were inside the military and not a result of any "defects" in American society. It also concluded that the antiwar movement had no discernable impact on the quality or motivation of "officer material." If the crisis was, and is, internal to the army, the solution must also be. Yet, those who rose to the most senior levels of military command were precisely the bureaucrats who benefited by the corruption. The army's own study, in stunning bureaucratic language, acknowledged that for this very reason, reform was unlikely: "The fact also that the leaders of the future are those who survived and excelled within the rules of the present system militates in part against any self-starting incremental return toward the practical application of ideal values."[88] That is to say, reform must and cannot be internal.

The grunts understood that they were endangered by the guerrillas, the regular army of North Vietnam, and their own temporary, rotating officers, in no particular order of threat.

They knew that the home front did not support what they were doing. If no one cared about them, they could not care about the rules or established authority. Occasionally, around 1970, grunts would scribble UUUU on their helmets: the unwilling, led by the unqualified, doing the unnecessary, for the ungrateful. Other helmets proclaimed POWER TO THE PEOPLE, KILL A NONCOM FOR CHRIST, or NO GOOK EVER CALLED ME NIGGER. It was finally as if all that they could believe and remember were pain and death. One young man from the Bronx, for example, was cited for heroism:

> They gave me a Bronze Star and they put me up for a Silver Star. But I said you can shove it up your ass. I threw all of the others away. The only thing I kept was the Purple Heart, because I still think I was wounded.[89]

A wound is the most intimate souvenir.

It cannot be surprising that the grunts found ways to resist corrupt officers in a war that could not be understood. Desertions, excluding AWOLs, in the army alone rose from 27,000 in 1967 to 76,634 in 1970, a rate increase of 21 per thousand to 52 per thousand.[90] The marines were even worse with 60 desertions per thousand.[91] According to the Department of Defense, the rate of desertion in Vietnam was higher than in either Korea or World War II, and the rate increased as the intensity of the fighting declined and absurdity increased. As President Nixon began withdrawing troops, many of the grunts remaining on the ground lost even more conviction about why they should stay and fight. The desertion rate from 1965 to 1971 increased by 468 percent.[92]

Fragging, defined as an attempt to murder by using a grenade, reached astonishing levels in Vietnam. It was usually a result of the fear and hatred felt by the workers toward their bosses. For example, marine Private Reginald Smith testified in a court-martial that his lieutenant was so slow in setting up a listening post that by the time he sent three marines out, the NLF was waiting and killed two of them. The troops were discussing the incompetence of this lieutenant just before he was killed by a fragmentation grenade.[93] It was frequently said that combat squads raised a bounty to be awarded to anyone who would "waste" a particularly hated officer. The Criminal Investigating Department of the Third Marine Amphibious Force said there were more than 20 fraggings in eight months of 1969, according to the transcript of a court-martial. The Defense Department admits to 788 fraggings from 1969 to 1972.[94] This figure does not include attempts to kill officers with weapons other than "explosive devices," such as rifles. Richard Gabriel calculated that "as many as 1,016 officers and NCOs may have been killed by their own men,"[95] but he points out that this figure includes only men who were caught and tried. There is no precedent in American military history for violence against officers on anything like this scale.

Another response of the "workers" was to "strike," that is, to disobey a combat order, that is, to commit mutiny. The Pentagon kept no records of mutinies, but Senator Stennis of the Senate Armed Forces Committee said that there were 68 mutinies in 1968 alone.[96]

Yet another form of resistance by grunts was the pandemic use of hard drugs. In the spring of 1970, 96 percent pure white heroin appeared in Saigon; by the end of the year it was everywhere, sold in drugstores and by Vietnamese children on street corners. This junk was so pure and cheap that the troops smoked or sniffed, with only a minority reduced to injection. Its use was not remarkable in Vietnam because smoking was usually a group activity, accepted by almost everyone, and common for clean-cut midwestern boys as well as for city kids. Nothing in all of military history even nearly resembled this plague. About 28 percent of the troops used hard drugs, with more than half a million becoming addicted.[97] This was approximately the same percentage of high school students in the States who were using drugs, but they were using softer stuff. In Vietnam, grass was smoked so much it is a wonder that a southerly wind did not levitate Hanoi's politburo.

The failure of senior officers is partly reflected in the fact that they knew what was going on and did nothing to stop it, and did not protest. Richard Gabriel and Paul Savage concluded that "the higher officer corps was so committed to expedience that the organized distribution of drugs was accepted as necessary to the support of the South Vietnamese government, which often purveyed the drugs that destroyed the Army that defended it."[98] The CIA and the diplomatic corps in Vietnam prevented other governmental agencies from getting at the truth, while individuals with the CIA, if not the Agency itself, helped to fly drugs into Vietnam from Laos.

Despite an occasional attempt to do something—usually punishing the troops—about the blizzard of skag, neither the U.S. government nor the military ever accomplished anything worth mentioning. The much advertised urine testing (to be conducted in what the GIs called The Pee House of the August Moon) was ineffective because the tests were unreliable, the troops who were not hooked could flush their bodies before the tests, and no one was prepared actually to help the soldiers who were addicts. One scholar concluded that "in not rooting out the sources of heroin in Laos and Thailand, the government had simply made a calculation that the continued political and military support of those groups profiting from the drug traffic was worth the risk of hooking U.S. soldiers."[99] General Westmoreland, as usual, blamed everyone but his own senior officers: "The misuse of drugs . . . had spread from civilian society into the Army and became a major problem. . . . A serious dilution over the war years in the caliber of junior leaders contributed to this. . . ."[100]

Racial conflict was suffused throughout the war, from 1968 until the end. Every service, including the previously calm air force, had race riots of varying magnitude. As some of America's cities burned, or rather as the ghettos in some cities burned, the domestic rage found its counterpart in the military. Fraggings were sometimes racially motivated. One battalion commander said, "What defeats me is the attitude among the blacks that 'black is right' no matter who is right or wrong." One black soldier said, "I'd just as soon shoot whitey as the VC."[101] In one incident that is what actually happened: Two white majors were shot trying to get some black GIs to turn down their tape recorder.

White officers were sometimes offended by expressions of black solidarity, including ritual handshakes, the closed fist, swearing, black jargon, and, especially, blacks arguing that they were being forced to fight "a white man's war." (The North Vietnamese and the NLF often tried to exploit that theme through various forms of psychological warfare.) The weight of the military justice system was lowered on black GIs far out of proportion to their numbers. The congressional Black Caucus did a study in 1971 that showed that half of all soldiers in jail were black.[102] The next year, the Defense Department learned that blacks were treated more harshly than whites for identical offenses. The occasional race riots were invariably triggered by the increasing militance of American blacks in general, the peculiarly obtuse social attitudes of many older military officers, the frustrated hopes of the Great Society, the sense of an unfair draft, and an unfair shake in Vietnam.

Trying to make it to DEROS, that miraculous day one year after they had stepped foot onto Vietnam's red soil, the foot soldiers did what they could to survive the guerrillas or North Vietnam's army or their officers. For most of them, the point of the war was the clock ticking toward the shortening of their time, and, finally, the last day, the wake up call, and home. Others, in a daze of battle, tried to put home out of mind. Many others, probably most, became increasingly cautious as their "sentence" wore down, and the ingenuity expended by the short-timers in avoiding combat, occasionally simply by threatening a hard-driving officer, was inspirational, almost enough to revive the American dream of self-reliant citizens. No one wanted to die with only hours, or days, or weeks, or months, left to serve. No one wanted to die in any case, but it was even more unbearable to think about with only a short time to go. The idea of home, the idea of making it, became increasingly real as the war became increasingly surreal.

They left Vietnam as they came, suddenly, by air, usually alone, and engulfed by impressions and anxieties that were too cascading to sort out. "We went to Vietnam as frightened, lonely young men. We came back, alone again, as immigrants to a new world," William Jayne, a marine rifleman, wrote. "For the culture we had known dissolved while we were in Vietnam, and the culture of combat we lived in so intensely for a year made us aliens when we returned."[103] They were aliens for a great variety of reasons, some because they had grown up while their former buddies who had not gone to Nam seemed as if they had been frozen in time; they were still late adolescents whose lives revolved around six-packs, cars, and chasing girls. Others because they were stunned by the nation's refusal to welcome them home as returning warriors. Others because of the continuing pain of flesh and memory. Yet others because the war had destroyed their earlier faith in "the World," in American institutions.

The men recorded in *Charlie Company* each had his own trip

home, some burdened by uncontrollable anger, flashbacks, and nightmares. Most returned relatively smoothly. Many did not. Thomas K. Bowen thought when he got home that the entire war had been a "mistake," and said, "I mean I have no—absolutely no—respect for my government." Still others could not get jobs, and some resented the women and the nonvets who were working. Joe Boxx finally decided that "bein' a Vietnam vet didn't mean shit." Skip Sommer had re-upped to survive, but finally could not endure the army and deserted; he eventually gave himself up and was later dishonorably discharged. He was a haunted, enraged man even twelve years later. But, he said, "I don't remember anything I really am ashamed of, besides the fact that I survived." Alberto Martinez was losing his mind and in despair killed himself. Edmund Lee became an expatriate in Australia. Frank Goins, back home in south Georgia, remembered the democracy of races in the foxholes, but discovered, "When we got home, they still didn't want us to go to Mr. Charlie's cafe by the front door...." David Brown was not even given the usual four or five days off the line at the end of his tour; one day he was in combat and the next night the freedom bird landed him in San Francisco. He drank too much for a year or two. Charles Rupert said: "I risked my life for my country, and now nobody gives a shit. If I have a son, I won't let him go. I'll send him to Canada first." J. C. Wilson: "We were fools."[104]

On the other side, Lieutenant Robert Kennish, a commander of Charlie Company: "I did pretty well. No problems at all, really, that are going to afflict me for the rest of my life. I think I gained more from my experience in the military and in Vietnam than I lost." What mattered to him most was that he grew in his own self-esteem as a man. An anonymous veteran grunt said that he simply grew up in the war. David Rioux, a devout Catholic who was blinded in the war, understood and approved the war as a struggle against Communism, one that he was proud to have fought. Michel, David's brother, fought in David's company and feels that David's faith prevented him from committing suicide. David said about himself and his brother: "We both knew why we were in Vietnam, and the men around us didn't, for the most part, or saw it only confusedly, but we saw why we were there and we were proud to be there, defending a people who were being oppressed by Marxist Communism. We were doing something that was commendable, in the eyes of God, our country and our family."[105]

The stereotypes at loose in the nation when the troops began returning were largely shaped by the reports of My Lai as well as television reports of the heroin nightmare. Many Americans assumed the returning vets were junkies. Some vets were persistently asked how it felt to kill a human being. All the vets were subjected to an embarrassed national attitude about the war, and about their role in it. It got worse when the North overran Saigon, and television showed the pictures of the scramble to evacuate the remaining Americans. Then the question became even more insistent: What did we accomplish by fighting? For the veterans who had believed in the cause, Saigon's surrender was a terrible blow. Both the Rioux brothers, along with other traditionalists, believed that "giving up" was the mistake, not intervening in the first place. For the others, those who had decided the war was not worth fighting while they were fighting it, the fall of Saigon confirmed their opinion. In any case, the veterans faced an unprecedented social and political fact when they finally made it back: The nation did not know what to do with them, and would just as soon forget, or try to forget, the entire sorry "episode." None of the vets could forget.

They were not only not welcomed home, some of them were abused for their uniforms, their decorations, and their short hair. There was a revealing false rumor that antiwar critics were shooting vets as they climbed out of their planes. It is a mass delusion, of course, but thousands of vets claim that they were spat upon when they first arrived home. (The return of the Iranian hostages, with symbolic yellow ribbons all across the nation, with ticker-tape parades and presidential attention, brought it all back for thousands of them. It proved, once more, that only prisoners are recognized. Something was wrong.)

Most of the veterans returned home reasonably whole, as whole as returning veterans from earlier wars. The majority were not dopers, did not beat their wives or children, did not commit suicide, did not haunt the unemployment offices, and did not boozily sink into despair and futility. Yet, some prisons are still populated with black vets; the VA hospitals still do their bureaucratic thing too often and fail to help. Some vets, more than a decade later, have not yet recovered, and some never will. The government has done less for these veterans than for those of other wars. The vets had to build their own monument. Now they are struggling to force the reluctant government to face up to the hideous question of the degree to which our war technology had poisoned our own men with Agent Orange. More than a decade after most of them had come home, the government in 1984 began to make small progress in admitting its responsibility in this issue.

Nonetheless, the majority returned home and found there was life after Vietnam. Tim O'Brien, a former grunt and prize-winning novelist, thought the adjustment was too good. He feared that the vets' experience was becoming too mellow, too nostalgic. He had hoped their recoil from war would have been more of a brake on national saber-rattling. He wished they could have retained the passion and convictions that sustained them while they were boonie-rats. He wrote, "We've all adjusted. The whole country. And I fear that we are back where we started. I wish we were more troubled."[106]

When some grunts in Vietnam heard the news that the war was over, everyone began shouting. "They were ecstatic." One of them finally asked, "Who won?" They were told the NLF won. "They didn't care."[107]

EIGHT

THE AMERICAN LULLABY

War is a product of culture. It is an expression of the way a culture thinks of itself and the world. Different cultures go to war for different reasons and fight in different ways. There is an American way of war. Our Vietnam War was started and fought in ways our culture required.

All the critics of General Westmoreland's "strategy" of a conventional big-unit war of attrition argued that he failed to understand that the guerrillas were more important than the conventional forces of North Vietnam. Most of the "pacification" devotees made the same point. None of them understood the relationship between American culture and the American way of war.

Lieutenant Colonel Zeb B. Bradford was a better cultural critic than the civilian and academic experts. He explained that Americans could not have fought successfully as guerrillas or antiguerrillas. It was thus necessary for Americans to have concentrated on our own way of war:

> The great strength of US fighting forces historically has been precisely that they have exploited their peculiarly American qualities and attributes. Highly mechanized and technical warfare reinforces our tendencies and talents and

serves as a vehicle for evolutionary advance—counterinsurgency goes against the grain. We are a rich, industrial, urban country. Highly technical forces are compatible with our characteristics and resources.[1]

Zeb Bradford wrote what is indisputable: Mostly white, English-speaking soldiers could not fight as guerrillas in Asia. We would make superb guerrillas if we were fighting in the United States.

The counterinsurgency fad was a direct consequence of President Kennedy's uninformed enthusiasm, and it confused the American effort for many years after his death. When the army Chief, General George Decker, told President Kennedy that "any good soldier can handle guerrillas,"[2] the President first lectured him and six months later fired him. The military brass got the message. On the surface, counterinsurgency was in. JFK's support of the stylish Green Berets was consistent with his athletic patriotism, and was based on the assumption that military training could somehow overcome culture and race. Peer De Silva, the CIA's chief of station in Saigon, remembered that Robert and John Kennedy believed that "if a Vietcong *can* lie for hours under water in a rice paddy, breathing air through a straw, so *can* we."[3] It was harder to train them to climb out of the water, mix with the villagers, and remain undetectable. The American way of life and war meant that we could not succeed as counterinsurgents.

American political culture—the self-righteousness of our nationalism—merged with the impulses of our technological culture—tell us what to do and we'll do it, no questions asked. President Kennedy's enthusiasm for counterinsurgency led the nation to assume that we could successfully intervene in Vietnamese politics in ways that were foreign to America's genius. Our managerial sophistication and technological superiority resulted in our trained incompetence in guerrilla warfare.

The conclusion is obvious: If this nation cannot use its managerial and technological strengths in international conflict, it would be wise to avoid engagement. If our expensive weapon systems will not contribute to victory, it would be wise not to pretend that we have other resources.

The only circumstance where this conclusion does not apply is when the imbalance between us and our enemy is ludicrous, as in the adventure on the island of Grenada. This conclusion, however, did apply to our peacekeeping force in Lebanon, where our massed technology could not protect the marines from one terrorist's truck. Our Vietnam experience had revealed that we could not stop what we did not stop in Lebanon. That is because military intelligence, not missiles or an armada of warships, is necessary to stop terrorism. If the intelligence is available, one bullet may be all the technology necessary. If it is unavailable, our soldiers will surely die.

The entire ecology of America's military bureaucracy depends on weapons—increasingly complex, difficult to maintain, and expensive. Thus, General Westmoreland's strategy of conventional war was consistent with the realities of American culture, obviously including its bureaucratic and corporate values. There was nothing else he could do. In a gigantic confusion of means and ends, the Pentagon, both then and now, appears to conceive of its weapons as national strategy and its budget as foreign policy. This is a revealing symptom of the technicians' mentality: Quantity shall overcome. The Israelis and the North Vietnamese might have taught us otherwise. This dependence on quantity has some meaning in conventional warfare, but certainly not in guerrilla war, and, within limits, probably not in the calculus of nuclear deterrence.

The technician's mind is organized around the question *how*. He is motivated by a desire, sometime a need, to solve problems. He is rational, practical, hardheaded, and believes that if an idea can be transformed into a solution that actually works, the idea was true. Most of the war's planners exhibited these traits. Three other attributes of the technological mentality had an even more direct impact on the war. The technician's language is amoral, dispassionate, and optimistic. For example, Secretary McNamara's perception of Vietnam as a limited war reveals all these habits of mind: "The greatest contribution Vietnam is making—right or wrong is beside the point—is that it is developing an ability in the United States to fight a limited war, to go to war without the necessity of arousing the public ire."[4]

A technician's war would be muddied by the public's passion. Thus, the Vietnam War was cold-blooded. Secretary Rusk said that "we tried to do in cold blood perhaps what can only be done in hot blood, when sacrifices of this order are involved."[5] None of the Presidents attempted to stir passion about this war. General Westmoreland mistakenly said that the reason was that the political leaders "were more afraid of stirring up the hawks than the doves, a very ironical development. . . . Therefore, a policy decision was made to keep the war low key."[6] The war was fought for reasons of state, not out of anger. If the American public was whipped into anger, the political engineers might not have been able to attempt to fine-tune Vietnam to just the right level of death. They might not have been able so precisely to control a more passionate war. The very idea of limited war was at stake.

According to Colonel Harry Summers, an operations officer in Vietnam, the cold-bloodedness was a result of the academic sources of the theories about limited war. "As we . . . read the writings of the political scientists and systems analysts on limited war, they are noteworthy for their lack of passion. The horror, the bloodshed and the destruction of the battlefield are remarkably absent." He quoted Karl von Clausewitz, the classic theorist of war, who wrote about 150 years ago: "It would be an obvious fallacy to imagine war between civilized peoples as resulting merely from a rational act on the part of the government. . . ." Crackpot rationalism, to paraphrase C. Wright Mills, was understood a very long time ago. Colonel Summers mistakenly believed that the academics could be forgiven for their bloodless rationalism, "but we in the military knew better." The military was guilty of not talking, of cooperating with the deceptions, and of not forcing the issue when the Presidents decided to avoid exciting the middle class.[7]

The belief that the public should coolly and unemotionally support a war was a result of the desire to make the war conform to the technological mind. We were to fight the war for calculated reasons. This was not war as the American people fondly remembered their good wars, especially The Big One. When the people finally became angry, their anger was more often aimed at the Presidents than at the enemy. Americans, as others, need to perceive the enemy's threat, and the threat needs to be real enough to frighten them, and the fright needs to be metabolized into anger. Then they will support war.

A war over ideology is not enough for the people, however exercised over the abstractions the leaders and other "responsible" elites became. These groups believed in abstractions: dominoes, national credibility, and the significance of

counterinsurgency. They were merely convinced, not passionate. That is never enough for the people. It is right to insist on
becoming fighting mad. Anger could not be factored into the
technician's equations.

North Vietnam finally won its war because it was willing to
accept more death than we considered rational. That is why the
bombing campaigns failed. It is not that our technology failed.
Our cultural perceptions failed when so many intelligent men
in high positions simply assumed that our enemy's culture was
sufficiently like ours that he would quit at a point where we
believed we would quit.

We lost the war because we were never clear about the guerrillas, their popular support, the North Vietnamese, or ourselves. Our marvelously clever technology did not help us to
understand the war and, in fact, confused us even more because
it created our unquestioning faith in our own power. Finally,
the North's decision to continue fighting, and our decision to
stop, were each consistent with the cultural imperatives of each
nation. Because the army of South Vietnam was trained by us
to fight in the American style, it was forever dependent on a
supply of hardware and fuel. That army was incongruent with
the culture it was trying to defend.

This is why the military's continuing claim that we could
have won the war if it had been allowed to fight differently is
pointless. We could not have fought it differently. The constraints on the tactics of the war, and the absence of a political
goal to shape those tactics, were products of American culture
at the time. It is meaningless to argue that "next time we'll do
it differently and win." The only reasonable prediction about
the cultural pressures surrounding a "next time" is that they
will at least resemble those that existed in the 1960s and exist
now.

Americans continue to believe that managerial expertise and
war technology will contribute to the security of the nation and
the peace of the world. Such a belief is consistent with who we
are, but inconsistent with our experience in Vietnam. We did
not know when, where, or how to make use of our tools. It is
important to have the right tools. We have them. But it is also
important to know when and how to use them. This is why the
debate about whether anything useful can be learned from Vietnam is not very enlightening. What we must learn from Viet-

nam is not tactics or strategy, not technique, but who we are, what our culture requires.

One of the slogans used to tranquilize the people in George Orwell's *Nineteen Eighty-Four* is "Ignorance is Strength." In America since Hiroshima, that slogan turned out to be backward. For postwar America, strength was ignorance. We were so strong, we thought we did not need to know about others. We mistakenly thought we knew ourselves and that was all that mattered. Our power was thought somehow to immunize us against failure, at least against colossal failure.

Because culture creates war, it also creates peace. Some people now argue that the peculiar set of circumstances we encountered in Vietnam will never occur again. There are many ways to remain ignorant about Vietnam. The best way is to remain ignorant about America. Another is to insist that the war was unique, so different from other wars that it holds no important lessons. Every historical event is unique, after all. James Thomson, who resigned from the NSC in 1966, expressed this idea much too cleverly: "The only lesson we should learn from Vietnam is never again to fight a nationalist movement dominated by Communists in a former French colony."[8] This emphasis on Vietnam's uniqueness has three implications: it ignores American culture; it dismisses Vietnam as an aberration; and, it does not prevent future intervention on what is now thought to be the inappropriate model of Vietnam.

For all the criticism that the Vietnam War was unnecessarily militarized, a parallel fact was that America's managerial fetish "civilized" the military. General Westmoreland was the chief bureaucratic supervisor who reported to the bureaucratic Joint Chiefs who reported to Secretary McNamara who wrote the book on bureaucracy in the Defense Department. The symptoms of an increasingly managerial military establishment were evident in the military's conception of itself as just "doing a job," of its men as managers and workers, and its careerism, bureaucratic sensitivities, and fixation on accounting controls and statistical indexes. These are the lasting legacies of Secretary McNamara's indisputably brilliant tenure. The military's overwhelming investment in engineering was (and is) severely criticized. But this emphasis was (and is) consistent with our national values. It produced the weapons. The Pentagon could not do otherwise.

Colonel Summers acknowledged that the job of the political leaders of the war was to provide the political strategy of the war, its reasons and purpose. The job of the systems analysts was to provide the means to accomplish the purpose. What was missing was a military strategy for the use of the available means to accomplish the stated purpose. He thought we had the *why* and the *what*, but not the *how*. Yet, true to his trade, Colonel Summers swept politics under the rug. We could no more answer why we were in Vietnam than we could explain how to use our cascade of weapons. The single great American accomplishment of the war was in supplying the weapons, and that was not enough.

Having weapons without a purpose or a strategy led to the policy of attrition. If we exploded enough bombs and fired enough rounds, we assumed the enemy would quit. At some point, he would have. General Westmoreland always knew where that point was. The alternative to attrition, he said, was "a war of annihilation."[9] The military struggle could have succeeded only if all of Vietnam had been utterly devastated, with the people dead and buried, or at least dead. Someone once said that the military wanted to carry Vietnam away in the ashtrays of its cars.

Our most important questions cannot be answered by managers or technocrats. This is a shame because they are our specialists in quick fixes. They are the only ones who can deliver what we think we want on the cheap and on time. Our admiration of people who "deliver the goods" contributed mightily to the self-defeating delusions we carried into Vietnam. It contributes to the relative emptiness of our political culture. If America does not have wonder weapons or other magic, it will necessarily be reduced to an incredible combination of isolationism, clumsy military interventions, the careless use of troops who are "just doing a job," and incessant self-congratulation about our self-importance. The fundamental weakness revealed in Vietnam was our strength: management and technology. What was missing was a little maturity—a recognition that the need for the house matters more than the tools required to build it.

The Vietnam War's chief planners—the Bundys, Hilsman, Taylor, McNamara, McNaughton, all the Whiz Kids, Rostow, and Kissinger—the best and the brightest, assisted in engineering a catastrophe for Vietnam and a tragedy for America. By some trick of cultural evolution, the values they represented and the culture they embodied have now become characteristic of the upwardly mobile middle class. The bureaucratic success of the war's thinkers reveals that a value-free dedication to pleasing the boss pays off. How many veterans have been rehabilitated in our law, engineering, and business schools, and have in the process turned themselves into the bureaucratic technicians who sent them to war in the first place?

Management and engineering are today the most popular fields of study in America. Our universities are "producing" graduates in these disciplines in record numbers, and many campuses cannot cope with the demand. The students and their families are responding to the job market, to the understandable desire of young people to get a good job. The universities' reflexive investment in these areas of study weakens other fields of study. Our difficulty is not that we are now training technicians in record numbers, but that we are educating fewer people to think critically, to contribute to the knowledge needed for a stronger political culture, or to be able to conceive of alternative futures. The question that finally emerges is profoundly serious. Are America's bureaucratic values consistent with the need to prepare broadly educated citizens who will surely be needed to keep the technicians in their place, away from political and military decision making? Vietnam demonstrates that the answer to this question may be the difference between an arms race and disarmament, between success or failure in the world, and between war and peace.

We cannot rely on either industry or the universities to help. Both institutions have become bureaucratized in the same way as the military in Vietnam. Across America's central institutions, leadership has been replaced by management. The analogy of the body count in Vietnam is the head count in academia and the bottom line in industry. As the body count created incentives to damage the military in Vietnam, head counts and bottom lines do the same to their institutions. All three require deception to succeed, a concentration on the short term, an inability to contemplate future consequences, an emphasis on pleasing the supervisor (with the resulting prohibition on dissent, that is, creativity) rather than on doing the work, requiring loyalty to individuals rather than to an objective, an inability to define purpose, and uncontrollable careerism.

The head count in higher education constitutes the basis of funding campuses, especially public ones, across the nation. The distortions created by this index, by this managerial impulse of the inchworm, does two things: It provides educational managers with control; and, it allows legislators, trustees, faculty, and the public to judge success by the numbers. The result, as in the war, is corruption, psychic withdrawal, and failure. But there is control.

The bureaucratization of higher education on an industrial model has altered the purpose of higher education, as it also deformed senior army officers. It induced careerism, self-indulgence, and alienation—bad institutional citizenship. What followed were mountains of regulations that were rarely enforced, procedures in place of substance, and manipulation instead of competition. It has turned the university from developing the intellect to supplying the market's demand, and to deceptive public relations that attempts to persuade people to invest their dreams and their hopes in an institution that is prepared to satisfy neither.

It is characteristic of Americans to think of education as some sort of panacea, as the "remedy" for what went wrong in Vietnam. Harrison Salisbury wrote that what was needed was "education, education, education."[10] If he meant self-education, he is right; if he meant the sort of education that occurs in our colleges and universities, he is simply relying on another myth. The idea that education is a vehicle for individual betterment is proved millions of times by the people whose degrees awarded them the chance to earn more money than their parents. In this sense, education pays off. But we have generalized from the cash benefits of higher education to other assumed benefits. This generalization is a myth.

At least in large public universities, which I know best, higher education is as bureaucratic in its form and substance as the military. It rewards what it can measure, and so favors "productivity" rather than creativity, quantity rather than quality. It prefers professors with high head (body) counts in large classes, with long lists of publications. It does not quite know how to support professors with merely excellent classes and excellent publications. A senior academic bureaucrat favors decisions made by lower-level bureaucrats, so that the senior officer almost invariably supports deans who invariably support department chairmen. The procedurally correct decision may be substantively correct, but this is less compelling. "Staying in channels" and "playing by the rules" play into the hands of the conforming members of the academic community, favor the majority as against minorities, and have a powerful tendency to punish dissent, including intellectual dissent. Smart students pick up these attitudes almost immediately and deduce the sort of behavior that is likely to get them the high grades they and their parents demand.

The reality of the bureaucratic university is the bureaucratization of the intellectual life itself. Students are made to jump through required hoops whose purposes are often elusive, such as the accumulation of a magic 120 hours of credit for graduation. It is always the case that a quantitative requirement is arbitrary. Why does an undergraduate degree take four years? Such requirements are arbitrary only in an intellectual sense, however, because they prepare students to accept our bureaucratic society's quantitative definitions of success.

The professoriate is at least as manipulated by quantitative requirements as students. I have always accepted the publish or (and) perish rule. Intellectually vital scholars need to go public to benefit from the criticism of strangers. But the rule's distortion into lists of more than one hundred publications by individuals, mostly in the sciences, reveals that something is awry. The fetish of quantity, the academy's version of the military's numbers racket, assumes that each publication is the equivalent of another. This has several consequences, all of which I experienced as a chief academic officer: It forces bureaucrats who make promotion decisions to betray their deepest academic instincts; it forces faculty members to publish what in a saner world they would happily never have written; it turns everyone's attention away from quality.

Formal education, in short, is not likely to improve the political culture of Americans. Our universities are not prepared, not equipped, and not inclined to educate for deeper and truer political understanding. The current emphasis on technical areas of study, usually in professional schools, goes in exactly the other direction. As we have seen, the technician accepts the world as given, the problem as formulated by someone else. He works within predefined boundaries and is not trained to ask a different question. His training deliberately leads him away from the question *why*. The technological mentality accepts the steady evolution of technology, but within a fixed social context. This mentality, however, is not only produced by schools of business and engineering, as the careers of the liberally educated war managers—such as professors Bundy, Hilsman, Rostow, and Kissinger—reveal. Some individuals apparently can absorb these attitudes through the skin.

Because formal education reflects the values of American culture, it is unhelpful to think of it as an antidote to culture. Education and culture, as war and culture, are inseparably linked. The conclusion is inescapable: Education, or its lack, and war are inseparably linked. Only the individual can do anything about his educational deficiencies and he is unlikely to do so. To join Mr. Salisbury and others in hoping that education can be the counterweight to dangerous American cultural assumptions is not facing the miserable facts: The universities can't and the people won't. This helps to explain the ignorance that led us to Vietnam.

America's business enterprise exhibits similar symptoms. In business, the emphasis on the bottom line provides an incentive to seek instant gratification. Rotation of officers in industry was never as grotesque as in the military, but the average length in office of industry's chief executive officers is now seven years. This aggregate figure obviously hides much faster spinning. In one recent six-year period, for example, RCA had four chief executives. The results are predictable. The short tour breeds defensiveness, an eye to the next job, a desire to avoid risk, a need to ignore the future in the interest of accomplishment in the present, and a slapstick quest for the secret of Japan's success.

All these indexes of "success"—the body count, head count, and bottom line—are reverse alchemy, a way for bureaucracies to turn gold into lead. A long time ago, in 1782, De Crèvecoeur, an American farmer and a shrewd observer, asked his countrymen a question that has never stopped reverberating: "What then is the American, this new man?"[11] Our understanding of the Vietnam War and of its sustaining culture provides the most recent answer. What then is the American? He is a bureaucrat.

* * *

Bureaucratic man at war in Vietnam, at work in the Pentagon, or wherever else—in the university's administrative offices and classrooms, in the executive suites of American industry, in the unions and the civil service, and throughout the professions—is and must be dedicated to the proposition that his personal needs and desires take precedence over the basic purposes of his institution or profession. This is not new. More important, these bureaucratic organizations require that their employees, especially their most senior officers, seek to subvert the goals for whose accomplishment the organizations were created in the first place.

Bureaucracy is as old as organized armies, as the administration of imperial Rome, as the Catholic Church, and as the courtiers who minced into the presence of emperors. What is modern, and what the Vietnam War revealed about America, is that the bureaucratic personality is contagious. It spread with the spread of higher education, doubly important, first to train professionals, and also to reclassify older activities as professions which now require training, such as management and engineering.

With higher education, bureaucratic attitudes have spread throughout the middle class. America is a nation of employees. In 1965, excluding agriculture, 85 percent of the work force was employed by others, against .09 percent self-employed. By 1980, these figures changed to 88 percent against .07 percent, and are rising. More important than the gross statistics is that the attitudes of middle-class Americans, especially those in the expanding world of the professions, have been transformed into the attitudes required of upwardly mobile bureaucrats.

The modern bureaucratic organization is the only major social institution that brings large numbers of people together in a way that prevents them from developing a commitment to each other or to the enterprise. It requires that they be bad citizens of their organization. People who work in bureaucracies have learned, usually without being taught, that their individual fortune depends on the approval of their supervisors. This has always been true for employees, in bureaucracies or not. What is peculiar about the contemporary bureaucracy is the way this approval is won.

The white-collar employee, increasingly identified as a member of a profession, or of a service bureaucracy, characteristically works with words or numbers. More and more senior employees are hired for their judgment rather than for more specific skill. Approval from the supervisor is won by providing him with what he considers to be desirable language or numbers, that is, good advice.

The question is what constitutes desirable and, therefore, persuasive advice? There are always three considerations. Does the subordinate's work make a contribution to the function (killing guerrillas, educating the young, selling merchandise) of the organization? Does it contribute to the welfare of the organization (bigger profits, bigger budgets)? Does it contribute to the welfare of the supervisor (making the supervisor look good to *his* supervisor)? The first two always seem more abstract than the third. At every bureaucratic layer, the approval of the supervisor is more real, more important, and, finally, more rewarding than a concern with either institutional function or welfare.

In a bureaucracy everyone has a boss, everyone is a subordinate. Bosses have bosses, if not within their own institution, then in a governing organization that plays a directing role. Thus, to function effectively in a bureaucracy is to master the fine art of subordination. The more responsibility one has, the more important one is, the more one has to learn humiliation. Everyone's advancement is contingent on pleasing the boss. Everyone must learn to please. The psychic cost of this is known to prostitutes, waiters, and stand-up comedians.

The higher one rises in a bureaucracy, the more important charm becomes, because the more important the bosses of the boss are, the more they are "generalists," the less they know, and the more they must rely on charm as an instrument of manipulation. Indeed, if one really goes high enough, the major questions of the board of directors, of the electorate itself, are questions of personality. Charm is the response to such questions. The art of bureaucratic success is the art of charming the ignorant, and humiliation is the price.

The bureaucratic professionals are thrown back on themselves, on their personal hopes and dreams, on their own desire to make it. That is the implication of careerism. Improving one's career becomes one's career. The organization becomes the vehicle for personal advancement. When this occurs, there is only a small possibility that the employee, however elevated on the promotion ladder, will develop citizenship, loyalty to the organization or to co-workers. What usually occurs has variously been described as me-ism, narcissism, or "looking out for #1." These slogans describe the symptoms. The social disease of the separated self is a result of the psychology of bureaucrats and of the fact that the only effective way to organize people to do the work of the modern state and the modern economy is bureaucracy.

The self, as many cultural critics have said, becomes the center of the universe. This is not because of unfortunate toilet training, or because of the break-up of the traditional family. It is because it works, delivers the salary, security, and the career ladder. Young American professionals have learned that the bureaucracies want from them what they want for themselves. The bureaucracies hire people sufficiently self-interested to focus on technique, not goals; on self-advancement, not group loyalty; on the career, not tradition; on their own futures, not politics, not policy. This was illustrated by the behavior of some of Vietnam's senior officers.

Attending to the needs of the self produces the skills valued in bureaucratic organizations. It produces the necessary language, the emphasis on manipulation, and the vital knowledge that colleagues are enemies. It sensitizes the aspiring professional to the necessary knowledge that his success depends upon the failure of others, or that the success of others will mean his failure.

Peter Cohen, a Harvard MBA, described these attitudes in *The Gospel According to the Harvard Business School:*

> You learn in school not to give a shit if the people you climb over are weak or sick or small or blind. You understand that everybody is your enemy, and you learn to fear and hate people, to live in crowded isolation for the rest of your days. . . . You didn't really feel all that good even about seeing people you liked. Because from today on, they would again become the standard against which you would have to prove yourself. Only now you knew how good some of these guys are, how hard they drive themselves, and how difficult they are to beat.[12]

When such vague social movements finally work their way into mass culture and become specific in the process, become a kind of advice to the lovelorn, the reality of the change is indisputable. *Cosmopolitan* magazine is a more accurate social barometer than the Bureau of Labor Statistics. In a recent issue it displayed on its cover the title of an article: "How Loving a Company Can Spoil a Career." The article counseled: "Don't be so loyal to your co-workers that you couldn't bear to be promoted above them."[13] For its young audience, it is likely that this advice was not hot news.

The formula for personal success becomes clear in almost no time: Someone's success is everyone else's failure. A person's most immediate colleagues necessarily become an impediment to happiness. This is not quite what Hobbes meant when he described society as the war of all against all, because the bureaucrat's weapon of choice is never open conflict. If this is a war, it is fought with personality as the weapon. It is a struggle of images. It is a war where process replaces content, where the greatest tactical error is to make accurate predictions that are perceived to be unhelpful to the boss, as George Ball learned in the State Department, as Robert McNamara finally learned in the Defense Department, as the junior staffman Sam Adams learned in the CIA, as Henry Kissinger's staff learned in the White House, and as the always silent senior officers learned in the military.

The modern bureaucracy organizes people around a common task that is far less important, if it is important at all, than the psychology of pleasing or, to speak more plainly, seduction. For example, when General Westmoreland wanted a marine commander to carry out an order, he sent a letter that began, "I would like to see a plan. . . ." In World War II, a similar letter would start: "You will. . . ."[14] Westy's subordinates understood that he was giving them an order, but his use of language made it seem that they should do as he "suggested" because he would "like" it and them.

The contemporary Don Juan is on a ladder, not to his lady's boudoir, but to the vacant box one layer up on the organization chart. In both cases, the appearance of being pleasing is required to cross the threshold. In both cases, success merely whets the appetite for more. In both cases, process replaces content, anxiety replaces pleasure, and the ladder finally has no last rung as it disappears into the clouds.

Contemporary American anxiety is traceable to the rootlessness required by the imperial self that is valued by bureaucratic organizations. The bureaucratic personality is trained to live inside his own skin. He cannot comfortably live in a stable family. He understands manipulation too well to cooperate by reflex, and too well to sustain friendship. With the agony will come the manipulation that ensures defeat and the self-importance that pretends it does not matter. The pain is enough to screen out the world.

By definition, the poor cannot play this game. The Vietnam grunts, especially the large majority who came from working-class backgrounds, had a different set of aspirations from that of the senior officers, especially the professionals who had been educated to their craft and who had made it a career. The working-class conscripts and enlisted men blew the whistle on the misconduct of their officers, as in the case of Sven Eriksson and at My Lai, not because they were inherently more noble, although many were, but because they had nothing to lose by telling the truth, and the officers did.

For the bureaucratic personality the future is more real than either the present or the past. What he will become after the series of promotions he is counting on is more exciting and gratifying than what he is or was. Because in America the career identifies the individual, the anticipated future of the career identifies what the person wishes to be. Members of the non-bureaucratic working class seek identity and pride in their collective past. Thus, the search for roots, for ethnic pride and cohesion, is a mark of rejection. The celebration of ethnic culture in contemporary America is a symptom of being closed out of the dream.

After President Nixon abolished the draft to secure his reelection, the most privileged young Americans, thanks to the all-volunteer force, had the great luxury of indulging their distaste for public issues. This attitude can be summarized as a sequence: The war first caused a rejection of leadership and institutions, then the authority of culture, and, finally, a retreat to all that ultimately mattered, to the isolated self. For example, Nicholas Lemann was only nineteen when the American killing stopped in 1973. He later said of the postwar generation:

> . . . people like me assumed that the enterprise was not noble, rebelled against it for a time, and then joined it, not

out of the sincere beliefs of our parents, but because there was no other choice. That's why today, although we're better educated than they were, we vote less. It's why survey after survey shows us to feel no loyalty to our employers. It's why marriage and children scare us. There is no large example from our lives that shows us connections like these producing anything but pain. So we stay loose and free and that way at least stave off being disappointed.[15]

The world is right to worry about America's future actions. The new professional American middle class would also be worried if the concern were closer to home, if it had a sense of home; and it would worry about the future if it had a genuine sense of the future, which depends on a sense of time, including the past. Members of this class would share their political concerns with their friends if they or their friends had a sense of politics or citizenship. If they had a sense of friendship. As the world continues to burn, and threatens to explode, these anxious Americans will surely continue to be the hungriest people on earth, at least in their need for affection and approval.

Political authority, legitimate or not, need not concern itself with them. They will neither criticize nor resist. There is no time. It is risky and unimportant. It would not be professional or courteous. It is not rational. It would not be pleasing. And they will surely continue to be the most anxious to please on the face of the earth: "Have a nice day."

In pleasing they do not intend to give pleasure. They mean to profit from the pleasing. They mean to move up. They mean, if you please, to take your job, if it is worth taking. They believe they have a right to it because they can do it better. They are moved by efficiency and cost-effectiveness, by rationality. They are stonily indifferent to other people, to politics, to history, to goals, and to democracy. These emotional and intellectual handicaps were all part of the baggage that induced us to intervene in Vietnam in the first place. They are now more debilitating and more dangerous.

With the profusion of new professional technicians, enormously skilled in analysis and management, American "know-how" has never been stronger. The Vietnam War was the most professionally managed war in history. That is why it was misguided from the start and futile at the end. The sophistication of technique, already very great, continues to grow. We can now calculate the costs and benefits of a proposed activity with marvelous accuracy. Yet, we seem unable to declare without mumbling what we stand for.

Nothing now can soothe the anxieties of the bureaucratic Americans. The cultural transformations of American life have run too wide and too deep. The President, Congress, politics in general, cannot move them. As an external force, politics has no shaping relevance to the self. It exists only as wordnoise, background static, occasionally interesting revelations about "personalities" (that is, other selves), and a generally depressing parade of newsclips about unpleasant things happening out there. The "cures" for this depression constitute our mass culture, and substantially support the medical, psychiatric, pharmaceutical, entertainment, and recreational industries. The relentless inwardness of these professionals has, fittingly enough, made them politically pointless.

This definition of the ego as the world is partly attributable to the reaction to the Vietnam War, and was reinforced by the characteristic American solipsism that contributed to our intervention in the first place. Many have said that the war's lasting legacy was the decline of respect for authority. One result of this was the conclusion that there was no legitimate authority external to the self. Thus, the emotional distance between the demands of citizenship and the claims of bureaucratic man could hardly be more dramatic. A national discussion of war and peace cannot occur. Those are the problems of other people.

What we are finally left with is two social facts of some importance: a nation without citizens, and a people without politics. When these two facts are considered with a third—possession of the greatest power on earth—it is a reasonable conclusion that America has transformed itself from a moral example to a threat to the security of its own and other people.

Our superbly trained professionals will make it worse. Although it is unlikely, it may be that American business and universities, along with the professions, can prosper with the bureaucratic personality. The nation cannot. It may be that as we invented South Vietnam, we may now have to invent America. We deluded ourselves that the social chaos and incompetence of the leaders of South Vietnam was good enough for our purposes. It was futile there and it is not working here.

What is needed is more passion, more compassion, less misleading precision, and more wisdom. Everyone knows that this is a pipe dream. How can we even imagine such a reformation? An answer requires an angry citizenry. But if the citizen is dead, what then? Then we will go on as we are going on. The elites will believe that this is good enough. They have already killed with the use of their skills. They will do so again.

If we stretch our credulity beyond the breaking point, maybe it is possible to imagine the rebirth of an idea. The citizen is dead; long live the citizen. Maybe the dead middle-class citizen can be brought back to life. It is easy to smile knowingly because this is too much to believe, and I concede our fatigue and skepticism and distraction in advance. Following the death of the citizen, as Vietnam revealed, there is death, but not metaphorical or symbolic death. As our technicians and their bureaucratic supervisors continue to do their work, it is reasonable to conclude that next time America will be more efficient, not more effective, merely less wasteful of our resources. As they say, more bang for the buck.

All this is reason enough to disinter the citizen. Because it is not an immediate self-interest, everyone knows that this will never happen. Americans do not know what to do. We will rely on others—the President and his experts, along with the cream of American bureaucratic institutions—to help us, to keep us safe from war, especially nuclear war. Let us pretend, against the repressed knowledge of Vietnam, that our leaders want peace more than power. If we wish to live off fairy tales, it may be instructive to remember that the tooth fairy demands a piece of our children before she pays up, and we have to supply the cash.

We are in the calamitous position of having to choose between an unrealistic faith in the possibility of reinventing the nation and a suicidal delusion that what we have is good enough. If we are too busy to think about this, others will choose for us. Because they are careerists, they will choose, as they have chosen, the delusion. That way they will again appease the right wing, and so will not be accused of being soft. They will always choose to be "realistic" and tough. In the short run they benefit from the world as it is. They rely on technical experts in the nuclear disarmament waltz. It takes more gullibility to believe that they know what they are doing than it does to imagine a new citizenry that will defend itself against them, not only the political leaders, but the technicians who give them aid and comfort, and not only them, but our very own cultural values that give us comfort while threatening our survival.

Our bureaucratic culture is in control. One antidote to folly is experience. Vietnam gave us the necessary experience. But, as President Eisenhower and other Americans boast that we are not "helpless prisoners of history,"[16] we are prone to unlearn experience. We are still the world's pastless barbarian, now not in a coonskin cap, but under our nuclear umbrella. The world had better hope that, for once, the Americans will find a way to become more thoughtful.

The American barbarian is at large in the world. Only its own fears can restrain it. But it is not very practiced in fear. It would rather act than think. It knows how to act much better than it knows when or why it should or should not. It does not know what to do. It is not so much cornered as bewildered. Others must decide whether this confused nation is an adequate defense against an unknown future. It may be that the future is even more dangerous because we exist, and because we have persuaded ourselves that we, as a nation, will protect both ourselves and the rest of the world. That is the wrong question. What we must ask is how we may learn to protect ourselves from ourselves.

There is no reason to believe that the Soviet Union is immune to its own myths. Soviet culture, just as any other, creates war and peace. It is not enough to insist that the conflict with the Soviets is their fault, even if it is. The conflict is between their culture and ours, their myths and ours, between Holy Russia and God's Country.

Of course the Soviet Union is a competitive force in the world. The best way to restrain it is to reduce world tensions. The second best way is for us to stop creating the Soviets' allies and our own enemies. We may someday decide to risk unilateral intelligence. The worst way is to believe our own national cheerleaders, to relish the idea of an exciting international scrimmage, or to follow the advice to shoot first and ask questions later. In its clumsiness, the USSR is easily recognizable as a bureaucratic behemoth. America does sometimes defend freedom by frustrating the Soviet Union. Still, we expect more from America. It owes us more because we owe it more. We are in its debt for its earlier example of freedom, however flawed. Ho Chi Minh recognized this when he used the Declaration of Independence as part of the enabling charter of North Vietnam.

It is intolerable, therefore, when America crashes around the world in the dumb and murderous way it did in Vietnam. It is not enough for it to be against the Soviets, or even against Communism. It must be for something. And because of its history and traditions, it has no choices. It must be for progressive change at home and in the world. Such change will occur in any case, so the question is whether we shall kill to prevent it in the short run, or work to assist in reducing the carnage. America must be for freedom, for dignity, for genuine democracy, or it is not America. It was not America in Vietnam. It runs the risk of forgetting how to be America. That is intolerable to American citizens. If there are any who survived Vietnam.

The ingenious solution to the problems created by the assault on the idea of citizenship and by middle-class antagonism to the Vietnam War was the all-volunteer military. This eliminated the draft, created a professional army, safeguarded the affluent, relied on the need of the poor to enlist, and destroyed the classic democratic need for the citizen-soldier. It also meant that future Presidents would be freer to act militarily because now they could depend on the compliance of a middle class whose sons would be safe. It meant that America would now rely for its defense on men who had been denied opportunity at home. It was the last turn of the screw: Poor Americans would protect, perhaps with their lives, richer Americans whose private pursuits would be undisturbed. As Joseph Califano, who had served in the Pentagon and the White House during the war, said, "It is truly Kafkaesque thinking for public officials who call themselves liberals to support this six billion dollar investment of scarce public sector resources so the lower class can fight our wars."[17]

The all-volunteer force diluted the Americans' sense of obligation to country, just as the Vietnam War did. James Webb, a marine veteran of Vietnam, said that America must "stop being afraid to ask the men of Harvard to stand alongside the men of Harlem, same uniform, same obligation, same country."[18] This idea would have to rest on a sense of citizenship in the middle class. The American citizen was one of the major casualties of Vietnam and the all-volunteer force guarantees the continuing free pursuit of collective self-indulgence. An essential step toward the re-creation of an American citizenry would be a requirement for compulsory public service, including, but not limited to, military service, for every young American, rich and poor, male and female, every race and religion, and the handicapped who can work. No educational exemptions.

An understanding of the cultural sources of our Vietnam experience may help us in the future. We must become conscious of the myth of the city on a hill, of our technological and managerial fetishes, of our bureaucratic tangles, and of our political incompetence. Perhaps we will never be able to give up the pleasure of chanting "We're Number One." Perhaps we will always prefer either to forget Vietnam or to interpret it in ways that will permit us to replay it. Although there is nothing inevitable about self-imposed amnesia, we must also remember that health is not contagious. It is never clear why great numbers of people will stir themselves to think about themselves in the world. It is very clear why the new, young, affluent bureaucrats will remain satisfied with themselves and the world that rewards them with the ease everyone pronounces good. They will continue to organize their lives to please their superiors. As a result, they must be written out of the equation for peace. They will not help, but they will not hinder.

The exception are those in Washington and the military. They became a national menace when they were handed the levers and buttons of political and military power. When Lyndon Johnson excitedly described these clever people to Sam Rayburn, that old political hack said that he would feel better if any of them had ever run for political office, even for sheriff. He was right if he meant to suggest that a sense of accountability to the public was not characteristic of the arrogant and intelligent men whom President Kennedy assembled. Political involvement guarantees nothing, obviously, but it does require thinking about a constituency beyond the universities, beyond the Oval Office and the Tank in the Pentagon. Such involvement is necessary, but not sufficient. Nothing is sufficient except the refusal of the people. And the people wanted Vietnam as it was gathering its deadly force.

That is why national self-knowledge, our barely conscious national values, and our understanding of why we are dangerous is vital. That is why we must understand our Vietnam experience. The Presidents did not bring us Vietnam. Had LBJ asked for a straightforward declaration of war in 1964, instead of the devious Tonkin Resolution, the Congress and the public would have approved. The Communists did not bring us Vietnam either; they merely created what we thought was a problem which we converted into a disaster. We brought it on ourselves, and are likely to do it again.

Americans supported the war for so long because we assumed that our leaders knew what they were doing, because of our chronic panic about Communism which is so patently dangerous that evidently we do not need to understand it, and because we assumed that it would all be easy. We were wrong on every count. Our history in Vietnam is therefore an ideal case study that reveals what is wrong with us.

The way we described the Vietnam War to ourselves and the world was even more self-defeating. All the Presidents told the world that Americans were in Vietnam to prove our reliability, to prove that our word is our bomb, and to safeguard the world. When these things had been said, they became true. Our rhetorical escalation of the stakes for which we fought created those stakes. They were too important to us and the world to trust the Vietnamese. We were fighting in Vietnam, all the Presidents said when they described the dominoes, to protect the free world. This is why the Soviets could rely on their proxy and we could not rely on ours. The North was fighting an unlimited war for the unification of their country. We were fighting a limited war to protect all of humanity. Thus, we could not afford to let the South Vietnamese take over our war. It was too important to risk.

It is another irony that President Nixon counted on American technology to prevent the North from winning. He had secretly promised President Thieu that America would continue to bomb if the North violated the terms of the "peace." Yet, the earlier decisions to bomb the North created the American prisoners of war—the pilots—whose release was the only prize we won in negotiating the peace. In other words, we made peace in order to recover the pilots who had been taken as a result of our reliance on technology to win the war.

Another consequence of our prodigal use of technology was the satisfaction, such as it could be, of discovering that the Communists could not solve Vietnam's economic and social problems after they won. We had conducted ourselves in a way that guaranteed that they would win a broken country, with nothing of economic value left standing in the North, with thousands of square miles of dead forests in the South, along with the flooding and erosion of the top soil that follows. We left them a moonscape of poisoned water, dead land, and a corrupted southern population, what Senator Fulbright once called "a society of prostitutes and mercenaries."[19] A Senate Subcommittee on Refugees estimated the *civilian* casualties of the war in the South as 400,000 killed, 900,000 wounded, and 6,500,000 refugees. Altogether, 2,000,000 Vietnamese were killed, and about 4,500,000 more were wounded, about 10 percent of the population. These horrors made economic reconstruction somewhat awkward. Some Americans point to postwar Vietnam as a showcase of the fact that Communism does not work, and that other Communist-inspired wars of national liberation will lead to the same result of ashes and dust. We only lost the military war, some say, but because of the misery of postwar Vietnam, they claim that we are supposedly winning our larger worldwide war of ideas.

If we do not learn the central facts about Vietnam, that is, the facts about ourselves, we will continue to fumble this war of ideas. The military is not helpful when it insists that civilian interference caused us to lose the war. An infantry colonel bitterly described the war Presidents:

> What the hell did we have? A PT-boat commander with a talent for self-advertisement and a couple of Navy logrollers who never saw action. How do you expect them to make intelligent decisions, even if their advisers are smart and forceful, when they have no background that helps them understand the situation? No way, Mac.[20]

Another colonel had a wider view: "We've thrown over the old 'can do' idea. Now we want to know exactly what they want us to do and how they think we can accomplish it."[21] When any American rejects the old "can do" spirit, it is reasonable to conclude that he has been badly hurt. When the military rejects this article of faith, it is reasonable to conclude that the earlier easy confidence in American hardware, even the unexamined confidence in American institutions themselves, may be in the balance. The military, despite the agony of Vietnam, felt then and feels now that they did not lose the war. They think that victory was denied them by political decision makers who liked to play with soldiers.

The argument that civilian interference prevented the military from winning has been widely accepted, with almost half of the American public (and 82 percent of combat vets) agreeing. This easy assignment of blame obviously permits all of us to growl at the politicians and be done with it. But the ticket-punching careerist officers were not invented by civilians. The utter failure to develop military tactics effectively to utilize the technology was not the fault of civilians. The strategy of attrition and the dizzying rotation of officers were not made in Washington. The cover-ups and deceptive optimism were the military's own. The interservice rivalries were not required by politicians. The bureaucratization of William Westmoreland's mind was the military's own. The unwillingness to stop the blizzard of heroin was the military's own. The subversion of the Special Forces, the insistence on using B-52s, and spreading the use of Agent Orange were all military decisions.

It is, however, true that the military could not have "won" the war. Neither it nor the politicians knew what *winning* meant. By sheer force of firepower the military won its battles, but it could never have made these victories add up to victory. What was the military's responsibility for the failure of the Presidents and their aides to formulate a strategy? It was not the fault of the politicians that the leading generals and admirals bit their tongues when their candor was indispensable. Unless, of course, they had nothing to say. Colonel Summers, for one, rejected the military's argument that politicians' meddling prevented a victory: "Our problem was not so much political interference as it was the lack of a coherent military strategy—a lack for which our military leaders share a large burden of responsibility."[22] In any case, the military's traditional emphasis on its own experience and judgment was unavailable to the nation's leaders as the Chiefs routinely snapped off a salute with the standard "Can do, sir!" Wind-up bureaucratic dolls should not complain that others did not let them win.

* * *

The question of our intervention in Vietnam remains. The most basic issues are necessarily hypothetical and speculative. They all involve actions *not* taken and, therefore, consequences *not* experienced. This is not a mere intellectual game. It is not possible to understand why the war Presidents made their decisions unless we have some understanding of what they were attempting to avoid. We must speculate about a rejected alternative.

What would have happened had President Truman answered his mail? The postman rang eight times. What would have happened if the United States agreed to assist Ho Chi Minh in his repeated requests for moral support in creating a new Vietnam in the aftermath of the Japanese occupation of his country, and in what many mistakenly thought was the end of French colonialism? Dean Rusk, who was in charge of military intelligence in Southeast Asia at the time, said in 1977: "If there was ever any chance of helping Ho Chi Minh to move off in a different direction, it would have been I think late 1945 and early 1946 and that opportunity was lost if there ever was one."[23]

The "realistic" justification for this failure is that at the time Vietnam's eventual significance to the United States was not and could not have been perceived, that the United States could not give aid and comfort to a Communist, and that such aid would have strengthened the Kremlin at the very moment when the cold war was congealing relationships all over the world. It was apparently impossible. Yet, at least one intelligence officer at the time reported that Ho Chi Minh was more of a nationalist than a Communist. Cold warriors automatically assumed that *he was probably duped.* There is the suicidal assumption, the flash point in our sorry Vietnam story. This assumption might, of course, have been true. But how will we ever know? Was it worth anything, including 58,000 dead American soldiers, to have explored this proposition? In saving the cost of a postage stamp did America force Ho Chi Minh to find help in Moscow? Had we helped, might something have turned out differently? Would America, not to mention all of Indochina, have been better off if we had worked with people whose politics we did not like, and would our help necessarily have resulted in a more powerful Kremlin?

There is obviously a beginning to the unfolding realities in international politics, although it is difficult to perceive it at the time. After the realities begin creating other realities, the possibility of change becomes increasingly difficult. America has often created its own enemies by being offended by someone's actions and forcing them into the open arms of the Soviet Union. We should not be so easily offended, and we should be more thoughtful about what is in our own best interest. Out of its anti-Communism, the United States may have created North Vietnam as an anti-American, pro-Soviet regime. This was also the case with Fidel Castro in Cuba. It was also to be the case in Central America. The point at which to concentrate the attention is early enough when progressive and popular local leaders ask for help. After the help is denied for reasons of domestic American politics, a line is crossed, rifles appear, and the intractability of facts takes over. At that point we condemn the violence, support free elections, and worry about our "position in the world." How do we get off so deadly a carousel?

America's strategic embrace of stability, its fear of change, and the Presidents' distrust of the electorate, all conspire to prevent this sort of early intervention on the side of change, on the side of struggling people. If Vietnam teaches only one thing it must be that supporting an unpopular regime is extremely dangerous, to the people, the regime, and us. Thus, we installed the Shah of Iran and supported him beyond any American interest except stability. We created the Shah just as we created South Vietnam, in the interest of stability. Stability is only advantageous to the already comfortable. A great advantage of stability is that it does not require any thought. It is presumed to keep the world in a comfortable configuration for us, what Dr. Kissinger called "order," that permits Americans, including our leaders, to go about our affairs without having to think.

We have not had a new or constructive idea since the Marshall Plan of 1947. That was a time and an idea that brought together America's wish to be both altruistic and anti-Communist, and it succeeded in the ways intended. Since then, in Korea, Berlin, Cuba, and Vietnam—every significant postwar crisis—our responses have been the reflexes of the obsessed. The question is not, What would have happened had we failed to act as we did in Korea, Berlin, Cuba, and Vietnam? The question is, What might have been done to prevent those crises from developing?

The Cuban missile crisis is even now celebrated as one of the supreme achievements of American international management. It is integral in the continuing mythology about President Kennedy. That crisis brought the world closer to nuclear war than ever before or since. At the time the American people, along with millions of others, were sick with fear. It was the single greatest failure of American statecraft in the postwar period because it was caused by President Kennedy's humiliation over the silly Bay of Pigs invasion, and his failure to convince Premier Khrushchev that the President was an adult who should be heeded. It was caused by the outrage Americans were led to feel when Fidel Castro was still a guerrilla fighter in the Cuban mountains. Both Presidents Eisenhower and Kennedy, by their failures over Cuba, had engineered a set of circumstances that the Soviets believed they could exploit.

It is entirely imaginable that Americans could have assisted Fidel Castro to create a decent social revolution against what almost everyone agreed was a corrupt and ruthless dictatorship. If that can be imagined, President Kennedy's deadly serious threat to vaporize the earth may not seem quite so glorious. Should we assume that if the Soviet premier had not behaved rationally, an act of the American President would have meant that we would not be alive today? That so many Americans continue to take pride in having made "the other guy blink" illustrates that we do not know how to think about the world because we do not know how to think about ourselves.

Similarly, it means little to say that Vietnam was a fact staring us in the face. We must wonder about what we can never know: Had we worked with Ho Chi Minh in 1945 and 1946, would he have been the same man we heard about twenty years later? Then the question becomes whether we did what was possible before our fragile war Presidents began to face what each of them called "the facts" of Vietnam. Once those facts intruded on the consciousness of the leaders, the bureaucracy, and the people, it may have been too late. Once Vietnam became a fact instead of a chance, it may have been too late. Vietnam became more factual in 1950, and from then on the facts became progressively heavier and more stubborn. With wisdom, of course, it is never too late.

At last there is one remaining question: What should we *do* now? This is a very American question, based on the mad assumption that political problems, like technological ones, necessarily have solutions. What should we do about what? Our culture? We are not so simple a problem to "solve." The "solution" to a flawed culture is its perceived failure. The tragedy of Vietnam provided us with the experience necessary for careful reflection. To learn from this experience we must reject the military's alibis and the politicians' lullabies. We must struggle with the oyster until we grasp the black pearl: We are what went wrong in Vietnam. We did not pay attention when the chain to Vietnam was being built. We were too pliant under a President's charm, and, for a while, under another's pleading, and, for a while, under another's deceit. Our spirit was lifted by "decisive action," such as mining Haiphong's harbor, when we should have known that it, like every other desperate decision, would backfire. We must learn from our experience in Vietnam. It is perhaps still too soon to test whether we are either able or willing to do so. But it is time to acknowledge that our political leaders do not speak thoughtfully about Vietnam. We should not expect them to do so. In any case, the war was our responsibility. So is the aftermath.

We must develop the long-term resilience and knowledge to act in our own best interest. But our inattention, our bad political education, the insecurity of our leaders, and the obsessions of the technocrats, all seem to move in exactly the other direction—rigidity and ignorance. Given our technological power and our complacency as a people, we seem to be able to survive these defects. Strength is ignorance. Our power and complacency led us into the Vietnam War. Our rigidity and ignorance kept us there, at costs we continue to pay. It may, for example, already have happened that we have taken military actions merely to prove that we are really stronger than we showed in Vietnam; and, that we have not taken actions for fear of "another Vietnam."

Our power, complacency, rigidity, and ignorance have kept us from incorporating our Vietnam experience into the way we think about ourselves and the world. When the remaining Americans were lifted off the roof of the embassy in Saigon, President Ford told the nation that it was time to restore America's pride. For one brief historical moment, later in the 1970s, it looked as if we had developed some doubts about our international and cultural moorings. It looked as if we might have the nerve and wisdom to be concerned not only about Vietnam, but about ourselves. But there is no need to think unless there is doubt. "The era of self-doubt is over,"[24] President Reagan assured the West Point cadets. Freed of doubt, we are freed of thought. Many Americans now seem to feel better about themselves.

The old tinder, now probably more flammable, is at hand. After Ronald Reagan lost the nomination to Gerald Ford in 1976, he talked to a group of his young volunteers who were at the Republican Convention. He wanted them to persist in the good fight. He concluded his plea in a soft voice: "We who are privileged to be Americans have had a rendezvous with destiny since the moment, back in 1630, when John Winthrop, standing on the deck of the tiny *Arbella* off the Massachusetts coast, told his little band of Pilgrims, 'We shall be as a city upon a hill.' " Many of his followers wept at the emotional intensity of the moment. Governor Reagan then predicted, as he would in his 1979 announcement that he would run again: "We will become that shining city on a hill."[25]

NOTES

1. GOD'S COUNTRY AND AMERICAN KNOW-HOW

1. Stephen Young in W. Scott Thompson and Donaldson D. Frizzell, eds., *The Lessons of Vietnam* (London: Macdonald and Jane's, 1977), p. 228.
2. Steve Harper interview in Murray Polner, *No Victory Parades* (New York: Holt, Rinehart & Winston, 1971), pp. 25–26.
3. Maxwell D. Taylor, *Swords and Plowshares* (New York: W. W. Norton & Co., 1972), p. 401.
4. Larry Berman, *Planning a Tragedy* (New York: W. W. Norton & Co., 1982), p. 76.
5. Seymour M. Hersh, *The Price of Power* (New York: Summit Books, 1983), p. 569n.
6. Norman Podhoretz, *Why We Were in Vietnam* (New York: Simon & Schuster, 1982), pp. 46–47.
7. Tad Szulc, *The Illusion of Peace* (New York: Viking Press, 1978), pp. 140–41.
8. Henry Kissinger, *White House Years* (Boston: Little, Brown & Co., 1979), p. 226.
9. Peer de Silva, *Sub Rosa* (New York: Times Books, 1978), pp. 273–74.
10. Interview in Charles J. Levy, *Spoils of War* (Boston: Houghton Mifflin Co., 1974), p. 11.

11. Tim O'Brien, *If I Die in a Combat Zone* (New York: Delacorte Press, 1969–73), pp. 45–46.
12. William C. Westmoreland, *A Soldier Reports* (Garden City, N.Y.: Doubleday & Co., 1976), p. 250.
13. Interview in Levy, *Spoils of War,* p. 21.
14. Michael Herr, *Dispatches* (New York: Alfred A. Knopf, 1977), pp. 125–26, 133.
15. Interview in Al Santoli, *Everything We Had* (New York: Ballantine Books, 1981), p. 170.
16. Daniel Lang, *Casualties of War* (New York: McGraw-Hill, 1969), pp. 26, 102, passim.
17. *Ibid.*, p. 20.
18. Herman Melville, *White Jacket* (London: Oxford University Press, 1924), p. 189.
19. John Winthrop, *Papers,* A. B. Forbes, ed. (Boston: Massachusetts Historical Society, 1931), Vol. II, p. 295.
20. John F. Kennedy, *Public Papers of the Presidents,* Jan. 20, 1961 (Washington, D.C.: G.P.O., 1962), p. 3.
21. Worthington Chauncey Ford, ed., *The Writings of George Washington* (New York: Putnam's Sons, 1889–93), Vol. XIII, p. 317.
22. Saul Padover, ed., *The Complete Jefferson* (New York: Irvington Publishers, 1943), pp. 385–86.
23. *The Vietnam Hearings* (New York: Random House, 1966), p. 115.
24. *Ibid.*
25. Arthur M. Schlesinger, Jr., *The Bitter Heritage* (Boston: Houghton Mifflin Co., 1967), p. 79.
26. David Halberstam, *The Best and the Brightest* (New York: Random House, 1972), p. 41.
27. Interview in Santoli, *Everything We Had,* p. 172.
28. Hubert Humphrey, "Building on the Past," in Anthony Lake, ed., *The Legacy of Vietnam* (New York: New York University Press, 1976), p. 358.
29. George W. Ball, "Have We Learned or Only Failed?" *The New York Times Magazine,* April 1, 1973, p. 13.
30. Walter H. Capps, *The Unfinished War* (Boston: Beacon Press, 1982), pp. 70–71.
31. Woodrow Wilson, *Public Papers* (New York: Harper and Bros., 1925–27), Vol. II, p. 302.
32. J. M. Keynes, *The Economic Consequences of the Peace* (New York: Cambridge University Press, 1920), pp. 38–39.

33. Sigmund Freud and William C. Bullitt, *Thomas Woodrow Wilson* (Boston: Houghton Mifflin Co., 1967), p. 204.
34. Harold G. Nicolson, *Peacemaking, 1919* (Boston: Constable, 1933), p. 256.
35. Keynes, *Economic Consequences*, pp. 42–43.
36. Freud and Bullitt, *Wilson*, p. 272.
37. *Ibid.*, p. 287.
38. Sigmund Freud, "The Disillusionment of War," in Philip Rieff, ed., *Character and Culture* (New York: Collier Books, 1963), p. 140.
39. *Ibid.*, p. 119.
40. Garry Wills, *Nixon Agonistes* (New York: Mentor, 1971), p. 439.
41. Kissinger, *White House Years*, p. 230.
42. Ezra Pound, "Hugh Selwyn Mauberley," in F. J. Hoffman, *The Twenties* (New York: Free Press, 1965), p. 438.
43. Lyndon B. Johnson, *Public Papers of the Presidents*, Jan. 20, 1965 (Washington, D.C.: G.P.O., 1966), p. 73.
44. *Ibid.*, April 7, 1965, p. 172.
45. Graham Greene, *The Quiet American* (London: Heinemann, 1955), pp. 11, 12, 27, 34, 101.
46. U.S. House of Representatives, Select Committee on Intelligence, *Hearings*, 94th Cong., 1st sess., Nov. 4, 6, Dec. 2–17, 1975, part 5, pp. 1706–7.
47. Douglas Kinnard, *The War Managers* (Hanover, N.H.: University Press of New England, 1977), p. 92.
48. *Public Papers of the Presidents*, Jan. 20, 1961, pp. 1–3.
49. *Ibid.*
50. Fox Butterfield, "Vietnam is Not Over," *The New York Times*, Feb. 11, 1983, p. A14.
51. Dwight D. Eisenhower, *Public Papers of the Presidents*, Jan. 20, 1953 (Washington, D.C.: G.P.O., 1960), p. 4.
52. *Ibid.*, p. 5.
53. Richard Nixon, *Public Papers of the Presidents*, April 7, 1971 (Washington, D.C.: G.P.O., 1972), p. 525.
54. Halberstam, *Best and Brightest*, p. 462.
55. Henry A. Kissinger, *Nuclear Weapons and Foreign Policy* (New York: W. W. Norton & Co., 1957), p. 427.
56. "Lessons from a War," speech at conference *Vietnam Reconsidered*, University of Southern California, Feb. 9, 1983.
57. James C. Thomson, Jr., "How Could Vietnam Happen?" *The Atlantic*, April 1968, p. 53.

58. Jacques Ellul, *The Technological Society* (New York: Alfred A. Knopf, 1964), p. 19.
59. U.S. Senate, Electronic Battlefield Subcommittee of the Committee on Armed Services, *Hearings*, 91st Cong., 2nd sess., Nov. 18, 19, and 24, 1970, p. 87.
60. Fulbright, *Vietnam Hearings*, p. 222.
61. Westmoreland, *A Soldier Reports*, pp. 217–23.
62. Thompson and Frizzell, eds., *Lessons of Vietnam*, p. 180.
63. James Crumley, *One to Count Cadence* (New York: Random House, 1969), p. 170; Norman Mailer, *Why Are We in Vietnam?* (New York: Holt, Rinehart & Winston, 1967), p. 12.
64. Mark Baker, *Nam* (New York: William Morrow, 1983), p. 101.
65. A. D. Horne, ed., *The Wounded Generation* (Englewood Cliffs, N.J.: Prentice-Hall, 1981), p. 174.
66. Herr, *Dispatches*, p. 160.
67. Horne, *Wounded Generation*, p. 33.

2. THE CHAIN TO VIETNAM

1. Franklin D. Roosevelt, *Public Papers*, Feb. 23, 1945 (New York: Russell and Russell, 1944–45), Vol. XIII, pp. 562–63.
2. Jean Lacouture, *Ho Chi Minh* (New York: Random House, 1968), p. 2.
3. Interview in Michael Charlton and Anthony Moncrieff, *Many Reasons Why* (London: Scolar Press, 1978), pp. 6–7.
4. Archimedes L. A. Patti, *Why Viet Nam?* (Berkeley: University of California Press, 1980), pp. 84–85, 87, 88.
5. *Ibid.*, p. 86.
6. Michael Maclear, *The Ten Thousand Day War* (New York: Avon Books, 1982), p. 6.
7. *Ibid.*, p. 7.
8. Interview in Al Santoli, *Everything We Had* (New York: Ballantine Books, 1981), p. 44.
9. Reprinted in Gareth Porter, ed., *Vietnam* (Stanfordville, New York: Earl M. Coleman Enterprises, 1979), Vol. I, p. 69.
10. *Ibid.*, pp. 65, 66.
11. *Ibid.*, Feb. 16, 1946, p. 95.
12. *Ibid.*, Fontainebleau conference, July 22, 1946, reprinted on p. 108.

13. William P. Bundy, "The Path to Viet Nam," *Department of State Bulletin*, Sept. 4, 1967, p. 276.
14. Reprinted in Porter, ed., *Vietnam*, April 21, 1945, Vol. I, p. 45.
15. George F. Kennan, "The Sources of Soviet Conduct," *Foreign Affairs*, July, 1947, p. 582.
16. John Lewis Gaddis, *Strategies of Containment* (New York: Oxford University Press, 1982), pp. 25–53.
17. Kennan, "Sources," *Foreign Affairs*, p. 582.
18. George F. Kennan, *American Diplomacy* (Chicago: University of Chicago Press, 1951), p. 153.
19. Harry S. Truman, *Public Papers of the Presidents*, March 12, 1947 (Washington, D.C.: G.P.O., 1963), p. 179.
20. James C. Thomson, Jr., Peter W. Stanley, and John Curtis Perry, *Sentimental Imperialists* (New York: Harper Colophon Books, 1981), p. 253.
21. Robert M. Blum, *Drawing the Line* (New York: W. W. Norton & Co., 1982), pp. 207–8.
22. Reprinted in Thomas Etzold and John Lewis Gaddis, eds., *Containment* (New York: Columbia University Press, 1978), p. 389.
23. Gaddis, *Strategies of Containment*, p. 116.
24. Reprinted in Etzold and Gaddis, *Containment*, pp. 388, 392.
25. *Ibid.*, pp. 432, 435.
26. Harry S. Truman, *Public Papers of the Presidents*, June 27, 1950 (Washington, D.C.: G.P.O., 1965), p. 492.
27. Lloyd Gardner, "From Liberation to Containment," in William Appleman Williams, ed., *From Colony to Empire* (New York: John Wiley & Sons, 1972), p. 371.
28. Harry S Truman, *Memoirs* (Garden City, N.Y.: Doubleday & Co., 1955–56), Vol. II, p. 321.
29. Gardner, "From Liberation," in Williams, ed., *Colony to Empire*, p. 382.
30. John Spanier, *The Truman-MacArthur Controversy and the Korean War* (New York: W. W. Norton & Co., 1965), p. 247.
31. *Congressional Record*, Jan. 30, 1949, 81st Cong., 1st sess., p. A993.
32. *Congressional Record*, June 14, 1951, 82nd Cong., 1st sess., p. 1602.
33. Harry S Truman, *Public Papers*, April 11, 1951, pp. 23–25.
34. *Ibid.*
35. *Ibid.*, Jan. 9, 1952, p. 13.

36. *Congressional Record,* March 14, 1951, 82nd Cong., 1st sess., p. 2397.
37. Richard Nixon, *Memoirs* (New York: Warner Books, 1978), Vol. I, p. 136.
38. Gardner, "The Dulles Years," in Williams, ed., *Colony to Empire,* p. 387.
39. Dwight D. Eisenhower, *Public Papers of the Presidents,* Jan. 20, 1953 (Washington, D.C.: G.P.O., 1960), p. 4.
40. *Ibid.,* Feb. 2, 1953, p. 18.
41. "Purpose of Resolution on Captive Peoples," Feb. 26, 1953, *Department of State Bulletin,* March 9, 1953, p. 372.
42. *Public Papers,* April 16, 1953, p. 183.
43. *Ibid.,* May 5, 1953, p. 258.
44. *Ibid.,* Aug. 4, 1953, p. 541.
45. *Ibid.,* May 5, 1953, p. 258.
46. "Foreign Policy for the Seventies," in Anthony Lake, ed., *The Legacy of Vietnam* (New York: New York University Press, 1976), p. 250.
47. Andrew H. Berding, *Dulles on Diplomacy* (Princeton, N.J.: Van Nostrand, 1965), p. 116.
48. "Morals and Power," June 16, 1953, *Department of State Bulletin,* June 29, 1953, p. 897.
49. Gaddis, *Strategies of Containment,* p. 132.
50. "The Power of Moral Forces," Oct. 11, 1953, *Department of State Bulletin,* Oct. 19, 1953, pp. 511–12.
51. *Ibid.*
52. *Public Papers,* April 7, 1954, p. 383.
53. *Ibid.,* Aug. 4, 1953, p. 541.
54. *Ibid.*
55. "Meeting the People of Asia," Dec. 23, 1953, *Department of State Bulletin,* Jan. 4, 1954, p. 11.
56. Gaddis, *Strategies of Containment,* p. 130.
57. "Meeting the People," *Department of State Bulletin,* pp. 12–13.
58. Bernard B. Fall, *Hell in a Very Small Place* (New York: J. B. Lippincott Co., 1967), pp. 20–21.
59. *Ibid.,* p. 28.
60. *Ibid.,* p. 51.
61. Maclear, *Ten Thousand Day War,* p. 32.
62. Fall, *Hell,* pp. 128–29.
63. Maclear, *Ten Thousand Day War,* p. 44.
64. Nixon, *Memoirs,* Vol. I, p. 184.

65. *Ibid.*, p. 185.
66. *Ibid.*
67. *Ibid.*, p. 186.
68. "Memorandum by the Chairman of the Joint Chiefs of Staff, Admiral Arthur Radford, for the President's Special Committee on Indochina," March 29, 1954, reprinted in Porter, ed., *Vietnam*, Vol. I, p. 510.
69. George Herring, *America's Longest War* (New York: John Wiley & Sons, 1979), p. 35.
70. *Ibid.*
71. Gaddis, *Strategies of Containment*, pp. 178–79.
72. Alexander Kendrick, *The Wound Within* (Boston: Little, Brown & Co., 1974), p. 67.
73. Matthew Ridgway, *Soldier* (Westport, Conn.: Greenwood Press, 1974), p. 277.
74. Townsend Hoopes, *The Devil and John Foster Dulles* (Boston: Little, Brown & Co., 1973), p. 222.
75. Herring, *America's Longest War*, p. 38.
76. Jean Lacouture, *Vietnam: Between Two Truces* (New York: Random House, 1966), p. 19.
77. *Ibid.*, p. 21.
78. *Ibid.*, p. 20.
79. Herring, *America's Longest War*, p. 44.
80. Ralph W. McGehee, *Deadly Deceits* (New York: Sheridan Square Publications, 1983), p. 25.
81. Gaddis, *Strategies of Containment*, p. 159.
82. Charlton and Moncrieff, *Many Reasons Why*, p. 55.
83. Edward G. Lansdale, *In the Midst of Wars* (New York: Harper & Row, 1972), p. 135.
84. *Ibid.*, p. 150.
85. "Report on Covert Saigon Mission," *Pentagon Papers* (New York: Times Books, 1971), p. 54.
86. *Ibid.*, p. 61.
87. Lansdale, *In the Midst of Wars*, p. 233.
88. Dwight D. Eisenhower, *Public Papers*, Oct. 25, 1954, p. 949.
89. Bernard B. Fall, *Viet-Nam Witness* (New York: Frederick A. Praeger, 1966), pp. 15–16.
90. Lansdale, *In the Midst of Wars*, p. 147.
91. Herring, *America's Longest War*, p. 55.
92. Maclear, *Ten Thousand Day War*, p. 53.
93. Herring, *America's Longest War*, p. 43.

94. Maxwell D. Taylor, *Swords and Plowshares* (New York: W. W. Norton & Co., 1972), p. 235.
95. Fall, *Viet-Nam Witness,* p. 181.
96. Frances Fitzgerald, *Fire in the Lake* (Boston: Little, Brown & Co., 1972), p. 28.
97. Lacouture, *Vietnam,* p. 31.
98. Fitzgerald, *Fire in the Lake,* p. 86.
99. Lacouture, *Vietnam,* p. 23.
100. Fall, *Viet-Nam Witness,* p. 112.

3. THE INVENTION OF SOUTH VIETNAM

1. David Halberstam, *The Best and the Brightest* (New York: Random House, 1972), p. 60.
2. Lloyd Gardner, "Cold War Counter Revolution," in William Appleman Williams, ed., *From Colony to Empire* (New York: John Wiley & Sons, 1972), p. 432.
3. "Memorandum of Conference on the Meeting between President Eisenhower and President-elect Kennedy on Laos," Jan. 19, 1961, reprinted in Gareth Porter, ed., *Vietnam* (Stanfordville, New York: Earl M. Coleman Enterprises, 1979), Vol. II, pp. 90–91; Arthur M. Schlesinger, Jr., *A Thousand Days* (New York: Fawcett, 1965), p. 156; Clark Clifford interview in Peter Joseph, ed., *Good Times* (New York: Charterhouse, 1973), p. 428.
4. "Memorandum of Conversation Involving Rusk, McNamara, the Joint Chiefs of Staff and Other Officials," April 29, 1961, in Porter, ed., *Vietnam,* II, pp. 96–99.
5. *The Pentagon Papers,* (New York: Times Books, 1971), p. 86.
6. Roger Hilsman, *To Move a Nation* (Garden City, N.Y.: Doubleday & Co., 1967), p. 32.
7. Theodore Sorensen, *Kennedy* (New York: Harper & Row, 1965), p. 305.
8. Halberstam, *Best and Brightest,* p. 69.
9. Schlesinger, *A Thousand Days,* p. 316.
10. John F. Kennedy, "Address before the American Society of Newspaper Editors," *Public Papers of the Presidents,* April 20, 1961 (Washington, D.C.: G.P.O., 1962), pp. 305, 306.
11. *Ibid.,* p. 306.
12. Hilsman, *To Move a Nation,* p. 413.

13. *Ibid.*
14. *Ibid.*
15. Gustav Gillert, Jr., "Counterinsurgency," *Military Review,* April 1965, p. 25.
16. *Ibid.*, p. 26.
17. Michael Herr, *Dispatches* (New York: Alfred A. Knopf, 1977), p. 257.
18. Theodore Milton, "Air Power: Equalizer in Southeast Asia," *Air University Review,* Nov. 1963, pp. 6, 8.
19. Maxwell Taylor, *Swords and Plowshares* (New York: W. W. Norton & Co., 1972), p. 249.
20. Hilsman, *To Move a Nation,* p. 466.
21. *Ibid.*, p. 419.
22. *Ibid.*, p. 56.
23. Warren Cohen, *Rusk* (Totowa, N.J.: Cooper Square Publishers, 1980), p. 137.
24. Schlesinger, *A Thousand Days,* p. 363.
25. William Westmoreland, "Vietnam in Perspective," *Military Review,* Jan. 1979, p. 35; Halberstam, *Best and Brightest,* p. 76.
26. "Thoughts on Vietnam," in W. Scott Thompson and Donaldson D. Frizzell, eds., *The Lessons of Vietnam* (London: Macdonald and Jane's, 1977), p. 47.
27. Halberstam, *Best and Brightest,* p. 66; but compare Schlesinger, *A Thousand Days,* p. 425: "Bitched again."
28. Stanley Karnow, *Vietnam* (New York: Viking Press, 1983), p. 214.
29. *Pentagon Papers,* May 23, 1961, pp. 133–35.
30. Porter, ed., *Vietnam,* June 9, 1961, Vol. II, p. 109.
31. Harry G. Summers, *On Strategy* (Novato, Cal.: Presidio Press, 1982), p. 171.
32. Porter, ed., *Vietnam,* Oct. 10, 1961, Vol. II, p. 134.
33. Taylor, *Swords and Plowshares,* p. 253.
34. Hilsman, *To Move a Nation,* p. 523.
35. Taylor, *Swords and Plowshares,* p. 237.
36. *Pentagon Papers,* Nov. 1, 1961, pp. 146–48.
37. *Ibid.*, Nov. 3, 1961, p. 152.
38. Schlesinger, *A Thousand Days,* p. 377.
39. Porter, ed., *Vietnam,* Nov. 1, 1961, Vol. II, p. 136.
40. George C. Herring, *America's Longest War* (New York: John Wiley & Sons, 1979), p. 84.
41. Morton Halperin, *Bureaucratic Politics and Foreign Policy*

(Washington, D.C.: The Brookings Institution, 1974), p. 70.

42. Herring, *America's Longest War,* p. 82; Schlesinger, *A Thousand Days,* p. 363.
43. Arthur M. Schlesinger, Jr., *The Bitter Heritage* (Boston: Houghton Mifflin Co., 1967), p. 20.
44. Interview in Al Santoli, *Everything We Had* (New York: Ballantine Books, 1981), p. 7.
45. James C. Hasdorff, "Vietnam in Retrospect," *Air University Review,* Jan. 1974, p. 3.
46. Schlesinger, *A Thousand Days,* p. 897.
47. Michael Maclear, *The Ten Thousand Day War* (New York: Avon Books, 1982), p. 64.
48. Herring, *America's Longest War,* p. 97.
49. Herr, *Dispatches,* p. 50.
50. Maclear, *Ten Thousand Day War,* p. 65.
51. Nguyen Chi Thanh, "Who Will Win in South Viet Nam?" (Peking, 1963), Porter, ed., *Vietnam,* Vol. II, p. 184.
52. "Untold Story of the Road to War in Vietnam," *U.S. News & World Report,* Oct. 10, 1983, p. 8.
53. *Pentagon Papers,* Aug. 24, 1963, pp. 200–201.
54. *Ibid.,* Aug. 29, 1963, p. 203.
55. *Ibid.,* Aug. 31, 1963, p. 208.
56. John F. Kennedy, *Public Papers of the Presidents,* Sept. 2, 1963 (Washington, D.C.: G.P.O., 1964), p. 652.
57. Interview in Michael Charlton and Anthony Moncrieff, *Many Reasons Why* (London: Scolar Press, 1978), p. 99.
58. Hedrick Smith, "The Overthrow of Ngo Dinh Diem," *Pentagon Papers,* p. 179.
59. *Pentagon Papers,* Oct. 5, 1963, pp. 221–22.
60. *Ibid.,* Oct. 30, 1963, p. 227.
61. Interview in Charlton and Moncrieff, *Many Reasons Why,* p. 98.
62. *Ibid.,* p. 216.
63. Maclear, *Ten Thousand Day War,* p. 80.
64. Schlesinger, *A Thousand Days,* pp. 909–10.
65. Halberstam, *Best and Brightest,* p. 77.
66. "Untold Story," *U.S. News & World Report,* p. 10.
67. George Ball, "Have We Learned or Only Failed?" *The New York Times Magazine,* April 1, 1973, p. 13; Larry Berman, *Planning a Tragedy* (New York: W. W. Norton & Co., 1982), p. 86.
68. Berman, *Planning a Tragedy,* p. 108.

69. Bernard B. Fall, *Viet-Nam Witness* (New York: Praeger, 1966), p. 200.

70. *Pentagon Papers,* Oct. 30, 1963, p. 233.

71. John Lewis Gaddis, *Strategies of Containment* (New York: Oxford University Press, 1982), p. 213.

72. Doris Kearns, *Lyndon Johnson and the American Dream* (New York: Harper & Row, 1977), p. 171.

73. *Ibid.*, p. 209.

74. *Ibid.*, p. 177.

75. Lyndon B. Johnson, *The Vantage Point* (New York: Holt, Rinehart & Winston, 1971), p. 42.

76. Kearns, *Johnson,* pp. 181–82.

77. Porter, ed., *Vietnam,* Nov. 26, 1963, Vol. II, p. 222.

78. *Ibid.*, p. 223.

79. *Ibid.*, Dec. 6, 1963, p. 227.

80. *Pentagon Papers,* Dec. 21, 1963, p. 280.

81. Porter, ed., *Vietnam,* Dec. 21, 1963, Vol. II, p. 233.

82. *Ibid.*, p. 234.

83. Hilsman, *To Move a Nation,* p. 507.

84. Porter, ed., *Vietnam,* Jan. 22, 1964, Vol. II, p. 235. Also see *Pentagon Papers,* pp. 130, 158–60.

85. Hilsman, *To Move a Nation,* p. 508.

86. *Pentagon Papers,* Jan. 22, 1964, p. 283.

87. *Ibid.*, pp. 282, 284–85.

88. Neil Sheehan, "The Covert War and Tonkin Gulf," *Pentagon Papers,* p. 248.

89. Fall, *Viet-Nam Witness,* p. 105.

90. Sheehan, "Covert War," *Pentagon Papers,* p. 262.

91. *Ibid.*, p. 264.

92. Porter, ed., *Vietnam,* June 12, 1964, Vol. II, p. 287.

93. George W. Ball, *The Past Has Another Pattern* (New York: W. W. Norton & Co., 1982), p. 379.

94. Lyndon B. Johnson, "Special Message to the Congress on U.S. Policy in Southeast Asia," *Public Papers of the Presidents,* Aug. 5, 1964 (Washington, D.C.: G.P.O., 1965), p. 931.

95. Porter, ed., *Vietnam,* Aug. 7, 1964, Vol. II, p. 307.

96. Sheehan, "Covert War," *Pentagon Papers,* p. 273.

97. Halberstam, *Best and Brightest,* p. 419.

98. Sheehan, "Covert War," *Pentagon Papers,* p. 277.

99. Cohen, *Rusk,* p. 321.

4. WAR BY THE NUMBERS

1. Lyndon B. Johnson, *The Vantage Point* (New York: Holt, Rinehart & Winston, 1971), p. 110.
2. Theodore H. White, *The Making of The President, 1964* (New York: Atheneum, 1965), pp. 336, 374.
3. Doris Kearns, *Lyndon Johnson and the American Dream* (New York: Harper & Row, 1976), p. 264.
4. William C. Westmoreland, "Vietnam in Perspective," *Military Review,* Jan. 1979, p. 37.
5. William C. Westmoreland, *A Soldier Reports* (Garden City, N.Y.: Doubleday & Co., 1976), p. 409.
6. Larry Berman, *Planning a Tragedy* (New York: W. W. Norton & Co., 1982), pp. 34–35.
7. Eric F. Goldman, *The Tragedy of Lyndon Johnson* (New York: Alfred A. Knopf, 1969), p. 404.
8. Berman, *Planning a Tragedy,* p. 37.
9. *Ibid.*, p. 39.
10. "Memorandum for the President from McGeorge Bundy," Feb. 7, 1965, reprinted in Gareth Porter, ed., *Vietnam* (Stanfordville, New York: Earl M. Coleman Enterprises, 1979), Vol. II, p. 349.
11. *Ibid.*, p. 351.
12. *Ibid.*, p. 353.
13. *Ibid.*
14. *Ibid.*, p. 355.
15. *Ibid.*, p. 356.
16. *Ibid.*, p. 357.
17. Johnson, *Vantage Point*, p. 128.
18. *Ibid.*
19. *Ibid.*
20. *Ibid.*
21. Berman, *Planning a Tragedy,* p. 44.
22. *Ibid.*, p. 45.
23. *Ibid.*, p. 50.
24. Johnson, *Vantage Point*, p. 125.
25. Ralph W. McGeehee, *Deadly Deceits* (New York: Sheridan Square Publications, 1983), p. 140.
26. Johnson, *Vantage Point*, p. 132.
27. *Ibid.*
28. Michael Maclear, *The Ten Thousand Day War* (New York: Avon Books, 1981), p. 125.

29. Johnson, *Vantage Point*, p. 138.
30. *Pentagon Papers*, March 24, 1965 (New York: Times Books, 1971), p. 442.
31. Maureen Mylander, *The Generals* (New York: Dial Press, 1974), p. 8.
32. William C. Westmoreland, *A Soldier Reports*, p. 28.
33. *Ibid.*, pp. 105–6.
34. *Ibid.*, p. 112.
35. *Ibid.*, pp. 112–13.
36. *Ibid.*, pp. 119–20.
37. *Ibid.*, p. 120.
38. *Ibid.*
39. *Ibid.*, p. 122.
40. Donald E. McQuinn, *Targets* (New York: Tor Books, 1980), p. 60.
41. Matthew Ridgway, *Soldier* (Westport, Conn.: Greenwood, 1974), p. 277.
42. Westmoreland, *A Soldier Reports*, pp. 137–38.
43. *Ibid.*, p. 130.
44. Bill Moyers interview, PBS, "LBJ Goes to War," *Vietnam: A Television History*.
45. *Pentagon Papers*, House of Representatives, ed. (Washington, D.C.: G.P.O., 1971), Vol. VI, pp. 38, 41, 44.
46. Maxwell D. Taylor, *Swords and Plowshares* (New York: W. W. Norton & Co., 1972), p. 339.
47. Mary McCarthy, *Vietnam* (New York: Harcourt, Brace & World, 1967), pp. 18–21.
48. *Pentagon Papers*, Oct. 14, 1966, p. 555.
49. "Outlook Now for the War in Vietnam," *U.S. News & World Report*, Nov. 21, 1966, p. 66.
50. Arthur M. Schlesinger, Jr., *The Bitter Heritage* (Boston: Houghton Mifflin Co., 1967), p. 44.
51. John Lewis Gaddis, *Strategies of Containment* (New York: Oxford University Press, 1982), p. 255.
52. John Henry II, "February, 1968," *Foreign Affairs*, Fall 1971, p. 29.
53. Gaddis, *Strategies of Containment*, p. 262.
54. Philip Geyelin, *Lyndon B. Johnson and the World* (New York: Praeger, 1966), p. 155.
55. Bui Diem, draft "Note," at *Vietnam Reconsidered* conference, University of Southern California, Feb. 9, 1983, p. 2.
56. Maclear, *Ten Thousand Day War*, p. 141.

57. *Ibid.*, p. 148.
58. Berman, *Planning a Tragedy*, p. 87.
59. *Ibid.*, p. 95.
60. *Ibid.*, p. 106.
61. *Ibid.*, p. 110.
62. *Ibid.*, pp. 112–19.
63. Maclear, *Ten Thousand Day War*, pp. 142–43.
64. George C. Herring, *America's Longest War* (New York: John Wiley & Sons, 1979), p. 157.
65. Maclear, *Ten Thousand Day War*, p. 143.
66. Westmoreland, *A Soldier Reports*, p. 153.
67. Maclear, *Ten Thousand Day War*, p. 143.
68. Douglas Kinnard, *The War Managers* (Hanover, N.H.: University Press of New England, 1977), p. 43.
69. Michael Herr, *Dispatches* (New York: Alfred A. Knopf, 1978), p. 47.
70. John A. Parrish, *12, 20 & 5* (Baltimore, Md.: Penguin Books, 1972), p. 270.
71. Don Oberdorfer, *Tet!* (Garden City, N.Y.: Doubleday & Co., 1971), p. 158.
72. David Halberstam, *The Best and the Brightest* (New York: Random House, 1972), p. 145.
73. Gaddis, *Strategies of Containment*, p. 255.
74. Herring, *America's Longest War*, p. 178.
75. Kearns, *Johnson*, p. 336.
76. Herring, *America's Longest War*, p. 179.
77. Johnson, *Vantage Point*, p. 151.
78. Clark M. Clifford, "A Viet Nam Reappraisal," *Foreign Affairs*, July 1969, p. 607.
79. *Ibid.*, pp. 610–13.
80. Henry, "February, 1968," *Foreign Affairs*, p. 21.
81. Westmoreland, *A Soldier Reports*, p. 357.
82. Henry, "February, 1968," *Foreign Affairs*, p. 23.
83. Lyndon B. Johnson, *Public Papers of the Presidents*, March 31, 1968 (Washington, D.C.: G.P.O., 1970), p. 476.
84. Moyers interview, PBS, "LBJ Goes to War," *Vietnam.*

5. THE POLITICS OF EGO

1. Richard Nixon, *RN: The Memoirs* (New York: Warner Books, 1978), Vol. I, p. 399.

2. *Ibid.*, p. 401.
3. *Ibid.*
4. Seymour M. Hersh, *The Price of Power* (New York: Summit Books, 1983), p. 14.
5. *Ibid.*, p. 20.
6. Theodore H. White, *The Making of the President, 1968* (New York: Atheneum, 1969), p. 380.
7. Henry Kissinger, *The White House Years* (Boston: Little, Brown & Co., 1979), p. 10.
8. Nixon, *Memoirs*, Vol. I, p. 421.
9. Kissinger, *White House Years*, p. 11.
10. Nixon, *Memoirs*, Vol. I, p. 422.
11. Kissinger, *White House Years*, p. 12.
12. Nixon, *Memoirs*, Vol. I, p. 422.
13. Kissinger, *White House Years*, pp. 13–14.
14. *Ibid.*, p. 14.
15. Tad Szulc, *The Illusion of Peace* (New York: Viking Press, 1978), p. 26.
16. Nixon, *Memoirs*, Vol. I, p. 424.
17. *Ibid.*, p. 427.
18. William Shawcross, *Sideshow* (New York: Washington Square Press, 1979), p. 87.
19. Henry Kissinger, "The Viet Nam Negotiations," *Foreign Affairs*, Jan. 1969, pp. 211–12.
20. *Ibid.*, p. 218.
21. *Ibid.*, p. 231.
22. Shawcross, *Sideshow*, p. 77.
23. *Ibid.*, p. 87.
24. Henry Kissinger, "Domestic Structure and Foreign Policy," *Daedalus*, Spring 1966, p. 506.
25. Richard Nixon, *Public Papers of the Presidents*, July 1, 1970 (Washington, D.C.: G.P.O., 1971), pp. 546–47.
26. Shawcross, *Sideshow*, p. 87.
27. *Ibid.*, p. 90.
28. H. R. Haldeman with Joseph DiMona, *The Ends of Power* (New York: Times Books, 1978), p. 83.
29. Szulc, *Illusion of Peace*, pp. 150–51.
30. White, *Making of the President, 1968*, pp. 430–31.
31. Kissinger, "Domestic Structure," *Daedalus*, pp. 509–10.
32. Quoted in Nixon, *Memoirs*, Vol. I, p. 431.
33. Hersh, *Price of Power*, pp. 79–80.
34. Haldeman, *Ends of Power*, p. 82; Nixon, *Memoirs*, Vol. I, p. 432.

35. Richard Whalen, *Catch the Falling Flag* (Boston: Houghton Mifflin Co., 1972), p. 139.
36. Szulc, *Illusion of Peace*, p. 196.
37. Shawcross, *Sideshow*, p. 91.
38. Hersh, *Price of Power*, p. 60.
39. *Public Papers*, May 14, 1969, p. 372.
40. Richard Evans, Jr., and Robert D. Novak, *Nixon in the White House* (New York: Random House, 1971), p. 83.
41. Matthew Ridgway, "Indochina: Disengaging," *Foreign Affairs*, July 1971, p. 592.
42. Shawcross, *Sideshow*, p. 100.
43. Hersh, *Price of Power*, p. 108.
44. Nixon, *Memoirs*, Vol. I, p. 536.
45. *Public Papers*, June 30, 1970, p. 536.
46. Szulc, *Illusion of Peace*, p. 283.
47. Shawcross, *Sideshow*, p. 146; Hersh, *Price of Power*, p. 190.
48. *Ibid.*, pp. 190–91.
49. William Safire, *Before the Fall* (New York: Ballantine Books, 1975), pp. 186–87.
50. Shawcross, *Sideshow*, p. 152; Nixon, *Memoirs*, Vol. I, p. 562; Hersh, *Price of Power*, pp. 192–93.
51. Safire, *Before the Fall*, p. 190.
52. Hersh, *Price of Power*, p. 308.
53. Gareth Porter, *A Peace Denied* (Bloomington, Ind.: University of Indiana Press, 1975), p. 104.
54. Lyndon B. Johnson, *Public Papers of the Presidents*, Feb. 2, 1968 (Washington, D.C.: G.P.O., 1970), p. 163.
55. Kissinger, *White House Years*, p. 1301.
56. *Ibid.*, p. 1121.
57. Hersh, *Price of Power*, p. 584.
58. Nixon, *Memoirs*, Vol. II, p. 195; Porter, *A Peace Denied*, p. 129; Kissinger, *White House Years*, p. 1372.
59. Kissinger, *White House Years*, p. 1325.
60. *Ibid.*, p. 1327.
61. Porter, *A Peace Denied*, p. 127.
62. Henry A. Kissinger, *American Foreign Policy* (New York: W. W. Norton & Co., 1969), p. 32.
63. Haldeman, *Ends of Power*, p. 95.
64. Hersh, *Price of Power*, p. 606.
65. *Ibid.*, p. 568.
66. Kissinger, *White House Years*, pp. 1328–29.

67. *Ibid.*, p. 1399.
68. Porter, *A Peace Denied,* pp. 134–35.
69. Nixon, *Memoirs,* Vol. II, p. 207.
70. *Ibid.*, p. 242.
71. Thomas L. Hughes, "Foreign Policy: Men or Measures?" *Atlantic,* Oct. 1974, p. 56.
72. Nixon, *Memoirs,* Vol. II, p. 250.
73. *Ibid.*, p. 247.
74. *Ibid.*, pp. 242–43.
75. Richard Nixon, *Public Papers of the Presidents* (Washington, D.C.: G.P.O., 1975), March 29, 1973, p. 235.
76. Nixon, *Memoirs,* Vol. II, p. 243.
77. *Ibid.*, p. 244.
78. Quoted in Kissinger, *White House Years,* p. 1469.
79. Nixon, *Memoirs,* Vol. II, p. 245.
80. *Ibid.*, p. 253.
81. *Ibid.*, p. 254.
82. George Eade, "Reflections on Air Power in the Vietnam War," *Air University Review,* Nov.–Dec. 1973, p. 7.
83. George C. Herring, *America's Longest War* (New York: John Wiley & Sons, 1979), p. 248.
84. Nixon, *Memoirs,* Vol. II, p. 246.
85. U.S. Congress, House of Representatives, Subcommittee of the Committee on Appropriations, *Department of Defense Appropriations, Hearings,* 93rd Cong., 1st sess., 1973, p. 30.
86. Nixon, *Memoirs,* Vol. II, p. 258.
87. Hersh, *Price of Power,* p. 631.
88. McGeorge Bundy, "Vietnam, Watergate and Presidential Powers," *Foreign Affairs,* Winter 1979–80, p. 406.
89. Nixon, *Memoirs,* Vol. II, pp. 29–30.
90. Shawcross, *Sideshow,* p. 160.
91. C. P. Snow, *Science and Government* (Cambridge, Mass.: Harvard University Press, 1961), p. 73.
92. *Public Papers,* May 24, 1973, p. 560.
93. Hersh, *Price of Power,* p. 314.
94. *Public Papers,* Feb. 25, 1971, p. 221.
95. *Ibid.*, p. 222.
96. Interview in Peter Joseph, *Good Times* (New York: Charterhouse, 1973), p. 455.
97. Robert Jay Lifton, *Home from the War* (New York: Simon & Schuster, 1973), p. 450.

6. ENABLING IGNORANCE

1. Morton H. Halperin, *Bureaucratic Politics and Foreign Policy* (Washington, D.C.: The Brookings Institution, 1974), p. 292.
2. Richard Neustadt, *Presidential Power* (New York: John Wiley & Sons, 1960), p. 9.
3. Halperin, *Bureaucratic Politics*, p. 245.
4. Richard Nixon, *Memoirs* (New York: Warner Books, 1978), Vol. I, p. 436.
5. Henry Kissinger, *White House Years* (Boston: Little, Brown & Co., 1979), p. 1199.
6. Frank Snepp, *Decent Interval* (New York: Vintage Books, 1977), p. 115.
7. Arthur M. Schlesinger, Jr., *A Thousand Days* (New York: Fawcett Books, 1965), p. 377.
8. *Ibid.*, p. 379.
9. James Fallows, *National Defense* (New York: Random House, 1981), p. 77.
10. Maxwell D. Taylor, *Swords and Plowshares* (New York: W.W. Norton & Co., 1972), p. 416.
11. Gustav J. Gillert, Jr., "Counterinsurgency," *Military Review*, April 1965, p. 26.
12. Richard Betts, *Soldiers, Statesmen, and Cold War Crises* (Cambridge, Mass.: Harvard University Press, 1977), p. 132.
13. *Ibid.*, p. 133.
14. Ward Just, *Military Men* (New York: Alfred A. Knopf, 1970), p. 185.
15. Taylor, *Swords and Plowshares*, p. 201.
16. *Ibid.*, p. 202.
17. Roger Hilsman, *To Move a Nation* (Garden City, N.Y.: Doubleday & Co., 1967), p. 426.
18. *Ibid.*, p. 579.
19. Henry L. Trewhitt, *McNamara* (New York: Harper & Row, 1971), p. 232.
20. Halperin, *Bureaucratic Politics*, p. 262.
21. Cincinnatus, *Self-Destruction* (New York: W. W. Norton & Co., 1981), pp. 105–6.
22. Interview in Al Santoli, *Everything We Had* (New York: Ballantine Books, 1981), p. 46.

23. Gregory Palmer, *The McNamara Strategy and the Vietnam War* (Westport, Conn.: Greenwood Press, 1978), p. 78.
24. Alain C. Enthoven and K. Wayne Smith, *How Much Is Enough?* (New York: Harper & Row, 1971), p. 296.
25. *Ibid.*, p. 297.
26. *Ibid.*, p. 305.
27. William Westmoreland, *A Soldier Reports* (Garden City, N.Y.: Doubleday & Co., 1976), p. 161.
28. John Lewis Gaddis, *Strategies of Containment* (New York: Oxford University Press, 1982), p. 251n.
29. U.S. Congress, House of Representatives, Committee on Armed Services, *Hearings on Military Posture*, 90th Cong., 2nd sess., 1968, p. 8883.
30. U.S. Congress, House of Representatives, Committee on Appropriations, Subcommittee *Hearings*, 90th Cong., 1st sess., 1967, p. 43.
31. Taylor, *Swords and Plowshares*, p. 308.
32. Joseph Martino, "Systems Analysis and Counter-Insurgency," *Air University Review*, Sept–Oct. 1966, p. 33.
33. Eliot Cohen, "Systems Paralysis," *American Spectator*, Nov. 1980, pp. 26–27.
34. James Schlesinger, *On Relating Non-Technical Elements to Systems Studies* (Santa Monica, Cal.: RAND Corp., Feb. 1967), pp. 12–15.
35. Palmer, *The McNamara Strategy*, p. 123.
36. Peer De Silva, *Sub Rosa* (New York: Times Books, 1978), p. 212.
37. *Ibid.*, p. 220.
38. *Ibid.*, p. 227.
39. *Ibid.*, p. 242.
40. *Ibid.*, p. 243.
41. *Ibid.*, p. 245.
42. *Ibid.*, pp. 257, 261.
43. Robert S. McNamara, *The Essence of Security* (New York: Harper & Row, 1968), p. 91.
44. Westmoreland, *A Soldier Reports*, pp. 86–87.
45. Gaddis, *Strategies of Containment*, p. 253.
46. Robert Komer, "Was Failure Inevitable?" in W. Scott Thompson and Donaldson D. Frizzell, eds., *The Lessons of Vietnam* (London: Macdonald and Jane's, 1977), p. 269.

47. Robert Gallucci, *Neither Peace Nor Honor* (Baltimore, Md.: Johns Hopkins University Press, 1976), p. 84.
48. U.S. Congress, House of Representatives, Select Committee on Intelligence, *Hearings*, 94th Cong., 1st sess., 1975, p. 1727.
49. Kissinger, *White House Years*, p. 1112.
50. Thomas Thayer, "Air Power," in Thompson and Frizzell, eds., *Lessons of Vietnam*, p. 146–50.
51. Sam Adams, "Vietnam Cover-Up," *Harper's*, May 1975, p. 41.
52. *Ibid.*, pp. 41, 42.
53. *Ibid.*, p. 43.
54. *Ibid.*, p. 44.
55. *Ibid.*
56. *Ibid.*, p. 62.
57. U.S. Congress, House of Representatives, Select Committee on Intelligence, *U.S. Intelligence Agencies and Activities: Hearings*, 94th Cong., 1st sess., 1976, p. 1703.
58. *Ibid.*, p. 1711.
59. Adams, "Vietnam Cover-Up," *Harper's*, p. 65.
60. House Select Committee on Intelligence, *Hearings*, p. 1703.
61. *Ibid.*, p. 1655.
62. *Ibid.*, p. 1703.
63. *Ibid.*, p. 1685.
64. Robert Komer, *Bureaucracy Does Its Thing* (Santa Monica, Cal.: RAND Corp., Aug. 1972), p. 59.
65. House Select Committee on Intelligence, *Hearings*, p. 1710.
66. *Ibid.*, p. 1699.
67. Komer, "Was Failure Inevitable?" in Thompson and Frizzell, eds., *Lessons of Vietnam*, p. 270.
68. Adams, "Vietnam Cover-Up," *Harper's*, p. 65.
69. Interview with Sam Adams, Oct. 29, 1983.
70. House Select Committee on Intelligence, *Hearings*, p. 1656.
71. Adams, "Vietnam Cover-Up," *Harper's*, p. 65.
72. Interview with Sam Adams, Oct. 29, 1983.
73. Adams, "Vietnam Cover-Up," *Harper's*, p. 68.
74. *Ibid.*, p. 73.
75. U.S. District Court, Southern District; *Gen. William C. Westmoreland* v. *CBS, Inc.*, *et al.*, 82 Civ. 7913, "Memorandum in Support of Defendant CBS's Motion to Dismiss and for Summary Judgment," May 23, 1984, pp. 6–7, fn 5.
76. *Ibid.*, p. 17. Cf. "Plaintiff General William C. Westmoreland's Memorandum of Laws," Ch. III.

77. *Ibid.,* p. 18.
78. *Ibid.,* p. 24ff.
79. *Ibid.,* p. 21.
80. *Ibid.,* p. 29ff.
81. Halperin, *Bureaucratic Politics,* p. 160.
82. "The Pike Papers," *The Village Voice,* Feb. 16, 1976, p. 77.
83. W. W. Rostow, "Memorandum," Nov. 1967; MACV, *Statistics on the War in Vietnam,* "VC/NVA Strength." Copies of these documents are in my possession.
84. Thomas Powers, *The Man Who Kept the Secrets* (New York: Alfred A. Knopf, 1979), p. 189.
85. *Ibid.,* pp. 81–82.
86. Seymour Hersh, *The Price of Power* (New York: Summit Books, 1983), p. 207.
87. Komer, *Bureaucracy Does Its Thing,* p. ix.
88. Westmoreland, *A Soldier Reports,* p. 216.
89. William Colby and Peter Forbath, *Honorable Men* (New York: Simon & Schuster, 1978), p. 272.
90. *Ibid.,* p. 268.
91. Snepp, *Decent Interval,* p. 12.
92. Tad Szulc, *The Illusion of Peace* (New York: Viking Press, 1978), p. 234.
93. *Ibid.,* p. 235.
94. Colby, *Honorable Men,* p. 273.
95. Szulc, *Illusion of Peace,* p. 236.
96. Powers, *The Man Who Kept the Secrets,* p. 216.
97. Interview with Sam Adams, Oct. 29, 1983.
98. David Halberstam, *The Best and the Brightest* (New York: Random House, 1972), p. 203.
99. "A War Being Lost Because an Ally Won't Fight?" *U.S. News & World Report,* Sept. 16, 1963, pp. 40–41.
100. David Halberstam, "The Ugliest American in Vietnam," *Esquire,* Nov., 1964, 114ff.
101. For his future career as a senior officer in CORDS, see *The New York Times,* May 24, 1968, p. 4, and June 10, 1972, p. 1, and June 14, 1972, p. 46; *U.S. News & World Report,* May 31, 1971, pp. 29ff.; *Newsweek,* June 19, 1972, pp. 43–44; and *Time,* June 19, 1972, pp. 24–25.
102. Douglas Kinnard, *The War Managers* (Hanover, N.H.: University Press of New England, 1977), p. 58.
103. Kissinger, *White House Years,* p. 27.

104. Halperin, *Bureaucratic Politics*, pp. 268–69.
105. Westmoreland, *A Soldier Reports*, p. 304.
106. Douglas Blaufarb, *The Counterinsurgency Era* (New York: The Free Press, 1977), p. 297.
107. Stanley Karnow, *Vietnam* (New York: Viking Press, 1983), pp. 534, 602.
108. Robert Komer in Thompson and Frizzell, eds., *The Lessons of Vietnam*, p. 110.
109. Karnow, *Vietnam*, p. 603.

7. THE WARRIORS

1. Murray Polner, *No Victory Parades* (New York: Holt, Rinehart and Winston, 1971), p. 37.
2. Paul Starr, *The Discarded Army* (New York: Charterhouse, 1973), pp. 8–9.
3. Veterans Administration, "Myths and Realities," submitted to the U.S. Senate, Committee on Veterans' Affairs, July 1980, p. 7.
4. Starr, *Discarded Army*, p. 192.
5. Lawrence M. Baskir and William A. Strauss, *Chance and Circumstance* (New York: Alfred A. Knopf, 1978), p. 9.
6. *Ibid.*, p. 10.
7. James Fallows, "What Did You Do in the Class War, Daddy?" *The Washington Monthly*, Oct. 1975, p. 7.
8. James Webb, *Fields of Fire* (New York: Bantam Books, 1972), p. 1.
9. Polner, *No Victory Parades*, p. 27.
10. Baskir and Strauss, *Chance and Circumstance*, p. 7.
11. William Westmoreland, "Vietnam in Perspective," *Military Review*, Jan. 1979, p. 37.
12. Martin Binkin and Mark J. Eitelberg, *Blacks and the Military* (Washington, D.C.: The Brookings Institution, 1982), p. 33.
13. Martin Luther King, Jr., "A Time to Break Silence," *Freedomways*, 2nd Quarter, 1967, p. 106.
14. Mark Baker, *Nam* (New York: William Morrow, 1983), p. 36.
15. Tim O'Brien, *If I Die in a Combat Zone* (New York: Delacorte Press, 1973), p. 69.
16. Lee Childress interview in Al Santoli, *Everything We Had* (New York: Ballantine Books, 1981), p. 64.

17. Henry L. Trewhitt, *McNamara* (New York: Harper & Row, 1971), p. 238.
18. Luis Martinez interview in Santoli, *Everything We Had*, p. 160.
19. Robert Jay Lifton, *Home from the War* (New York: Simon & Schuster, 1973), p. 33.
20. Herb Mock interview in Santoli, *Everything We Had*, p. 85.
21. Robert Santos interview in *ibid.*, p. 132.
22. William Hauser, *America's Army in Crisis* (Baltimore, Md.: Johns Hopkins University Press, 1973), p. 103.
23. William C. Westmoreland, "A Report to the Congress by the Commander of U.S. Military Forces in Vietnam," April 28, 1967, *Department of State Bulletin*, May 15, 1967, p. 741.
24. Seymour M. Hersh, *Cover-Up* (New York: Random House, 1972), p. 103.
25. *Ibid.*, p. 52.
26. *Ibid.*, p. 35.
27. Westmoreland interview in Michael Charlton and Anthony Moncrieff, *Many Reasons Why* (London: Scolar Press, 1978), p. 148.
28. William Peers, "Leadership Requirements in a Counterinsurgency Environment," March 18, 1970, reprinted in Cincinnatus, *Self-Destruction* (New York: W. W. Norton & Co., 1981), p. 197.
29. *Ibid.*, p. 196.
30. Douglas Kinnard, *The War Managers* (Hanover, N.H.: University Press of New England, 1977), p. 175.
31. Baker, *Nam*, pp. 171–72.
32. Hersh, *Cover-Up*, p. 20.
33. *Ibid.*, p. 21.
34. Joseph Ellis and Robert Moore, *School for Soldiers* (New York: Oxford University Press, 1974), p. 164.
35. *Ibid.*, p. 166.
36. Hersh, *Cover-Up*, p. 237.
37. William C. Westmoreland, *A Soldier Reports* (Garden City, N.Y.: Doubleday & Co., 1976), p. 375.
38. Hersh, *Cover-Up*, p. 264.
39. Baker, *Nam*, p. 151.
40. "General Westmoreland Reports on Vietnam War," *U.S. News & World Report*, Nov. 28, 1966, p. 48.

41. James B. Stockdale, Foreword in Richard A. Gabriel, *To Serve with Honor* (Westport, Conn.: Greenwood Press, 1982), p. xiv.

42. William C. Westmoreland, "Progress Report on the War in Viet-Nam," Nov. 21, 1967, *Department of State Bulletin*, Dec. 11, 1967, p. 788.

43. Cincinnatus, *Self-Destruction*, p. 112.

44. Maureen Mylander, *The Generals* (New York: Dial Press, 1974), p. 12.

45. Starr, *The Discarded Army*, p. 12.

46. Bruce Lawlor in Santoli, *Everything We Had*, p. 176.

47. Herb Mock in *Ibid.*, p. 183.

48. William C. Westmoreland, "Analysis of Moral and Professional Climate in the Army," April 18, 1970, in U.S. Army War College, "Study on Military Professionalism," Carlisle Barracks, Pa., June 30, 1970, p. 53.

49. *Ibid.*, p. i.

50. *Ibid.*, p. iv.

51. *Ibid.*, pp. 13–14.

52. *Ibid.*, p. v.

53. *Ibid.*, p. B44.

54. *Ibid.*, pp. 12, 15.

55. *Ibid.*, p. B29.

56. *Ibid.*, p. 20.

57. *Ibid.*, p. 21.

58. *Ibid.*, p. B1, B5.

59. *Ibid.*, p. 25.

60. *Ibid.*, pp. B1–2.

61. *Ibid.*

62. *Ibid.*, p. B1–14.

63. A. D. Horne, ed., *The Wounded Generation* (Englewood Cliffs, N.J.: Prentice-Hall, 1981), pp. 143–44.

64. David Shoup, "The New American Militarism," *The Atlantic Monthly*, April 1969, pp. 51–56.

65. Kinnard, *The War Managers*, p. 174.

66. Cincinnatus, *Self-Destruction*, p. 144.

67. Santoli, *Everything We Had*, p. 219.

68. Office of Systems Analysis, Office of the Secretary of Defense, "Experience in Command and Battle Deaths," January 1968, p. 24; Center of Military History, Department of the Army.

69. Office of the Deputy Chief of Staff for Personnel, Department of the Army, "Study of the 12-Month Vietnam Tour," June 29, 1970, Appendix: "Advantages and Disadvantages of 12-Month Hostile Fire Area Tour," p. 1; Center of Military History, Department of the Army.

70. Mylander, *The Generals*, p. 74.

71. Haynes Johnson and George C. Wilson, *Army in Anguish* (New York: Pocket Books, 1972), p. 76.

72. Office of Systems Analysis, "Experience in Command," p. 25.

73. *Ibid.*, p. 27.

74. *Ibid.*, p. 29.

75. *Ibid.*

76. *Ibid.*, p. 30.

77. *Ibid.*, "MACV Rebuttal," p. 15.

78. Oscar Grutsky, "The Effects of Succession," in Morris Janowitz, ed., *The New Military* (New York: Russell Sage Foundation, 1964), p. 89.

79. Westmoreland, *A Soldier Reports*, p. 417.

80. Army War College, "Study on Military Professionalism," p. 23.

81. *Ibid.*, p. 26.

82. Santoli, *Everything We Had*, p. 43.

83. Kinnard, *The War Managers*, p. 75.

84. *Ibid.*

85. Peter Goldman and Tony Fuller, *Charlie Company* (New York: William Morrow, 1983), p. 98.

86. Kinnard, *The War Managers*, p. 172.

87. James Fallows, *National Defense* (New York: Random House, 1981), p. 121.

88. Army War College, "Study on Military Professionalism," p. 29.

89. Lifton, *Home from the War*, p. 178.

90. Richard A. Gabriel and Paul L. Savage, *Crisis in Command* (New York: Hill and Wang, 1978), p. 182.

91. Hauser, *America's Army in Crisis*, p. 94.

92. Gabriel and Savage, *Crisis in Command*, p. 42.

93. Charles J. Levy, *Spoils of War* (Boston: Houghton Mifflin Co., 1974), p. 46.

94. Gabriel and Savage, *Crisis in Command*, p. 183.

95. Gabriel, *To Serve with Honor*, p. 4.

96. Gabriel and Savage, *Crisis in Command,* p. 45.
97. Gabriel, *To Serve with Honor,* p. 3.
98. Gabriel and Savage, *Crisis in Command,* p. 48.
99. Starr, *The Discarded Army,* p. 114.
100. Westmoreland, *A Soldier Reports,* p. 371.
101. Baskir and Strauss, *Chance and Circumstance,* p. 137.
102. *Ibid.,* p. 138.
103. William Jayne, "Immigrants from the Combat Zone," in Horne, ed., *Wounded Generation,* p. 161.
104. Goldman and Fuller, *Charlie Company,* pp. 207, 209, 220, 249, 251–56, 276, 281.
105. *Ibid.,* pp. 245, 263.
106. Tim O'Brien, "We've Adjusted Too Well," in Horne, ed., *The Wounded Generation,* p. 205.
107. Starr, *The Discarded Army,* p. 4.

8. THE AMERICAN LULLABY

1. Zeb B. Bradford, "US Tactics in Vietnam," *Military Review,* Feb. 1972, p. 75.
2. Harry G. Summers, *On Strategy* (Novato, Cal.: Presidio Press, 1982), p. 73.
3. Peer de Silva, *Sub Rosa* (New York: Times Books, 1978), p. 277.
4. Summers, *On Strategy,* p. 18.
5. Michael Charlton and Anthony Moncrieff, *Many Reasons Why* (London: Scolar Press, 1978), p. 115.
6. *Ibid.,* p. 137.
7. Summers, *On Strategy,* pp. 13, 35.
8. Earl C. Ravenal, *Never Again* (Philadelphia: Temple University Press, 1978), pp. 23–24.
9. Cincinnatus, *Self-Destruction* (New York: W. W. Norton & Co., 1981), p. 73.
10. Harrison E. Salisbury, ed., *Vietnam Reconsidered* (New York: Harper & Row, 1984), p. 320.
11. J. Hector St. John (De Crèvecoeur), *Letters from an American Farmer* (Philadelphia: Mathew Carey, 1793), p. 46.
12. Peter Cohen, *The Gospel According to the Harvard Business School* (Garden City, N.Y.: Doubleday & Co., 1973), pp. 169, 186.
13. Marilyn Mercer, "The Company Neurosis," *Cosmopolitan,* March 1983, p. 307.

14. Douglas Kinnard, *The War Managers* (Hanover, N.H.: University Press of New England, 1977), p. 61.

15. Nicholas Lemann, "The Post-Vietnam Generation," in A. D. Horne, ed., *The Wounded Generation* (Englewood Cliffs, N.J.: Prentice-Hall, 1981), p. 211.

16. Dwight D. Eisenhower, Jan. 20, 1953, *Public Papers of the Presidents* (Washington, D.C.: G.P.O., 1960), p. 4.

17. Joseph Califano, "Doubts About an All-Voluntary Army," *New Republic*, March 1973, p. 11.

18. James Webb, "Why the Army Needs It," *Atlantic*, April 1980, p. 44.

19. Noam Chomsky and Edward S. Herman, *After the Cataclysm* (Boston: South End Press, 1979), p. 8.

20. Drew Middleton, "Vietnam and the Military Mind," *The New York Times Magazine*, Jan. 10, 1982, p. 37.

21. *Ibid.*, p. 90.

22. Summers, *On Strategy*, p. 143.

23. Charlton, *Many Reasons Why*, p. 18.

24. Howell Raines, "Reagan Vows U.S. Will Press to Build Defenses," *The New York Times*, May 28, 1981, p. 1.

25. Peter Hannaford, *The Reagans* (New York: Putnam Publishing Group, 1983), pp. 136, 218.

INDEX